MARIA CALLAS

Also by David Bret and published by Robson Books

The Piaf Legend
The Mistinguett Legend
Maurice Chevalier
Marlene, My Friend
Morrissey: Landscapes of the Mind
Gracie Fields
Tallulah Bankhead: A Scandalous Life
Living on the Edge: The Freddie Mercury Story

MARIA CALLAS
The Tigress and the Lamb

David Bret

 Robson Books

First published in Great Britain in 1997 by Robson
Books Ltd, Bolsover House, 5-6 Clipstone Street,
London W1P 8LE

British Library Cataloguing in Publication Data
A catalogue record for this title is available from the
British Library

ISBN 1 86105 110 7

Set in Plantin by Derek Doyle & Associates, Mold,
Flintshire. Printed and bound in Great Britain by
Creative Print and Design Wales, Ebbw Vale.

Contents

This book is dedicated to Montserrat Caballé, Monica Solash and Les Enfants de Novembre.

N'oublie pas . . .
La vie sans amis c'est comme
un jardin sans fleurs

Acknowledgements

Writing this book would not have been possible had it not been for the inspiration, criticisms and love of that select group of individuals whom I still regard as my true family and *autre coeur*: Barbara, Irene Bevan, Montserrat Caballé, René and Lucette Chevalier, Jacqueline Danno, Hélène Delavault, Marlene Dietrich, Tony Griffin, Roger Normand, Betty Paillard, Annick Roux, Monica Solash, Terry Sanderson, John and Anne Taylor, François and Madeleine Vals. God bless you all!

Very special thanks to my tireless agent, David Bolt, and to the superb publishing team at Robson Books. An especial thanks, too, to Kathryn Burton of EMI. Most important of all, *chapeau bas* to you, Maria, for contributing to *Le Ring* and making all this possible . . . and to Jeanne, against all odds still the keeper of my soul.

David Bret

Foreword

I first met Maria Callas in New York, when I was singing 'Don Carlo' and 'Luisa Miller' as part of the 1968–9 season. We spoke after a rehearsal, when I told that I had been dissatisfied with my performance. Her face lit up and she said, 'That's a good thing! When you can admit that you've sung badly, you also know that you can do better if you try. The day you start thinking and telling everyone how wonderful you are, that's the day you should take a long vacation!' That evening she invited my husband and me to dine with her and Pasolini, and we remained best friends until she died.

My greatest regret is that I never saw Maria on the opera stage – I attended one of the Juilliard master-classes, and I was in the audience towards the end of her career when she sang in that wonderful concert at Carnegie Hall with di Stefano. Other than that, like many people I had to make do with the recordings of her performances. And yet, if those recordings are so unique, imagine what she must have sounded like on the stage at the time she was the ultimate Puccini and Verdi heroine!

Maria was *the* supreme professional, by far the best worker there has ever been in our particular factory. And work for her was almost a form of religion. 'I prepare myself for rehearsals like I would for marriage,' she once told me, although I feel that the marriage between Maria and her public was much more than the conventional one. She was like a nun who has taken her final vows: the stage was her altar, the theatre her Sanctuary. She dedicated her life to her vocation – Body, Heart and Soul – and when she spoke about the way in which she prepared her roles, always following the dictates of the composer, she would pronounce his instructions as if reading from the Bible. Yet in the end it was not lack of faith which broke her spirit, it was a lack of understanding and compassion from other human beings which brought about the end of her life.

If Maria was difficult in her professional life, it was because she *was* a professional, and some of the others were not always so. On one occasion, she told me, she turned up for a rehearsal at La Scala, and instead of singing, the other artists were having a heated discussion about football! She was *very* upset about that! Maria was only difficult with mediocre people, the ones who were not completely dedicated to their art ... those conductors, directors and singers who had no devotion at all towards the opera, only in what was in it for themselves. The 'cash-and-carries', she called them. And so many of these hated her success. There is nothing so deeply ugly as jealousy.

During my formative years, Maria was always there to offer me advice. For example, when La Scala offered me 'Macbeth', she told me not to accept it. 'They *must* offer you operas which will suit your voice,' she said. ' "Macbeth", needs an *ugly* voice, not a beautiful sound like yours, and it also needs an angrier person!'

She also advised me about personal issues. I knew that she was having problems of her own, but we never spoke about those and I never once heard her complain. Maria cared for the welfare of her closest friends because they were so few. 'Real friends are very special,' she would say, 'but you have to be careful because some-times you have a friend and you think they are made of rock, then suddenly you realise they're only made of sand. It's a terrible thing to go through life thinking that you have a rock on your side when you haven't.'

The Callas that I knew was a fine artist, a wonderful woman and friend, *and* a rock. We shall never see her like again.

Montserrat Caballé,
Barcelona, 3 June 1997.

Introduction

Hers was the archetypal tale of the ugly duckling who by sheer willpower and courage of conviction transformed herself into the most beautiful of swans. Maria Calogeropoulos, the shy, awkward daughter of Greek immigrants who rose like a shooting star from the backstreets of Manhattan to become the greatest operatic diva of this century. A sublime talent and remarkably humble woman, an enigma whose artistry and vulnerability appropriated her to that privileged coterie of female entertainers – Piaf, Monroe, Garland and a mere handful of others – whose every triumph and tragedy we willingly anticipated and shared.

As a communicator and supreme authority on the human condition, Callas was without equal. By applying the experiences and emotions of her own troubled life to her art, she was able to climb inside the skin of each of her heroines and transcend the limitations of her predecessors, contemporaries and most of her successors by bringing these often wretched women to *life!* And because she had never been afforded the luxury of a normal, contented childhood – dominated as she had been by a mother whose psyche bordered on insanity – Callas sought and was offered love by the audiences which flocked to see her, in particular that oft-oppressed section of our society which she lovingly labelled 'The Callas Boys'.

Norma, Lucia, Violetta, Lady Macbeth, Leonora, Medea, Amina and Tosca. These are but some of the roles, many of them previously neglected, that Callas made her own, often taking uncalculated risks, though with integrity and an almost uncanny intuition she turned even the most obscure work or drabbest production into the box-office event of the season.

Yet Callas's greatest role was herself: the temperamental diva whose tantrums and walk-outs were almost as sensational as her entrances. The consummate professional who had neither time nor patience for time-wasters or second-raters. The voluptuous siren whose ability to seduce brought her a series of relationships which were destined only to be doomed: Mario and Oscar, the enemy soldiers who were so cruelly wrenched from her; Rossi-Lemeni and Mangliveras, the opera stars who used her, only to have the tables turned on them; Serafin and Bagarozy, her early mentors; Meneghini, the man who fashioned her career and married her, only to find himself dumped because he had been unable to tame the tigress; Aly Khan, the irascible playboy who died so tragically; Visconti, Bernstein and Pasolini, voracious homosexuals whom she attempted and failed to 'cure', di Stefano, who helped her through her final triumphant tour, when the fans were at their most hysterical, and the critics at their most condemning. And the greatest love of her life – Aristotle Onassis – whose death set her on that rapid downward spiral of depression, drug-dependency and solitude where there was no division between day and night.

On and off the stage, Maria Callas was *the* Sacred Goddess.

This is her story.

1

O Caro Sogno . . . O Dolce Ebbrezza!

To load a child so early with so much responsibility is something there should be a law against. A child, taken away from its youth, becomes exhausted before its time.

Maria was born in New York's Flower Hospital (subsequently renamed the Fifth Avenue) on 4 December 1923. Her parents, who had emigrated to the United States just four months previously, were Jiorgos (George) Calogeropoulo, a 37-year-old pharmacist from Meligala, and Evangelia (Litza) Demitriadis, the 25-year-old daughter of a fairly well-to do army officer from Stilida, Northern Greece. The actual date of her birth has persistently caused problems for biographers. Her passport clearly states 2 December, that in the Registry of Births at New York's City Hall, 3 December. The singer herself believed differently, as she explained – albeit sarcastically – to Anita Pensotti of the Italian magazine, *Oggi*, in January 1957:

My mother maintains that she brought me into the world on the fourth. You choose whichever date you prefer. I prefer the fourth because, firstly, I have to believe everything my mother tells me, and secondly because it's St Barbara's Day, the patron saint of artillerymen, a proud and fighting saint whom I especially admire!

The Calogeropoulo marriage was almost entirely loveless from the start. Litza's father was General Petros Demitriadis, a hero of the Balkan Wars of 1912–13, who in his twilight years enjoyed much success locally as an amateur tenor. It was he who advised Litza against marrying a man with a reputation for being a womaniser. However, when Petros died suddenly of a stroke just six weeks before the wedding was scheduled to take place in August 1916, Litza's mother told her to follow the dictates of her heart. For the next fifty years, this most extraordinary woman would complain to all and sundry that she had married beneath her.

For a while, the Calogeropoulos had settled in an impressive house in Meligala, on the Peloponnese, where George, a graduate from Athens University, had run his own very successful pharmacy – the only one for miles – and where Litza, still only eighteen, had begun fulfilling the duties expected of her: organising the household with its small coterie of servants, turning a blind eye to her husband's extra-marital flings, and having children. Their first daughter, Jackie (Yacinthy), born on 4 June 1917, had initially been regarded by George as a disappointment – traditionally, in most Greek households, females were seen as secondary citizens and incapable of continuing the family line. Then, in 1920 Litza had given birth to Vassily (Vasiliakis) – only to lose him, three years later, to meningitis.

Vassily's death signalled the beginning of the end for the Calogeropoulos marriage. Distraught beyond belief, and without even discussing the matter with his wife, George sold the pharmacy and their house, and bought three steamer passages to New York to which one of his closest friends, Leonidas Lantzounis, had emigrated the previous year, to take up a surgeon's position at the New York Orthopaedic Hospital.

The first Litza heard of George's plans was just twenty-four hours before they were due to set sail. Yet in an age and culture where it was compulsory for wives – in this case, one who was without independent means, uneducated and five months pregnant – to be subservient, Litza had no option but to obey.

Neither George nor Litza could speak a word of English when they arrived in New York on 3 August 1923, at a time when the

American nation was mourning its twenty-ninth president, Warren G Harding, who had died suddenly the previous day in the midst of the corruption scandal which had rocked his party. The trio were met at the harbour by Leonidas Lantzounis, who had secured them a small rented apartment in 'Little Athens' – the small Greek community in Astoria, Long Island. It took them some time to adjust, particularly Litza, who from now on would have to do her own cooking and cleaning whilst her husband – self-demoted from entrepreneur to 'lowly immigrant' – had to submit to working for someone else as a pharmacist's assistant.

Having been told by a village quack that the child she was carrying would be a son to replace the much-lamented Vassily, Litza set about turning her new home into a near replica of their house in Meligala – even down to the tiny icons in the bedrooms, whose flames were kept burning day and night. And when she was not decorating and scrubbing, Litza was knitting baby clothes – blue, of course, and dreaming up names for the new baby. Subsequently, such was her shock and abhorrence at being delivered of a twelve and a half pound *girl* that she flatly refused to hold the baby for several days, let alone think of giving her a name – a rejection which would haunt Maria for the rest of her life. Worst of all was the fact that it took her parents until 26 February 1926 to have her baptised, when at the Greek Orthodox Church on East 74th Street, she was given the names Maria Anna Cecilia Sophia. Leonidas Lantzounis was her godfather. Soon afterwards, she was also given a new surname when, following complaints from his American clients that his name was unpronounceable, George went to court and had it changed, legally, to Callas.

By the end of 1927, George Callas had made sufficient headway – and enough money – to open his own drugstore, The Splendid Pharmacy, on 39th and 8th Avenue, in Manhattan. The family's new apartment boasted a pianola and a wind-up gramophone, two items which would quickly inspire Maria towards chosing a musical career which she had thus far never contemplated – particularly when she first heard the distinguished soprano, Amelita Galli-Curci, singing the lovely 'Vissi d'arte' from *Tosca*, an aria she would one day make her own.

Listening to her mother's rapidly increasing collection of gramophone records, and borrowing more from the local library, offered the youngster a sense of belonging which only intensified when the pianola was replaced by a piano: the thrice-weekly lessons she and Jackie now began taking compensated for a distinct lack of parental affection. Nevertheless, Litza's musical preferences and not theirs were the order of the day, as Jackie remembered some years later: 'We took it as absolutely natural that the only music worth spending time on was Bellini and Verdi ... we were raised to the sounds of grand opera and my mother's incessant nagging.'

These aspirations were almost dashed in July 1929, when Maria was hit by a car outside her home, and dragged some ten yards along the street. She was rushed to the hospital on Fort Washington Avenue, where doctors initially suspected brain damage, and told her parents to expect the worst. George Callas, in a rare caring mood – allegedly because he feared accusations of neglect from the authorities – immediately brought in a specialist friend from the Greek community who diagnosed nothing more than severe concussion. Even so, Maria was hospitalised for three weeks, and when she was discharged became quite a handful – throwing tantrums if she could not have her own way, and abusing her mother with the colourful language she had picked up from some of her less reputable neighbours.

To an extent, of course, she was only repaying Litza for her persistence in reminding her that 'ugly ducklings' with spots, spectacles and a tendency towards obesity invariably ended their lives unloved, childless spinsters. No wonder, then, that the poor girl spent her entire adolescence tormented by bouts of self-pity and near-suicidal depression. And yet, even her slimmer, prettier sister was having an equally tough time coping with Litza's tyranny.

Speaking of her own suicide attempt, at the age of ten, Jackie describes in her memoirs, *Sisters*, published in 1989, how Litza had demanded absolute obedience, adding she attributed her mother's periods of deep melancholia to the moon's phases. 'I would watch the night sky from our bedroom window and dread the diminishing crescent as a herald of bad days to come,' she wrote, describing

Litza's 'punishments' of pepper on the lips for telling lies, and of clothes being dumped in the street if the girls were untidy.

Hot on the heels of Maria's accident came October's Wall Street Crash, a devastating event which forced George Callas to sell his pharmacy at a loss – setting in motion a downward spiral in the family's finances which resulted in an almost annual moonlight flit from any number of cheap, tawdry apartments and seven changes of school for the Callas girls. This in turn both severely disrupted their education and prevented them from getting close to anyone in whichever district they happened to be living.

Such near-poverty taught Maria how to control her emotions, as she told Edward Downes many years later: if she and George passed an ice-cream parlour, she would tug at his jacket, but not say a word. 'I'd just look at him – not at the ice-cream parlour. Then he would play the comedy and say, "What *are* you asking for?" And I wouldn't say a word. I would just keep on looking at him like mad!'

Incredibly, Litza blamed George for the sudden decline in their standard of living, and in a fit of pique she swallowed a handful of pills – a futile attempt at drawing attention to herself, Jackie Callas later declared, for had her mother *really* wanted to die she would have taken something from George's poison cabinet. What Litza did not anticipate was her husband's reaction to her suicide bid. Wholly unsympathetic, he had her committed to the infamous Bellevue Lunatic Asylum, where she remained for several weeks … long enough to come to terms with the fact that George no longer cared what she did, so long as she was out of his hair. She also had to accept the fact that he would once again have to work for someone else, for whilst Litza was in the asylum, George took a job as a travelling salesman with a pharmaceutical company. As a result, Litza now concentrated her ambitions on her daughters. She was not overtly fond of them, but she was determined to use them as a means of re-ascending the social ladder. A friend of the family – a part-time singing coach – had heard Maria accompanying herself at the piano and singing 'La Paloma', and he now agreed to give her free tuition. Litza also insisted on the continuation of her daughter's piano lessons, whether George could afford them or not, and decided that Maria, as the one with the most talent, would succeed through *her*, even if it meant sacrificing personal happiness.

By the summer of 1935, Litza felt convinced that her daughter was ready to be presented to the world, so she entered her in an amateur talent contest with the Mutual Radio Network. Until now, Maria's only 'public' performances had been concerts and plays at the Public School 164 in Washington Heights, but with Jackie now relegated to accompanist, she sang 'La Paloma' and walked off with first prize – a handsome gold-plated Bulova wristwatch which she wore for several years, until she lost it.

Litza was impressed, so much so that she paid to have Maria's voice recorded professionally. Dated 4 July 1935, this relatively primitive rendition of 'Un bel di vedremo' from *Madama Butterfly* is preceded by a short speech. But it is not the name Maria Callas which appears on the label – striking out for independence, Maria had insisted on the pseudonym Nina Foresti.

Shortly after making this recording, Maria came second in a juvenile talent contest in Chicago, where her prize and certificate were presented to her by the comic, Jack Benny. She may have convinced herself that she would always be ugly on the outside. Within, however, she had proved to herself that she had much more to offer the world than mere looks – she had a voice, albeit one which needed a little coaxing and polishing around the edges, but a remarkable voice all the same which, time and time again during these unhappy years, would levitate her way above the heads of her so-called loved ones, whose only goal in life appeared to be making *her* feel inferior to them.

For Litza, however, talent contests *were* inferior and – as her husband had uprooted his family to come to America in the first place, telling no one – she decided to return with her daughters to Greece, without including George in her plans. Only there, she declared – with her *own* family to fall back on for moral and financial support should things not go according to plan – would Maria receive the tuition Litza knew she merited.

The move began at the end of 1936. Jackie had recently enrolled at a modelling school and, unlike Maria, had made several friends in the neighbourhood. Even so, she was packed off to Athens – on her own – where within a few weeks of her arrival she found herself accepted on a secretarial course. Litza and Maria waited to leave until February 1937, when Maria graduated from the school she had loathed, by which time her mother had crated their personal effects. George paid for their passage on the Italian liner, *Vulcania*, pleased to be free of them at last so that he could spend more time with his latest mistress. According to Jackie, his exact words upon learning that this troublesome woman was leaving him – once he had fallen to his knees and crossed himself – were, 'At last, my God, you have pitied me!'

For two days, whilst the ship ploughed through a series of tempests, Maria suffered from terrible seasickness. Then, one afternoon when she was feeling better, against her mother's wishes, she entered the tourists' lounge, calmly sat at the piano, and sang Gounod's 'Ave Maria' with all the gusto of a seasoned diva. Overheard by the captain, she was next invited to sing at that evening's officers' party in the *first*-class lounge!

Without even bothering to ask her mother's permission, Maria accepted, and leaving her ungainly spectacles in her cabin she repeated the Gounod piece, sang 'La Paloma', and – audaciously for a girl of just thirteen – concluded with the boisterous 'Habañera' from *Carmen*, tossing a flower from the vase atop the piano into the captain's lap! He, on the other hand, presented her with her first bouquet ... and her first doll, which she naturally hid from her mother.

In early March, the *Vulcania* docked at Patras, in the north-west Peloponnese, where Maria and her mother boarded the train for Athens. Exactly how Maria felt seeing her homeland for the very first time cannot be readily discerned, for here was a girl brought up to believe that she did not belong anywhere. She certainly must have felt confused by the scenario which awaited her in Athens – Litza's six brothers and sisters, and dozens of in-laws, friends and neighbours crowded onto the platform to ogle at this ungainly, myopic 'blazing talent' of Litza's letters, and by and large she was treated like some kind of freak.

Neither was Maria allowed to become accustomed to her strange new environment before Litza resumed her machinations. Driven to Grandmother Dimitriadis's house in the Sopolia district of the city – the Callas home for the next few weeks, until their apartment in Terma Patission was ready to move into – Maria was not even allowed to unpack her hand-luggage before Litza had arranged her first audition, for the following morning! Her plan, however, was overruled by her brother, Efthimios, an amateur tenor, who as head of the family declared that Maria should first get to know her new country and relatives. Not without a fight, Litza cancelled the arrangement and it was Efthimios himself – Maria's first ally – who organised her first audition at the beginning of December 1937.

Not one to do things by halves, Efthimios had arranged for his niece to participate in an amateur talent contest with a difference – at a taverna outside Athens. Once again she sang 'La Paloma', and though she did not win first prize, after her spot she was congratulated by Yanni Kambani, an up-and-coming young tenor with the National Lyric Theatre who promised to get her an introduction to his teacher, the renowned Maria Trivella of the Athens National Conservatory.

This audition too was tantamount to a family outing, with half the Dimitriadis clan in tow, taking turns to encourage and nag her – so much so that in a fit of rage Maria is alleged to have sworn never to sing again, should she fail. Singing the 'Habañera' from *Carmen*, she won, and Trivella, a finicky woman, was so overwhelmed by Maria's voice that she agreed to take her on for singing and French lessons – 'doctoring' her application form by declaring that her new pupil was sixteen, the legal age requirement for entry into the Conservatory. Incredibly, it was only now that Maria saw her first full-length opera, Verdi's *La Traviata*. She also began taking drama lessons with George Karakandis, while at around the same time Jackie began studying piano under Tassia Filtsou.

Over the next two years, under Trivella's tutelage Maria was to a certain extent able to break free of her mother's manipulations. By now, however, most of the damage had already been done and for the rest of her life she would never be entirely independent, or capable of making major decisions for herself. She also very quickly became almost oblivious to everything in her life *but* her work – for several months practising the scales for hours on end, learning popular songs and operetta before tackling the more serious arias so that her vocal cords would not be damaged whilst she was training. Her only pleasure outside music was eating, and she was capable of gorging on as many as eight full-sized meals in any one day, as she later confided in Anita Pensotti.

I have no particular recollections of my childhood other than the vague intuition that my parents were unsuited towards each other. I was deprived entirely of the joys of adolescence and by way of compensation became fat. Adopting the excuse that one has to be hefty to sing well I stuffed myself day and night with pasta, chocolate, bread and zabaglione. I was round and rosy, with pimples which drove me insane ...

At home, in the bird-room, Maria taught herself her legendary coloratura trill ... by mimicking Litza's pet canaries, singing so loudly that, according to one report, one of them went deaf! Yet because of her sheer determination to be the best pupil the Conservatory had ever had – both Litza and Maria Trivella urged her to aspire towards nothing less – Maria was unpopular with her fellow pupils, and just as in her New York schools, she did not make one single friend whilst she was there.

The hard work – and the tantrums – paid off handsomely when, on 11 April 1938, Maria joined the Conservatory students for a concert at the Parnassos Hall. Striking a blow for independence from her mother, she asked to be billed as Maria Kalogeropoulo – a name which she would retain for several years. The programme included works by Weber and Gounod, besides a selection of Greek folk songs, but it was Maria and Yanni Kambani who stole the show, closing the proceedings with a duet which earned them a standing ovation – Maria's first. Her success, and the ones which followed over the next year, established her reputation in Athens and enabled her to cope with the increasing misery of her personal life.

On 2 April 1939, she appeared in the students' production of Mascagni's *Cavalleria Rusticana*, singing the mezzo soprano role of Santuzza ... with a raging toothache. This and most of her subsequent Italian roles in Athens were sung in their original language, and not in Greek, as has been stated. On 22 May she sang five arias at the Parnassos Hall, including the difficult 'Ritorna vincitor' from Verdi's *Aida*, and the following evening she sang arias by Weber and Massenet at the same venue. On 25 June, the programme was even more demanding for a girl of fifteen – besides 'Innegio il Signor' from *Cavalleria Rusticana*, there was the whole of Act Three from *Un Ballo In Maschera*.

During this otherwise pleasant summer of 1939, Maria was considerably less perturbed by the gathering war clouds – the fact that Mussolini's troops had marched into neighbouring Albania, and now posed a Fascist threat to Greece – than she was by her sister's engagement to one of the country's most eligible bachelors, the wealthy shipping heir Milton Emberikos, whose mistress Jackie had been for some months. The actual engagement party took place on board his yacht, the *Eleni*, so named after his mother, whilst it cruised between the Greek mainland and Corfu. Whilst Litza and Jackie were dressed to the nines Maria, in her old-fashioned, dowdy clothes, was made to feel decidedly out of place and reminded yet again that no young man worthy of his name would ever want to marry someone who looked like *her*.

For Maria, redemption was waiting around the next corner in the bulky form of Elvira di Hidalgo, a fifty-nine-year-old Spanish former coloratura of ambiguous sexuality, of whom Maria jokingly told her French friend Roger Normand, 'She was the first lesbian I never had!' Many years later, she would applaud her mentor as 'an unforgettable and superlative Rosina' and ' a splendid interpreter of other very important roles'. She was of course being a tad *too* liberal with her praise. Di Hidalgo's few great performances had taken place before or during World War One, and though she had been considered skilful enough to partner Caruso and Chaliapin and grace the stages of some of the world's foremost houses, she had proved no match for contemporaries such as Tetrazzini and Galli-Curci, and is now largely remembered only for her association with Callas. By 1923, the year of Maria's birth, she was already considered past her prime, and today she is not even included in compilation record re-releases. Like her celebrated pupil, Elvira di Hidalgo was a tetchy, hard-to-please woman, though as a teacher she was reputed to have been second to none. Because of her reputation in this field she had recently taken up a post with Greece's most accomplished Conservatory – the Odeon Athenon – initially for just one season. On account of the hazardous political climate, she stayed on for several years as the company's artistic director – and Litza, naturally, was one of the first to contact her and *demand* that her daughter be offered an audition. This took place a few days later, with de Hidalgo initially dismissing Maria – all 185 pounds of her – as 'laughable'. The miracle occurred, of course, when the girl began to sing. Maria had chosen an unusually mature piece – 'Ocean! Thou Mighty Monster' from Weber's *Oberon* – but what de Hidalgo later remembered as 'violent cascades of sound' propelled her into taking Maria on as her personal pupil, free of charge to Litza.

Recognised as Maria Callas's first surrogate mother, Elvira di Hidalgo was an initially kindly Svengali who in one fell swoop delivered her of much familial oppression. As the years passed, however, she would become increasingly jealous of her ex-pupil's success ... whilst Maria never stopped extolling Elvira's praises, declaring that she owed all her preparation and artistic formation to this woman, including, 'She could say more about me than any other person because with Madame Elvira more than anyone else, I had contact and familiarity.'

Maria was by no means an easy student, and a weaker, less patient teacher might well have sent her packing. She was ill-educated, virulently bad-tempered, frequently rude and abusive to the other students, ungainly, and in those days she had a tendency to bite her nails until her fingers bled if she could not get her own way. Her vocal range was restricted, her gestures and stance were contrived, if not wooden, because she was myopic and terrified of moving around and bumping into things. Because of this problem, she had also convinced herself that she was stupid. In addition, as her mother had drilled it into her that as an 'overweight frump' she was unworthy of decent clothes, she had absolutely no dress-sense.

De Hidalgo single-handedly helped Maria to correct most of these faults, though it would take more than a decade to come to terms with and conquer her weight problem, and even then she would take a very pessimistic view of herself, saying once, 'Even when people look at me with great affection, I get very angry and think to myself, "People are staring at me with admiration! Why should they when I don't deserve it?" '

Elvira di Hidalgo's greatest gift to Maria, however, was her extensive knowledge of the bel canto repertoire which she passed on to her pupil. Throughout the western world, barring perhaps Italy, opera was virtually dying on its feet with opera houses closing at an alarming rate, or at best playing to half-capacity audiences who were tired of listening to the same old, churned-out roles. Many so-called 'minor' works of the great early-19th century composers had been largely forgotten or overlooked. *Norma* and *I Puritani*, which Bellini had written for the great soprano Giulia Grisi in 1834, and even Verdi's *Don Carlos* were rarely performed; Ponchielli's *La Gioconda* and Spontini's *La Vestale* were almost forgotten. In time, Maria would, through di Hidalgo's coaxing and influence, not only resurrect these and many other bel canto roles, but with her exemplary dramatic interpretative skills and formidable three-octave range, she would also make them her personal property. Over the next few years, not content to pore over and memorise every full score she could lay her hands on – 'It was a case of having to,' she later confessed, 'because I was so short-sighted, I would never have been able to read the cue-cards or see the prompter!' – she meticulously researched every one of her romantic or tragic heroines and, with the dexterity and skill of a Duse or Bernhardt, climbed inside their individual skins until she *became* whoever she was portraying on the stage.

2

Printemps Qui Commence

Music is the most beautiful thing in the world, and to be able to conquer certain difficulties with a fragile instrument like the voice brings such satisfaction that it's like something out of your soul.

On 28 October 1940, the Italian invasion of Greece began when the latter's prime minister, Ioannis Metaxas, received an ultimatum from Mussolini – unless his troops were allowed on the Greek mainland, Greece would be declared an enemy of Italy and Germany and there would be a full-scale war. Metaxas, already a sick old man, refused to capitulate and, for a few months at least, the Greek nation believed that their position in the conflict would remain neutral.

As for Maria, she was so deeply immersed in her work with the Conservatory that she never had the time to read newspapers, and only switched on the radio to listen to operas or recitals. On 23 February 1940 she had performed the duet 'Mira, o Norma' with Arda Mandikian, and on 3 April she had made her first radio broadcast with Mandikian, another of di Hidalgo's pupils, performing arias from *La Gioconda*, *Norma* and *Aida*. On 16 June, again at the Odeon Concert Hall, she had sung the lead in the Conservatory's production of *Suor Angelica*, a role which she had repeated on 27 November at the National Theatre, and again on 21 February 1941 at the Palace Theatre. In at least one of these performances, her sister Jackie sang in the chorus.

On 6 April 1941, the Germans came to Italy's aid and bombed Salonika, causing mass destruction and loss of life. Ioannis Metaxas had recently died but his successor, Alexander Koryzis, now left his country wide open to attack by committing suicide.

By 27 April Athens was under Nazi occupation, forcing King George II and his government to go into exile. Milton Emberikos, who had been called up but allowed to take an office job so as to remain in control of his business affairs, used his considerable influence and wealth to secure Litza and her daughters passages on a steamer from Piraeus to Egypt, where they would be safe. For several months Litza had been virtually shunned by her relatives. George Callas had recently been hospitalised in New York, and now that he was out of work there seemed no hope of his ever sending his wife and money, so the Dimitriadises saw no reason to support her, either. The Callases had been forced to rely on Milton's benevolence, moving to a smaller apartment in Harilaou Trikoupi, which he had furnished and on which he was paying the rent. Even so, Litza refused to even consider Egypt where, she declared, Maria would never get anywhere with her blossoming career.

Maria tried her best to ignore the Occupation, as incredible as this might seem. The city's schools, theatres and many of its shops had been closed, and a 6pm curfew imposed, but she refused to be told what to do, especially by foreigners, returning home from her studies at Elvira de Hidalgo's house when she had finished, even if it was after midnight. 'I was fascinated by listening to *all* of Madame Elvira's students,' she later told her friend, Lord Harewood, with a slight touch of the trademark arrogance which she had by then turned into an admirable quality, adding, 'For even with the least talented pupil you can learn something that you, the most talented, may not be able to do.' She actually scolded one German officer, the first time she was apprehended after curfew without an essential permit, telling him, 'I'm just doing my job, the same as you!' She was equally obstreperous when the Germans issued a decree banning all noise in public places. Dragging her piano onto the balcony of her apartment, she would let rip, rapidly attracting an interested audience which included more Germans and Italians than Greeks, so much so that in Maria's street at least, this particular ruling was reversed! Indeed, she was able to strike up a pact with some of these soldiers, who turned up time and time again to hear her sing, stipulating that she would *only* sing providing they brought food for her family, which of course they did until shortages became severe. By the end of the summer, however, many restrictions had been lifted, and when the theatres opened again, Maria learned that she had been appointed a full-time member of the recently formed Athens Opera.

The appointment made her extremely unpopular with a number of students at the Conservatory. Some of the older ones, who had been there several years but made little or no progress, were naturally envious of her success, and accused di Hidalgo of favouritism, and more – for one of the Conservatory's sponsors was none other than General Speidel, the Nazi military commander of Athens.

From a professional perspective, attention was drawn to the flaws in Maria's voice: the vibrato and occasional lack of purity in its upper reaches brought about by sudden emphasis on its dramatic intensity – setting a precedent which would dog her for the rest of her career. Maria, however, proved herself hard as nails and flung herself more intensely into her work, looking down her nose at these 'nondescripts' and treating them with all the contempt she felt they deserved.

Maria also pleased herself regarding who she should or should not fraternise with during these troubled times. In her opinion no race – save the Germans – was inferior to another, and even if they *were* the enemy she could never hate the Italians because they had given the world some of its most beautiful music. It is therefore no surprise to learn that Maria's first lover, during the summer of 1941, was a twenty-one-year-old Italian soldier named Mario, who won his way to her heart the only way anyone could in those days – by taking her to local restaurants and cafés and feeding her.

When she confided in Elvira de Hidalgo about Mario, far from dissuading her, her teacher encouraged Maria, and urged her to begin learning Italian. She would then be able to better understand

her lover, she could only speak a few words of Greek and English –
and be prepared to relocate to Italy as soon as the war was over, for
Italy was the only country in the world where the true career of any
great opera star could begin. Incredibly, Maria learned 'the
language of Dante' as she called it, in less than six months.

Maria also became involved, platonically, with two young British
officers who had escaped from enemy custody after the evacuation
of Crete – even going so far as to hide them in the cellar of the
apartment block at Patission 61. Litza may not have approved of
the idea – particularly as the harbouring of so-called enemy soldiers
meant on-the-spot execution – but Maria, now almost eighteen,
was by this time too important a star to be challenged. Hardly a day
went by when she did not threaten to leave home.

On 3 July 1941, Maria again played Beatrice, this time at the
Park Summer Theatre. This would be her last public appearance
for more than a year as Greece entered a period of tremendous
suffering and hardship. The British had blockaded all the major
ports, preventing food from being imported into the country, and
malnutrition temporarily became a greater adversary than the
occupying powers. The Callas family, supported by Milton
Emberikos's connections on the black market, ate reasonably well,
though they suffered the same as everyone else that winter when
Athens had its first snowfall in twenty years and there was a short-
age of fuel. Maria, aided by Mario, ate better than most: she stuffed
herself with pasta, cabbage and tomatoes, eating twice as much as
she should have, and her fondness for ersatz ice cream made from
rotten vegetables and pig fat is thought to have been responsible for
an outbreak of unsightly boils.

Maria's biggest break so far occurred at the Royal Theatre on 27
August 1942, when Remoundou, the soprano scheduled to sing
Tosca with the Athens Opera was taken ill, and Maria was asked to
replace her. Needless to say, she consented, though the company's
wardrobe master, Nikos Zografos, was presented with an almighty
dilemma trying at such short notice to find a costume big enough
to fit her. In the end, Zografos borrowed an outsized black velvet
smock from the National Theatre, and adapted it as best he could –
though it has to be said that if appearances were anything to go by,

Maria's co-star left much to be desired. Playing Cavaradossi was an immensely fat tenor named Antonis Dellendas, at the time one of the biggest opera stars in Greece, particularly idolised by the Italians, who formed a large part of the audience.

Because she was still dissatisfied with Maria's clumsy gestures, Elvira de Hidalgo personally paid for her to have several lessons with Renato Mordo, an Italian operetta director who was working in Athens at the time. 'Mordo taught me two things which became vital for my career,' she later said. 'One, never to move your hand unless you can follow it with your mind and your soul. Two, to always react on stage towards your colleague as if you're hearing his lines for the very first time. This is, after all, how you would react in a real-life situation.'

The role of Tosca also presented Maria with her first, though by no means the last, off-stage drama, when Remoundou, one of many people who had objected to Maria's appointment with the Athens Opera, tried to sabotage the performance by sending her husband to the theatre, where he waited for Maria in the wings and attempted to prevent her from entering the stage. When he grabbed her by the shoulder, however, Maria turned on him like a vixen and clawed his face with her nails. He responded by laying into her with his fists, and though the injuries sustained by Maria were nothing like those he received from her Italian lover, she was compelled to perform the whole of *Tosca* with the left-hand side of her face shaded by a wide-brimmed hat on account of a black eye.

Litza hovered in the wings all evening, mouthing instructions which were ignored, fanning Maria with a towel between acts, and generally getting on everyone's nerves. Most of those involved with the production expected it to be a failure without its original leading lady. Antonis Dellendas, in particular, so feared that his reputation would be tarnished by playing opposite an eighteen-year-old 'upstart' that he told the director of the open-air Summer Theatre in Klauthmonos Square, where the next performance of *Tosca* was scheduled to take place on 8 August, that he would not sing with Maria. He was subsequently replaced by the lesser-known Leonidas Couroussopoulos. In fact, though not entirely perfect in the role, Maria was singled out for particular praise by the local press. Alexandra Lalaouni wrote of her, 'No matter the value of the training she has been given, the musical instinct and the dramatic sensibility, both in the highest degree, are gifts that *cannot* have come from the classroom, especially not at her age. She was *born* with them.'

Maria was not the only one in her family to have been involved with an Italian soldier at this time. Litza, too, was benefiting from her association with Colonel Bonalti, though with her there had to be an ulterior motive, in this case not an entirely selfish one – food for her family, and advancement for Maria, which no doubt explains why the liaison was tolerated by the immensely patriotic Milton Emberikos.

It was Bonalti who selected Maria, along with five other singers from the Athens Opera, to travel to Salonika in October 1942 for a command performance commemorating the 150th anniversary of the birth of Rossini – a move which was violently opposed by Emberikos, for in performing before an exclusively Italian military audience, such actions could only be regarded as tantamount to collaboration by the public at large. Either Maria was oblivious to this, as has been suggested, or she simply did not care who she was singing to so long as she *was* singing – and earning her family a large food parcel.

Maria was however sensible enough to turn down several other 'command' performances, and did not work again until 19 February 1943, when she appeared in the chorus of Manolis Kalomiras's *Ho Protomastoras* (The Master Builder), a modern opera based on the book by Nikos Kazantzakis, who a few years later would achieve world-fame with *Zorba The Greek*. This was followed a few days later by a benefit concert to provide meals for impoverished children, a charitable deed which earned her the respect of those detractors who had attacked her appearance at the concert in Salonika. Unfortunately, her next engagement only caused her to be even more severely criticised.

Maria's romance with her Italian soldier was still going strong, so much so that he divulged his 'secret' to his superior, Major di Stassio, who reciprocated by inviting the pair to dinner at the Casa d'Italia – a cultural centre at that time funded by the Italian embassy, to which few Greeks could be admitted. A friendly rivalry began between the two men for Maria's affection, the first round of which was won by the much older di Stassio when he arranged for Maria to top the bill in a spectacular concert at the Casa d'Italia. Litza, wisely for once, forbade her daughter to become involved in such a project, particularly when she learned that di Stassio and Maria's lover were both working for Italian Intelligence. Maria only pleased herself. The concert, for which she and Arda Mandikian sang Pergolisi's 'Stabat Mater', was also broadcast on *Radio Athens*, but neither Maria's mother nor her sister were in the audience.

On 17 July, Maria sang *Tosca* for the third time, at Athens' Summer Theatre – an unpleasant experience, for although Antonis Dellendas now changed his tune and *demanded* to work with her, Maria would never forgive him for calling her an upstart. Four days later, she gave her first solo recital at the Kosta Moussouri Summer Theatre – offering a taste of what was to come in future years by choosing a delection of arias which many of her established contemporaries would have found gruelling. This ranged from Handel's 'Cara Selve' from *Atlanta* to Cilea's 'Poveri Fiori' from *Adriana Lecouvreur*, to several arias from *Il Trovatore*, rounding the evening off in a blaze of patriotism with a Greek folk song! Yet whilst the critics were still raving over this concert, Maria incensed them by returning to Salonika for another Italian command performance – making matters worse this time by singing a programme consisting mostly of Brahms and Schubert.

Professionally, Maria was making good if not uncontroversial progress. Her first love, however, was now wrenched from her life as quickly as he had come into it, when at the beginning of September the Allies advanced into Italy, forcing the government there to surrender. The move caused great despondency amongst the Italian troops stationed in Greece, most of whom had suffered as much from hunger and hardship as the people they had occupied, and they asked to go home. The Germans were merciless. Rounding up *their* former allies like so many cattle – dealing with resisters by slaughtering them in the streets – they shipped them to labour camps. Major Bonalti's fate would not be revealed to Litza for some time, but Maria learned just one week later that her handsome soldier had been brutally murdered long before reaching his destination.

For Maria, to have lost the very first person in the world who had cared for her for unselfish reasons, the mental anguish must have been unbearable. She had absolutely no one to turn to, not one human being whom she considered capable or indeed worthy of trust. For this reason, she coped with her grief the only way she knew how, by burying herself completely in her work. Her sister Jackie, who erroneously refers to Major di Stassio as Maria's wartime lover, recalled, 'That she was able to go on performing showed how much the theatrical life had already replaced the world of real emotions for her.'

On 26 September, Maria gave a recital at the Olympia Theatre, singing Mozart's Mass in C Minor, arias from *Fidelio*, *Thaïs* and *Aida*, once again ending with two popular songs. Most of this programme was repeated at the Cotopouli-Rex Theatre on 12 December, when the proceeds were donated to tuberculosis sufferers. Maria had recovered as much as she expected she ever would from Mario's death, and was amorously involved with a man so far removed from him that, had their relationship not been brief and discreet, she would have rapidly become a laughing-stock. Because of the difference in their sizes, some of the locals in Terma Patission had labelled Maria and Jackie 'Laurel and Hardy'. The new man in her life, temporarily, at least, was the Greek baritone Evangelios Mangliveras, some twenty-five years her senior, and tipping the scales at 280 pounds!

During the spring of 1944, Maria actually insisted on playing opposite Mangliveras – when no other singer with the Athens Opera would even consider such a thing – in the German-funded Greek première of Eugen d'Albert's *Tiefland*, a decision which raised more than a few eyebrows. Mangliveras, past his best and suffering from ill-health, was rumoured to be a Nazi sympathiser, and there had never been doubts regarding the composer's political leanings. Born in Glasgow of mixed parentage in 1864, d'Albert had studied with Liszt in London in 1886, and at the advanced age of fifty he had enlisted to fight in World War One – only to turn traitor and cross over to the Germans. The fact that this work was about to be staged in Greece was symbolic of Germany's ousting of Italy as the country's occupying power. For as long as anyone cared to remember, the Italians had had a monopoly on opera, and now it was Germany's turn to prove to them that they were just as good – or so they thought. Maria sang the central role of Marta, the perplexed wife of a wealthy landowner who seeks solace in the arms of a young shepherd, then runs off with him to the mountains. Unfortunately, compared with the masterpieces by Verdi and Puccini, most music critics dismissed *Tiefland* as insignificant, though this particular production, which had the first of its six performances at the Olympia Theatre on 22 April 1944, did enable Maria's fame to spread beyond Athens, as it was reviewed in most of the German language newspapers. Friedrich Herzog of the *Deutsche Nachtrichten In Griechenland* praised her 'earthy natural-ness', adding, 'What other singers must learn, she possesses by nature ... her voice at the top displays a penetrating metallic power, and in quiet moments she knows how to reveal all the colours of her precious, youthful and innately musical soprano voice.'

The audience for the première of *Tiefland* was of course almost exclusively German, and one young lieutenant was so captivated by Maria's performance that he rushed to her dressing room after the performance and presented her with a bunch of flowers – again, the first time this had ever happened to her. His name was Oscar Botman, and over the next few months he and Maria became virtu-ally inseparable. But aside from an obvious mutual physical attrac-tion, the young couple's relationship was cemented by a bond of sadness. Oscar had been badly wounded during a skirmish and was not in the best of health, and like Maria he had lost someone dear to him – his fiancée had recently been killed in a road accident. Stranded far from home, he had no one to turn to and help him through his grief. Maria and he socialised a lot – she was never perturbed by the shocked stares of passers-by, or of the fact that Oscar always wore his uniform and jackboots. Such was her naivety that she never realised that she might have been doing something foolhardy, and she even invited him to her home, incensing her mother and Milton Emberikos – who, of course, had a right to complain because the Callas apartment was registered in his name.

Maria's relationship with Oscar also caused a rift between her and Evangelios Mangliveras, who suddenly asked her to marry him – a proposal which she turned down flat and, it is said, not at all politely, dismissing him with, 'I can't marry you. You're too old, too fat, and too ugly!' Henceforth, though they would have little option but to work with each other, few pleasant words would pass between them.

It was Oscar Botman who escorted Maria to the Olympia Theatre on 21 May where, with her old sparring partner Antonis Dellendas, now a reasonably close friend, she appeared in *Cavalleria Rusticana*. Oscar was also with her the next morning when she sang an aria from *Norma* at a benefit concert for impoverished opera singers, and again at the end of July when she gave two further performances of *Ho Protomastoras* with Mangliveras at the open-air Herodes Atticus Ampitheatre.

It was at this venue on 14 and 19 August 1944 – the eve of the Liberation – that Maria gave her most challenging performances thus far, performances which allowed the press to refer to her for the first time, at just twenty, as *diva*.

By now, Maria's family and acquaintances – there were still very few friends – had become accustomed to her bursts of patriotism, slotted between her 'enemy' work, but this time she pulled out all the stops when invited to sing Leonora in Beethoven's only opera, *Fidelio*, billed in the German-language press as 'a hymn to fidelity, liberation, and the symbolic passage from darkness to light'. Knowing that the entire front row of the ampitheatre would be occupied by the cream of the German command, she vowed to sing in Greek, a decision which had to be supported by not just her co-stars, Dellendas and Mangliveras, but by Oskar Walleck, the director of the Prague Opera who had been brought in to stage it. For Mangliveras, who sang the role of Pizarro, this would be his final role. That September he died of a heart attack, and Maria was one of the few mourners at his funeral.

A few weeks later, the Liberation of Greece began when the Germans marched out of Athens, allowing the Free Greek Army to return from Italy, and for several days there was jubilation on the streets of the city. For Maria, there was only more sorrow. Oscar Botman had not even been given time to say goodbye – three weeks later Maria was devastated by the news of his death. The official verdict was that he had succumbed to blood-poisoning, though she never stopped believing that, like her beloved Mario, he had been murdered.

For the people of Athens, the next few months proved infinitely more harrowing than almost anything that had happened during the German Occupation. The British entered the city, and at the end of November fighting broke out between ELAS (the Communist Resistance Group) and several other resistance groups when the British commander, General Scobie, ordered the dissolution of the former. Many thousands of people were killed when the fighting spread to the city-centre ... the day following Maria's twenty-first birthday, which was celebrated with just three cards and a letter containing $100 from her father, but with no clue as to his whereabouts.

In her later years, Maria would attempt to confuse biographers and journalists by persistently reinventing her past, sometimes in the space of two interviews telling completely different versions of the same event. In 1957, for the benefit of a gullible public and probably hoping to exonerate herself from the 'collaborationist' rumours which still lingered after all those years, Maria told Anita Pensotti that immediately after her performance of *Fidelio*, the Athens Opera had given her three months off so that her mother could find her a job distributing secret mail for the British. She even claimed to have been ensconced at their headquarters, but that she had insisted upon being driven to Patission 61 by jeep so that her mother would not be left on her own. This would have been a nice gesture, had it been true. The fact is, Milton Emberikos, whose father had recently died, managed to get Jackie away from the danger zone – the area surrounding Terma Patission – but Maria and Litza were unable to leave their apartment for more than a month, and would have starved had it not been for one of Milton's friends, who dodged the rooftop snipers to take them food ... a paltry sack of dried beans.

The two women were eventually rescued from almost certain

death at the hands of the partisans – Maria's name had been added to a hit-list on account of her 'involvement' with a German soldier – by an unnamed British officer who smuggled them into the Park Hotel, where they stayed until the New Year, by which time much of the aggression had subsided.

On 14 March 1945, very much against her will, Maria once again appeared in *Tiefland*. Her performance was well received by the audience at the Olympia Theatre, though as she entered the stage-door the other members of the cast jeered and spat at her. A few days later, when her contract came up for renewal, the director of the Athens Opera issued the statement: 'Maria Calogeropoulu has not had her contract renewed – she has played too active a part in the last months of the Occupation.' In effect, without actually using the word, her peers had branded her a collaborator for her liaisons with Mario, Mangliveras and Oscar Botman, and threatened strike action should she be allowed to stay with the company ... when in fact all she had searched for had been a little love and understanding.

Maria announced at once that she now intended leaving Athens to its own devices. As she told Lord Harewood in their televised interview of 1968, 'I had completed, shall we say, my schooldays. I had learned, I had known how far I can go, what I must do.' There was also the not inconsiderable threat that, as an American citizen, should she leave it too long before returning to the country of her birth now that she was an adult, that citizenship might have to be relinquished.

Maria still had the money sent to her by George Callas, and in April she learned that a boat had been commissioned to leave the port of Piraeus for New York in mid-September, exclusively for the repatriation of American citizens. Maria had but one contact in New York – the Greek bass, Nicola Moscona, a resident of the Metropolitan Opera and friend of Elvira di Hidalgo. Therefore, after dashing off a letter to Moscona explaining her intentions, the very next morning Maria presented her papers to the appropriate authorities – ignoring her mother's and di Hidalgo's pleas – and secured herself a passage. She then set about re-establishing her reputation, by no means an easy task now that she had been blacklisted by the Athens Opera. Working independently, she arranged a matinée at the Olympia Theatre for 20 March – rubbing salt into the wounds of these colleagues who had snubbed her – for British troops, her way of thanking them for saving her life. This was to be her only recital of exclusively British songs and included works by Vaughan Williams, Purcell and Sir Landon Ronald. The concert was successful enough for her to organise another, this time to raise money for herself, to augment the $100 she already had for the trip to America.

The 'Maria Calogeropoulo Farewell Recital' took place on 3 August at the Cotopouli-Rex Theatre. Accompanied by one of her few allies from the Athens Opera, the pianist Alice Lycoudi, Maria sang a powerful selection of arias from her favourite operas: *Il Trovotore*, *Aida*, *Oberon*, *Don Giovanni*, and Rossini's little-performed *Semiramide*, along with a curious set of Spanish folk songs which proved that, if nothing else, she knew how to offer her audiences variety. Her effort earned her several thousand drachma, which she added to her savings – a far cry from the story she later invented, that she had flashed an empty purse at Customs officials on leaving the country. Even so, it was an incredibly brave venture for an unattached, inexperienced young woman to be undertaking, though not one which overtly perturbed her, as she would later recollect: 'It was not simply a question of courage. It was something deeper, an unlimited faith in the divine protection that I was certain would not fail me.'

In fact, this concert was so successful that, with incredible nerve, the director of the Athens Opera approached her with a view to 're-negotiating' her contract, and offered her the lead in the Lyric Theatre's new production of Karl Millöcker's *Der Bettelstudent*. Maria accepted the offer. Hardly anyone believed that she could carry out her threat and actually leave Athens, and even Elvira de Hidalgo was confident that within a few months, her most cherished pupil's 'indiscretions' would have been forgotten. The première took place on 5 September, but for Maria, there would be but one performance. True to her word, she exacted her revenge on the Athens Opera by leaving them in the lurch – the Millöcker role was an exceedingly difficult one, and she knew that no one else would ever be able to sing it. Then, on 14 September after a hurried lunch with the Mayor of Piraeus – and refusing to allow anyone to accompany her to the harbour but Elvira de Hidalgo, to whom she owed *everything*, with her meagre belongings packed into two battered suitcases, Maria boarded the SS *Stockholm*, and promised herself that she would never set foot in Greece again.

3

O Scetto, Alfin sei Mio!

I accept advice. I seek it. But my friends must never be clumsy! I cannot be taken *too* abruptly because then I become truly wild!

When Maria arrived in New York in late September 1944, she was astonished to find her father waiting for her outside the Customs Hall. George Callas, now running a small but successful pharmacy on West 157th Street, had seen her name in the passenger list of the SS *Stockholm*, printed in one of the Greek-language newspapers. 'Sobbing from joy, I hugged him as though he had been raised from the dead,' she later recalled, again for the benefit of the legend. Maria was pleased to see her father, and happy that he was settled with his latest mistress, one who seemed to be taking care of him – Alexandra Papajohn, a jovial, buxom woman in her mid-forties. Maria found herself getting on well with Alexandra, though this did not compensate for the fact that she still regarded her father as tiresome because of his lack of interest in opera, and she hoped that she would not be staying with him for too long.

For the time being, however, Maria had no option but to accept her father's hospitality. Nicola Moscona, the man who had made her promise to seek him out as soon as she landed in America, at first refused to have anything to do with her. Since receiving

Maria's letter, Moscona had received others from friends in Athens detailing some of her 'activities' during the Occupation. Such a rebuff, however, only fuelled her determination. She reverted to the name Maria Callas, and began doing the rounds of impresarios, opera houses and theatre companies, clutching her slender but impressive portfolio of Greek newspaper clippings, which she had translated herself during the sea voyage – the German ones she had dispensed with. Very soon, though, she realised that she was wasting her time, coming to the self-ingratiating conclusion that absolutely no one in this rich, powerful city would ever engage a fat, Greek soprano. Despondency then turned to bitterness when the great tenor, Giovanni Martinelli, *did* take the time to listen to her before dismissing her with a curt, 'You show great promise. Why not start taking lessons?'

Not taking Martinelli's insult lightly, Maria pestered Nicola Moscona day and night until he agreed to meet her, principally to get her off his back. Then, with incredible nerve, she told the bass that unless he secured her an audience with Toscanini, she would never speak to him again! Regarded by many as the greatest conductor who ever lived, Arturo Toscanini had enabled La Scala in Milan to become the most famous opera house in the world. In 1936, since he opposed the Fascist regime, he had relocated to New York, where he now ruled supreme with the NBC Symphony Orchestra. Moscona, however, refused Maria's request, and she was good to her word – even when they worked together a few years later, the hatred was still present and much of their communication was conducted through an intermediary.

Over the next two months, Maria treated herself to something she had never had before – a social life. Her godfather, Leonidas Lantzounis, had recently married an American girl, Sally, who was about the same age as Maria and who helped her to shop for a new wardrobe – not an easy task, for Maria's taste in clothes was bizarre to say the least. The last few months of the Occupation had caused her to lose weight, but in a city rich with treasures on every street corner – pizzas, hot-dogs, hamburgers, pancakes in maple syrup – Maria's resistance was nil, and she rapidly piled on the pounds until, by the end of the year, she weighed a not very flattering fifteen stone.

Finally, in January 1946 Maria auditioned for the former mezzo soprano, Louise Caselotti, who ran a successful opera school in New York with her ex-lawyer husband Eddie Bagarozy. Initially, Caselotti disliked Maria – she found her arrogant, loud, and more than a little flirtatious with her husband. Bagarozy, on the other hand, initially only fell in love with the voice – a little raw around the edges, perhaps, and strident in its upper register, but a voice with quite phenomenal promise. He immediately compared her with Emmy Destinn (1878–1930), his favourite soprano whose 1924 recording of his best-loved aria, 'Suicidio' from Ponchielli's *La Gioconda*, had yet to be surpassed. He therefore took her on as a non-paying student, and within a week Maria's Machiavellian charm had captivated Louise Caselotti, who told her to treat the Bagarozy's Riverside Drive apartment as if it were her own. This was one offer Maria found hard to refuse, for she was beginning to find her father's company as stifling as Litza's had been. What Caselotti did not know, of course, was that Maria and Bagarozy were sleeping together when she was not around.

What happened next, however, staggered Maria's new friends and all but saw her completely ostracised by the operatic world. For some time, Bagarozy had been planning on founding his own company, for which he had teamed up with an Italian impresario, Ottavio Scotto, who had been married to Claudia Muzio, one of the greatest but most temperamental divas of pre-war years. It was a shrewd move. In the aftermath of the war many European opera houses were still waiting to re-open, and their singers and musicians were so desperate to work – and eat properly – that they were willing to do so for a fraction of their regular salaries. Between them, Bagarozy and Scotto engaged Hilde and Anny Konetzni of the Vienna Opera, the Wagnerian tenor Max Lorenz, the Italian bass Nicola Rossi-Lemeni, and the conductor Sergio Failoni. Maria was then signed to sing opposite Rossi-Lemeni, with Failoni conducting, in the company's debut production: Puccini's *Turandot*, a relatively new work which the composer had left unfinished. It had been premièred at La Scala in 1926, with Rosa Raisa singing the title role, but since being performed in Chicago on the eve of the war it had virtually disappeared from the operatic repertory.

Meanwhile, Bagarozy arranged for Maria to audition for the Met, confident that she would at least get a part in the chorus to tide her over until *Turandot* could be financed and a date set for its première. The company's General Manager, Edward Johnson, was so overwhelmed by what he heard that he offered her the leads in *two* English language productions, *Fidelio* and *Madama Butterfly*, for the Met's 1946-7 season. What Maria offered him in return, however, was a near heart-attack, for in front of his entire staff and a bevy of the most influential reporters in New York, she turned Johnson down flat! She, Maria Callas, would *never* consider singing Beethoven's beautiful work in other than its own language – she had obviously forgotten that, only recently, she had sung it in *Greek* – and she certainly had no intention, at fifteen stones, of playing a supposedly frail, fifteen-year-old Japanese girl!

Such a decision, retrospectively a wise one, was at the time regarded as sheer ingratitude, and for the rest of that year Maria was not only virtually ignored by her peers, her name also became the butt of cruel jokes. She auditioned for lessons with Romani Romani, the former maestro of Rosa Ponselle, only to be told that she did not need them. By way of contrast she was heard by Gaetano Merola, the head of the San Francisco Opera, who advised her to make a name for herself in Italy, after which he *might* consider offering her a contract. Her response, peppered with enough expletives to make a docker blush, was that if she did such a thing, she would not return to work for him were he the last impresario on earth. Then, at her wits' end – in an act which may only be described as two-faced selfishness, bearing in mind the events of the past – she penned an impressive plea to her mother in Athens, begging her to come to New York and help her!

Maria's letter was conveyed to Litza by Leonidis Lantzounis, who was about to spend his summer holidays in Athens. Until now, Maria's missives to her mother and sister had been frequent but unrevealing. She had fought long and hard to get away from this tyrannical woman, and pride had prevented her from divulging what a tough time she was having in America. Now, the truth was out – or at least most of it – and Lantzounis was content to fill Litza in on all the details: the obsessive eating habits, the tantrums, the rejection of a contract with the Met.

Litza knew, of course, that between them there would always be this impossible-to-live-with, impossible-to-live-without situation, but once again she had been given a heaven-sent opportunity to take control, and she grasped it with both hands. Milton Emberikos's mind had been made up for him by his family, following a fierce squabble with them over his father's estate. He had realised that he would never be able to marry the 'lowly' Jackie Callas, and he was no longer supporting her mother, whose only hope now was to borrow the money for her passage from Lantzounis. Then, there was the problem of travelling to New York – much more complicated than travelling *from* there to Greece just after the war, and a lengthy procedure. Eventually, Litza secured herself a passage on a ship to Marseilles – travelling steerage – from where she took the train to Paris and the boat-train to England before boarding the *Queen Elizabeth*, arriving in New York on Christmas Eve 1946.

Maria realised at once that sending for her mother had been a grave mistake. The tremendous show of manners which Litza put on when her husband and daughter met her off the *Queen Elizabeth* was dispensed with once they reached the apartment. Barging into George's bedroom, Litza packed Alexandra Papajohn's clothes and effects into as many bags as she could find, and flung them out of the window into the busy street below. This had an unexpected effect, however, when George subsequently elected to exercise his conjugal rights – a ruse which backfired, as his daughter Jackie reported second-hand in her memoirs. 'His advances in this quarter were met with noisy hysteria as Mother barricaded herself in Mary's room and threatened to commit suicide if he so much as touched her.' Litza's reaction to George's actions, once she had calmed down, was to take up where she had left off when the Callases had last been a family – nagging and bullying her husband and daughter publicly, telling all and sundry how useless the one was, and how successful the other would be now that *she* had resumed control. It is little wonder, then, that Maria referred to her mother at this time as, 'My best friend and my worst enemy'.

Litza also insisted on sitting in on Maria's rehearsals at the Bagarozys' apartment whilst *Turandot* was taking shape, and was largely instrumental in the extensive press coverage this suddenly attracted – though at first she had declared her daughter 'too fat and too drab' for such an exotic role. She also despised Bagarozy's idea that Maria should 'Frenchify' her name to Maria Calas: unable to do anything about this, however, she attempted to 'rectify' Maria's weight problem by demanding that her Chinese princess's costume be made two sides too *small* – before giving her daughter just six weeks to lose almost as many stones!

The première for *Turandot* was set for 6 January 1947, prior to which the entire company transferred to the Chicago Opera House. By this time, Maria and the twenty-six-year-old Rossi-Lemeni had become lovers, though she was still involved with Bagarozy – the photographs taken at the time reveal them as an impressive-looking but mismatched pair. At 5 feet 9 inches Maria was almost as tall as he was, but she was heftier, and whereas he looks immaculate in his pinstripes and Borsalino hat, Maria looks anything but in her Litza-bought clothes.

then, unexpectedly, the American Chorus Singers Union demanded payment upfront for the singers in the chorus, who unlike Maria and her Italian colleagues were not working for a pittance. The impresario's real problems started when he admitted that he did not *have* enough money left. The opening night was postponed several times, until Bagarozy was forced to concede defeat. Instead of *Turandot*, the Chicago Opera House was host to a benefits concert, the $6,000 proceeds of which went towards sending most of Ottavio Scotti's artistes back home. Soon afterwards, Eddie Bagarozy was declared bankrupt, and though he was allowed to keep his New York apartment because it was in Louise Caselotti's name, he was forced to sell his Long Island house, his cars, and his wife's jewellery collection to pay off his debts.

Avoiding her mother as much as possible, Maria sought solace within the arms of her new lover, though her disappointment at having had *Turandot* wrenched from her grasp was short-lived. At the beginning of February the couple returned to New York, where they more or less took up residence in the Bagarozys' apartment.

Here, Rossi-Lemeni, a nephew of the great conductor Tullio
Serafin, introduced Maria to Serafin's friend, the renowned tenor
Giovanni Zenatello, then aged seventy and the artistic director of
the prestigious Verona Festival.

Zenatello had already contracted Rossi-Lemeni for the next two
Festivals, but his current concern – hence his trip to New York –
was to search for a soprano to sing the title-role in his imminent
production of Ponchielli's rarely performed *La Gioconda* opposite
Rossi-Lemeni's Alvise. Several names had been already put
forward, including Zinca Milanov, the Met's pride and joy, but
Zenatello had considered these too expensive. Therefore, when
Bagarozy told him that Maria was so desperate to be launched on
the Italian circuit that he was certain that she would be willing to
perform for next to nothing, the maestro agreed to audition her.
Accompanied at the piano by Louise Caselotti, she sang 'Suicidio',
plus a duet from *La Gioconda* with Zanatello, and without hesitation she was signed up for a paltry 40,000 lire a performance
(around £18 or $60), far less than she had been offered by the Met.

Maria immediately flung herself into financing her trip to Italy
– not an easy task, for in those days she was always broke. Her
godfather, Leonidas Lantzounis, provided her with the fare whilst
Litza supplied her with a wardrobe – the dowdiest she could devise
for this, Litza declared, was all Maria deserved, given her current
obesity. Maria was to be accompanied on the journey by Nicola
Ross-Lemeni and Louise Caselotti, who herself had secured a
number of engagements in Italy, and Maria had the satisfaction of
telling her mother that Litza would be staying in New York this
time, with a husband she loathed and who, in spite of her protests,
had retained his mistress. Nevertheless Litza was allowed to
accompany her to the harbour and kiss her goodbye, for the sake of
publicity, when on 27 June 1947 Maria boarded the SS *Rossia* for
Naples. Before leaving, Maria also signed a ten-year contract with
Eddie Bagarozy – something he had apparently been pestering her
to do for weeks – nominating him her 'personal representative'.
This meant that in return for the usual ten per cent of everything
she earned, Bagarozy would be ultimately responsible for finding
her only the most lucrative engagements. It was a move which

Maria would bitterly regret, years later.

Although there were only to be five performances of *La Gioconda*, Maria was fêted like a true prima donna when she arrived in Verona on 29 June – exhausted not from the ten-day sea voyage but from the overnight train journey from Naples, where she and her companions had taken turns to occupy the only vacant slatted seat in the stifling carriage. She was greeted at the railway station by Gaetano Pomari, the director of the Verona Arena, and after a brief respite at the Academia Hotel escorted her to the plush Pedavena restaurant, where she and her co-stars – Nicola Rossi-Lemeni and the American tenor, Richard Tucker – were guests of honour at a dinner attended by a host of local dignitaries, the most important of whom was a rich building materials industrialist, Giovanni Battista Meneghini, a passionate opera enthusiast who served as the Festival's official escort for visiting artistes.

From the moment they met, Maria and Meneghini got on like the proverbial house on fire. He was not an attractive man – shorter than Maria, he was plump, stiff-stanced and twenty-eight years her senior – but she could not get over his kindness and quite unaffected compassion once she began confiding in him about her background and upbringing. Meneghini – whom she quickly baptised 'Titta' – was the only man she had known since Oscar Botman who, though keenly interested in her work, actually liked her for herself ... indeed, he was so fabulously wealthy that no matter how successful she became, she would never be able to offer him anything but herself. Therefore, when he asked her during the dinner if he might see her again, socially, she readily agreed to a sightseeing trip to Venice the next day – ignoring Nicola Rossi-Lemeni's protests. Her current lover, who may not yet have been jealous of his rival's attentions – or indeed been aware that he *had* a rival – warned Maria that Meneghini's reputation as an elderly Lothario had spread way beyond the confines of Verona, and to be careful. She told him to mind his own business, then dropped the bombshell that their relationship was over – setting a precedent for ending relationships with violent quarrels, only to begin them again, often years later, with equally forceful demonstrations of affection.

After just one week in his almost constant company, Maria was ready to admit that she was falling in love with Meneghini. Indeed, such were her feelings for this unusual little man that she would have been more than willing to make the ultimate sacrifice, as she told Anita Pensotti some years later:

> I went to Venice with Battista, and during that trip our love was born at a single stroke ... if Battista had wished, I would have abandoned my career, without regret, because in a woman's life (that of a *real* woman) love is more important, beyond compare, than artistic triumph.

Three weeks after meeting Meneghini, and happier than she had ever been in her life, Maria was introduced to the man who almost single-handedly transformed her into the greatest prima donna of this century. In 1913, aged thirty-five, Tullio Serafin had conducted his first performance at the Verona Arena, since which time he had become one of the most famous and respected maestri in the world, alternating between Milan, Rome and the New York Met where, in 1925, he had directed Rosa Ponselle in her first *Norma*. Now, he was to direct Maria in *La Gioconda*, and though he was the first to admit that her voice was nothing short of exceptional, he refused to listen to her until she had been put through her paces by the Arena's voice-coach and chorus-master, Ferruccio Cusinati, whose fees were secretly paid by Meneghini.

Serafin did tell her point-blank that her upper register needed to be worked on, and that she should refrain from studying the libretto until she had learned the music – for only within the music would she discern how the opera was meant to be acted. Maria took this one step further, some years later admitting to Derek Prouse of the *Sunday Times* that, whenever the words were not in keeping with the music, she had great difficulty remembering them. 'You just hate saying them,' she declared, adding, 'Sometimes when I first read the libretto I can't help laughing and I think, "Well, I *hope* I can keep serious at this phrase – it's really the most!" But, when I *feel* the music I can generally manage to give a better impression of the words.'

More than anyone else in the world at this time Maria respected

Serafin, telling her friend Lord Harewood, 'He taught me that there must be an expression, there must be justification. He taught me exactly the depth of music. He was the first and, I'm afraid to say, he's the last of those kinds of maestri.' And now, she flung herself almost paranoically into every rehearsal at the Adelaide Ristori Theatre, whilst Meneghini watched lovingly from the back of the auditorium, unaware that Serafin too had fallen in love with her – though in his case Maria did not respond.

At the end of July, Meneghini presented Maria with what she always claimed to be her most prized possession – even after he ceased to be an integral part of her life. This was a priceless miniature of the Madonna, attributed to Cignarolli, which would henceforth accompany her everywhere. Unlike some of her more superstitious contemporaries, Maria never refrained from wearing green or walking under ladders, and though the role was not part of her regular repertoire she considered *Macbeth* a lucky opera, and often deliberately whistled its arias in her dressing room to put the wind up her colleagues. She did however always cross herself before going on stage and on several occasions, if the role was considered 'iffy', she actually knelt to kiss the floorboards ... but above all, she never let her 'talisman' out of her sight.

The première of *La Gioconda* took place on 3 August 1947 before 25,000 extremely discerning spectators at the massive Verona Arena, with a terrified Maria limping on to the stage. During the previous afternoon's dress-rehearsal she had slipped and twisted her ankle, but determined to finish the performance uninterrupted – another 'minor' superstition – she had refused to let anyone look at it. Subsequently it had swollen to twice its normal size, and she was now compelled to wear a bandage and thick stocking under her shoe, which had the appearance of being club-footed. The applause which greeted each aria, however, and the standing ovation at the end of this and the next four performances were more than enough to compensate for her frayed nerves, even though she knew that in such a vast arena she was way out of her depth. The audience, too, did not know quite what to make of this clobbering sixteen-stone soprano, whose on-stage dramatics – culminating in an extremely realistic suicide wherein she hit the deck with an almighty thud, having lost her balance on account of her injured ankle – compromised certain sections of her range. Despite Serafin's teachings now the problem seemed to be her harsh middle register, particularly during the aria, 'Suicidio!'

It was because of this perfectly fathomable 'dilemma', of which Maria was well aware, that Maria refused to sing 'La Gioconda' at Vigerano, near Milan, when approached by the director, Liduino Bonardi – though she did add, snootily he thought, that the venue was beneath her. This point was picked up by Mario Labroca, the artistic director of La Scala, who all but promised her the role of Amelia in his forthcoming production of *Un Ballo In Maschera*, despite what he termed her 'rectifiable vocal defects'.

After the final performance of *La Gioconda* on 17 August, and whilst awaiting Labroca's contract, Maria devoted herself to one exhaustive shopping spree after another with Meneghini, making up for the miseries of New York when Litza had only been interested in making her look a mess. Meneghini lavished money on her like he had no other woman. Maria's taste in clothes was dire, to say the least, but only because she had been brought up to believe that fat meant ugly, therefore meant cheap. She was now taken to the most exclusive fashion houses and beauticians and made to look and feel as though, her music aside, she was serving a purpose. The photographs taken of her at this time show her looking large but regal, and suggest that Meneghini had succeeded in his quest to cure her of her introversion – enough at least to enable her to handle the shock she received in the November, when she heard that Mario Labroca had given the part of Amelia to someone else. For a few days Maria ranted and raved, calling Labroca all the filthy names she could think of and threatening to scratch his eyes out, until Meneghini took her to Milan – to cool off, but ostensibly to look for work.

It was a good move. Just days after arriving in Milan, Maria was auditioned by a representative of Venice's La Fenice Theatre and offered the part of Isolde in the company's Italian-language production of Wagner's *Tristan Und Isolde*, scheduled for the end of December – as well as the lead in *Turandot*. Such was her excitement – the first production was to be conducted by Tullio Serafin with whom, amazingly, she had already lost touch – that she signed the contract without even realising that she had but a few weeks to learn and perfect Isolde, a role she was largely unfamiliar with. Serafin, however, promised her that she would master the role with a good deal of study and determination, and this – along with the 50,000 lire she was being paid for each performance – was all the encouragement she needed.

The first performance of *Tristan Und Isolde* took place on 30 December, when Maria shared the limelight with the Bulgarian bass-baritone, Boris Christoff, whose debut recital had taken place in Rome the previous year, and who had since triumphed at La Scala. It was, however, Maria's *Turandot*, at the end of January 1948, which really got her noticed. By the final performance on 10 February she had been inundated with so many offers of work that she did not know which to choose first. To compromise, therefore, and not miss out on the experience and delights of performing for as varied an opera audience as possible, she accepted *every* one! By the end of November 1948 she would have sung *Turandot* in Udine, Rome, Verona and Pisa, Leonora in *La Forza Del Destino* in Trieste, Isolde in Genoa, and *Aida* in Turin and Rovigo.

Maria's *Turandot* placed an unquestionable strain on her friendship with Louise Caselotti, who had failed to make the career she had hoped for in Italy, and who now begrudged Maria's success with the role which, in effect, had virtually brought about her husband Eddie Bagarozy's downfall. Maria may have been willing to contend with such petty-mindedness, had this been Caselloti's only *faux pas*. However, when she criticised Maria's *voice* – applauded by Beppe Broselli of *Corriere del Popolo* as 'a majestic, splendid instrument, vibrant, warm, smooth and equal in every register', – Maria turned on her with venom and spat out that she never wanted to see Louise again.

There were further problems at the end of 1948 when Maria took *Turandot* back to Verona. For almost a year, she and Meneghini had been virtually inseparable, but when she arrived for her first rehearsal at the Arena, clutching the arm of her old flame Nicola Rossi-Lemeni, tongues began wagging. Although Maria tended to blow very hot or ice cold where relationships were concerned, platonic or otherwise – her friend Roger Normand, of whom more later, told me, 'One day, she would be calling you the sweetest person in the world, and the next day you would be dismissed as a shit for absolutely no reason than she was feeling a little off colour!' – she still had a soft spot for the bass, and had insisted on him appearing with her in *Tristan Und Isolde* in Genoa. Now, he was to sing the role of the exiled king, Timur, in *Turandot* as he had the previous August.

The news of Maria's 'exploits' was now conveyed to Meneghini's aggressive, domineering mother who branded her a 'gold-digger' and 'stage harlot'. Maria was surprised that a fifty-three-year-old man could still be dictated to by his elderly mother. She soon learned, however, how spiteful Madame Meneghini could be when society doors began slamming in her face and when she stopped being invited to *'hoi polloi'* dinners and receptions. Her own mother, too, voiced her opinion from the other side of the world for here, irrevocably, was one situation which Litza could *not* control. Maria did receive encouragement from her godfather, Leonidas Lantzounis – he too had found contentment later in life with a woman much younger than himself.

Maria's reaction was to completely ignore her mother's protests and, so far as the Meneghinis were concerned, she assigned her 'rose-between-thorns' situation, like her future, to Fate.

4

Je Marche sur Tous Les Chemins

What is there in life if you do not work? If you do not
work there is only sensations, and there are but *few*
sensations! You cannot live on them! You may only live
on work, *by* work and *through* work!

During the late summer of 1948, meticulously guided by Tullio
Serafin, Maria prepared for the role which would become synonymous with her name – Bellini's *Norma*, one of the most trying in
the whole operatic repertoire which had first been performed by
the legendary Guiditta Pasta, at La Scale in 1831.

More than any other role in her career, Maria became obsessed
by the formidable Druid priestess who falls in love with the Roman
Governor, Pollione, the arch-enemy of her people ... not surprising,
perhaps, when one takes into account the inevitable comparisons
between the artiste and the character. Both were forceful, domineering, passionate but occasionally cold and seemingly heartless
women – and Maria, like her *alter*-heroine, also knew the dilemmas
and intricacies of falling in love with the enemy. Both knew what it
was like to be worshipped, and to be betrayed by the men they
loved. In all, Maria sang the complete opera ninety times and its
most famous aria, 'Casta Diva', more times than she ever cared to
remember.

The Italian critics, by and large, were no more enthusiastic over Maria's Norma than they had been her Gioconda or Isolde. Initially, there were only two performances at Florence's Teatro Comunale, on 30 November and 5 December, and in those days no one knew, of course, how important the role would become, or how it would be developed over the years. *La Natione* called her 'a soprano of truly significant ability', and praised her technique as 'secure and perfectly controlled'. Control, in effect, was the operative word under the circumstances, for halfway through the first performance she was stricken with appendicitis – refusing surgery until after the second performance, by which time she was in such pain she could hardly stay on her feet. She had planned to sing *Aida* at the end of the month, so this had to be cancelled, yet no sooner had she come around from the anaesthetic than she was rehearsing her next role – Brünnhilde in Wagner's *Die Walküre*.

It was traditional in those days for many Italian opera houses to import German singers for these hugely demanding roles, but Serafin wanted only Callas and, as she flatly refused to sing in German, an Italian libretto had to be found, *Die Walküre* was one of two new productions being mounted by La Fenice for its 1949 season, both to be conducted by Tullio Serafin. The other was *I Puritani*, Bellini's last opera and a work which so tested its singers' resources that it was hardly ever performed. La Fenice had engaged Margharita Carosio, one of Italy's most fêted sopranos, to sing the central role of Elvira, but she now fell ill with influenza, posing Serafin with a seemingly insurmountable dilemma – even an artiste of Carosio's calibre had not been exactly right for Elvira, but she had been the best he could find. In effect, it was Serafin's wife who helped get him out of a very tight corner when, on 7 January 1949 – the day before the première of *Die Walküre* – she overheard Maria singing an aria from *I Puritani* in her hotel room, and was so moved that she rushed to tell Serafin that in her albeit humble opinion, she was convinced that his protégée would be more than capable of taking on two very differing roles at once.

The next morning at ten – very early for her – Maria was summoned to Serafin's suite at the Regina Hotel, bleary-eyed and still in her dressing gown, where she came face to face with the maestro and the artistic director of La Fenice, who instructed her to sing the aria which Madame Serafin had overheard the previous evening. Maria obliged, but when Serafin asked her how much of *I Puritani* she actually knew, she responded that she was only familiar with this one aria, which Elvira de Hidalgo had taught her in Athens. Years later, Maria explained to Lord Harewood what had happened next:

> He said, 'Look, Maria, you're going to do this role in a week!' I said, 'I'm going to do *what* in a week?' He said, 'You're going to sing *Puritani* in a week. I undertake that you study it!' I said, 'I can't. I have three more *Walküries*!' He said, 'I *guarantee* that you *can*!' So, I thought to myself, if a man like Serafin, who is no child, knows his job, can guarantee me a thing like that, I will be no fool to say no! And I said, 'Well, Maestro. My best I can do – more than my best I cannot promise!'

Maria's best, of course, *was* good enough, and in her series of extensive interviews with Anita Pensotti she was justifiably proud of her unprecedented achievements during the first three months of 1949 which, as she rightly pointed out, had much more to do with sheer good luck than the exaggerated ambition she was accused of by some of her contemporaries.

> That very day, Wednesday, I studied *Puritani* for several hours and sang *Walküre* in the evening. Thursday, several more hours of study, and again on Friday with a performance of *Walküre* in the evening. Saturday, with understandable nervousness, the first dress-rehearsal of *Puritani*. The next day, the final matinée of *Walküre* and the dress-rehearsal of *Puritani* … this went on stage on Tuesday. Then I sang *Walküre* in Palermo, and *Turandot* in Naples, *Parsifal* in Rome, and so on …

Maria's Brünnhilde, the critics had approved of. Her Elvira they positively raved about, even though in learning the role hastily she had improvised some of the words – the beautiful aria, 'Son vergin vezzoza' (I am a blithesome virgin) came out as 'Son vergin vizioza' (I am a *vicious* virgin!). No that anyone cared! Until *I Puritani*, Maria had been just another soprano – albeit a fine one. Now, the Italians regarded her as a phenomenon, referring to her for the first time simply as 'Callas', praising her 'limpid, beautifully poised voice', her 'vivid temperament', and her 'awesome, sinister and inexorable upper register'.

There had also been an amusing moment during the rehearsals for the Rome *Parsifal* when Maria had refused to kiss her onstage lover, sung by the Viennese baritone Hans Beirer, screaming at Serafin, 'His breath stinks of God knows what!' Beirer had been promptly dispatched to scrub his teeth, but Maria had still refused to kiss him, this time claiming that she did not know *how* to kiss a man in public. Serafin had then mounted the platform and shown her how – planting a long, lingering 'smacker' on the baritone's mouth which, Maria later declared, both men had enjoyed immensely.

Maria's success and a reluctant sense of duty had not prevented her from dashing off the odd letter to her mother or sister since her arrival in Italy. Though she now knew that she could manage perfectly well without the former, she still had some feelings for Jackie, and in the February she invited her sister to spend a holiday with her and Meneghini in Verona. Jackie jumped at the chance, and not for entirely unselfish reasons, as she later recalled: 'Perhaps, I fantasised, I could take up the piano again and Mary and her new friends would help me get started. Anything was possible.'

The trip was a disaster. Jackie saw nothing of the Italy Maria had promised to show her, and hardly anything of Maria herself who was constantly accompanied by Meneghini – when not rehearsing for a forthcoming visit to Argentina, she spent most of her time eating and was now described as 'immensely fat'. She had also become extremely bossy. 'After those first days she had ceased to be warm and sisterly and had gradually adopted the sort of mannerisms I imagine she used in the theatre to give herself the authority she needed,' Jackie remembered. 'Bit by bit she was becoming Maria the diva and was no longer Mary the sister.'

It is interesting to note that from this point in her memoirs

Jackie Callas – who has infuriated the reader by persistently calling her sister *Mary*, allegedly because Maria had infuriated *her* by publicly addressing her as Cynthia – only refers to her as *Maria*. Jackie also spoke of Maria's indifference, if not cruelty, to others. If she is to be believed – and there seems to be no valid reason why she should have fabricated such a story – at the beginning of the year, Maria had received a letter from Colonel Bonalti. Her mother's former lover had read of her success in the Italian newspapers, but sadly was now terminally ill in a hospital not far from Verona and had begged Maria to visit him so that he might rekindle some happy memories before he died. According to Jackie, Maria refused to see him.

A few days after seeing Jackie off at the railway station, Maria cut her first gramophone records for the famous Cetra label. This session came about after the company's managing director tuned in to her broadcast for *Radio Italia*, from Turin on 7 March, in which she had sung arias from *Norma, I Puritani* and *Aida*. Several of these were now committed to shellac, along with the 'Liebestod' from *Tristan Und Isolde* – to be issued towards the end of the year on three 12-inch 78 rpm records. *All* are thought to have been recorded in single takes.

Meanwhile, according to Jackie Callas, who later claimed that *she* had been largely instrumental in forcing his hand, Meneghini had proposed to Maria during her sister's stay in Verona. The couple decided to get the wedding over with before Maria left for Argentina on 21 April – because of business commitments, Meneghini would not be accompanying her. The marriage presented Maria with certain difficulties, for despite her deep affection for the man she was hopefully going to spend the rest of her life with, she did not wish for any unnecessary red-tape to get in the way of her career, and she wanted absolutely no involvement with his family or her own. Also, as she was Greek Orthodox and Meneghini a Catholic, it was necessary to acquire a papal dispensation before the ceremony could be arranged – which left her doubting whether they would be married before she left Italy. She therefore decided to set the ceremony for later in the year, and chose her nameday, 15 August, Meneghini, however, declared that this would be too late because several of his relatives had already objected to the marriage. He was also afraid that being separated from Maria for too long, and by thousands of miles, might just tempt her to change her mind – though he does seem to have been convinced that she was not in the least worried over the difference in their ages. 'I knew very well that when I was seventy, Maria would only be forty-two,' he recalled in his posthumously published memoirs. 'I had called her attention to this fact many times, but it did not matter to her. She wanted to marry me, no matter what.'

With his phenomenal wealth, Meneghini was able to cut corners. Just before three in the afternoon of 21 April – Maria was sitting in her hotel suite, surrounded by her luggage – a car arrived to take her to the Town Hall at Zevio, just outside Verona, where the civil ceremony took place. Two hours later, she and Meneghini were married in a side-chapel of Verona's Chiesa dei Fillippini. Aside from the priest and sacristan, the only others present were the witnesses: Meneghini's brother-in-law Dr Giovanni Cazzarolli, and a business acquaintance named Mario Orlandi. Meneghini's other relatives knew nothing of the time or location, and the first Maria's parents learned of the wedding was the next day when they received a telegraph – somewhat insultingly composed in Italian: SIAMO SPOSATI E FELICI (We are married and happy).

Although Maria appears to have initially been deliriously happy with Meneghini, she would always regret that her wedding had been 'a rushed job'. 'We exchanged vows and swore eternal love,' she told Anita Pensotti. 'I hadn't even the time to buy a new dress. Once again I had been denied the joys and fantasies dearest to a woman's heart – the wedding preparations, the gifts, the flowers.'

Neither was there to be a honeymoon. Immediately after the ceremony, Meneghini drove her to a hotel in Genoa and early the next morning she boarded the SS *Argentina* for Buenos Aires. She did, however, have one consolation for her alleged misery – Nicola Rossi-Lemeni, her ex-lover who would be supporting her on the tour, was waiting for her on the ship.

On 20 May, at the Téatro Colón in Buenos Aires, Maria sang the first of her four *Turandots* to a mixed reception from the Argentinian critics who did not know quite what to make of her on-stage histrionics – frequently overplayed at the expense of her voice, and badly affecting her range. Maria took such adverse criticism badly, simply because it was largely petty and unwarranted. The role of Turandot has always been regarded as 'vocal suicide' by sopranos – the recording Maria made of 'In Questa Reggia' in 1954, for example, is a powerhouse performance equalled by no one else in operatic history, and leaves little doubt as to why, singing with such ferocity, her voice burned itself out whilst Maria was still in her prime. After the final performance on 22 June, she vowed never to sing Turandot again on the stage.

Maria's salvation in Argentina was her four performances of *Norma*. 'A vigorous and human dramatic interpretation', enthused *La Prensa* – though by 2 July and her one-off *Aida*, never one of her preferred roles, their enthusiasm had plummeted once more. Much better received was her 'farewell' concert seven days later, still at the Colón and with Serafin at the helm, in honour of the 133rd Anniversary of Argentina's Independence, where 'Casta Diva' earned her a standing ovation.

Maria's nights may have been consoled by Nicola Rossi-Lemeni: he, however, was merely able to satisfy her physical cravings and, so far from home, she was indescribably lonely. Besides composing a series of astonishingly passionate and romantic letters to her husband, Maria telephoned or cabled him every day, insisting that the bill be footed by the management of the Téatro Colón, whom she held responsible for her misery! Many of these letters, despite Maria's insistence that they should never be read by anyone else, were published in his account of their years together, *My Wife Maria Callas*. By this time, of course, Meneghini felt so badly done by that he no longer cared what the world thought of his betrayal of her confidences, so long as he could get one over on Onassis.

Meneghini had also instructed the theatre director – again at his own expense – to cable Verona with every one of Maria's press reviews, only to berate the unfortunate man each time these were unfavourable or unflattering! It is hardly surprising then that the staff at the Téatro Colón were pleased to see the back of Maria, making it quite clear that she would never sing there again if they had any say in the matter.

When Maria returned to Verona in August 1949, her husband was no longer ensconced in their hotel suite, which he had only rented in the first place because life at the Meneghini family home had been made impossible by his mother. During Maria's absence, Meneghini *had* attempted a reconciliation with this nasty old woman, to no avail, hence his decision to buy the plush penthouse over his company offices at 21 San Fermo, overlooking the Arena. He had the penthouse decorated in the most garish fashion – not that Maria minded the shocking-pink wallpaper and curtains, the bright green carpets, and the wealth of gold-plated mirrors, for her tastes in decor were just as bizarre as his. For several weeks, too, she took on the role of an Italian housewife, dusting and polishing, and cooking mostly inedible meals for her husband and his friends, weeks which are said to have been amongst the happiest of her life ... until the novelty wore off, and she flung herself back into her work.

Maria's first engagement – which saw her billed as Maria Meneghini Callas – took place on 18 September at St Peter's Church, Peruga, when she sang the role of Herod's daughter in 'San Giovanni Battista', Alessandro Stradella's little-known oratorio which she only performed as a favour to the conductor, Gabrielle Santini ... an experience which she so detested that she swore never to sing another oratorio as long as she lived. On 31 October she gave a concert at the Arena – 'I might as well, seeing as it's just across the road!' she cracked – when the programme included her usual Norma, Isolde and Elvira, plus her first public performance of 'Ombra leggiara' from Meyerbeer's *Dinorah*, and an aria from Verdi's *La Traviata*. On 24 November she sang Act 2 from *Tosca* and Act 4 from *Manon Lescaut* on *Radio Italia*. Then, on 20 December, at the Téatro San Carlo in Naples, she sang the role of Abigaille in the first of three performances of Verdi's *Nabucco*, opposite the acclaimed baritone, Gino Bechi. Her interpretation of this very difficult role – the first Callas opera to be recorded live, in its entirety – was aggressive to say the least. It pained her that Bechi, in the title role, might steal some of her thunder and she was having none of *that*, she told Vittorio Gui, the conductor at the San Carlo. Thus, when the time came for the couple to take their curtain-call, she 'accidentally' nudged him aside, receiving rapturous applause which was nevertheless well deserved.

Until now, Maria's greatest ambition – to sing at La Scala, Milan, the very pinnacle of the operatic world – had evaded her, and 1950 looked like being another 'routine' year. There was *Norma* in Venice, Roma and Catania, *Aida* in Brescia; *Tristan Und Isolde* in Rome. Maria had never forgiven Mario Labroca for the way in which he had snubbed her and robbed her of her chance of singing Amelia in *Un Ballo In Maschera*, and though she was desperate to add her name to the glittering pantheon of artistes who had trodden the theatre's hallowed boards, she had steadfastly maintained that when *she* played La Scala – there was never any question of *if* – it would be strictly on her own terms. She very quickly changed. her mind about this, however, when at the end of March she was approached by La Scala's Antonio Ghiringhelli, the theatre's priggish, thoroughly unpleasant superintendent. Having seen one of her performances in Brescia, he asked Maria if she would replace the stricken Renata Tebaldi in his production of *Aida*, which was being mounted as part of that year's Milan Fair. Without hesitation, and despite the fact that she and Ghiringhelli took an instant dislike to one another, she accepted.

One year Maria's senior, the great Italian soprano had made her debut at Rovigo in 1944, and her big break had occurred two years later when Toscanini, looking for singers to re-open La Scala after the war, had engaged her to sing Verdi's *Requiem*, telling the press, 'She has the voice of an angel!' In 1947, when Maria had been making a tremulous debut at the Verona Festival, Tebaldi had been wowing the city's critics as Margéerite in Gounod's *Faust*. In October 1948, she had been sitting in the audience when Maria had sung *Aida* at Rovigo – at the end of the performance Tebaldi had leapt to her feet to lead the *bravos*, so now it was only logical that Maria should step into her shoes.

In her 'memoirs' recounted to Anita Pensotti, Maria declared an unswerving respect for and adoration of Tebaldi, in those days her peer, saying, 'From that day in Rovigo we became clear friends, exchanging advice about clothes, hairstyles, and even our choice of repertoire. Renata admired my dramatic force and my physical endurance – I, her sweet singing.' Some years later, however, she would be expressing very different opinions about her rival.

Maria had been known in Italy for a little over two years, criticised more than praised, and she should have been grateful to have been awarded this golden opportunity. Inwardly she was apprehensive but delighted, though her stubborn pride – inherited from her mother – would never have allowed her to broadcast such a thing publicly. A few days after accepting the role, she and Meneghini arrived in Milan, where she made it perfectly clear during her next encounter with Ghiringhelli, whose knowledge of opera and in particular bel canto was surprisingly limited – Meneghini was told to remain in their hotel suite – that she was not just another 'chorine' who could be badgered into sleeping with him, as several of his prima donnas and many of the female chorus had done, in the hope of furthering their careers. Indeed, because she stood up to him, the Superintendent would always respect her – but loathe her just the same.

The atmosphere was no less convivial the next morning when Maria faced her first major press conference, sitting next to an ashen-faced Ghiringhelli and setting a precedent by responding to every question with witty but aggressive repartee. Yes, of *course* she was thrilled to be appearing at La Scala, but as she was so short-sighted, it was no different from any other theatre! Yes, of *course* she cared about her public, so long as *they* cared about *her*! No, she did not care what the critics wrote about her voice – it was hers to use whichever way she saw fit! No, she did not have an enviable lifestyle – moving from one hotel room to the next! No, she was not nervous to be singing in front of the Italian president, and she certainly was not going to be photographed embracing Antonio Ghiringhelli – she did not even *know* the man. And finally, yes, she was deliriously happy, married to a man old enough to be her father – why indeed should she not be?

The first of Maria's three performances of *Aida* took place on 2 April, but though the public accepted her sufficiently to give her a standing ovation, the critics were largely hostile – Renata Tebaldi had already given six performances of the role, and in their eyes could do no wrong. One even went so far as to suggest that Maria had made up the notes as she went along, another declared that her diction was 'muddy', a third that she should perhaps begin taking lessons again! Maria was undaunted, blaming all *her* faults on a second-rate production which had been staged for a soprano – Renata Tebaldi – less talented than herself, and vowed that when she returned to La Scala, she and not 'that perverted little man' would be calling the shots. Only *then* would the critics realise what they had been missing for many years! For his part, Ghiringhelli – like so many others who had been at the sharp end of her tongue – swore that he would never work with her again, and instead of walking away from La Scala with the contract she had anticipated, Maria resigned herself to the few engagements in her diary – four *Aida*s in Naples, to be followed by a series of engagements in Mexico where she was to sing Tosca, Aida, Norma and Leonora in *Il Trovatore* at Mexico City's notoriously hard-to-please Palacio de Bellas Artes.

On 13 May 1950, en route to Mexico with her friend, the mezzo soprano Giuletta Simionato, Maria stopped off in New York to see her parents for the first time in three years. As with her last trip overseas, Meneghini had stayed behind on account of business matters. The reason for this visit was two-fold: since realising that her mother had almost always been behind her family's woes, she had become genuinely fond of her father, but she also wanted to rub salt into Litza's wounds by showing her how rich and famous she had become without her interference.

Perhaps Maria was disappointed that Litza was not on the quayside to see her bedecked in furs and jewels – a few days earlier, Litza had been hospitalised with an eye infection – but George took her there at once. For an hour or so, the reunion between mother and daughter seemed sincere, particularly when Maria invited Litza to join her in Mexico City as soon as she was well enough to travel. Later, there was an incident in her parents' apartment when Giulietta Simionato asked for a cold drink – George Callas was not in the room, and the lemonade bottle which Maria took from the refrigerator actually contained insecticide. Worse still, according to Maria, was the accusation levelled at her that, had Giulietta not recovered from her ordeal, *she* would have been found guilty of poisoning her and Litza, who it emerged had hidden the bottle in the refrigerator, would have done absolutely nothing to defend her.

A few days later, Maria left for Mexico City, where the conductor Guido Picco and most of the singers from the ten productions which were to follow were waiting to greet her at the Hotel Prince. All received an embrace or a handshake save Nicola Moscona, the man who years before had failed to get her an introduction to Toscanini. Maria walked straight past him, and ignored him all the way through rehearsals, though by 23 May, when the curtain rose on the first *Norma*, they were firm friends – united against the backstage tantrums and irrational behaviour of the German tenor Kurt Baum, who was singing Pollione. Baum, a firm favourite with the Met, simply could not relate to all the attention Maria was getting from the press, and in particular from Antonio Caraza-Campos, the womanising director of the Mexico City Opera. Baum constantly referred to her as 'the fat Greek', and Maria for her part tried to outbitch him during rehearsals by reminding him that he was too stupid to read his lines, let alone memorise them ... a fact which comes across only too clearly in the recording of the performance.

The critics adored Maria's *Norma*, unanimously concluding that she was the greatest soprano to have graced a Mexican stage since Rosa Raisa, the very first Turandot who had performed there during the twenties. 'In the Greek soprano there exists the quality of pure gold,' enthused *Excelsior*'s Mario Paes, who trailed Maria virtually everywhere like a camp-follower, whilst Julius lamented in the same publication, 'We were enchanted, and if anything saddened us at the conclusion of such a glorious performance, it was that we would never again hear another such *Norma* in our life.'

At the Palacio de Bellas Artes, Maria derived untold pleasure from giving Kurt Baum his comeuppance. Usually, if she did not care for a singing partner, the sparring would be reserved for the studio or dressing room. However, the spark for this particular display of fireworks was ignited during the première of *Aida*, when the German upstaged both Maria and Nicola Moscona by deliberately elongating his top-notes in an attempt to drown them and monopolise the applause.

During this first performance, Maria and Moscona graciously conceded defeat, though they were seething within and refused to share their curtain-call with Baum. During the next performance, however, they exacted their revenge – Moscona out-bellowed Baum when he was least expecting it and, in the 'Triumph' scene at the end of Act II, Maria sang an entire *octave* higher than Verdi had intended, holding an ear-splitting E-flat for fifteen seconds! The audience went wild with delight, stamping and cheering for a full five minutes. 'This woman's vocal organ rose to the most glorious height, leaving us literally knocked out!' wrote Mariano Paes, adding for the benefit of her detractors, 'She played her role with such authority, such refinement, such musicality, that whatever objections certain critics have made about her middle register disappear before her more important merits.' Karl Baum, however, was far from impressed and sloped off the stage in disgust.

Later, confronting her in her dressing room, Baum swore that not only would *he* never work with her again, he would personally see to it that she would never sing at the Met. Maria's cutting response to this was, 'And *I'll* see to it that everybody gets to know of your activities during the war!' She was, of course, merely stabbing in the dark – she knew absolutely nothing of Baum's past – though she does appear to have struck a nerve. For the next *Aida*, Baum was as good as his word – feigning illness, he had to be replaced at the last moment by Mario Filippeschi. Though nowhere near as talented as the German, Filippeschi certainly was more amenable, but within a matter of days Baum was back on the scene. Working with La Callas may have more than occasionally been an ordeal one would not wish to inflict on worst enemy, but it gave one prestige!

The next day, Maria's mother arrived in Mexico City, to a welcoming committee which might have befitted a visiting monarch ... something which Maria had orchestrated as a prelude to the biggest but least vociferous showdown of her life. Litza was given a room next to Maria's at the Hotel Prince, which Maria insisted should be filled with flowers throughout her sojourn, and over the next few days – sufficiently naive not to realise that she was being set up – she was introduced to just about every available city dignitary at a succession of luncheons, dinners and receptions. Photographers snapped the pair embracing – Litza wearing a fake smile and the most expensive fur coat her daughter had been able to find, and Maria cursing under her breath. Behind the scenes, few polite words passed between them. After each performance, whilst Maria went off to a club or bar to unwind with Giulietta Simionato or Nicola Moscona, Litza stayed in her room – where she had been assigned the task of clipping Maria's reviews and washing the *Aida* dye out of her underwear.

The première of *Il Trovatore*, with the 'forgiven' Kurt Baum singing the role of Manrico, took place on 20 June. It was a very special production, being the first that Maria had prepared for herself – as she had never sung Leonora before, and as he was not conducting her, Tullio Serafin had refused to help her. Not to be outdone, she excelled herself by returning to the original score and singing the role exactly as the composer had intended. Like the other Mexican premières, this was recorded and one is able to discern her nervousness, but also how the tension between Maria and Kurt Baum had slackened since their *Aida*. Indeed, the two former protagonists seem to be having a whale of a time during their battle for top-notes he ad-libbing an incredible twenty second D-flat during the trio 'Un instante almen dia loco' in Act One – so much so that their 'victim', the baritone Leonard Warren, left Mexico after this first performance ... claiming that he was suffering from altitude sickness!

The final *Il Trovatore* took place on 28 June, and the next morning Maria was driven to the airport. Her mother accompanied her, and the two women kissed goodbye a few minutes before Maria boarded the plane for Madrid, where she was to meet her husband. Litza was to stay on at the Hotel Prince for a few more days, at Maria's expense, before returning to New York to await what she assumed would be the next available 'call-to-arms'. What she did not know what that Maria had made up her mind never to see or speak to her again ... and that this time there would be absolutely no going back on her word.

5

Vi Calmate è Mio Marito

*I am personally incapable of enjoying what I have done
well because I see so magnified the things I could have
done better.*

The Mexican trip had exhausted Maria. During the flight back to
Madrid she suffered a debilitating migraine which did not improve
when she returned home, and Meneghini persuaded her to spend a
few days in bed – her immediate diary only included four 'minor'
Toscas in the provinces and an *Aida* at the Rome Opera. Whilst resting, she began working through the score of Rossini's *Il Turco In
Italia*, her only truly comic role, more's the pity. 'I too certainly
have the right to amuse myself once in a while,' she told Anita
Pensotti, adding that she had looked forward to escaping her habit-
ual tragedies for at least a little while.

The idea that Maria should sing the role of Fiorilla came from
Italy's leading film director, Luchino Visconti, by whom she was to
become fascinated to the point of obsession – until much of her
ardour cooled when she discovered that he was homosexual.

Visconti, the wealthy, aristocratic darling of the Associazone
Anfiparnaso, a coterie of Roman intellectuals and opera buffs, had
first seen her in *Parsifal* at the city's Opera House in February 1949,
since which time, he claimed, he had not missed one of her perfor-

mances in Italy. Many years later, Visconti would speak of this *Parsifal* in a French television interview, remembering how Maria had worn 'a tiny Circassian stool' on her head, which had kept dropping down over her nose, adding, 'I thought to myself, "That woman needs a good costume designer, one who makes hats that won't fall over her nose whilst she's singing!" ' Now, he was truly honoured to be working with her – his movement was sponsoring a two-week season at the Téatro Eliseo, having commissioned four new operas and two revivals – and he told reporters, 'At last the time has come to give Callas a decent hat!'

Maria learned the part of Fiorilla with her usual lightning speed, though she was not convinced that she would make it work. Admitting that she only ever felt optimistic when offered a new role, but that the novelty very quickly wore off, she later told Derek Prouse, 'My first reaction is, "This is something I should love to do, and I know I'll do it beautifully." But the moment I start to work, self-dissatisfaction is constantly hovering. One is a prey to the worst doubts and fears: "I'm incapable. I don't have any voice. I should never have taken on the job!" '

The rehearsals for *Il Turco in Italia* were initially tense, on account of Maria's and Luchino Visconti's unswerving awe of one another – they rarely comprised less than two three-hour sessions each day. Visconti touched her by attending every one. 'Maria is the most disciplined professional material I have ever had occasion to handle,' he later recalled, whilst she more simply observed, 'Bigger than di Hidalgo, even bigger than Serafin, Visconti was my god.' Visconti was of course falling not in love with her, but under her spell, as do many in the presence of a mighty diva, which was what Maria was rapidly becoming. She, for her part, was captivated by his intelligence, his gracious manner, and above all his sound knowledge of opera. Against Meneghini's wishes, the pair socialised in the anfiparnaso bars and cafés along Rome's Via Nazionale, where she got to meet many of his equally cultured friends, including the actress Anna Magnani, someone she had always admired.

The première of *Il Turco in Italia*, on 19 October 1950, was a grand affair attended by the cream of Rome society – some of whom half-expected this tragédienne to be way out of her depth as the vivacious Neopolitan strumpet who falls for the visiting Turkish prince. In fact, she only proved that she could sing absolutely everything, as the Italian magazine *Opera* reported: 'Maria Callas was the surprise of the evening in that she sang a light soprano role with utmost ease ... making it extremely difficult to believe that she can be the perfect interpreter of Turandot and Isolde.' Maria also repeated the 'truc' which had driven her Mexican public wild – letting rip with an ear-splitting, lengthy E-flat at the end of Act One.

Immediately after *Il Turco in Italia*, Maria began preparing two major new roles with Tullio Serafin – Elisabeth de Valois in Verdi's *Don Carlos*, and Violetta in his *La Traviata*, to be performed in. Naples and Rome at the end of the year. On 20 and 21 November she sang Kundry in *Parsifal* for *RAI Turin*, pleased to be working once more with Boris Christoff, who sang the role of Gurnematz. It was her way of saying goodbye to Wagner, with whom she had always felt uncomfortable, and the performances were recorded, albeit badly. Even so, the albums are valuable in that, aside from the elusive 1947 *Tristan Und Isolde*, they represent the only complete works by Wagner in the Callas discography.

At this time Maria's migraines were not getting any better, and on account of her weight she is thought to have also been suffering from water-retention. In addition there were rows with Serafin, for now that she was no longer quite so much in awe of her mentor – this had been transferred to Visconti – she was not afraid of criticising him if she thought he was wrong. Serafin knew, of course, that she was unwell, but he allowed her to soldier on, aware that this would be the lesser of two evils – until she collapsed with jaundice. Even so, she would have continued had it not been for her husband, who now *ordered* her to rest. Anyone else would not have got away with telling her what to do, but Maria had known since meeting him that Meneghini only had her welfare at heart, and she was putty in his hands. Reluctantly, she cancelled *Don Carlos*, though when she was feeling a little stronger she went to Florence to continue rehearsals for *La Traviata*, declaring that the role of the dying *demi-mondaine* would be easier to grasp if she too was ill.

La Traviata premièred at the Téatro Comunale on 14 January 1951 as part of the city's tribute to Verdi in this, the fiftieth year of his death. On 27 January, the actual anniversary, she sang *Il Trovatore* in Naples. This had the veteran tenor Giacomo Lauri Volpi singing the title-role, a man who would henceforth carry a torch for Maria, often championing her if he thought she was being unjustly treated by audiences or the press. Lauri Volpi had first heard her in the Rome *Norma* of February 1950, after which he had recorded in his journal, 'Norma is divine! I enjoyed it to the very depths of my soul! Voice, style, bearing, force of concentration and that vital pulsation of the spirit – all these rise to uncommon heights in this artiste!' Now, he dashed off a letter to the editor of a Neapolitan newspaper, attacking the San Carlo audiences for their 'lamentable' treatment of Maria, urging them, 'Open your ears and give the woman a chance!' In fact, Maria had received a healthy ovation each evening and it was Lauri Volpi himself who had been booed for singing flat, so much so that after the second performance this 58-year-old Manrico had been compelled to withdraw from the production.

In the middle of February – she was singing *Norma* in Palermo – Maria received a call from Ghiringhelli, urging her to come back to Milan. For *what*, he arrogantly declared, she would have to wait until they were face to face. Maria may still have hated the man, but she had been awaiting the summons from La Scala for so long that she would have accepted almost anything – save being asked once more to stand in for a stricken Renate Tebaldi, *and* in another *Aida*. Her response to Ghiringhelli remains unprintable, and she slammed his office door so hard that it almost came off its hinges.

Maria's outburst was also partly responsible for her not singing the role of Magda in what would have been, apart from the earlier *Ho Protomastoras*, her only modern opera – Gian Carlo Menotti's Pulitzer Prize-winning *The Consul*. Menotti wanted to stage his work at La Scala, and Ghiringhelli had instructed him to choose his own cast. However, when the composer plumped for Maria, the director refused to have her in his theatre other than as a guest-artiste. Menotti asked Maria all the same, and received only a slightly less vociferous response – she would sing at La Scala as neither guest nor understudy, but as its *star*. Ghiringhelli would pay for his folly for the rest of his life!

Meanwhile, there was one offer which Maria could not refuse. She was approached by Contessa Wally Castelbarco-Toscanini, the daughter of the legendary conductor and a friend of Visconti, who acted as a go-between in securing her an audition for the role of Lady Macbeth in Verdi's *Macbeth*. Toscanini, now aged eighty-four and very frail, was planning to put this on first for Bussetto, near the composer's birthplace, to be followed by a season at the New York Met. Maria passed the audition, even though she argued with the tyrannical old man over the score, but sadly the project was abandoned a few weeks later when he suffered a stroke.

At around this time, Maria accepted a tour of South America to begin in that July. She was disappointed that Serafin would not be travelling with her this time – he would be in Buenos Aires, but conducting Gigli, though he personally assured her that she would get on famously with his 'stand-in', Oliviero de Fabritiis. Also, in what was a successful bid to reassure her father that she still loved *him*, she wrote to George and informed him that she wanted him to meet her husband, who would be travelling overseas with her for the first time. Litza took the rebuff badly, declaring that if her husband could go off in search of adventure, then so could she. Unfortunately, this involved foisting herself upon her elder daughter in Athens. 'I could hardly bear it,' Jackie later lamented. 'I had forgotten her incessant nagging, her almost constant library of complaints about how badly treated she was.'

By now, Jackie Callas had given up hope of ever marrying Milton Emberikos, though the couple were still inseparable. Milton, however, flatly refused to support his unwelcome visitor, so Litza wrote to Maria in Verona, asking for a monthly allowance which, she declared, was only hers by right, considering all she had sacrificed to set Maria on the road to success. This was partly true, of course. Even so, Maria ignored the letter.

Meanwhile, on 26 May, for the opening of Florence's May Music Festival, Maria sang Elena in the first of four productions of Verdi's virtually forgotten *I Vespri Siciliani*. This was her second major work in six months with Boris Christoff and, like the first, it was recorded. Her performance compelled Newell Jenkins of *Musical America* to enthuse, 'Miss Callas is certainly among the best singers on the opera stage in Europe today, and a fine actress as well.' Conducting these performances and making his Italian debut was the much loved, legendary Austrian-born maestro, Erich Kleiber, a man whom Maria would always admire on account of the stance he had taken against Nazi Germany. In 1923, at the age of thirty-three, he had become director of the Berlin State Opera, but twelve years later he had turned his back on the country which had adopted him, moving to South America, where he had become an Argentinian citizen – only returning to his former post after the war. 'Kleiber and I had so much in common,' Maria later said. 'Born in one country, forced to travel to another for the sake of our careers, then forced by circumstance to relinquish our nationalities when in truth we never really felt as if we belonged anywhere.'

Within hours of the curtain coming down on *I Vespri Siciliani*, the news of Maria's triumph had reached Antonio Ghiringhelli, who set off for Florence immediately to offer her the same role to open La Scala's new season on 7 December, along with *Norma*, and the role of Constanze in the Italian-language production of Mozart's *Die Entführung aus dem Serail*. Maria was grateful, of course, but hardly surprised – and she was still referring to Ghiringhelli's kingdom as 'just another theatre'.

For several months, Maria had been negotiating with Rudolf Bing, the director of the New York Met who had only recently heard her for the first time – in a tape-recording of her Mexican *Aida* sent by his friend, Erich Engel of the Vienna State Opera who had actually been sitting in the audience. Enthralled by her voice, yet knowing absolutely nothing about her – not even her age and nationality! – Bing had contacted his Italian representative, Liduino Bonard, and asked him to negotiate a contract with her. Bonard had caught up with her after the *Trovatore* in Naples, where in view of the rumours circulating about her temperament he had found her surprisingly amenable. There was of course a sound reason for this: Meneghini had not been present at the meeting.

Maria had told Bonard that she would be prepared to sing up to eight performances in the Met's 1951-2 season for $700 each, plus expenses, and providing she would not be expected to stay in New York for longer than a month. These conditions, however, had not been accepted by Bing, a man renowned for being surly, tight-fisted and rude to some of his artistes. His response was that Maria would have to remain in New York for at least two months, to accommodate three weeks of rehearsals, and that as an 'unknown quantity' in the United States, to eliminate risks he would not be able to pay her more than $400 a performance, out of which she would have to pay her own expenses.

Upon hearing this, Meneghini hit the roof: Maria *would* spend the required two months in New York, he declared, but only for $600 a performance. Maria had then complicated matters by informing Bing that she was so anxious to prove her worth at the Met that she would be willing to sing there for just $200 a performance, providing he allowed her to choose her opening role. Bing did not accept this, either. His heart was set on her singing the role that had brought her to his attention in the first place – 'Aida'. For this, he informed her through Liduino Bonard, she would be paid the original $400 a performance and offered the option of a spring tour of the United States, *plus* possibly top-billing in the Met's 1952-3 season. Maria agreed to meet him halfway: she would sing *Aida* as requested, plus one or two operas of her choice, but Bing would have to cough up her husband's expenses. On top of this, she did not foresee any reason why rehearsals should exceed ten days, particularly as in Italy she was renowned for learning new roles in less than a week!

Bing had been livid, knowing that he had finally met his match, yet such was his keenness to engage her that he now arrived in Florence – using the pretext that he was visiting the Festival – to plead with her in person. Seeing Bing, of course, was proof enough that she was more than worthy of the Met, and she now knew that she would be able to barter to her heart's content. She took an instant dislike to him, and he too was not impressed by what he saw – 'she was monstrously fat and awkward,' he recalled. She also refused to audition for him, saying sharply, 'You've listened to me, tonight. That's the *only* audition you're going to have!' Bing then attempted to bluff, telling her in front of reporters, 'Miss Callas, in my opinion you still have much to learn before you can be a star at the Met!' Maria's only response to this was to smile politely, and walk away. Antonio Ghiringhelli had very quickly succumbed to the idea that having Callas in one's establishment was no longer an option, but an *obligation*.

On 9 June, again in Florence, Maria was tackling yet another new, entirely different role – Euridice in Haydn's posthumously published *Orfeo ed Euridice*, a work which had been written in 1791 and was now receiving its world première! The critics, however, gave it a definite thumbs-down. No less demanding was the material which Maria selected for that year's two major radio concerts. On 12 March, for *RAI Turin*, she had sung 'Io son Titania' from Thomas's *Mignon*, 'Leise, leise' from Weber's *Der Freischütz*, and Proch's *Variations*. The latter, with its stunning three-octave range, was repeated in her broadcast of 11 June – Maria's last performance before leaving for South America – from Florence's historic Grand Hotel.

When Maria and her husband arrived in Mexico City at the end of June, George Callas was already there to witness the mass hysteria at the airport and, rather than shake hands formally, the two men hugged on the tarmac and continued to get on famously during George's two-week stay in Mexico – in spite of the fact that George did not speak Italian, and Meneghini's English was shaky. During this time, too, Maria's father found himself becoming more and more interested in the one art he had never understood – opera!

The tour kicked off with three performances of *Aida* at the Palacio de Bellas Artes, where the role of Rhadamès was sung by Mario del Monaco who, like Kurt Baum before him, clung to his top-notes and overacted in such a way that some of the critics lampooned him, whilst going way over the top with their praise of Maria. 'She is a beauty of majestic and distinguished comportment,' fawned Junius of *Excelsior*. 'She has the maximum degree of grace for acting, elegance for dressing, temperament for attracting and moving, and above all a voice for singing. And *what* a voice!'

The press, however, did not know what to make of Maria's husband. Her former escort, Nicola Rossi-Lemeni, had not been that much to write home about, one critic declared, but he had certainly been more attractive and lively than this 'funny little man with his black leather bag'. Insisting that she should be paid only in gold dollars, Meneghini would take his bag to the superintendent's office each evening after her performance to collect Maria's fee, emerging like some victorious biblical tax-collector.

After *Aida* and a concert on the Mexican radio, Maria gave five performances of *La Traviata* with Cesare Valetti, the pal of Visconti's who had sung with her in *Il Turc in Italia*. By the last one, however, on 22 July, though her voice was in tremendous form, Maria was beginning to show signs of physical exhaustion – a combination of altitude sickness, insomnia and water-retention which caused her ankles to swell. When she reached Sao Paulo, to be reunited with Tullio Serafin who was to conduct her *Norma* and her alternating Violettas with Renate Tebaldi, she was so ill that only the *Norma* of 7 September and one *Traviata*, two days later, could take place.

singing with Maria in the latter were two young men who would later work with her around the world and become firm friends – the tenor Giuseppe di Stefano, and the baritone Toto Gobbi, who had fond memories of this first collaboration when writing his 1980 autobiography, *My Life*:

> Looking back, I cannot believe that anyone else in the whole history of the work ever sang that first act as she sang it then … I find it impossible to describe the electrifying brilliance of the coloratura, the beauty, the sheer magic of that sound which she poured out then … It was something one hears only once in a lifetime. Indeed, one is *fortunate* to hear it once!

Initially, Maria was pleased to see Renate Tebaldi, and whilst she was recovering in Sao Paulo, the pair socialised quite a lot, chatting over old times, and looking forward to the next few weeks when both would be making their debuts in Rio de Janeiro. Unfortunately, what Maria had termed 'a close friendship' would soon disintegrate, largely because of over-inflated egos and artistic licence, and only partly due to their differing views of opera. 'I was a little ahead of her and maybe she was insecure about that,' Tebaldi told the *Sunday Telegraph*'s Mel Cooper in 1991. 'For me, opera had to start with the singing. Maria was willing to sacrifice technique, even beauty of sound, to dramatic demands. I felt that the drama had to be expressed beautifully, musically – that opera was all in the throat.'

Tebaldi's *La Traviata* opened at the beginning of September, and earned her huge critical acclaim. Then, on 12 September, Maria sang *Norma* in a sparkling performance which brought the house down and earned her nine curtain-calls, inadvertently sparking off a vendetta which would drag on for many years, and not just against Renate Tebaldi. As Sergio Segalini, a leading authority on opera, pointed out in his 1979 portrait, *Callas: Les images d'une voix*, 'Callas was about to wage a war to the death against that world which had drained singing of its most subtle inflexions, its liveliest imagination, and of its most telling variations in *vibrato.*'

This 'war' began hotting up one week later when both sopranos were on the same bill in a benefit concert at the Municipal Theatre – benefiting who or what was never made clear. Each of the artistes had agreed upon a single item – Maria had chosen 'Sempre libera', Tebaldi the 'Ave Maria' from Verdi's *Othello*. After her aria, Maria took a deep bow and left the stage. Tebaldi, however, went against the rules by singing two encores.

Maria was livid, but this was only the tip of the iceberg in what seemed a vindictive conspiracy. On 24 September she sang her first *Tosca* at the same theatre – only to be summoned after the performance to the office of the director, Barreto Pinto, to be told that her three remaining dates had been cancelled owing to public disapproval. She had, in fact, received a standing ovation! Maria's initial reaction, and an unusual one given her character, was to remain calm and remind Pinto of his contractual obligation – that she be paid for the second *Tosca* even though she was not to sing it, and that her two *Traviatas* should take place unless he wanted to be sued. Pinto had no option but to give in, though he exacted his revenge on Maria by replacing her in *Tosca* with Renate Tebaldi. He then added insult to injury after the second sell-out *Traviata*, when she stopped off at his office to collect her fee. Pinto's remark

– 'So, you want money as well as glory?' – pushed her completely over the top and, grabbing the ink-stand on his desk, she would have smashed this over his head had it not been for Pinto's secretary, who wrestled it from her grasp.

Before returning to Italy, Maria signed a contract with the New York division of Cetra Records – the meeting, arranged by Meneghini, took place in the lounge of New York's Idlewild Airport, and was headed by the company chairman, Dario Soria. Although Maria had yet to perform on an American stage, her three 78rpm recordings had been imported into the country, where they had received considerable airplay, so it was merely a question of time. The contract stipulated that she would record four complete operas for the company by the end of 1952: *La Gioconda*, *La. Traviata*, *Manon Lescaut*, and Boito's *Mefistofele* – and Maria's husband saw to it that her remuneration would be more than adequate.

1951 was also the 150th anniversary of Bellini's birth, an event which almost certainly would have been overlooked had it not been for Maria's all but single-handed revival of the composer's work. Therefore, after two *Traviata*s in Bergamo at the end of October, she headed for Catania in Sicily – Bellini's birthplace – where on the actual anniversary, 3 November, she sang the first of four *Norma*s, alternating with four performances of *I Puritani*, all with Boris Christoff. Even her harshest critics hailed this as a considerable feat – in the past, these two hugely demanding roles had usually been interpreted by different kinds of soprano. She told the press in Catania, 'Bellini is my favourite composer, even more so than Puccini or Donizetti. This is because as a person he was stronger, and dare I say, more masculine.' Cynics have since maintained that this latter statement was an example of Maria's dry sense of humour – not only had Bellini suffered poor health for most of his short life, he had also been an effeminate, promiscuous homosexual.

As the La Scala première drew closer, Maria and Meneghini temporarily relocated to a suite in Milan's Grand Hotel. Antonio Ghiringhelli was a frequent but unwelcome visitor – fawning over his 'new star' whilst well aware that she could not stand the sight of him, nor he her. Neither did she get on too well with Victor de

Sabata, La Scala's resident conductor who persistently addressed her by her surname, though she did find invaluable allies amongst the cast – Boris Christoff again, and the baritone Enzo Mascherini. Rehearsals were nevertheless fraught and explosive. Maria had no patience whatsoever with time-wasters and singers who were not as fanatically dedicated to their art as she was – in other words, almost everyone.

Maria also had the annoying habit – at least from her colleagues' point of view – of singing full-voice at rehearsal, an unusual practice which more than a few could not cope with, and of which she once defended herself by saying, 'When a cyclist is training for a big race, he doesn't train at half-speed, otherwise he will never know how he's going to fare in the final. That is how it is with me, and if my colleagues don't like it, they can lump it!'

The first performance of *I Vespri Siciliani* took place on 7 December – the customary start of each La Scala Season, a cultural event which was shared by the entire city, for this was the feast-day of St Ambrose, the patron saint of Milan. Maria proved a sensation, though she was nervous when making her entrance. Sensing her apprehension, *Il Corriere della Sera*'s Franco Abbiati wrote, 'The miraculous throat of Maria Meneghini Callas did not have to fear the demand of the opera, with the prodigious extension of her tones and their phosphorescent beauty, especially in the low and middle registers, and with her technical agility, which is more than rare – it is unique.'

On 9 January 1952, between the final *Vespri Siciliani* and the La Scala première of *Norma* one week later, Maria sang a roisterous Elvira in Florence, opposite Nicola Rossi-Lemeni. At the end of this performance, for the first time though certainly not the last, the orchestra – whom she had screamed at and cursed during rehearsals – were the ones who turned towards the stage to offer her a standing ovation!

If anything, Maria's La Scala *Norma* was an even greater triumph than her Elena, even though the sets were pre-war and rickety. Newell Jenkins of *Musical America*, one of her staunchest and most supportive champions, labelled her Italy's finest dramatic-lyric soprano, adding, 'She electrified the audience by her very presence even before singing a note. Once she began to sing ... her tones came out round and full, with a legato like that of a stringed instrument.'

In mid-March, Maria returned to Catania, this time by public demand, for three performances of *La Traviata*, though she was largely preoccupied with learning a new role – that of Constanze in Mozart's *Die Entführung aus dem Serail*, which she insisted on singing in Italian. Maria did not like Mozart very much, and only agreed to sing the role because it formed part of her deal with La Scala, where it was being performed for the first time. She once denounced his music as 'dull', though with Callas's bel canto embellishments, arias such as 'Tutte le Torture' with its endless series of high Cs and Ds is anything but. Some years later, in one of her Juilliard masterclasses, Maria defended her particular style of singing Mozart, albeit she only brought him twice to the concert platform.

Mozart is usually sung with too much delicacy, as though the singer were on tiptoes, when his music should be performed with the same frankness and bel canto approach one would use in *Il Travotore*, for example. Mozart, after all, *was* a master of bel canto. So sing Mozart as though he were Verdi. There is no difference in the approach.

The première of *Die Entführung aus dem Serail* took place on 2 April, yet by the fourth and final performance – ignoring her husband's protests that she was not only exhausting herself, but on the verge of a breakdown – she had pledged Tullio Serafin that she would have learned another much more complex role by the middle of the month – Rossini's *Armida*, which the composer had written for his fiancée, the soprano Isabella Colbran, in 1818, and which was so difficult that it had not been performed for more than a century. In fact, Maria memorised the score in just five days – or at least thought she had, for at the Générale in Florence on 24 May – the dress-rehearsal attended by the press and local dignitaries – for the first time ever she forgot the words of her opening recitative, stopped the performance, and began again after a hurried study of the libretto. Not that anyone appeared to notice! 'One can readily believe that no one today save Maria Callas could possibly negotiate the incredibly difficult part and make it sound like music,' concluded Newell Jenkins in *Musical America*, whilst Andrew Porter enthused in *Opera*, 'Her presence is imperious, her coloratura not piping and pretty, but *powerful* and dramatic.

Whilst she was in Florence, Maria received a visit from Roberto Bauer, Rudolf Bing's new Italian representative, who asked her if she would be interested in opening the New York Met's 1952-3 season with *La Traviata*. When she asked him if Bing's terms were the same as they had been before, and Baum replied that they were, Maria told him, 'Mr Bauer, go fry an egg!'

Two days before her final *Armida*, Maria sang *I Puritani* at the Rome Opera House. She had been ordered to rest by her husband *and* her doctor as she was only weeks off another trip to Mexico, where for $1,000 a performance she was to be partnered by Giuseppe di Stefano. As usual, she knew best. Yet in spite of her already crippling schedule and heavy repertoire, she was learning two new roles to be tried out in Mexico before being presented to the more critical Italian audiences – Gilda in Verdi's *Rigoletto*, and Donizetti's equally challenging *Lucia di Lammermoor*.

It was as if Maria imagined time to be running out, this quite indefatigable hunger for work. It certainly could not have been for the high fees she was now commanding, for married to Battista Meneghini, she was already technically a multi-millionairess. It was as if she was also still trying to make up for the ugliness of her childhood, as if she was afraid that the bubble might burst at any moment and that she would find herself miserable again, compelled to live in some awful tenement block with her mother, whom she believed to be behind every inhibition and anxiety.

Maria's tenacity impressed the critics. Cynthia Jolly, hailing her as 'one of the singing heroines of the 20th century', wrote in *Opera*:

This all-purpose soprano, a prototype of the legendary singers of old, makes a buxom Elvira who is vaguely disconcerted when she has no virtuoso flights in view. Her tone is not uniformly beautiful but the general impression is overpowering. Her bel canto style is liable to sudden bursts and protuberances which disappear entirely in passages of agility, so that her descending scales are like rippling water.

Maria was in fact effectively little more than an automaton, a skilled technician wholly able to 'drift' from one character to the next and *still* climb inside that woman's skin, unaware of the long-term damage she may have been inflicting on herself, her voice, and those around her. Maria, however, did not feel that she might have been doing harmful things by interpreting roles usually associated with different types of sopranos. A few years later she explained to Derek Prouse, one of her favourite journalists, 'My particular voice *can't* stay in one repertoire. Or rather, my voice has one *main* repertoire, that of Bellini, Donizetti and Rossini, and it comprehends more than one of the modern categories of voices. It is soprano. Period! Pasta and Grisi did *Norma*s and *Fidelio*s, and I'm only doing what they did.'

I Puritani opened Maria's 1952 season, again at the Palacio de Bellas Artes, on 29 May. There were two performances, followed by two *Traviata*s, before the spectacular première of *Lucia di Lammermoor* on 10 June. Based on Sir Walter Scott's novel *The Bride of Lammermoor*, and considered by many to be Donizetti's finest work, this was one of the most demanding in the Italian repertoire – and a work which could almost have been conceived with Maria in mind, with its tale of passion, sexual intrigue, madness and mayhem. When Maria told her Juilliard students in 1972, 'Opera is filled with people who go mad,' there were a few chuckles from the audience. Twenty years earlier in Mexico City, however, the public initially found Lucia's infamous 'Mad Scene' disturbing, though nevertheless thrilling. The applause lasted twice as long as the aria and brought her no fewer than *sixteen* curtain-calls. Even so, the perfectionist within her dismissed this impressive performance – which was recorded, to prove the point – as 'mediocre', and she would not be satisfied with the way she interpreted the role until some years later.

The critics, however, did not like Maria's *Rigoletto*, which she had not wanted to sing in Mexico, claiming that the rest of the cast were under-rehearsed. Quite likely, she could just as easily have given a couple more *Traviatas* and the public would have been appeased – however, Caraza Campos, the director of the Opera Nacional, made her stick to her contract and the ensuing, almost farcical performance was summed up in a few choice words by *Musical America*'s Solomon Khan: 'As an anti-climax came a pedestrian performance of *Rigoletto*, for Mr Campolonghi, the jester, was neither socially nor histrionically up to Verdi's demands. Mr di Stefano's Duke, far from outstanding, and Miss Callas's Gilda, not an ideal role for her, did not improve the situation.'

Maria flew into a rage when she read Khan's review, and if her 'salvation' lay in the final *Lucia* of 26 June and her two *Toscas* a few evenings later – this failed to placate her. Allowing one adverse criticism to obliterate the memory of her many triumphs, she left Mexico vowing that she would never set foot in the country again … and stuck to her word even when, the following year, Antonio Caraza-Campos offered to double her salary. There would also be no more *Rigolettos* on the stage. Back in Italy, however, there was more upset: her mother, silent for almost a year, had re-surfaced to make Maria's life a misery once again.

Having failed to get her own way with her other daughter, and finally admitting that her marriage was over, Litza had returned to New York where she had successfully sued George for maintenance, set by the courts at $100 a month. Then, whilst in New York she had learned of the recent drastic changes in the Greek monetary system where the Treasury had devalued the drachma one hundred per cent against the US dollar – in other words, George's allowance, modest by American standards, would be worth a small fortune if sent to Greece. Litza therefore decided to return to Athens – not a good move, for her husband was now able to get away without paying her a penny, and Litza was unable to do anything about it unless she went back to the court in New York.

Not to be outdone, Litza wrote to Maria, demanding that she pay her the $100 allowance she was not getting from George. The plea was ignored, and the letters became more vindictive. Meneghini, Litza declared, was immensely rich and it was therefore his duty to support the mother-in-law he had never met – on top of this, both of them should sponsor Jackie's new career as a singer. Maria tried to keep the letters a secret from her husband, but Meneghini found them and had them translated. He then wrote a polite missive to Litza, informing her that he was now responsible for Maria's well-being, and that under no circumstances would he allow her to be upset. Maria, however, saw no reason to spare her mother's feelings. Jackie Callas, suffering the brunt of Litza's carping, remembered the reply:

> She went on to tell Mother that as she, Maria, had to 'bark' for a living why didn't Mother also get a job. But it was the ending that shocked us both: 'It is now good weather. Now that it is summer, go to the shore and get some fresh air. If, as you say, you still have no money, you had better jump in the river and drown yourself.'

6

Si Colmi Il Calice ...

We labour for years to make ourselves known, and when fame finally follows our steps everywhere we are condemned always to be worthy of it, to outdo ourselves so as not to disappoint the public which expects wonders of its idols.

On 19 July 1952, five years after making her debut with the role in the same city and at the same venue – the Verona Arena – but this time for 500,000 lire a performance, Maria sang the first of two *Giocondas*. News of her disastrous Mexican *Rigoletto* had reached the Italian critics, and though the public loved Maria's singing, and her 'authentic' touch of dyeing her hair Titian red so that she would not have to wear the traditional Gioconda wig in the torrid heat of an Italian summer, the newspapers generally gave her a bad time. Hearing her for the first time on the stage was the *Chicago Tribune*'s Claudia Cassidy – an ardent, usually unbiased Callas fan who would become a trusted friend and subsequently follow her around the world with scarcely a detracting word. It was to Cassidy that Maria remarked, upon introducing her to Meneghini, 'There *is* a God, Claudia. I should know because I have been touched by His finger.'

Cassidy, however, though 'self-confessedly crazy' about the woman, was not over-enthusiastic about this role.

She is young, pleasant to look at ... She has three voices: a truly beautiful mezza voce of opulence and warmth, some faked, rather hollow chest tones and a puzzling top voice. They tell me she sings high E and F in dazzling coloratura, and it may be that to do this she has sacrificed her dramatic tones. For her Gioconda had trouble with high C, which was wobbly, forced and shrill. The report is that she will not sing the role again. This would be wise, for she has neither the voice nor the ardent personality to bring it to life ...

On 21 July, Maria signed a recording contract with EMI of London. The company's director was Walter Legge, the husband of soprano Elisabeth Schwarzkopf who had been employed by the company since the early thirties and who had recorded, amongst others, Karajan, Beecham, Flagstad, Fischer-Dieskau, Christoff, and of course his wife. Legge had been trying to secure Maria since first hearing her *Norma* at the Rome Opera House, but without success. Although Meneghini was nothing less than fanatical about making money – and even more so about hanging onto it – at that time Maria had been perfectly content to remain with Cetra. Since then, however, her friend Dario Soria had left the company to work for EMI's American label, Angel Records. Therefore, when Legge had approached her once more in the spring, she had at least shown interest and would have signed there and then, had it not been for her ever-suspicious, parsimonious husband.

The Meneghinis, Legge was told, adhered to an old superstition wherein it was considered bad luck to sign any legal document for two weeks – for once a deal had been mutually agreed, there was no going back on an Italian's word of honour. Walter Legge apparently swallowed the story, which of course was only a ruse by the wily Meneghini to get his wife more money – one which worked, for when Legge returned to Verona a few weeks later, Meneghini told him that the contract had not been signed and returned because EMI's offer had been grossly inadequate. When Maria was asked for her opinion, she replied that she did not have one – her husband, she added, was in charge of the financial aspects of her career. The next morning, however, the contract was signed on

Meneghini's terms – and with Maria's insistence that *all* her complete operas should be recorded on the stage of an empty La Scala, on account of the theatre's formidable acoustics. What she probably did not know was that Walter Legge would have agreed to almost anything, for Maria Callas was too valuable a commodity for EMI to even consider turning down.

On 2 August, still at the Arena, Maria sang *La Traviata* in what Peter Dragadze of *Opera* called 'an unforgettable experience'. Elisabeth Schwarzkopf was so impressed by Maria's interpretation that when she and Walter Legge joined the Meneghinis for supper, afterwards, Schwarzkopf vowed that having heard such perfection she would never sing the role herself. The elder soprano is also thought to have been present at the sessions in Turin, several weeks later, when Maria recorded *La Gioconda* and *La Traviata* as part of her four-opera deal with Cetra – a contract which, on account of Soria's defection and her increasing affection towards Walter Legge, Maria now refused to honour. A few years later she would record *Manson Lescaut* with Tullio Serafin, but sadly there would never be a complete *Mefistofele*. There was, of course, a forfeit of several thousand dollars for breaking the contract, which Meneghini paid willingly.

Another influential individual who had to claw his way past the grasping 'Mr Callas' was Royal Opera House Covent Garden's 'trouble-shooter', Sandor Gorlinsky, who had attempted to secure Maria for a season there shortly before she had left Italy for her last Mexican tour. Since first hearing her in 1947, Lord Harewood – a member of the company's Board of Governors – had never stopped singing her praises, and it was he who had persuaded the General Administrator, David Webster, to make her an offer.

Initially, Maria had been reluctant to take on more engagements than she could handle, and she had asked Gorlinsky to contact her upon her return to Verona. Meneghini, of course, now demanded a salary which Covent Garden could not possibly afford – but as she was far less concerned about earning fabulous fees, in these days at least, than she was about conquering the British public, Maria slipped Gorlinsky a note, begging him to visit her apartment when her husband was out. Subsequently it took but a moment for her to negotiate and sign the contract: £2,000 plus expenses, for five *Norma*s, the first to be staged at Covent Garden since Rosa Ponselle's headlining season of 1929.

Maria and Meneghini arrived in London at the end of October 1952, to a fanfare of publicity mainly organised by David Webster, who introduced Maria to the rest of the cast, most of whom she had worked with already. One, a young Australian soprano named Joan Sutherland whom Webster had signed for the minor role of Clotilde, was already a name on the London operatic stage and some years later would also be acclaimed for her Norma and her Lucia.

Battista Meneghini, naturally, insisted on the opera company renting a suite for them at the Savoy – henceforth Maria's base whenever she was in London – yet even he with his flair for ostentatious publicity could not have orchestrated the vast sea of flowers which awaited her – over one hundred baskets and bouquets sent by British fans she never knew she had, so many of them that they overflowed into the corridor and the foyer. For the first time in her life, Maria broke down and wept that these strangers, whom she would probably never be able to thank personally, could have loved her so much.

Maria was also terrified that she might be being showered with too much attention before being allowed to prove to the British public that she was worthy of such an honour. 'The moment I stepped onto the stage,' she later recalled, 'I thought that my heart had suddenly stopped beating ... I was terrified that I would not live up to their expectations.'

Maria regarded the London première of *Norma* on 8 November 1952 as one of her proudest achievements. The event was a tremendous success, but if the audience were wildly enthusiastic, the critics fought amongst themselves to see who could produce the most acerbic or pseudo-intellectual piece on this phenomenon that they were hearing for the first time. 'Callas's fioriture were fabulous,' proclaimed Cecil Smith of *Opera*, adding, 'The chromatic glissandi held no terrors for her in the cadenza at the end of "Casta Diva".' John Freeman of *Opera News*, however, steered clear of the technical jargon by commenting, 'Perhaps the main cause of discussion as to her greatness, and the one which causes people to think her over-rated, is a fairly frequent lapse into a masked tone in the middle register, which at times makes her sound as if singing with a mouthful of hot marbles.' And whereas Maria was delighted by Philip Hope-Wallace's description, 'She is tall and splendid – like a Millais portrait of a Victorian diva,' she was incensed by the comments of the distinguished opera critic, Ernest Newman, a man who like some of his American contemporaries could 'make or break' a production with a few well-chosen words. Newman dismissed her as 'slightly subnormal', and told reporters, 'Yes, she *is* wonderful, but she is *not* a Ponselle.'

In fact, what it boiled down to was that many of these so-called experts were as baffled as their Italian counterparts had been, during those early performances in Verona when they had failed to comprehend the reason for her on-stage histrionics. Unable to categorise her, simply because she was unique in her own sphere, they made futile attempts to transcribe her magnitude into column inches, failing miserably to convey her true art to the masses who were yet to see or hear her.

From London, Maria and her husband flew back to Verona, where a 'surprise' awaited her – a pale green Alfa Romeo with leather seats and dashboard, an early birthday present from Meneghini which she detested on sight, not because of its 'unlucky' colour but, it is alleged, because she considered 'working-class automobiles' way beneath her status. Whatever the reason, it did not take her long to come up with a 'stock' statement each time she was stopped by a reporter, getting in or out of it: 'If an ordinary artiste drives a Cadillac or a Rolls-Royce, dear, how can I do the same? Aren't I *expected* to be different?'

The very next day Maria began rehearsing the first of her three roles for La Scala's new season: the exceptionally taxing Lady Macbeth, which she declared would adhere exactly to the composer's specifications. Lady Macbeth was a role which required not just a powerful singer, but also a dramatic actress capable of conveying the neurasthenia and psychological instability of history's archetypal madwoman. Verdi himself had requested of the first Lady Macbeth in 1848 (Marianna Barbieri-Nini) that she should be 'wicked and ugly, with a stifled, dark voice' – translated into Maria's no-nonsense parlance as 'a hard-bitten bitch', in a performance which was certainly unforgettable. What is sad is that she only performed the role five times.

The highlight of La Scala's *Macbeth*, premièred on 7 December 1952, and the first of Maria's operas to be televised, was undoubtedly the sleepwalking scene wherein the tormented Lady Macbeth – her hands covered in blood – sings 'Una machia' whilst reliving Duncan's brutal murder. Even though someone in the auditorium got up and whistled – on the Continent an expression of severest disapproval – Maria was given a standing ovation and took seven curtain-calls. The following week, Signe Scanzoni wrote in *Opera News*, 'We saw Maria Meneghini Callas as a Lady Macbeth whose vocal cords apparently must have been granted some extra strength which gives this voice an almost inhuman quality.'

At La Scala, on Boxing Day – just nine days after Maria's final *Macbeth* – she was partnered by Giuseppe di Stefano, still smarting after being hammered by the Mexican critics, in the first of six productions of *La Gioconda* – yet another role she would not sing again on the stage. These were followed early in the New Year by a season of *Traviata*s in Venice and Rome, commemorating the centenary of the work, which were panned by local critics, many of whom virulently disapproved of the fragile, consumptive Violetta being portrayed by a sixteen-stone woman.

What the critics did not know was that, supervised by her doctor and a dietician, Maria had decided to rid herself of this excess fat which, she declared, had been affecting her health for some time. At the beginning of the year she had had to cancel a concert at London's Royal Festival Hall – Verdi's *Requiem* with Beniamino Gigli, no less – because of illness, and she was convinced that her size had much to do with her tendency to succumb to every bug that was going around.

That summer, Maria had elected to sing a new role – Cherubini's *Medea*, not in the French but in Italian – and she was determined to *look* the part of the beautiful enchantress who seduces Jason, the leader of the Argonauts. Strictly adhering to her diet of fresh fruit and vegetables and nearly-raw meat, Maria sought inspiration in achieving her greatest goal from the pretty, elfin actress, Audrey Hepburn, the young star of William Wyler's film, *Roman Holiday*.

Maria met Hepburn at a party in Rome, along with her co-star from the film, Gregory Peck ... and when Peck remarked that there was a distinct facial resemblance between the two women, Maria was in seventh heaven, and at once adopted Hepburn as a role-model. Another tremendous influence was the Milanese couturier, Madame Biki, to whom she was introduced by Wally Toscanini. For most of her life, Maria had been taunted about her appearance – first by her mother, then by insensitive journalists and critics. For his part, Meneghini had done his utmost to make her aware of her quite potent femininity by buying her expensive furs, gowns and jewels, but so far her choice of clothes had been left to Maria herself, a woman who had absolutely no fashion sense. Biki had dressed both Hepburn and Anna Magnani, another 'frump' who had been turned into a princess with a minimum of effort, and she now took Maria in hand. Besides becoming her personal (and of course extremely well-paid) fashion adviser, she also became a cherished friend.

In the meantime, there were Maria's first Italian performances of *Lucia di Lammermoor* in Florence, Genoa and Catania and, sandwiched between, her La Scala debut of *Il Trovatore* with her friend, the powerful mezzo-soprano Ebe Stignani. *Opera*'s Peter Dragadze, having denounced her Rome Violetta as 'untraditional', was filled with enthusiasm now. 'This *Trovatore* was worth waiting for, and had the success it truly merited,' he wrote. 'Maria Callas again passed a difficult task ... her handling of the dramatic content of her part was a masterpiece of artistry.'

In February 1953 Maria also recorded *Lucia di Lammermoor*, her first complete opera for EMI, with Tito Gobbi and Giuseppe di Stefano. A few weeks later, still with di Stefano and her former lover, Nicola Rossi-Lemeni, she recorded *I Puritani* – the first time this had ever been recorded.

If Maria's Lady Macbeth had been hysterically evil then her Medea, which she sang for the first time in Florence on 7 May – indeed, the work had not been done in Italy since Ester Mazzolini had, according to most of the critics, messed it up in 1909 – was arguably the vilest creature to have been characterised on the opera stage, though Maria did not think so. 'The way I *see* Medea is the way I *feel* it,' she explained. 'Fiery, apparently very calm but very intense. The happy time with Jason is past. Now she is devoured by her misery and fury.'

Having enabled Jason to acquire the Golden Fleece, Medea has fallen in love with him and borne him two sons. However, he becomes betrothed to Glauce, the daughter of Creon, the Corinthian king who has already banished Medea from his realm. Plotting her revenge, Medea kills Glauce by way of a poisoned crown and cloak which she has sent as a wedding-gift, then murders her children before setting fire to the temple.

And yet there was always something about Maria's Medea – her tenderness towards Jason, and her large, pleading eyes before perpetrating the heinous deed – which evoked pity amongst subsequent audiences. 'I have compassion for her,' Maria told the *Observer*'s Kenneth Harris, in 1970, 'She kills her children because she feels she has no other choice, and because, being a goddess, she can remove them from this bitter and bloody world and enable her to join them in everlasting life. She kills so they may live in peace and dignity. She knows there will be no hope of that for them in this world, so she commits them to the next.' On stage, though the actual murders are not seen, this closing scene was enacted with such realistic malevolence that several members of the audience fainted.

For Maria's Medea there were *no* detractors. 'Maria Callas has surmounted a challenge that today perhaps no other singer would even be able to attempt,' wrote *Il Gazzettino*'s Giuseppe Pugliese – earning himself a thank-you note from Maria, and a rebuke from her husband for omitting the obligatory 'Meneghini'. Teodoro Celli of *Corriere Lombardo* told his readers, 'Maria Meneghini Callas *was* Medea ... she went beyond the notes, directly to the monumental character of the legend, and she handed it back to the composer with devotion and humble fidelity.' Many years after the event, Sergio Segalini still remembered this first, definitive performance, and negotiated a brave psychoanalysis wherein for once it was probably appropriate to associate the singer and actress with the part. In his moving, eulogistic study, *Les Images d'Une Voix* published in 1979, Segalini wrote, 'Callas probably recognised herself to some extent in this sorceress in search of justice. Was *she* not the sorceress of song in search of *musical* justice? When one listened to her Medea, it was easy to understand why that voice lasted a shorter time than others.'

In her dressing room after the première of *Medea* Maria was again approached by Rudolf Bing's Italian representative, Roberto Bauer who – having already dismissed her as 'a waste of time' – now followed instructions and offered her several engagements with the New York Met for the January and February of 1954. Bing had also propositioned Maria's then most-preferred baritone Ettore Bastianini, hoping that he might provide the necessary 'bait' to catch the big prize. The roles for which she had been considered, Maria was told, were *La Traviata*, *Lucia di Lammermoor*, and of course, *Aida*. Maria then suggested that it might be better to substitute one of these with *Norma* – to which Bauer responded that this would be impossible as this opera was the 'property' of the great soprano, Zinka Milanov, Rudolf Bing's favourite singer. This time, Bauer was shown the door and Meneghini told the press, 'My wife will never sing at the New York Met whilst Rudolf Bing is in charge, and that is that!'

Maria, meanwhile, focused her attention on her second season at London's Covent Garden. For around £350 a performance – with absolutely no arguments from either side – she had been engaged to sing three of her most familiar roles: *Aida* under the baton of John Barbirolli – *Norma* again with Joan Sutherland – and *Il Trovatore*. This being Coronation year, Covent Garden had commissioned Benjamin Britten to write an opera, *Gloriana*. Singing her first *Aida* just two days after the actual Coronation, and her first *Norma* on 15 June, Maria was therefore up against fierce competition.

Once again the critics were divided, many of them paying more attention to the way Maria looked than how she sounded. She had been furious to learn that Margherita Wallman, the director of the La Scala *Medea*s, had described her as 'looking like one of the caryatides on the Acropolis,' and she had tried to discover the identity of the reporter from the *Observer* who had described her as 'a large Junoesque figure, striding about the stage with a curious, loping roll' ... before printing her earlier response when a friend had invited her to go on a shopping expedition. Slapping her thigh she had cracked, 'What, and drag all *this* around with me?'

Her *Trovatore*, on the other hand, was adored by the critics, with *The Times* leading the plaudits: 'Madame Maria Callas sang and acted everyone off the stage. She is not an artist given to gesturing, but when she moves an arm the audience sits forward, gripped by the stimulus of a dynamic personality in action.'

After her London season, Maria tried to take things easy for a few days at her Verona apartment – learning Alessandro Scarlatti's. forgotten baroque opera, *Mitridate Eupatore*, which was to open her La Scala season at the end of the year. At the end of July she recorded *Cavalleria Rusticana* in Milan with Rolando Panerai and Giuseppi di Stefano. Incredibly, the sessions took place on Maria's days off from her performances of *Aida* in Verona – the last time she sang the role on stage – and once these projects had been completed, she 'took things easy' by recording *Tosca* with di Stefano, Tito Gobbi and Victor de Sabata!

Maria's 1953 *Tosca* is generally regarded as *the* definitive version of the work. It was also the end result of a series of vociferous and sometimes vulgar differences of opinion, insults, and bitchy on-stage squabbles which all but shook La Scala to its foundations. Tosca's every recitative and line of libretto was dissected and psychoanalysed by Maria, who declared that the whole work *must* be sung and enacted as if in front of an audience. Her line after she has killed the scheming chief of police, Scarpia – 'E evanti a lui tremava tutta Roma!' (And before him, all Rome trembled!) – was repeated forty-seven times before she nodded to de Sabata that she was satisfied!

Maria's criticisms, however, were not just directed at herself. She was so dissatisfied with her first scene with Tito Gobbi, who decided that *he* was not up to scratch, that they insisted on twenty-nine takes for just a few minutes of music when, according to the conductor, the first take had been perfect!

The jewel in *Tosca*'s glittering crown, of course, has to be the sublime 'Vissi d'arte', aside from 'O mio babbino caro' Maria's most requested showpiece, and without any doubt one of the most beautiful, heartfelt arias she ever sang. It is her particular hymne à l'amour, her personal credo still, two decades after her death. 'I have lived for art and love,' she opines, defying the listener to believe that these melancholy tapering phrases were not created for her alone, before concluding with the sob in the voice which was always for real, 'I have harmed no one. Secretly I have offered help when it was needed ... and my singing to the stars made them shine more brightly. In this hour of anguish, Lord, why is this my reward?' A masterpiece!

1953 was the sixtieth anniversary of Alfredo Catalini's death, and to commemorate the event La Scala revived his best-known work, *La Wally*. The following year, Maria would record its lovely aria, 'Ebben? me ne andrò lontana', but for the opening performance of La Scala's new season, the role was to be sung by Renata Tebaldi. It was a political decision. Ghiringhelli had wanted the work to be conducted by Toscanini, who had conducted the original in 1892, well aware that *La Wally* was his most cherished opera – the maestro had named his daughter after Catallani's heroine. Toscanini was however too ill to accept the engagement, but he told Ghiringhelli that had he accepted, there would only have been one Wally – his all-time favourite, Tebaldi. In Ghiringhelli's eyes, Toscanini's was the law, and the great soprano had been engaged ... not just for *La Wally* but also for *Tosca*, *Otello* and *Eugene Onegin*. Maria did not mind this, for in addition to *Mitridate Eupatore* she had been asked to sing Lucia, and the new roles of Gluck's *Alceste* and Elisabeth de Valois in Verdi's *Don Carlos*. Neither did she object to the fact that Tebaldi and not herself would be opening the season – she acknowledged that this would only be fair, seeing as she had opened the last two. What she did not reckon with, however, was her rival's unusual behaviour.

A few days before Tebaldi's première, one of Italy's top music critics, Emilio Radius of *L'Europeo* – Maria often referred to him sarcastically as 'my dear friend', though he was anything but – wrote a tongue-in-cheek piece for the publication saying how much more peaceful the opera world might be if its two leading lights were not constantly at one another's throats. Furthermore, Radius suggested a public meeting, for the benefit of their admirers and the press, wherein the two should shake hands. This may have been expecting too much from Maria, though she did devise a little plan of her own. She had intended going to Tebaldi's première in any case –it was always a good idea to study the competition, Maria declared, and how better to do so than as a member of the audience? Therefore, when the critics saw her sitting in a box and executing a polite curtsy to Toscanini for the benefit of the photographers, they assumed that the feud had finally been resolved. When, however, neither Tebaldi nor Toscanini turned up for the première of *Medea* on 10 December – and when it emerged that at Tebaldi's première, a note had been passed to Maria specifying that she should not go backstage after the performance, the critics forecast war.

What the critics were also unaware of were the backstage cat-fights which had preceded the opening of *Medea*. These had been sparked off at the beginning of November by Antonio Ghiringhelli when he had announced that, owing to the fabulous reviews *Medea* had attracted in Florence, this would now be replacing the work by Scarlatti. Maria welcomed the news, though not so the producer, Margherita Wallmann, who had ordered the sets and arranged for the final fittings of the costumes. Ghiringhelli told her not to worry – such was Maria's pulling power that he knew he would more than make up for any losses the theatre incurred, if not through this production then in the next three. Then, two weeks before opening night, Victor de Sabata suffered a heart-attack.

Ghiringhelli, who even had the audacity to suggest that Maria's tantrums may have been responsible for the conductor's illness, lost no time in finding a suitable replacement. Leonard Bernstein, a young American graduate of Harvard and the prestigious Curtis Institute of Music, had recently completed a successful concert tour of Italy. Thirty-five years of age, Bernstein had rocketed to fame in 1944 when, having composed the *Jeremiah Symphony* and the Hollywood musical, *On The Town*, he had stood in for the indisposed Bruno Walter to conduct the New York Philharmonic.

Initially, however, Bernstein was a tough nut to crack. He was suffering from influenza, acute bronchitis and hay fever, and he had never heard of Cherubini, let alone *Medea*. Furthermore, he announced, on account of her 'fuck-awful reputation', the last singer in the world he wanted to conduct was Maria Callas! The money offered by Ghiringhelli, and the fact that his very first involvement with an opera house was to be with La Scala, helped him to change his mind.

A further problem occurred with the actual scores for *Medea*, which were old and decaying and which Ghiringhelli saw no point in having reprinted, as the opera was only going to be performed three times in his theatre. Several of the musicians, including Bernstein himself, were allergic to dust and there was a great deal of coughing and sneezing – this can be heard when one listens to the pirated recordings of the performances.

There were few problems, however, between the conductor and his prima donna. As with Visconti, Maria was so enthralled by Leonard Bernstein's boyish good looks, ready wit and charm, and his quite impeccable manners that she became putty in his hands. Her naivety for the time being would not allow her to recognise the fact that like Visconti, Bernstein too was homosexual, and that when he came to her apartment with friends such as the handsome tenor, Franco Corelli, there was much about life she had yet to learn.

With Bernstein, there was just the one professional difference of opinion. In the so-called 'grovelling' scene of Act III, when Medea is about to murder her children whilst executing some of the most difficult vocal music ever composed, Bernstein hit upon an idea which they both knew would bring the house down. Instead of simply kneeling at the altar and singing, 'Numi, venite a me, inferni Dei!' – 'Come to my aid, infernal gods!' – Maria would *lie* face downwards on the steep temple steps, with her voluminous scarlet cloak spread about her, then slowly lift her head and gaze into the storm-clouds. Maria's only apprehension was that she might slip and injure herself – she still weighed just short of twelve stones – so Bernstein came up with a solution. Maria was positioned upon the steps *before* the curtain rose, and several members of the chorus stayed close at hand to assist her, should she get into difficulties. She did not, and this particular *Medea* remains one of the most exciting performances she ever gave.

A staircase provided the central feature of Maria's next production at La Scala – *Lucia di Lammermoor*, conducted by another musical luminary, Herbert von Karajan, of whom Maria was eternally suspicious. It was common knowledge that before World War Two, von Karajan had been a member of the Nazi Party. She agreed to work with him, however, when Antonio Ghiringhelli informed her that the Allies had 'de-Nazified' him in 1946.

In order to 'research' Donizetti's opera, Karajan had not just followed Maria's example by going back to the original score – he had also visited Scott's stark Scottish setting for his novel, subsequently transferring this to the bleak, poorly-lit stage. In the Karajan production of *Lucia* which was premièred on 18 January 1954, the infamous Mad Scene opened with the heroine standing at the top of the staircase, in her nightdress and with her hair the most frightful mess. Also, upon Maria's insistence – allegedly to prove to Karajan, the former Nazi, that *she* abhorred violence – this particular Lucia was not clutching a dagger. The audience, Maria declared, already knew the plot, so what was the point of exaggerating the bloodshed? In fact, even without the dagger and the fake blood, the scene was so realistic that the audience leapt to its feet halfway through it, applauding wildly. For reasons known only to themselves, Maria's admirers showered her with hundreds of red carnations. Maria, not to be put off easily even by mass adoration, incorporated these flowers into the scenario – stooping in her 'madness' to retrieve several of them, as if she were scooping up handfuls of blood ... then at the end of the scene, finally losing control of her emotions, she burst into tears over what one critic called 'this Callasmania'.

'The theatre seemed about to collapse under the deluge of the applause,' declared *Corriere della Sera*'s Franco Abbiate. 'This was not the ethereal Lucia one is accustomed to hearing, but the dramatic heroine of whom Donizetti perhaps only dreamed.' Cynthia Jolly of *Opera News*, who by this time had met *her* heroine, went one step further by making up for her past adverse criticisms:

Callas's supremacy amongst present-day sopranos lies in no mechanical perfection, but in a magnificently tempered artistic courage, breathtaking security and agility, phrasing and stage-poise ... and in a heart-rending poignancy of timbre which is quite unforgettable.

Following 'routine' performances of *Lucia*, *Medea* and *Tosca* in Venice and Genoa, Maria returned to La Scala on 4 April 1954, singing the lead in Gluck's *Alceste* which, on account of its unpopularity with the Italian public, had never been performed there before. Maria's metamorphosis from self-confessed ugly duckling to elegant, beautiful swan was by now almost complete. Her weight was down to just under eleven stones, enabling her to be carried above the bearers' heads into the temple at the close of Act Two.

On 12 April, with two *Alcestes* to go, Maria sang her first Elisabeth de Valois in *Don Carlos*, one of her favourite roles and one with which La Scala audiences were more familiar, resulting in more favourable reviews from the critics. Someone had to complain, of course, and in this instance it was Riccardo Malipiero of *Opera*, who opined, 'Callas's voice is not quite suited to Verdi's music, for this wonderful singer, so confident in difficult passages and powerful in dramatic ones, lacks the sweetness and softness necessary in moments of abandon.'

Halfway through the *Don Carlos* run, Maria began recording what is generally regarded to be her definitive *Norma* and for the first time she had a say in who would be recording it with her. She chose Ebe Stignani and Nicola Rossi-Lemeni to sing Adalgisa and Oroveso – no surprise, for they were two of her closest friends. Problems arose, however, when Walter Legge wanted Giuseppe di Stefano to sing Pollione, whilst Antonio Ghiringhelli demanded Franco Corelli. Maria had never stopped blaming di Stefano for the Mexican *Rigoletto* fiasco, and she was terrified of spending too much time with the almost ethereally handsome Corelli because she was falling in love with him, and did not know how she would handle cheating on her husband, if the crunch came. She therefore 'compromised' by deciding upon Mario Filippeschi, a tenor she positively loathed, and when Antonino Votto expressed his disapproval, Maria told him that he would not be conducting in any case – but Tullio Serafin! This resulted in an out-and-out row with Ghiringhelli, who would not allow the sessions to take place at La Scala. The opera was therefore taped at the Cinema Metropol … with very few tantrums. Here she was briefly interviewed by Martin Meyer of the American *High Fidelity* magazine, telling him minutes after a violent, expletive quarrel with Filippeschi, 'Every year I *must* do better than the year before, otherwise I would have to retire. I don't need the money, dear. I work for *art!*'

Maria also rejected Walter Legge's suggestion that she should record Verdi's *La Forza del Destino* and Boito's *Mefistofele*, claiming that she was not yet ready to do so. Though she would change her mind a few months later about the former, following the huge standing ovation earned by her Leonora at Ravenna on 23 May, her fans would have to make do with just the one recorded aria from the latter – 'L'altra notte' – and three from *Don Carlos*, which Legge also wanted recorded in its entirety: 'To che le vanita', 'Non pianger mia compagna', and Eboli's 'O don fatale'.

Although she never sang Nedda on the stage, Maria did consent to recording Leoncavallo's *I Pagliaci* with di Stefano and Serafin at the end of May 1954, and *Il Turco in Italia* with Nicola Rossi-Lemeni (but without Serafin) at the beginning of September … by which time she was preparing for the greatest and arguably most exciting challenge of her career … the conquest of America.

7

Partagez-Vous Mes Fleurs?

I stand on my own merits, and I want always to work with people who are included on theirs. I don't want to horse-trade my way across the world of opera. I'm concerned with art, not commerce.

The New York Met's Rudolf Bing was certainly not the kind of man to give up on a challenge. During the spring of 1954, via the by now extremely impatient Roberto Bauer, Maria was offered the establishment's ceiling fee of $1,000 for each of up to twenty performances – absolutely the most they paid anyone, including the 'royal favourites' Tebaldi and Milanov – to sing *La Traviata*, *Cavalleria Rusticana* and *Tosca*, in addition to two roles of her choice from a selection of four: *La Gioconda*, *Un Ballo In Maschera*, *Andrea Chénier* and *Aida*.

This time, Maria came very close to signing Bing's contract, despite her husband's protests, until he drew her attention to the small print and the clause, 'There shall be no strings attached as to visas for husbands, friends or concubines.' This time Bauer was sent packing with the message, 'Tell your dear Mr Bing that I would rather stop singing altogether than travel anywhere without my beloved Titta!'

For once, the repercussions proved beneficial. Maria's rejection of the Met reached the ears of Carol Fox and Lawrence Kelly, two enterprising young Chicago impresarios who had already succeeded where Maria's former mentor, Eddie Bagarozy, had failed – reviving the once prestigious Chicago Lyric Opera.

Fox and Kelly had first begun courting Maria in November 1953, after teaming up with a young conductor, Nicola Rescigno – all three were in their early to mid-thirties. Maria had been suitably impressed by the progress they had made since then, in signing up Nicola Rossi-Lemeni for the title-role in two performances of *Don Giovanni*, which had attracted fabulous reviews in February 1954. Now, Carol Fox was invited to spend the weekend with the Meneghinis in Verona, though this time when it came to discussing business, Maria's husband – who spoke virtually no English – was. casually dismissed whilst Maria and her new friend engaged in a little 'girls' talk'.

For Fox, getting Maria to sign the contract was little more than a formality, particularly as she herself could not have dictated better terms: two performances each of *Norma*, *La Traviata* and *Lucia* at $2,000 a performance – twice the Met's ceiling fee – plus unconditional expenses, a suite at the best hotel in town, the services of a chauffeur and personal maid, and as much time for rehearsals, within reason, as Maria deemed necessary.

The timing could not have been more perfect, for three of Maria's album sets – *Tosca*, *I Puritani* and *Lucia* – headed the American classical best-seller list. It was also a matter of course, now that Callas was on Fox's and Kelly's books, that several of her most important colleagues quickly followed suit. The pair already had Rossi-Lemeni, and over the course of the next few weeks they excelled their own expectations by signing Tito Gobbi, Giuseppe di Stefano and Giulietta Simionato to support Maria – then organised Simionato, Gobbi and Giacinto Prandelli for non-Callas productions of *La Bohème* and *Il Barbiere di Siviglia* for the same season.

Meanwhile, in the middle of September, and without her husband, Maria flew to London where in less than a week, under the baton of Tullio Serafin, she recorded her first two studio albums for EMI. *Puccini Heroines* and *Operatic Arias*, a unique concept in these early days of the long-playing record, contained several roles which she had not sung and subsequently would not sing on stage, including the heartrending 'Si, mi chiamano Mimi' from *La Bohème*, and the definitive 'O mio babbino caro' ... besides arias from *La Wally* and *Adriana Lecouvreur*, roles which had been sung with great success by Renata Tebaldi – and a positively hair-raising 'In questa reggia' from *Madama Butterfly*.

The Meneghinis arrived in Chicago at the end of October, where for the first time Maria found herself almost suffocated by the press, though she never minded when they were interested in her career as opposed to her personal life. What she did not know was that Meneghini had supplied several journalists – including Claudia Cassidy of the *Chicago Tribune* – with a series of 'before' and 'after' shots of his wife, some of the former hardly flattering, and these were now published side by side on various front pages. 'I wouldn't have recognised her without the advance pictures,' Cassidy reported, though having seen several of her performances over the last few years, she had witnessed Maria's transformation from close at hand. 'She is wand-slim, beautiful as a tragic mask, with a glint of gaiety.'

The tabloids in particular had more or less reinvented Maria's life story. Here was a poor immigrant girl from a loving family, who had lingered overseas but long enough to learn her art, and to acquire fame and a fabulously wealthy husband, and now she had come 'home' to take up her rightful crown. Everywhere the couple went, too, they were photographed arm-in-arm or kissing, and this portrait of marital bliss was embellished by pictures of a Biki-dressed Maria playing the perfect wife in the kitchen of their hotel suite – 'slaving' over a hot stove whilst fixing her husband's supper, or unpacking her carrier-bags after her latest trip to the local deli-catessen! The idea had come from Marlene Dietrich, who really did know how to act the *hausfrau*! On one occasion Maria had attended one of Marlene's dinner evenings and helped the great star to cater for a gathering of twelve, only to be invited to sit on Marlene's kitchen floor to share an omelette whilst the rest of the guests tucked in! But, as one biographer, George Jellinek, observed, 'who can resist a diva who is as handy with the gas-range as she is with the funeral pyre?' Fortunately, Maria's mother was too far away –

'visiting loved ones in Greece', according to the concierge at her apartment block – to make the press any wiser, and the arrival of George Callas from New York only added to this harmonious but contrived family picture.

Conducted by Nicola Rescigno, a man in whom Maria could see no wrong, the first performance of *Norma* took place on 1 November, and was a resounding success. 'Her range is formidable, her technique dazzling,' wrote Claudia Cassidy. 'She sang the "Casta Diva" in a kind of mystic dream, like a goddess of the moon briefly descended.' 'It was a great night for Chicago,' enthused Ronald Eyer of *Musical America*, adding as a postscript, 'It may prove an even greater night for opera in America.'

Seven days and innumerable personal appearances later, Maria sang her first *Traviata* which such perfection that Seymour Raven of the *Chicago Tribune* was prompted to comment, 'I'd like even to be around when she makes mistakes, for I guess you could rule carelessness out among any possible reasons.' *Opera*'s James Hinton, on the other hand, who had watched Maria leaving the Ambassador Hotel for a rehearsal – 'wearing enough stones to sink a ship' – was not impressed by her characterisation of Violetta, commenting, 'The idea of Miss Callas lying poor and neglected in a furnished room is too much to expect of *any* audience!'

The Chicago press had also been alerted to the fact that, where Callas was concerned, supreme artistry and arch-bitchiness more or less went hand in glove, so the tabloids were on the lookout for tell-tale signs of animosity between Maria and her colleagues. In this respect, she did not disappoint them.

Maria's first 'blue' occurred with Tito Gobbi, who was singing the role of the elder Germont. Gobbi always maintained that Maria's tantrums and tetchiness were the result of her self-imposed high standards. 'This meant that people demanded the impossible of her,' he wrote in his memoirs, 'so that she forever carried the burden of having to reaffirm her supremacy or else be regarded, by herself as well as by others, as in some sense failing.'

During the 8 November *Traviata*, after Gobbi had sung his aria at the end of the second act, only one half of the curtain fell. A technician was summoned, who immediately detected a fault with the mechanism. However, once the second half of the curtain had been brought down, the other section went back up again and stuck, much to the amusement of the audience, who began tittering in what was ostensibly a very dramatic moment in the plot. During the interval, Meneghini summoned the theatre manager and ordered him to fire the technician, only to be manhandled back to the auditorium and spark off a row between Maria and Gobbi which all but resulted in the rest of the performance being cancelled. As if commanding a lackey, Maria summoned Tito Gobbi to her dressing room, and for several minutes – whilst the audience were left wondering why the interval was dragging on for so long – she ranted and raved. Every now and then he interjected with a cutting remark, unaware that a small cluster of reporters was listening outside the door.

CALLAS: How *dare* you interfere with the success of my *Traviata*?

GOBBI: I was aware that it was Verdi's *Traviata*, Maria ...

CALLAS: It is *my Traviata*, and unless you watch your step, I will ruin your fucking career!

GOBBI: You may be an almighty power in the opera world, my dear Madame Callas, but don't forget that I've been in this business ten years longer than you ...

CALLAS: Get out of my dressing room, you shit, before I call the manager ...

GOBBI: No, Maria. *You* get out of your dressing room and onto that stage, otherwise I will personally repeat every single word of this conversation to the audience!

Needless to say, the air had been cleared, and once the problem with the curtain had been resolved and the audience given an explanation for the 'unavoidable' delay, the third act of *La Traviata* went well, and when Maria and Gobbi took their bows, then embraced, it was with the greatest sincerity. For the rest of her life he and Maria would be only the best of friends.

It was on Tito Gobbi's shoulder, not her husband's that Maria wept when her former agent, Eddie Bagarozy, not unexpectedly served her with a writ: since 1947, he claimed, he had spent $85,000 of his own money promoting her career, his wife Louise Caselotti had never been paid for giving Maria singing lessons, and he himself had not received one cent in commission, as per the terms of their contract. The total was a staggering $300,000, and Maria's American record company, Angel, was served with a warrant of attachment for this amount.

Maria immediately retaliated, declaring that she had been forced to sign Bagarozy's contract under duress – only to learn that Nicola Rossi-Lemeni, who had signed his contract on the same day as Maria, had also received a writ for a much smaller amount, and that after meeting with Bagarozy's lawyers an out-of-court settlement had been reached wherein the bass had parted with just $5,000. Maria was all set to follow her former lover's example. Tito Gobbi managed to talk her out of meeting Bagarozy face to face and carrying out her threat of 'knocking his goddam teeth down his throat', so she issued a statement declaring that she too was open to negotiation. Meneghini, however, flatly refused to pay Bagarozy so much as one cent, creating a dilemma which would only intensify over the next few years.

On 15 November, partnered by Giuseppe di Stefano, Maria gave her most stunning performance in this her first American season – a *Lucia* which earned her more than twenty curtain-calls. But what made it doubly important was that Maria, who had dyed her long hair 'Jayne Mansfield blonde' and taken to wearing lashings of Elizabeth Arden's 'Victory Red' lipstick, had inadvertently joined the ranks of sirens such as Dietrich, Monroe, Garland and Bankhead. Henceforth, her audiences would contain a largely gay element – hundreds of young men, her adored Callas Boys who flocked to the front of the stage after every performance to fling bouquets at her feet, or merely to touch the hem of her dress and be recompensed by a gracious smile or a handshake. And *nothing* inspired their frenzied worship more than Lucia's 'Mad Scene', detailed by Claudia Cassidy under the *Chicago Tribune*'s banner headline: WHICH IS MAD? THE CALLAS LUCIA OR HER

FRENZIED PUBLIC?

Maria Meneghini Callas has this town's opera-goers bewitched. An innocent bystander wandering into last night's *Lucia* in the Civic Opera House might have thought Donizetti had scored the 'Mad Scene' for the audience ... Remember that she just sang a glittering *La Traviata*. Then listen to *Lucia*'s first act, spun like warm silk, sometimes with an edge of steel ... None of this is fair warning for the 'Mad Scene', sung with a beauty and purity of coloratura and fioriture that can set susceptible folk roaring with joy ...

Maria's 'secondary' career as a gay diva had begun, and though she was initially puzzled by the demonstrations of what she called 'these odd little men' who were often at their most vociferous outside stage-doors or within airport lounges, she very quickly came to realise how utterly sincere and devoted they were. Many years later a young actor named Steven Mathers, who founded the excellent 'Callas Circle' fan-club, summed her up in *Gay Gazette*: 'She was a most assuredly glamorous creature within which there was an undeniable element of the drag queen, in her elegant dresses and slightly overdone eyeliner ... yet echoing gay men's body consciousness, she completely reinvented herself.'

Whereas some of Maria's heterosexual admirers have scorned the Callas Boys, accusing them of irreverence, it has to be said that even Maria said in Chicago, 'To them I'm the Bette Davis of opera, and *that* pleases me no end!' There is, however, considerably more to it than this, as Roger Baker pointed out in *Gay Times*:

The great mainstream operas are very heterosexual in their subject matter. But this heterosexuality is almost incidental, for what really characterises these distraught individuals who sing their way to death is the fact that they are either outsiders who break the moral code or who, by breaking a moral code, become outsiders ... The point is that we are being asked to share the emotions and suffering of a social outcast. Connected with this is the frequent portrayal of the contrast and tension between maintaining an acceptable public face while suffering some private agony ... It is not hard to see how a gay man, living by necessity a double life and aware of society's disapproval of his nature, can relate to these outsiders: Norma, Manrico, Carmen, Isolde, Butterfly, Lulu ...

The second and final *Lucia* took place on 17 November. A few days later Maria and her husband left for Milan, and the start of the new season. This time she was engaged to sing in *five* productions: besides *Medea*, *Il Trovatore* and a revival of her Rome success, *Il Turco in Italia*, there would be two new roles – Amina, in Bellini's *La Sonnambula*, and opening the season on St Ambrose's Day, she would be singing Giulia in Spontini's near-forgotten *La Vestale*. It would be one of La Scala's most enterprising, if not risky seasons: besides the productions with Maria, there would be premières of Gershwin's *Porgy and Bess*, Menotti's *The Saint of Bleecker Street* ... and Renate Tebaldi in *La Forza del Destino*.

The Spontini opera effected a reunion between Maria and Luchino Visconti – in her opinion the *only* person, she told Antonio Ghiringhelli, capable of directing a work which to some extent relied more on its stage effects than its weak plot and musical content, and one which had not been performed since Rosa Ponselle's 1933 Florence season. Ghiringhelli took some persuading, declaring he would never work with a man who was a promiscuous homosexual *and* a communist, and it was only when Maria threatened to rip up her contract that the ebullient Superintendent relented. Indeed, Antonio Ghiringhelli was so afraid of losing Maria that when he learned that Visconti's production would set him back a cool 85 million lire, he is said to have quipped, 'Is *that* all?'

Shortly before her trip to Chicago, Maria had been invited to appear in Visconti's fourth feature film, *Senso*, the story of a young Venetian countess who has recently married a wealthy nobleman thrice her age, and who cheats on him with a handsome but poor army lieutenant of her own age. Maria had flatly refused to play an adulteress, and after a further rejection by Ingrid Bergman, Visconti had plumped for the beautiful Italian starlet, Alida Valli, who had appeared in Carol Reed's *The Third Man*. Never one to give up on a challenge, Visconti had then implored Maria to at least accept a cameo role in his film – as the soprano in the opening scene at Venice's La Fenice, where the third act of *Il Trovatore* is just ending. Again, she had turned him down.

Maria was absolutely besotted with Visconti, and he was so *platonically* enchanted by her that over the next few years, in order to work with her, he more or less turned his back on what he was truly good at – making films. Also, since her 'transformation' Maria had come to realise that good-looking men were beginning to find her sexually attractive – and for the first time in her life she was not afraid of making the first move. *La Vestale* tells the story of Giulia, the daughter of an eminent Roman family who, having been forbidden to marry her soldier lover, Licinius, obeys her father's dying instruction and becomes a Vestal Virgin. Maria must have identified with the initially luckless Giulia, for singing Licinius, and making his La Scala debut, was Franco Corelli, a twenty-nine-year old Italian tenor of almost unbelievable beauty with whom she was positively aching to have an affair. What she did not know was that her other 'quarry', Visconti, had similar designs on the young man, though sexually Corelli was not interested in either of them.

The rehearsals for *La Vestale* were therefore uncustomarily amenable: one former lover, Rossi-Lemeni, two would-be ones, her friend Ebe Stignani whom Maria had insisted sing the High Priestess, and the occasional presence of Toscanini, now eighty-seven, fading fast, but still unable to resist a pretty, flirtatious young woman ... though he is said to have felt 'grieved' that Maria had reverted to her natural colouring and was no longer a blonde. The pictures of him, Maria, Visconti and the conductor Antonino Votto, grouped together whilst going through the score, are quite touching. The legendary maestro should have been conducting Verdi's *Falstaff* at La Piccola Scala, but he had been compelled to step down because of ill-health.

On and off the rehearsal platform, Maria wooed Franco Corelli and enthused to her friends about his 'magnificent thighs', whilst bending over backwards to please Visconti when the director made her go over the same lines or movements dozens of times, for no other reason than to experience the intense pleasure this brought him. She, who always detested the habit, was so infatuated by him that she even put up with his chain-smoking ... and for the time being she was too naive to realise that the young man who usually collected him from the theatre after rehearsals was also sharing his bed. 'Sexually, my husband was not able to fulfil my desires,' Maria later told her French friend, Roger Normand. 'And yet the two men I truly loved, more than any others in the world at that time, seemed more interested in each other than they were in me.'

Spontini had been a great favourite at the Parisian court of Napoleon, and for this reason Visconti opted for what he termed 'a cold as moonstruck marble three-dimensional' First Empire setting. He engaged the eminent designer, Piero Zuffi, who. enlarged La Scala's stage forward – in Spontini's day the singers had often performed on a proscenium – and flanked it with massive alabaster pillars. As for the singers' gestures, Visconti based these on the late-18th century paintings of the French neo-Classical artist, Jacques Louis David.

Anyone who was anyone, not just in Milan but in all Italy, was at the première of *La Vestale*, which was also recorded and widely broadcast across Europe. The revelation, however, came not just from her singing, for most of the audience were seeing the 'new' Maria – slimmer and lovelier than ever – for the first time. 'She also *looked* superb,' declared Peter Hoffer of *Music & Musicians*, adding, 'It is a pleasure to watch her, and one begins to *believe* at last in the action on the stage.' There was also a nice touch when Maria was taking her curtain-call at the end of Act Two. Her personal guest-of-honour, Toscanini, applauded her from the stage-box whilst she was assailed from all directions with hundreds of red carnations. Catching one in her hand, Maria crossed the stage, and with a deep curtsy presented it to the maestro. The audience went hysterical, and the photograph of the event subsequently appeared in newspapers around the world.

There were five performances of *La Vestale*, the last taking place on 18 December, before the Christmas break. On 27 December, in San Remo, Maria realised another ambition by appearing in a radio concert with Beniamino Gigli. The greatest lyric-dramatic tenor of his day, then aged sixty-four and coming towards the end of a mighty career, was in fine voice. At the last moment, however, he refused to sing a duet with Maria, confessing, 'I would very much like to, but I'm afraid she is just *too* good!'

This was a fine tribute indeed, and one only has to listen to the four arias which were recorded at this broadcast to realise *how* good Maria was, particularly in the acoustic renditions of Charpentier's 'Depuis le jour' from *Louise*, but more especially in Meyerbeer's 'Ombra leggiera', which really has to be heard to be believed. Indeed, some critics, upon hearing the San Remo version for the first time, were so mystified by Maria's 'echo' effect, created as a dialogue between Dinorah and her shadow companion – giving the impression that there were two different soprano voices – that they were publicly willing to swear that either some technical wizardry had been employed, or that Maria had smuggled another singer into the studio. There were of course dozens of witnesses, Gigli included, who were prepared to swear otherwise!

Maria's next La Scala production should have been *Il Trovatore* with Mario del Monaco singing the central role of Manrico. Just one week before the première, however, the tenor – who had recently scored one of the greatest triumphs of his career, singing the title role in Giordano's *Andrea Chénier* at the New York Met – told Antonio Ghiringhelli that he would only be content singing *this* role at La Scala.

There was in fact more to it than this. Del Monaco, regarded by many as the natural successor to Gigli, and certainly one of the finest tenors of his generation, is said to have been afraid of singing such a strenuous role in front of La Scala's critical audiences. Also, as an aficionado of Renata Tebaldi, who had confided in him that her next appearance at La Scala in the April would be her last unless between them they could cook up a plan to make Maria less popular, del Monaco was keen to push Maria into a role she did not know and hopefully watch her fall flat on her face.

Ghiringhelli, naturally, expected fireworks from his prima donna, at best that she would merely demand del Monaco's instant dismissal. In fact, she surprised them both by announcing that she would be *delighted* to sing the role of Maddalena di Coigny, the lover of the young French poet Marie André Chénier, who had fallen foul of Robespierre during the Revolution and been sent to the guillotine. And, if Maria had but five days to learn the score, so what? Had she not done the same thing before, with formidable results?

Unfortunately, the première was a disaster. Thirty or so fans of Renata Tebaldi were sitting in one of the galleries, and they disrupted the performance whenever Maria was on the stage by applauding in the middle of every scene. Maria was naturally tetchy. Her big aria was 'La Mamma morta', wherein Maddelena laments the death of her mother after the revolutionary mob has set fire to her house ... an emotional, demanding piece which has an extended high B which, on this occasion, wobbled so dreadfully that the so-called Tebaldiani began hissing, booing and stamping their feet. The critics, of course, knew what was happening and why, and offered her due consideration. 'She imparted amorous rapture and delicate abandon to the role, projecting with admirable talent the rich and plentiful sounds of her extended range,' wrote the *Corriere del Téatro*'s Quaglia.

Quaglia's defence, a congratulatory hug and bouquet from Giordano's widow, and a lengthy standing ovation resulting in innumerable curtain-calls, however, failed to pacify Maria, who vented her fury on del Monaco, whom she held wholly responsible for the fracas because he had persuaded Ghiringhelli to change the programme. And of course, when she was told of the tenor's connections with Tebaldi, he was declared an enemy of the lowest order and warned to watch his back, should he ever cross Callas's path again.

Maria also publicly accused Renata Tebaldi of sabotaging her première by paying for a 'claque' of professional applauders – a common practice in Italy, though these people were usually paid to lead the applause for a diva they liked, not to boo the opposition. When the press asked her, however, if she and Tebaldi were still rivals, Maria shook her head ... and delivered the statement which, when published in newspapers around the world – minus the obligatory epithets – could only be interpreted as an invitation to open warfare:

I live in another world. *She* is a *vocalist* of certain repertoire. *I* consider myself a *soprano* – one who does what they used to do once upon a time. *I* have taken music that has been long dead and buried, and I have brought it back to life once more. If the time comes when my dear friend Renata Tebaldi will sing *Norma* or *Lucia* or *Anna Bolena* one night, then *Traviata* or *Gioconda* or *Medea* the next – then and *only* then will we be rivals. Otherwise it is like comparing champagne with cognac. No – champagne with *Coca-Cola*!

By the time this remark reached Tebaldi's admirers, Maria had sung three further *Andrea Chéniers* with but little antagonism – though still vowing never to sing the role on stage again, a vow she kept. However, when she sang *Medea* in Rome on 22 January, pandemonium erupted in the Opera House and continued throughout the performance. During the curtain-calls, there was unexpected hostility from the usually placid Boris Christoff, who had sung the role of Creon. The great bass may have been willing to turn a deaf ear to Maria's quite obscene remarks about Renata Tebaldi, who was after all his friend, but he certainly was not going to be told by this 'Athenian' upstart that he needed more rehearsals to perfect his voice! Therefore, whilst the entire cast moved towards the footlights to take their bow, the burly Christoff purposely stood in front of her so that the audience could not see her. In the wings, she turned on him and spat out, 'The next time I see you, I hope you will be dying from the pox!'

At the end of January, on the verge of mental and physical collapse, and suffering from a painful boil on the back of her neck, Maria returned to Milan where over the next few days she stayed at home, playing hostess to Lawrence Kelly, just in from Chicago to tempt her to return there for the next season. Not surprisingly, considering the impact she had made on the Windy City the first time around – and the fat cheque she had pocketed at the end of it – Maria agreed. Kelly, however, was decidedly unimpressed by the Meneghinis' interpretation of hospitality – inviting friends to join them for dinner at the Biffi Scala, then expecting *them* to pick up the tab! Roger Normand remembers an occasion at around this time when Maria went shopping in Paris and asked him to meet her for tea at the Hôtel Continental, off the rue de Rivoli, for tea: 'The waitress brought the bill, and Maria asked her to take it back and make out *separate* bills. All we'd had were two small cups of tea. Then she said she didn't have any small notes on her, so I ended up paying for us both!'

Maria's next La Scala première, Bellini's *La Sonnambula* – to be directed by Visconti and conducted by Leonard Bernstein – had been set for 17 February, but Maria was so worn out that it had to be postponed until 5 March. Her obsession with Visconti had by now extended to having his movements monitored, and she suspected that her idol was getting a little too friendly with the dashing, extroverted Bernstein, who had never made any secret of his homosexuality. What she did not know was that, though the pair were not seeing each other, most of their nights were spent combing the city's red-light district for rent-boys and rough trade.

Meneghini, who had carried out a few investigations of his own – terrified, naturally, of *any* competition, let alone *two* suitors who were much younger and better-looking than he was – knew of the pair's nocturnal activities, and confident that his wife was not about to stray, at least not in their direction, he attempted to keep her content the only way he knew how, by wooing her with more material possessions. Maria already had more of these than she knew what to do with – jewellery, paintings, priceless pieces of porcelain and antiques, and a wealth of bric-à-brac most of which was neither of use nor ornamental. What she did not have, and what she had always longed for, was a home of her own. The apartment in Verona belonged to the Meneghini family, and whenever Maria was working in Milan, their suite at the Grand Hotel was costing her husband a fortune. Therefore, whilst in his words Maria was 'fluttering her eyelids at every queer who came along', Meneghini supervised the renovations of the four-storey house he had bought her at 40 via Michelangelo Buonarroti, in one of the city's most fashionable districts. Then, announcing that he wished to devote himself entirely to his wife's career – in other words, to keep an eye on her in case some handsome young man came along who was *not* gay, Meneghini sold his share of the business to his brother.

For as long as she cared to remember, Maria had yearned to sing the role of Amina in Bellini's *La Sonnambula*, which many years before had attracted rave reviews when sung by Elvira di Hidalgo at the New York Met. Amina is a Swiss orphan who is betrothed to Elvino, a young local landowner. Their relationship sours, however, when a stranger arrived – he is in fact Count Rodolfo, the lord of the castle who has been away from the village since he was a boy. Rodolfo spends the night at the inn, where Amina is seen entering his room, through the window. She is sleepwalking, and Maria was able to really enact this scene with her eyes closed because Visconti had placed a perfume-doused handkerchief on the bed. Elvino gets to know of this, and is outraged. The count is of course well aware of Amina's innocence, as is Lisa, the innkeeper, but as she too is in love with Elvino, she does not tell him. The truth is only revealed when he sees Amina sleepwalking with an unlighted lamp across a rickety bridge over the mill wheel. One of the planks gives way and Amina stumbles, dropping her lamp into the waters below. Then, as the villagers cry 'Viva Amina!', she awakens in Elvino's arms and the pair rush off to be married.

It was this final scene which had prevented Maria from singing Amina for so long, for Bellini's inspiration for this delectable, innocent creature is thought to have been the astonishingly delicate-looking Swedish-born Italian ballerina, Maria Taglioni, who had introduced *La Sylphide* in 1832, three years before Bellini's death. The composer's librettist, Felice Romani, had issued the instruction, 'This role demands an actress who can be playful, ingenuous and innocent, and at the same time passionate, sensitive and affectionate.' This of course was Visconti's exact perception of Maria, and as he too had always been fascinated by Taglioni, he decided to bring her back to life through Maria, aided by replicas of the great dancer's costumes, which Visconti told her to embellish with a liberal amount of her own jewellery. When Maria complained that the audiences would never believe in a village girl decked out in several million lires' worth of rubies and emeralds, Visconti told her, 'The audience won't be looking at a village girl. They will be looking at Callas *portraying* a village girl. There is a subtle difference, mark my word!' Perhaps for this reason, the Visconti-Callas

Sonnambula was all the more appreciated as a *visual* performance, though Maria's singing on the recordings is of course exquisite.

At the height of her fame, Taglioni's waist had measured just twenty-two inches, exactly the same as Maria's was right now. Maria also possessed the same outward fragility and grace, so teaching her how to walk like a ballerina and stand in the fifth position was not a problem, though trying to work out how she would sing as if in a trance, then fall from the bridge without hurting herself was.

Both problems were effectively solved by Maria herself. Just as she had applied her unique technician's skills when summoning Dinorah's shadow companion, so she 'veiled' her voice for the lovely aria, 'Ah, non credea mirarti', where she asks the flowers if it is possible that they will wither so soon, now that she has seemingly lost her love – accompanied by a solitary viola, her voice seems to be emulating the rippling stream beneath her. The 'fall' itself was one of the most spectacular moments in operatic history, particularly as Maria never moved! Whilst she was crossing the bridge, the stage-lights were dimmed so that Maria, wearing a replica of one of Taglioni's costumes from *La Sylphide*, could only be seen outlined against the mountain backdrop. She then breathed in very, very slowly, giving an impression that she was moving upwards. Then, at the crucial moment, she suddenly exhaled, creating such a realistic illusion that the audience gasped with astonishment, as though watching a trapeze artiste taking what could well be a fatal plunge, even though the safety-net would not allow this. Then, as she moved towards the footlights with her lover to proclaim, jubilantly, 'Ah, non giunge uman pensiero al contento and'io son piena!' (Ah, no one could understand the happiness I feel!), the stage and auditorium lights, including La Scala's magnificent crystal chandelier, all came on at once, in what has been declared by some critics as the most thrilling and noisiest climax to any Callas performance – the last few bars of which are completely drowned by hysterical appreciation in the live recordings of the opera which have survived.

With two *Sonnambulas* to go, on 15 April Maria opened with Nicola Rossi Lemeni in *Il Turco in Italia* – her very first comic role at La Scala. This time the director was Franco Zeffirelli, a close friend of Visconti and therefore a man she found she could trust. Born and educated in Florence, Zeffirelli had worked as an actor, playing Dimitri in Visconti's film of Dostoevsky's *Crime and Punishment* before turning his hand to set and costume design, then of course directing films of his own. His first opera, Rossini's *La Cenerentola* with Giulietta Simionato singing the title-role, had been staged at La Scala in 1953. Maria grew very fond of him – not without inciting the now tiresome Meneghini's jealousy – and during the run of the opera socialised with him and his friends, or simply dined with him and his disabled father. Although Zefirelli often remarked that Maria's greatest weakness had been her tendency to take herself too seriously – once telling a reporter, 'I lost count of the number of times that I said to her, "Maria, for Christ's sake, lighten up!" ' – she did prove herself an able comedienne in *Il Turco in Italia*, rolling her eyes and pulling faces at Rossi-Lemeni, giggling a lot, and even executing a hilarious tarantella. 'Maria Callas was brilliant ... singing and acting magnificently with the finesse, subtlety and artistic ability that usually one only dreams of,' wrote Peter Hoffer in *Music & Musicians*.

During the run of *Il Turco in Italia*, Maria received *another* offer from the New York Met, this time begging her to open the 1956-7 season with *Lucia di Lammermoor*. She agreed at once – until Roberto Bauer told her that the conductor would be the Met's resident Fausto Cleva, whom Maria could not stand, claiming that they had once had a violent quarrel in Verona. Bauer stood his ground when she insisted that Cleva would have to be replaced, and after some deliberation, Maria conceded – though Rudolf Bing's trump-card of unprecedented first-class hotel accommodation and up to $3,000 in expenses for herself and her husband helped her with her decision – until Bauer added that Bing also wanted her to sing *The Magic Flute* in English. Many years later, reflecting on how she had previously refused to sing *Fidelio* in English, she would tell Derek Prouse, 'I don't like opera in English, I'm sorry to say. If the opera is born in English by an English composer, that's quite a different matter.' Roberto Bauer was sent away with a flea in his ear, and was so upset by Maria's show of hysterics and her colourful language that he told Bing, at the risk of losing his job, 'The next time there's any negotiating to be done with that evil-tempered witch, you can do it yourself!'

For her final offering in La Scala's 1954-5 season, Maria once more turned to Luchino Visconti to stage a sensational *La Traviata*, the likes of which had never been seen before not just on an Italian stage, but anywhere in the world. This was Visconti's favourite opera, his favourite film was the Greta Garbo-Robert Taylor vehicle *Camille*, and as a child he had seen Sarah Bernhardt *and* Eleonora in the stage-play of *La Dame Aux Camélias*. His *Traviata*, however, would differ from all these interpretations of Dumas *fils*'s novel, published in 1848, in that it was centred entirely around Maria's complex persona. 'I did it to serve Callas, because one *must* serve Callas,' he said at the time.

Infatuated by the decadent period of recent French history known as La Belle Epoque, Visconti brought the setting of *La Traviata* forward to 1875, and engaged Lila de Nobili, an undisputed authority on the subject, to design the sets and Maria's costumes. De Nobili had recently scored a series of triumphs in Paris, notably with her work for Edith Piaf's musical-comedy *La Petite Lili* and the French adaptation of Tennessee Williams's *A Streetcar Named Desire*. She now dressed Maria in the bustles, bonnets and excruciatingly tight bodices of the period, and personally painted the sets, each one reflecting Violetta's mood and state of health. Thus in the first scene the drawing room is embellished in scarlet, gold and black, symbolising frivolity, riches and death, with the heroine in a black satin dress and elbow-length white gloves, clutching a posy of violets and flittering around the stage like an authentic *demi-mondaine*, entertaining her guests ... hard-faced but defenceless as Alfredo tells her, when they are alone, that he loves her. Then, when he is gone, she sluttishly loosens her hair and kicks off her shoes, as if ready for business, as she sings 'Sempre libera' – an act which caused some members of the audience to walk out of the theatre on 28 May, the evening of the première.

In complete contrast, de Nobili's set for Act Two, which takes place in Alfredo's and Violetta's country cottage, conveyed a simple, rustic aura wherein this young woman, in the final stages of consumption, enjoys the only peace of mind she has ever known, finally coming to terms with the fact that, after a lifetime of seeking favours and material possessions from heartless men, she is about to sacrifice the only true love she has ever experienced because Alfredo's father, Germont, has declared her status inappropriate. The settings here are in the most delicate pastel shades and Violetta, à-la-Garbo, wears a white lace-edged dress and bonnet, and carries a parasol.

Nothing could quite compare with Violetta's death-scene, as far removed from Hollywood as could be imagined. Just as Maria had seemed to sing in her sleep in *La Sonnambula*, so she allowed her voice and movements to declare her deteriorating health. Gazing into her mirror she sings 'Addio del passato' (Goodbye bright visions) as a veritable chanson-réaliste. And yet, there is hope! Violetta has sold her furniture and effects to pay off her debts, sharing Alfredo's precognitive dream that all will be well when he comes to take her away. 'Rinasce, rinasce ... m'agita insolito vigor' (My pulse beats and my strength is returning), she pronounces, though subconsciously she cannot evade the fact that death is imminent. Fumbling with her clothes, she is determined to dress herself but is unable to tie her cloak and bonnet, and in a desperate attempt to pull on her gloves she cries, 'Ah, gran Dio! Morir si giovane!' (Oh, great God! To die so young!) And when *this* Violetta dies, it is upright in her lover's arms, with her huge, wide-open eyes staring into the void beyond the footlights until the curtain has fallen. Needless to say, the first time this happened there was scarcely a dry eye in the house.

Most of the critics approved of this 'new' *Traviata*, though naturally there had to be some detractors, particularly the diehard devotees of Verdi who accused the producer and his prima donna of 'extreme irreverence'. Visconti was denounced in one publication for shifting the setting of the opera 'to the depraved world of Zola's *Nana*,' whilst Maria was accused of 'acting like a whore' in the 'Sempre libera' scene, and for dying with her hat and cloak on. She was further criticised for singing *pianissimo* during her death scene, though she soon put one journalist firmly in his place when he asked her who had been tired, Violetta or Callas – exploding, 'Neither of us were tired, you fool. She was dying. Now go away and find yourself another job!'

It was also revealed, the morning after the première, that Maria had had a massive bust-up with Giuseppe di Stefano – a formidably talented singer, but a somewhat wooden if not hammy actor, for whom gestures were often a secondary feature of any opera. Therefore, when both Maria and Visconti had arranged extra rehearsals in the hope of getting him to act, in the director's words, 'a little more like a lover than a lump of wood towards his dying mistress', di Stefano had persistently turned up late, incurring Maria's wrath and on one occasion having the door slammed in his face. 'I am *never* late, and I don't expect people to be late with me,' she bawled at him. 'Lateness is the very worst of bad manners!' The last straw had occurred during the première itself when, after Act Three, Visconti and the conductor Carlo Maria Guilini had urged Maria to take a solo curtain-call. In a fit of pique, di Stefano had stormed off the stage and out of the theatre, and one hour later, Visconti had received word that he would not be returning to the production.

Di Stefano was replaced by the more amenable but less satisfactory Giacinto Prandelli, who had sung with Maria in *Die Entführung aus dem Serail*, and the second performance of *La Traviata* on 31 May was just as well received by the audience as the first. During the third, however, as Maria kicked off her shoes – this time high into the air – for 'Sempre libera', someone in one of the galleries actually blew a whistle. Raising one hand, Maria stopped the orchestra, and there was an embarrassing moment whilst the offending man, an irate di Stefano fan, was forcibly removed from the theatre. Then, taking a deep breath, she resumed the aria, and at the end of the act, this time it was *she* who demanded a solo curtain-call. Admitting that she had received a number of anonymous letters which threatened disruptions of her performance, she later explained, 'I wanted the audience to tell me its opinion clearly and straightforwardly, and they did so, with a generous rain of applause which extinguished my fury.'

8

Elle Est Dangereuse ... Elle Est Belle!

I don't like fights and I don't like quarrels. I hate the
nervous, mental confusion they engender. But if I have
to fight, I'll fight. Up to now I've generally won, but
never with any feeling of elation.

In August 1955, Elvira di Hidalgo arrived in Milan to spend a
month's holiday with her brother, Luis, who lived in the city. Her
reunion with Maria was an emotional one – the two women had not
seen each other since Maria had left Athens, and for the last few
years, well into her sixties but still a highly respected and sought-
after teacher, di Hidalgo had been resident at the Ankara
Conservatory, in Turkey.

Such was Maria's possessiveness that di Hidalgo spent more time
with her than she did with her brother – accompanying her on day-
long shopping sprees for yet more bric-à-brac and gadgets for the
new house, visiting Madame Biki's and, most important of all,
sitting in on the recording sessions for *Madama Butterfly*, *Aida* and
Rigoletto. It is now known that Giuseppe di Stefano *should* have
been singing in all three, but that Maria had insisted upon him
being dropped at the last moment – her means of getting back at
him on account of his behaviour after the *Traviata* première.
Therefore, the role of Pinkerton in *Madama Butterfly* was sung by

Nicolai Gedda, and in *Aida* Richard Tucker sang Radames. By the beginning of September, however, Maria's anger had cooled and di Stefano returned to the fold to sing the Duke in *Rigoletto* – terrified of what the critics would make of this, particularly the ones who had savaged his performance in Mexico, three years before.

The sessions went so well, in fact – soothed no doubt by Elvira di Hidalgo's presence – that di Stefano was invited to sing Edgar in the first of the two productions of *Lucia di Lammermoor* for the Berlin Festival at the end of September. Maria also insisted on di Stefano travelling with her to Berlin on 24 September, leaving a somewhat confused Meneghini to follow a few days later. Several of those close to Maria have said that, just as difficulties only stimulated her, so she never truly appreciated a man's worth until she had had a blazing row with him and he had stood up to her. Although this would never happen with Mario del Monaco – on 29 June she had agreed to sing *Norma* with him in Rome only because it had been on the radio, where no one could see her glaring at him – it temporarily drew her closer to di Stefano, which worried Meneghini considerably, for this man was blatantly *heterosexual*. Later Maria and di Stefano would have a very passionate affair, but for now she was into yet another hiding for nothing, flirting with the great Greek bass, Nicola Zaccaria, who at the eleventh hour replaced the indisposed Giuseppi Modesti in the role of Oroveso. Even so, Meneghini became so flustered during the afternoon of the première, 29 September, that he missed the plane to Berlin – making Maria so tetchy that she refused to go on to the stage until he arrived, fortunately only ten minutes after the curtain was scheduled to rise.

The tickets for both *Lucias* had sold out within two hours of the box-office opening, with some fans camping out all night on the pavement, and many being snapped up by touts and re-sold for several times their original value. The première was also broadcast on the radio, and has since been made commercially available on any number of pirate recordings. Such was the enthusiasm of the Berliners that after the Mad Scene they came close to rioting – particularly when Maria, still in character, wandered around the stage picking up roses and tossing them to the orchestra, kissing one bloom suggestively before aiming it, with alarming accuracy for one so short-sighted, squarely into the flautist's lap!

The Berlin *Lucia von Lammermoor*, as it was tagged by some critics, is generally regarded as Maria's finest interpretation of the role, for in it her voice was absolutely flawless. 'It has a bell-like, tender, sustained pianissimo,' enthused *Der Tagesspieler*'s Werner Oehlmann. 'It has a modulation for every fluctuation of feeling and the floating lightness of a bird's voice that traces every arabesque in the melody. ' 'Oh yes, an artist to her fingertips,' proclaimed Desmond Shawe-Taylor of *Opera*, concluding, 'The real royal thing! I dare she will *never* sing any better than she does now!'

After the performance, there was a reception for the cast at the Italian Embassy. For once Maria had eschewed Madame Biki for the much more expensive Christian Dior, and she looked sensational as she entered the building flanked by her *beaux*, di Stefano and Zaccaria, with Meneghini trailing awkwardly behind with Zaccaria's wife, Efi. And of course it had to happen – whilst Maria was deliberating over the canapés, a young journalist who of course knew exactly who was who at the bash, asked her if he might escort her to a club after the reception ... providing she could get rid of her father. Maria merely smiled, and walked away, reminded once more that many people regarded her marriage as little more than a laughing-stock.

Two weeks later, the Meneghinis flew to Chicago for Maria's second season at the Civic Opera House, which was scheduled to open on 31 October with *I Puritani*, to be followed by *Il Trovatore* and Maria's stage debut of Puccini's *Madama Butterfly*. Heralding the season was a large spread in *Life* magazine, headed 'Voice Of An Angel', within which Robert Neville covered her career so far, throwing in her negotiations with Bing and the ongoing feud with Tebaldi for good measure. Maria, however, strongly disapproved of one of the accompanying photographs when shown the rough copy – a shot of the 'old' Callas taken during her 1949 Venice *Puritani* – and insisted on a re-shoot.

Once again, tension was anticipated. Whilst discussing the terms of her contract with Lawrence Kelly, in Milan, Maria had stipulated that he also engage Renata Tebaldi – regardless of the cost of having two massive stars on his budget – so that audiences would be able to decide for themselves which soprano they preferred, instead of being influenced by the critics. When asked what would happen should Tebaldi *not* appear, Maria had replied, 'Then Callas stays in Milan, dear!'

Tebaldi had welcomed the challenge, though she was not entirely happy that Maria was opening the Chicago season, instead of her *Aida*, which had been relegated to the following evening. Kelly then attempted to smooth relations between Maria and Tebaldi by arranging a joint press-conference within the master dressing-room, which had both their names on the door – but if Maria at least seemed to want to bury the hatchet, her rival was not buying and during the sojourn in Chicago, the pair never met.

As before, Maria's gay admirers turned out in their droves to hear her. In *I Puritani*, Elvira is first heard offstage as she pronounces, 'La luna, il sol, le stelle!' (The moon, the sun, the stars), so that the audience are well-prepared for her arrival. When she did walk on to the stage, however, her fans made such a row cheering that she completely missed her cue and, after taking a deep bow, she began again. Later in the performance, a sudden flurry of excitement forced her to throw an excruciatingly off-key high D ... and still she could do no wrong! 'No mistake about it – she's the premier singing actress of today,' declared Howard Talley of *Musical America*, whilst Claudia Cassidy raved, 'Whereas Lucia was a normal girl gone mad for love, Elvira is a fey, unstable creature who is off and on like Finnegan. And the singing is magnificent!'

Instability was certainly the order of the evening when Maria and her husband attended the première of Tebaldi's *Aida*. Lawrence Kelly had offered her seats in his box, but she had refused, declaring that she wished to eschew favouritism for once by sitting amongst the general public in the orchestra stalls. There was a sound reason for this, for halfway through Tebaldi's aria, 'O patria mia', Maria snatched at her necklace of cultured pearls, snapping the thread, and for the next ten minutes the performance was disrupted whilst she and a dozen spectators scrambled around on their knees picking up the pearls – aided by the flashlight which Meneghini just happened to have in his jacket pocket.

Il Trovatore, which had its first performance on 5 November, was just as enthusiastically received – besides Ettore Bastianini and Ebe Stignani, the production boasted in its central role the legendary Swedish tenor, Jussi Björling, then at the height of his powers, yet sadly at just forty-four approaching the end of his life. After the performance, Björling told reporters, 'I now know that there is perfection in the world. Her name is Callas.'

That evening, too, Rudolf Bing made his most desperate attempt thus far to secure Maria for the New York Met. Accompanied by his assistant, Francis Robinson, he flew to Chicago to plead with her in person, receiving a very cool reception from Lawrence Kelly and Carol Fox, who suspected that once she fell into Bing's clutches, Maria would never work for the Chicago Lyric again. For the first time ever, the Met was willing to exceed its $1,000 ceiling-fee and, having kissed Maria's hand and virtually gone down on his knees before her for the benefit of press photographers – something he did often, though such obvious fawning never cut any ice with La Callas – Bing took her aside and told her that what she would sing and for how many performances could always be discussed at a later date. For the time being, she could be assured of $1,200 a performance, plus $3,000 in expenses for herself and her husband, who would of course be welcomed to New York with open arms. Maria signed the contract at once!

Madama Butterfly which premièred on 11 November was, from the critics' point of view, the low-point of the Chicago season. Roger Dettmer of the *Chicago American* began his review enthusiastically enough: 'The Town, we all know, has been Callas-crazy for more than a year, and none has been more demented than I. In the proper role and in good voice, I adore the woman. I am a slave in her spell!' Here the praise halted as he concluded, 'Give her further performances and Mme Callas can be the "Butterfly" supreme in our time. Ideally, the Callas Butterfly (or anyone's faithful to the libretto and to the score) is scaled for an *intimate* house – the Piccola Scala, for example.' Claudia Cassidy was similarly unimpressed:

> As a decoration she was exquisite, with the aid of another *Butterfly* beauty of older days, Hizi Koyke, who staged the

performance. As a tragic actress, she had the inerring simplicity, the poignant power that thrust to the heart of the score. But in the first scene she missed the diminutive mood which is *Butterfly*'s essence. This was charming make-believe, but it was not Cio-Cio-San, nor was it the ultimate Callas.

When Maria signed her contract with Kelly and Fox, it had been for six performances only – two each of the three operas. She had also insisted on a clause wherein they and the management of the Civil Opera House would be fully responsible for protecting her from Eddie Bagarozy, who had threatened to have her arrested should she set foot in the city again. The security surrounding her for these six performances was therefore extremely tight, yet even then the District Attorney's process-servers had managed to get backstage – to within five yards of her dressing-room – only to be thwarted by a group of fans who had kept them successfully at bay. In the meantime Maria had escaped via the fire-escape and been somewhat unceremoniously bundled into the back of a van. Now, her undoing was effectively two-fold: the signing of the Met contract which meant that as their seasons clashed, Maria would be unable to sing in Chicago's 1956 season – and a supplementary *Madama Butterfly* on 17 November, by public demand, which ultimately was proof enough that not everyone heeded the critics, for all 3,500 seats were sold in just two hours. Unfortunately, the tremendous publicity this attracted enabled Carol Fox, whose relationship with Lawrence Kelly was now strained, to get her own back on Maria for allowing herself to be 'purloined' by Rudolf Bing.

Bagarozy lost no time in taking action, and as Maria finished taking her curtain-calls and rushed to her dressing-room, she was heavied by two burly men in Al Capone-style hats and raincoats – Deputy Sheriff Daniel Smith and Marshal Stanley Pringle – who informed her that they had been instructed to serve her with a writ. Maria, placing both hands behind her back, declared most haughtily, in an outburst which delighted the clutch of gay fans waiting for autographs, 'I will *not* be sued! I have the voice of an angel!' Sheriff Smith then brought her back to earth with a bump – the law requiring that a summons should make bodily contact with the defendant, he moved menacingly towards her and thrust the $300,000 writ inside her kimono.

What happened next completely dispelled the myth that most of Maria's 'difficulties' were but the invention of jealous rivals. 'Forty-four four-letter words in three minutes, like Mae West this little lady certainly proved herself no angel,' proclaimed one publication, describing how, her eyes ablaze with hatred and her Victory Red mouth twisted into a hideous grimace, Maria had charged after her persecutors. She almost certainly would have resorted to physical violence – if not to Smith and Pringle, then to the Associated Press photographer commissioned by Bagarozy to trail Maria and subsequently capture the 'raging tigress' scene for posterity – had she not been manhandled back to her dressing-room by Meneghini and Lawrence Kelly, screaming at the top of her voice, 'Chicago will be sorry for this. I'll never sing in this fucking horse-shit town again!'

Maria's outburst was certainly justified, though she was extremely lucky not to have been arrested on account of her bad language and her physical threats against the process-servers. Had this happened, and had she been detained in police custody, the chances are that she would not have been able to return to Milan in time for the next season. Meneghini therefore decided to get her out of the country before she did any more damage. That same evening he booked them on the first available flight out of Chicago – to Montreal, at dawn, where for two hours Maria hid in a corner of the lounge, camouflaged by dark glasses and a wide-brimmed hat, waiting for the connecting flight to Milan.

Two years later, after she had apologised to Daniel Smith and Stanley Pringle for her outburst, Maria spoke of the Chicago incident to Anita Pensotti, confessing, 'I was not indignant at those poor process-servers, who in the final analysis were only carrying out the orders they had received, but at those who had kept quiet about the trap and betrayed me.' She was referring to the fierce rivalry between Lawrence Kelly and Carol Fox, wherein Fox, hoping to secure Maria for another Chicago season but contracted exclusively to herself, had allowed the process-servers backstage, then told Maria that *Kelly* had been the guilty party, hoping to alienate her against him. This does not appear to have been true, however, for even the 'protection' clause in the 1955 Chicago contract would have been able to prevent Smith and Pringle from carrying out the law.

Maria was also defended by Tito Gobbi – valiantly so, for he too had suffered the sharp end of her tongue in this very theatre not so long before. Writing in his memoirs, the baritone criticised Smith for not having had the manners to remove his hat, and concluded, 'How dared this oaf lay his hand on someone who had just given 99 per cent of everything she had and was in her effort to serve her art and her public? Suppose she *did* owe money – the matter could have waited for a couple of hours. To attack any artist at such a time is contemptible.'

Back in Milan, there was more drama and cursing when Maria read the contents of an advertisement in the *Corriere della Sera* – next to a photograph of the 'new' Maria was an endorsement, signed by Dr Giovanni Cazzarolli, Meneghini's brother-in-law, who had been one of the witnesses at her wedding: 'In my capacity as Maria Meneghini Callas's physician, I hereby declare that the wonderful results achieved by her recent diet are mostly due to her eating Pantanella Mills physiological pasta.' Anyone else would have laughed off such nonsense, particularly as Maria had been paid handsomely for the endorsement, whether she had agreed to/been aware of it or not. However, when Pantanella's managing director – a nephew of Pope Pius XII – attempted to defend his company's reputation by using his 'holy-link' status to throw rank, Maria saw red. Still smarting from Chicago, she served the company with a writ – then told reporters that the true secret of her remarkable weight-loss had nothing whatsoever to do with diet: she had simply taken to swallowing tapeworms!

Incredibly, the Pope himself attempted to intervene between the warring factions, inviting the Meneghinis to a private audience – and getting more than he bargained for. Initially, Maria refused this immensely privileged invitation, telling a Vatican official, 'If his Holiness is so keen to meet me, tell him to come along to La Scala the next time I'm there!' Eventually, to please Meneghini she gave way, and another audience was arranged – one which ended badly, for Maria made it quite clear that she was not used to being ordered around, even by the Pope, who made the mistake of telling her that whilst *Parsifal* was his favourite opera, he had been surprised to tune in to *RAI Rome* and hear her singing Kundry in German. 'I do not sing in *German*,' Maria snarled. 'I do not sing in *any* language that I don't understand!'

The Pope was therefore on to a loser when he suggested that it might be the best for all concerned, including his own peace of mind, if she dropped her lawsuit against Pantanella Mills. Although she did not actually tell him to mind his own business, Maria intimated as much by saying, a little less forcibly than her earlier outburst, 'I will think about it. More than that I cannot promise.' In fact, she was now more determined than ever to strike out for what she believed was the right to protect her name from being 'just another advertising slogan', and though the case would take another four years of tough legal wrangling, in the end she did acquire substantial compensation, plus costs – but more importantly, Dr Cazzarolli and Pantanella Mills were compelled to publish a letter of apology in the *Corriere della Sera*.

Maria's 1955-6 La Scala season would be her busiest yet: besides nine *Norma*s and an unheard-of seventeen *Traviata*s there would be two new roles – five performances singing Rosina in Rossini's *Il Barbiere di Siviglia*, and six singing Fedora in Gïordano's half-forgotten opera of the same name. The sparks started flying, however, when she discovered that Mario del Monaco would be singing Pollione in *Norma*, which was to open the season.

Maria and the tenor she referred to as 'that goddam fiend' made every attempt to outbitch each other all through rehearsals. Del Monaco persistently reminded her of her 'indiscretions' in Chicago, and is alleged to have been responsible for pasting *that* photograph to her dressing-room door. Del Monaco's claque also proved considerably more rowdy than any Maria had heard before, and fearing trouble Antonio Ghiringhelli had appointed a former tenor, Ettore Parmeggiani – for obvious reasons, Maria nicknamed him 'Cheese Face' – to ensure that each rival faction was placed in that part of the theatre most appropriate to achieve maximum audience participation, depending on who was supporting whom.

Indeed, on the evening of the première there were so many of these professional detractors that the only way Maria's true admirers could make themselves discernible from the others was by applauding the recitatives!

This extraordinary behaviour continued throughout the next five *Norma*s, so incensing Meneghini – who henceforth would prove more trouble for Maria than he was worth, with his endless meddling only fuelling the fires of her temperament – that he formally complained to Ghiringhelli, who promptly told him to mind his own business and stop being so paranoid! The bellicose little man then threatened Mario del Monaco with a writ, warning him to quieten his 'claque', or else. Unfortunately for Maria, this only made matters worse.

One of the terms of del Monaco's contract was that *no one* should take a solo curtain-call, including himself. On New Year's Day 1956, however, the del Monaco 'claque' joined forces with the Tebaldiani, cheering so loudly that the tenor was compelled to break his own ruling and take a lengthy curtain-call after the first act which, according to Meneghini, he had not earned in the first place. And if this was not enough, during the interval Maria's husband marched into Ettore Parmeggiani's office and threatened to sue him unless he had the offending del Monaco supporters forcibly ejected from the theatre! Needless to say, this did not happen, and at the end of the performance when many of the audience were yelling for their tenor, Maria gave del Monaco a resounding kick on the shins – then whilst he was hopping around the wings in agony, she rushed on to the stage and stole all the applause!

The revival of Visconti's *La Traviata* was no less troublesome. Giuseppe di Stefano should have been singing the role of Alfredo, but upon hearing of Maria's 'antics' with his friend del Monaco, he had backed out at the last moment and had had to be replaced by Gianni Raimondo. Maria would remain convinced, however, that del Monaco alone engineered the incident which took place on 19 January, the evening of the première. During the actual performance there had been but little disturbance – just the odd hissing, and the whistle-blower in the gallery who was in fact one of Maria's biggest fans, and who on several occasions was invited to dine with her. Then, as she was taking her bows, reserving her deepest curtsy for Visconti, who was sitting in his family box, several bunches of radishes fell at her feet!

Maria later maintained that she had mistaken these vegetables for carnations, and over the course of her next few interviews they grew progressively bigger as she changed her story – first they were out-of-season carrots, suggesting that if she *was* to be pelted with vegetables, then at least someone had gone to the trouble of buying expensive ones. Then they were turnips, posing the question, of course: how on earth would anyone in obligatory evening wear be allowed into La Scala armed with turnips, and if so, was the admittedly myopic Maria *really* expected to be believed that she had mistaken them for flowers, even when pressing them to her breast?

By and large, Maria's subsequent *Traviata*s were trouble-free and extremely well received, though almost all the critics agreed that they lacked the sparkle of the earlier Visconti-de Nobili productions. *Il Barbiere di Siviglia*, on the other hand, which premièred on 16 February with Tito Gobbi singing the central role of Figaro, they hated almost to a man – 'a Rosina almost worthy of psycho-analytical study', was how Franco Abbiati summed up her interpretation in *Corriere della Sera*.

The problem with Maria's Rosina seems to have been two-fold. Firstly, though she was not naturally a maladive woman, influenced by the undeniably maudlin Meneghini, these days she'd fallen into the habit of always taking herself too seriously, and had absolutely no idea how to unwind. Secondly, as a *tragédienne*, without the guiding hand of a Visconti, as had happened with *Il Turco In Italia*, she did not know how to be funny on the stage. Some years later, running through 'Una voce poco fa', she would advise her Juilliard students, 'Sweeten up the beginning of the aria. It *must* have a smile in it!' In 1956, however, not only was Maria jeered and whistled at by a large section of the audience, who chatted loudly all the way through the second act, she also had to suffer the indignity of hearing the slamming up of seats as dozens of people left the theatre, as noisily as they could. As for the conductor, Carlo Maria Giulini, he was so humiliated that he announced that after this production, he would not be working at La Scala again.

Maria's La Scala season should have ended with six performances of *Parsifal*, conducted by Erich Kleiber who had recently, for the second time, given up his position with the Berlin State Opera – this time on account of ill-health – but even terminally ill, the great maestro had wanted to end his career on a high note, conducting for Callas. Now, he died unexpectedly, and she refused to even think of a replacement, electing instead for one of her most melodramatic roles for some time: Giordano's *Fedora*, based on Vittorien Sardou's play which had been written for Sarah Bernhardt in 1883. Singing opposite her was Franco Corelli, temporarily assigned to the 'enemy' camp ... for failing or refusing to have an affair with her. As usual, the 21 May première was interrupted by detractors, whom Maria ignored, though she hit the roof when Claudio Sartori of *Opera* denounced both her and Corelli's interpretation as 'perhaps overstepping the limits of good style'. Neither did she approve of the backhanded compliment from *Music And Musician*'s Peter Hoffer, 'Once again she proved that even if she is not the greatest singer, she is certainly one of the world's greatest actresses.'

Maria and Giuseppe di Stefano – forgiven for the umpteenth time – had been engaged to sing at the Vienna Staatsoper in La Scala's production of *Lucia di Lammermoor*, to be conducted by Herbert von Karajan as part of that year's Festival. Indeed, such was her hurry to get away from Milan after the final *Fedora* of 3 June that Maria left her beloved Cignaroli behind and would not sing a note until a friend had fetched it from her home.

The *Lucia* première, on 12 June, was attended by the Austrian president, Theodor Körner, and far from the petty jealousies of La Scala there was not a boo to be heard. The Sextet proved so popular that it had to be repeated, there was twenty-five minutes of hostility after the Mad Scene, and so many curtain-calls that everyone lost count. One in particular – shared by just Maria and von Karajan – brought an angry outburst afterwards from di Stefano, which for once she completely ignored.

Outside the theatre there were traffic-jams as Maria was mobbed by hundreds of over-excited young men, and though she would have been content to stay there for the duration, signing programmes and enjoying a for once friendly, appreciative audience, the humourless Meneghini flung a spanner in the works by summoning the police 'to restore order'. 'That was the night when I first realised what a miserable bastard my husband could be,' Maria later told Roger Normand.

At the end of June 1956, the Meneghinis travelled to the tiny island of Ischia in the Bay of Naples – Maria's first real holiday in years, where on account of the vast difference in their ages, she was able to break free of her husband most days to sunbathe, shop, and take in a little sightseeing. She spent some time with the composer Sir William Walton and his wife, who lived on the island, and several times took the boat to nearby Capri, a snobs' paradise which was nevertheless home to Britain's greatest ever entertainer, Gracie Fields, who was as down to earth as they came.

Maria had always admired Gracie's English interpretation of 'O mio babbino caro', and it was Sir William Walton who arranged for them to meet at Gracie's beautiful home, La Canzone del Mare, where she spent a few days spared of her husband's nagging and 'compared notes' with Gracie about New York. The British star had just returned from there after winning a Silvana Award for her appearance in a straight play, *The Old Lady Shows Her Medals*, and Maria had just been informed that her roles at the Met were to be Norma, Tosca and Lucia.

Capri offered Maria two, for her, important diversions. Firstly, she took a shine to Gracie's handsome caretaker, Mario Pollio. Although he refused to cheat on his young wife by having the fling with Maria which she obviously wanted, Mario did tell her that she was wasting her beauty and intelligence on a man like Battista Meneghini. Secondly, Gracie Fields was rehearsing several new songs for a forthcoming British tour, and one of these was the lilting theme from the film, *Summertime In Venice*, an extremely rare excursion outside the opera world which Maria actually sang – in Gracie's lounge, accompanied by her on the piano!

It was to Venice that the Meneghinis travelled at the end of July. Maria's New York debut was being sealed with an appearance on the cover of *Time* magazine – an infinite honour – but instead of the customary photograph, she was to be painted by Henry Koener, who met her whilst she was guest of honour at the 17th Film Festival. Meneghini declared that the sittings would have to take place at their home – with himself supervising, of course.

The couple then returned to Milan, where during the first week of August Maria was reunited with Giuseppe di Stefano, who had been contracted to partner her in two of her three recordings for EMI: *La Bohème*, which sadly she would never convey to the stage, was recorded at the end of August, and this was followed early in September by Verdi's *Un Ballo In Maschera*. Antonino Votto conducted on both. Prior to these, however, she recorded *Il Trovatore* in under a week, for which di Stefano had not been contracted to sing Manrico because the conductor, von Karajan, and Maria had wanted Richard Tucker. The American, however, had flatly refused to work with von Karajan because of his Nazi connections during the war.

In fact, all of these operas should have been conducted by Tullio Serafin, but at the end of 1956 he and Maria were not on speaking terms. Earlier in the year, Serafin had been asked to record – with Maria – *La Traviata* for EMI, but as she had recorded this for Cetra in September 1952, the terms of her contract with them dictated that she would not be permitted to record it again until September 1957. Serafin and Walter Legge both knew this, but they had apparently been unwilling to wait until Maria was free. *La Traviata* had subsequently been recorded with Antonietta Stella singing the role of Violetta – causing Maria to scream at the reporters who asked her if the rumours that she had ended her working partnership with Serafin were true, 'Don't speak to me about that insufferable little man! *I* shall never speak to *him* as long as I live!'

9

Vedro Le Mie Vendette!

My shyness and insecurity have often made me seem
arrogant – it's a form of self-protection of timid people.
A person who is really sure of herself does not need to act
like a dictator.

The Meneghinis arrived in New York on 15 October 1956, where
they were met at Idlewild airport by Maria's father, Dario Soria of
Angel Records, and the Met's Francis Robinson who, ever wary of
Eddie Bagarozy's process-servers, had brought a lawyer along.
Maria surprised everyone by demanding a meeting with Bagarozy's
lawyers – this took place in Soria's office when her settlement offer
of $25,000 was rejected. Bagarozy had made it clear that he would
settle for nothing less than the full amount. Over the next two
months, therefore, Robinson and his lawyer did not let Maria out
of their sight – even standing guard outside the door if she had to
visit the powder room. To his credit Rudolf Bing attempted to
minimise Bagarozy's threats to seize her American earnings –
something he was legally entitled to do, as the courts had granted
him a warrant of attachment – by suggesting to Maria that her fee
for each performance be paid into a Swiss bank. 'This meant that
she would have no salary in America for the Bagarozys to attach,'
he recalled in 1972, adding, 'We perfected this arrangement in great

detail, but Meneghini rejected it. In fact, he rejected all arrangements that did not involve payment to *him*, in *cash*, before the curtain rose, of his wife's fee for each performance. Towards the end, I had him paid in five-dollar bills, to make a wad uncomfortably large for him to carry.'

The advance publicity for Maria's first New York season took a decisive turn for the worse when on 27 October – two days before the *Norma* première – the first edition of *Time* with Maria's portrait on the cover hit the newsstands. In the ten days running up to its publication, with no advance warning of its contents as had been the case with the *Life* feature, one interview or function had followed another. Maria, with her cool beauty, intelligence and exemplary manners had exuded such charm that many journalists had actually been *disappointed* not to have been confronted by some screaming, hysterical vixen with a reputation of being able to outcurse a sailor on shore leave. If anything, New Yorkers had been surprised to learn that she had a sense of humour, albeit a dry, sarcastic one, when a young woman reporter had visited her hotel suite and asked, quite innocuously, 'Madame Callas, you were born in the United States, brought up in Greece, and now you are practically an Italian. In which language do you *think*?' – to which had come the response, 'I *count* in English, dear!'

The four-page *Time* editorial – penned by George de Carvalho, the winner of the 1952 Pulitzer Prize – did, however, offer its readers the completely wrong impression that Maria had been putting on an act for the benefit of the press, that the rumours *were* all true. In order to form a 'balanced appraisal' of Callas, the woman, the magazine's researchers had sent out questionnaires to a number of her friends and colleagues, and to several detractors who, no matter how much they were paid, would never find anything good to say about her. Giuseppe di Stefano had declared, in a statement made before the Vienna *Lucia* (since which time they had made up), 'I'm never going to sing opera with her again, and that's final!' Another 'colleague' who requested anonymity – Maria always swore it could only have been Mario del Monaco, whom Rudolf Bing had audaciously engaged to sing Pollione in *Norma* – stated, 'Callas is a diva more widely hated by her colleagues and more widely loved by her public than any other living singer.' The most spiteful condemnation of all, however, came from Maria's mother, whom *Time* had tracked down in Athens and who, of course, had not been averse to telling the world about her daughter's ingratitude and cruel streak. Litza had even supplied the magazine with a copy of Maria's last letter, and its contents truly shocked many of those who had spent hours queuing for hard-to-come-by, often extremely expensive tickets for *Norma* – touts were reported to be selling the already overpriced $35 orchestra-stall tickets for four times this amount. As one critic who was obviously only relating to one side of the story put it, 'How can one be expected to respect a sadistic young woman who has instructed her own mother to drown herself?'

The American public, therefore, was by and large out for their pound of flesh, and a considerable portion of the audience on 29 October were not in the least interested in opera – they wanted to see this 'curiosity' who had taken up such a wealth of newspaper column inches. As for the genuine opera enthusiasts, they wanted to find out, of course, if she could live up to the expectations created by her publicity machine. Rudolf Bing had ensured her plenty of competition: Zinca Milanov with a revival of Verdi's *Ernani*, and Renata Tebaldi in Tyrone Guthrie's sparkling new production of *La Traviata*.

Maria was more nervous than usual, particularly since whilst she was waiting in the wings there had been the occasional outburst of applause as some personality or other had entered the theatre, Edith Piaf and her best friend Marlene Dietrich, Zinka Milanov, and the 'holy terror' gossip-columnist Elsa Maxwell all received standing ovations as they were ushered to their seats – and now, as she entered the stage, there was an almost glacial silence. Maria was not in her best voice during her opening recitatives – New York was in the throes of an Indian summer, and she was having trouble with her sinuses. She almost dried up, too, when a handful of spectators – said to be del Monaco fans – began hissing during 'Casta Diva'. By the end of the first act, however, Maria had put up enough of a struggle to win over one of the toughest audiences of her career. 'She went on to tackle the formidable coloratura hurdles of the role with practised precision,' Winthrop Sargeant wrote in the *New*

Yorker, 'singing nearly everything in tune – a feat noteworthy in itself – giving each passage an appropriate elegance of style.' *Time* magazine, perhaps hoping to put right the irreparable damage of their feature, concluded after a lengthy, flagrantly sycophantic review which Maria dismissed as 'purest bullshit', 'Callas's voice and stage presence add up to more than beauty – namely, the kind of passionate dedication, the kind of excitement that invariably mark a champ.' The most honest review, however – the one Maria clipped – came from Howard Taubmann of the *New York Times*, a man who had seen Rosa Ponselle's legendary interpretation of *Norma* a quarter of a century before:

> It is a puzzling voice. Occasionally it gives the impression of having been formed of sheer willpower rather than natural endowments. The quality is different in the upper, middle and lower registers, as if three different persons were involved. In high fortissimos, Miss Callas is downright shrill. She also has a tendency to sing off-pitch when she has no time to brace herself for a high note ... Miss Callas may however be forgiven a lack of velvet in parts of her range. She is brave to do *Norma* at all, and she brings sufficient dramatic and musical values to her performance to make it an interesting one.

There was drama, of course, partly instigated by the grotesquely overbearing Rudolf Bing, who seemed to have a mania for grabbing Maria's hand and kissing it at every opportunity whenever they faced the press. It was something that made her cringe, and though she once referred to him as 'a perfect gentleman, an exquisite and solicitous director', she was only being sarcastic, applying the same tone of voice which was reserved for speaking of such 'dear friends' as Renate Tebaldi. Similarly, when Bing described Maria as 'girlishly wonderful to work with', no one who knew of the backstage screaming matches at the Met could possibly have taken such a remark with less than a huge pinch of salt. In order to appease his favourite prima donnas, Milanov and Tebaldi, Bing had *paid* some newspapers to place photographs of him signing them on either side of the one of him signing Maria, in Chicago, and this had brought an angry outburst from Mario del Monaco, who had accused Bing of favouritism. The tenor had exploded again upon hearing that Maria was to be escorted around New York by Francis Robinson – 'like some visiting queen' – and at considerable expense, Bing had been compelled to hire the tenor a bodyguard, for absolutely no reason at all!

The final straw, however, came when del Monaco threatened to walk out on the production should Maria take any solo curtain-calls, for Bing passed the instruction on to her. Offering not one word of argument, at the end of the première, flanked by del Monaco and the bass, Cesare Siepi, Maria took a deep bow before retrieving a huge bouquet of pink roses tossed onto the stage by a fan. Smiling radiantly, she plucked a bloom and offered it to Siepi, with a sincere, 'Thank you, darling!' Then, as the bass retreated to allow her to take the forbidden call, she plucked another and passed it to del Monaco, still smiling, and pronounced in English, 'You are a cunt!'

Maria had requested a post-performance party within the Trianon Room at the Ambassador Hotel – paid for by Angel Records and hosted by its director, Dario Soria – to which had been invited a galaxy of Hollywood stars, reporters, and several top diplomats from the Greek and Italian embassies in New York. Maria was escorted to the party by her husband, Soria and his wife, and a private detective-bodyguard employed by Windtons, the famous jewellers who had paid Maria $5,000 to wear and advertise over $1 million worth of their finest emeralds.

Maria spent much of her time chatting to Marlene Dietrich who, in the forties and fifties, played the role of a benevolent ambas-sadress, welcoming often disorientated European stars to America and introducing them to New York society. She had been responsi-ble for launching Edith Piaf's phenomenally successful Stateside career and had taken Maria under her wing immediately after the publication of the *Time* feature, when she had been a bag of nerves and unable to keep anything down. Sending out for ten pounds of fillet steak, Marlene had borrowed a liquidiser from the hotel kitchen, puréed it, and made Maria drink the juice. According to some reports, she is supposed to have asked Marlene, 'What brand of stock-cubes do you use?' Marlene later dismissed this as 'rubbish', telling me, 'Do you honestly think that Callas could have been that *stupid*? If you want to know, we talked about men – how most of hers were old enough to be her grandfather, and how *all* of them were unworthy of the love she had to give. Then we spoke about that tenor, the one she kicked. I told her, "Next time you must aim for the balls, Maria," to which she replied, "Isn't that where he keeps his *brains*?" '

In fact, Maria's feud with the tenor sorted itself out a few days later when, halfway through the *Norma* run, he was replaced by Kurt Baum, another singer who had caused problems in the past but who was now very loosely regarded as a friend. Then, in order to placate del Monaco, Bing dismissed Cesare Siepi and brought in another former sparring partner, Nicola Moscona.

On 15 November, with one *Norma* still to go, Maria sang the first of her two *Tosca*s, conducted by fellow Greek Dimitri Mitropoulos, with Giuseppe Campora as Cavaradosi and George London in the role of Scarpia. The following year, George London would be interviewed by *High Fidelity* magazine, and in a feature headed, 'Prima Donnas I Have Sung Against' would only praise Maria. Confessing that he had had a few forebodings about working with her – not helped by the comment from his wife, 'Look, she can't do more than actually *kill* you in the second act!' – London remembered how, before the curtain rose on the première, he had popped his head around her dressing-room door and told her, 'In bocca di lupo' – the Italian equivalent of 'break a leg'. Maria had been so moved that she had cupped both his hands between hers. 'She later told me that this insignificant courtesy had meant a great deal to her,' London said, before gallantly defending her reputation and tempestuous nature: 'I believe it is a good thing. It brings back a long-lost atmosphere of operatic excitement. There is nothing that can fire opera goers, and send them to opera box-offices, so surely as a desire to see a genuine member of that sublime species, the prima donna!'

The critics loved this Callas-London *Tosca*, with Irving Kolodin of the *Saturday Review* praising Maria as 'the most credible Tosca of our time', whilst Ed Sullivan demanded that Maria and London should re-enact the whole of Act II on his famous television show – not an easy task, for they were allotted just fifteen minutes on 25 November for a performance which, through no fault of their own, was acutely embarrassing. A shocked Claudia Cassidy wrote in the *Chicago Tribune*,

> I was not so naïve as to expect the whole second act on an hour's variety show. But I had *not* expected to find it butchered to a jigsaw of fifteen minutes, miserably crowded onto a clumsy stage, and so horribly photographed that Mr London resembled a bunch of old bananas and the lovely Callas was turned haggard as a witch. But there it was, just a dud, and what can such a mess possibly prove? People who never go to opera will be contemptuously certain they haven't missed a thing, and the ones who *know* opera will be outraged by this travesty.

Claudia Cassidy read her article to Maria over the telephone, just hours before her one-off reprisal of *Norma*, two evenings later at Philadelphia's Academy of Music – an act which sparked off an attack of nerves which affected her performance. 'Callas is a human being, not a goddess,' declared *Musical Courier*'s Sam Singer, adding glibly, 'And she certainly *sang* like no goddess.' By 3 December, however – the eve of her thirty-third birthday – and the première of *Lucia di Lammermoor*, Maria was in her customary sparkling form, sending the largely gay audience into paroxysms of hysteria after the Mad Scene and taking twenty curtain-calls.

Yet whilst Maria's Lucia earned her formidable praise from the critics, it unearthed a temporary enemy in the bulky form of Elsa Maxwell, a close friend of Renata Tebaldi who now decided, quite unnecessarily, to make Maria's life a misery.

It is not difficult to discern why, initially, Elsa Maxwell disliked Maria so much. As a 'new breed' of opera star, Maria's beauty, figure and potent femininity both attracted and repelled the horrendously unattractive but all-powerful lesbian socialite scandalmonger, whose viperish observations fed gossip columns in America and Europe in exchange for endless favours and handouts from the wealthy patrons she befriended and helped that bit further up the social scale. These handouts included rent-free suites at New York's Waldorf Astoria and Paris George V, plus free meals at the world's most exclusive eateries, open invitations to meet the crowned heads of Europe or stay at their palaces, and access to relationships with some of the world's most beautiful women, even at seventy-three. Her maxim, 'You supply the money, and I'll supply the imagination', had been her calling card for over three decades, and as the self-professed *arbiter eligantiarum* of the international set, her parties were without equal and her every comment treated like some latter-day gospel. If Elsa Maxwell spread the word that Maria Callas was 'a heartless bitch', then for many there was absolutely no arguing against the fact. In short, this woman could be an invaluable ally – or the most ruthless of foes.

Previously, Maxwell's only criticism of Maria had been to dismiss her as 'that devious diva', to which Maria had responded by calling her 'just another fat, ugly old horse'. Now, however, her spite tottered on the verge of vituperation. In the *Time* feature, in quotes, had appeared the comment, 'Tebaldi is unlike Callas ... she has no backbone!' – attributed to no one in particular, though everyone knew that it could have only been made by Maria. Now, Maxwell 'fixed things' with *Time*'s editor so that a letter from the wronged soprano could be printed in the next issue, part of which read,

> The signora admits to being a woman of character and says that I have no backbone. I reply: I have one great thing that she has not – a heart. That I actually trembled when I knew she was present at a performance of mine is utterly ridiculous. It was not Signora Callas who caused me to stay away from La Scala. I sang there before she did, and consider myself a *creatura della Scala*. I stayed away of my own free will, because an atmosphere not at all pleasant had been created there.

This last comment, of course, suggested that Maria's rival *had* left La Scala because of her, and she dismissed the whole letter as 'tripe', though she could hardly ignore Maxwell's own retort, 'I confess that the Great Callas's acting in Lucia's Mad Scene left me completely unmoved', – followed by barbed comments about Maria's 'misplacement' of the heroine's red wig, after Act Two, which had resulted in Lucia 'going completely nuts as a platinum blonde'.

A furious Maria decided, therefore, that she would 'have it out' with the ubiquitous Maxwell, once and for all, and a suitable public arena was arranged – a party to be held at the Waldorf Astoria, hosted by the Greek film-mogul Spiros Skouras, in aid of the US Hellenic Welfare Fund. In the meantime, there was another problem to be sorted out, one much closer to home.

After the première of *Lucia*, Maria had complained to Fausto Cleva – a conductor with whom she was working under extreme duress – that Enzo Sordello, the baritone singing the role of Henry Ashton with whom she claimed she had always worked with great dissatisfaction in the past, was not up to scratch. Cleva should of course have reported the matter to Rudolf Bing, but as he and the singer shared a common loathing – Maria – they decided that it might be a good idea to teach her a lesson. Unfortunately, their plan backfired. During the second *Lucia* on 8 December, Sordello produced an unwritten top note at the end of his second act duet with Maria which seemed to go on for ever, forcing her to cut short a high D, which gave the impression that she had run out of breath. Then, according to Bing, as Sordello's note finally trailed off, Maria yelled 'Basta!', which the audience interpreted as 'bastard', as did the tenor. This was completely untrue. The performance was broadcast live, and subsequently released on a pirate recording, so the only 'crime' committed appears to be Sordello's extraneous top note – and equally untrue are some of the reports that Maria had given Sordello a kick on the shins, as she had del Monaco. What *is* true is that after the performance an extremely agitated Maria reached Bing's office long before her opponent, to deliver the ultimatum, 'Either that creep goes, or I walk!'

Bing was sufficiently naïve, or perhaps stupid enough, to call Maria's bluff, and she promptly cancelled her performance of 11 December, an action which resulted in a near-riot outside the Met as hundreds of irate fans stormed the box-office. Bing had given out an announcement that there should be no refunds as Maria had been replaced by Dolores Wilson, a soprano whom few of them had even heard of. Dozens of policemen armed with batons were brought in to restore order, and Bing was compelled to reverse his decision. Sordello was given his marching orders, with strict instructions not to speak to the media – *if* he wanted to work again. Bing then issued a formal statement to the effect that the baritone had been dismissed following a disagreement with Fausto Cleva ... after which Sordello was depicted in newspapers across America, grimacing and ripping Maria's photograph in two, in a silent protest.

It was Marlene Dietrich who advised Maria, 'If you want to get even with Elsa Maxwell, whatever you do, don't try to out-bitch her. She has the power to write what she wants. Kill her with kindness, dear!' Maria did exactly this at the Skouras party, marching up to the woman Hedda Hopper had described as 'a cross between Marie Dressler and a bulldog' and announcing, 'Miss Maxwell, I esteem you as a lady of honesty, one who is devoted to telling the truth!' Maxwell – who in her most recent outburst had denounced Maria as 'Opera's Number One Hellcat' – was so taken aback by this unprecedented sweetness of tone that she promptly fell head-over-heels in love with her and, over the next few years, pursued her with almost reckless abandon. 'Boring old farts, promiscuous homosexuals and dykes with one foot in the grave,' Maria told her pal Roger Normand in 1976. 'You name it, and it came running after me. I wonder if Audrey Hepburn attracted all the dregs of society, the way I did?'

On 21 December, the morning of the Meneghinis' return to Milan for the Christmas holidays, a mink-clad Callas, clutching Toy, her tiny poodle, made an appearance at New York's Supreme Court having been served with a summons by Eddie Bagarozy. The hearing was set for 15 January, in Chicago. Then, still trailed by the press, the couple were driven to Idlewild airport, where in the lounge Maria came face to face with Enzo Sordello, who was booked on the same flight. The baritone, probably hoping to muscle in on Maria's popularity, marched up to her and extended a somewhat shaky hand of friendship. Maria turned her back on him and told reporters, 'I'm sorry, but I don't like that man taking advantage of my publicity.' When Sordello approached her again, on the plane, she swiped his hand away and growled, 'Fuck off!'

Even more astonishing were the comments made by Maria on the plane itself, about her husband. These were disclosed many years later by Walter Legge in his (unpublished) obituary of Maria – referred to by Michael Scott in his excellent *Maria Meneghini Callas*. When asked why she was travelling first-class whilst her husband had been relegated to the tourist section of the aircraft, Maria retorted, 'If those stinkers at the Met won't pay for him to travel first-class, I won't pay either. Anyway, I always order a second portion of whatever I eat, shove it in a vomit-bag and give it to the stewardess to take to him!'

By 11 January 1957, the Meneghinis were back in New York and Maria, now a fully fledged member of the jet-set, turned up at the Waldorf Astoria's Royal Ball – wearing $3 million worth of rented emeralds and dressed as the 18th dynasty Egyptian queen, Hatshepsut. For Elsa Maxwell, who turned up as a very unimperial-looking Catherine the Great, it was regarded as a quaintly amusing, ironic choice – for legend persisted that Hatshepsut had been a male ruler, and in contemporary art she had always been depicted wearing a beard!

Two evenings later, Maria was present at Edith Piaf's Carnegie Hall recital, regarded by many critics as *the* musical event of the year. Piaf was at this time the world's highest paid female entertainer, and for this one-woman show and two television appearances was being paid more than Rudolf Bing had paid Maria for her four *Lucias*! Then, on 15 January, Maria and her husband travelled to Chicago for the Bagarozy hearing which, as no agreement was reached by either party, was adjourned until later in the year. And here, in the 'horse-shit town' she had sworn never to set foot in again, Maria gave a superb concert at the Civic Opera House which enabled her to equal the world record set by Edith Piaf – $10,000 for a single performance.

In a programme which included arias from *La Sonnambula*, *Il Trovatore*, *Norma* and *Lucia* – collectively, already known as 'Callas's Greatest Hits' – the showstopper was 'In questa reggia', from

Turandot, a hazardous piece which Maria had earlier sworn never to sing again. Later she would admit that, though Puccini had earned her the most money from record royalties, he was a composer she had always disliked. 'Many lovely voices have speedily come to great careers singing Puccini,' she said. 'Then they amount to nothing because they're unable to sing anything else. *Tosca* is but Grand Guignol. *Bohème* a true work of genius. I dropped *Turandot* as soon as I could. I'm only sorry Puccini didn't die before he started *that* mishmash!' 'In questia reggia' was also Claudia Cassidy's favourite piece.

> She sang that cold, cruel aria with every ounce of strength she could summon, driving it like nails into the consciousness of the audience. It was not beautiful, for it was forced to a degree altogether perilous to the human voice so mistreated. But it was, for sheer courage and determination, for winning at all costs, magnificent!

After a short break at their home in Milan, the Meneghinis flew to London, where on 2 and 6 February Maria sang *Norma* at Covent Garden with Ebe Stignani and Nicola Zaccaria. 'Her histrionic presentation of the role is of the art that conceals art,' *The Times* declared, adding, 'It is her colleagues who appear to be acting, while Norma herself is real.' During the second performance, such had been the hysteria after 'Mira, o Norma', Maria's duet with Stignani, that the pair were compelled to break Covent Garden's cast-iron rules forbidding encores and to sing it again.

One of the extras playing one of Norma's children was Frank Johnson, who some years later told an amusing story concerning the time the Druid priestess clasped him to her bosom: 'I was the man able to go through life truthfully asserting that Maria Callas's left nipple had penetrated his right eye, and that therefore it was not true that a man who had spent much of his professional life in the Commons gallery had never glimpsed greatness.'

In London too there was a reunion with Tito Gobbi, when with Luigi Alva, Nicola Zaccaria and the conductor Alceo Galliera she recorded *Il Barbiere di Siviglia*, her first opera outside Italy, for EMI.

It was not a happy time with Walter Legge, however, for when Maria suggested that in the near future she would also like to record *Medea*, and possibly *Macbeth*, for EMI, Legge told her that this would be out of the question because such works were no longer popular with the public. Maria turned on him, snarling, 'A fat lot *you* know about opera!'

On 2 March, still with Zaccaria and with her latest unrequited love interest – the young tenor, Nicola Monti – singing the role of Elvino – Maria revived Visconti's *La Sonnambula* at La Scala – for which Claudia Cassidy flew in especially from Chicago, armed with a consignment of Maria's favourite Victory Red lipstick. 'She could have bought it anywhere in the word,' Cassidy recalled, 'but she always felt that if it had been purchased in the States, it would bring her luck.' Cassidy had never seen Maria's Amina, and she was knocked sideways by the spectacular lighting effects of the 'Ah! non giunge' finale.

Claudia Cassidy stayed on in Milan for Maria's next big opera revival, Donizetti's *Anna Bolena*. The idea to stage it had come from Maria's conductor friend, Gianandrea Gavazzeni who, like the composer, had been born in Bergamo, some thirty miles from Milan. First sung in 1830 by the great Giuditta Pasta, the opera whose Anne Boleyn is far removed from history's tragic queen, had for many years been considered Donizetti's masterpiece, yet it was now completely forgotten. Apart from a one-off production by a group of young singers which Gavazzeni had heard during a visit to Bergamo in October 1956, it had not been performed since 1881!

Antonio Ghiringhelli's initial reaction towards Maria's suggestion was that she must be mad. Rudolf Bing of the New York Met had already denounced *Anna Bolena* as 'an old bore of an opera'. However, when she and Gavazzeni told him that Luchino Visconti had agreed to direct, he too became interested and instructed La Scala's scenic director, Nicola Benois, to spare no expense on the sets. These were worked out at Visconti's sumptuous villa on the Via Salaria, where the pair spent hours poring over old textbooks, studying the architecture of Henry VIII's England and in particular Hans Holbein's Tudor portraits.

In New York, Maria had asked Marlene Dietrich how it was she always looked so superb in her sparkling Jean-Louis stage gowns, and Marlene had replied that she was sewn into them after they had been sculptured onto her body! Nicola Benois now applied this technique to his Anne Boleyn, dressing her in every shade of blue and covering her in huge jewels so that she stood out against his foreboding black, white and grey sets – these cleverly created an optical illusion, giving the impression that the stage was three times its actual depth. In contrast to Anna, Benois dressed the glamorous Giulietta Simionato, who was singing Giovanna (Jane Seymour) in scarlet.

The première of *Anna Bolena*, the highlight of that year's Milan Fair, took place on 14 April, and was an unqualified success. In his study of Maria, Sergio Segalini called it, 'Probably the most electrifying performance of Callas's career.' The *Corriere della Sera* declared, 'Her vibrant voice, stage deportment, the artistry of her singing and her stupendous stylisation – *everything* makes of Callas an Anna who can have no rivals today.' Even the sets were given resounding applause as each one was revealed, and Maria's standing ovation at the end of the performance lasted almost as long as the second act!

In all, there were seven performances of the Donizetti opera, each more enthusiastically received than the last. Yet, whilst Maria was riding high on the crest of her particular wave, a fool-hardy remark coupled with her husband's rapidly increasing greed were to burst the balloon. Following the phenomenal success of her *Lucia* the previous summer, Erich Engel of the Vienna State Opera had engaged her to sing *La Traviata*, with a ten per cent increase in the fee he had paid her. Maria had seemed content with the deal, which was way above Engel's ceiling-fee, and the prospect of working with Herbert von Karajan once more only delighted her. Meneghini, however, threw a spanner into the works by telephoning Engel and demanding double the amount he had offered – and Maria made matters worse by telling the press, 'I don't *care* about the money side of my work so long as I'm being paid more than anyone else!' Urged by von Karajan, who branded Maria 'a grasping tyrant', Engel therefore had no option but to cancel her contract.

Meanwhile, Elsa Maxwell arrived in Milan to catch one of the latter performances of *Anna Bolena*, and to inform Maria that Meneghini had asked her to organise a party, in her honour, which would take place in Venice that September. The pair were photographed embracing at Milan's Malpenso airport – one newspaper captioned the result: The Two Tigresses. Now, switching roles from polite society hostess to acid-tongued hack, ignoring the fact that not so long ago no one had been more anti-Callas than herself, Maxwell launched a ferocious attack against Maria's detractors. 'Horrified' by the way 'her' star had been heckled at La Scala, she told a press conference, 'Someone has been spreading lies about one of the most touching individuals I have ever known. Whoever they are, and wherever they may be, I'll track them down. Nothing can destroy the supreme art of Maria Callas!'

Flattered by such championing, Maria flung herself into rehearsals for her fifth Visconti production – Gluck's *Iphigénie en Tauride*, his final work, which he had completed in Paris in 1779. This would be Visconti's first excursion into non-Italian opera, though most of Gluck's operas had been composed in the Italian style – and, though neither of them knew it at the time, it would be their last collaboration.

Once more, Nicola Benois was commissioned to design the costumes and sets – and he and Visconti immediately ran into a row with Maria because they had decided to transfer the plot, based on the fifth century BC stories by Euripides, to a rococo setting of ancient Greece: this comprised a massive central staircase, flanked by columns and statues and featuring an altar to the goddess Diana, behind which lay the sea. Maria's protests, that she wanted this to remain a Greek story enacted by a Greek, fell on deaf ears and initially she told Visconti that she would not wear Benois' costumes, even if they promised to be more stunning than his designs for *Anna Bolena*. Then Elsa Maxwell saw them and agreed that Maria's gowns – inspired by the works of the 18th century Venetian decorative painter, Giovanni Battista Tiepolo – in silk and satin brocades with huge, voluminous trains, were the most beautiful she had ever seen.

The première of *Iphigénie en Tauride* on 1 June 1957 offered La

Scala's audience the most thrilling entrance from a prima donna it had ever witnessed. The opera opens with a fierce storm, with Maria, her hair and bodice looped with strings of pearls, walking up the steep staircase, then rushing down it again with her 70-foot train billowing about her – always hitting her high note the instant her foot touched the eighth step.

Unfortunately, although Visconti declared it his best work with Maria, most of the critics did not agree with him. Lionel Dunlop of *Opera* may have considered her 'a humane princess ... a constant and exciting joy', but many of his colleagues declared that Maria's singing only *seemed* exemplary because she was the only singer on the stage worth listening to. Sergio Segalini likewise came to what he reckoned to be the only logical conclusion: 'Sadly, this new production, despite a rarely achieved plastic beauty, was not very cautiously cast, therefore Callas was lost in a somewhat heterogeneous musical company.'

On 19 June, Maria flew to Zurich in Switzerland, where she sang two arias in a concert at the Town Hall. Two evenings later, back in Milan, the Italian president Giovanni Gronchi bestowed upon her the title of *Commendatore* – an honour rarely awarded to women, let alone foreign women – for her services to Italian opera. Immediately afterwards, leaving her husband at home, Maria and Elsa Maxwell embarked on a brief 'girls-only' trip to Paris. Here, for the first time since staying with Gracie Fields, she allowed herself several days of unfettered, un-nagged freedom – being fêted by one of this century's most notorious womanisers, Prince Aly Khan.

For several years, one of Elsa Maxwell's pet projects had been the championing of the Aga Khan's wayward son against the press's incessant criticism of his private life, which had resulted in the position of spiritual leader to the 20 million Muslims of the Ismaili sect – formerly held by his father – being passed on to his son, Karim, shortly before Aly met Maria.

Born in Italy and raised in Europe, Aly had inherited a fortune from his mother. Although he was highly respected as Pakistan's delegate to the United Nations, and he had been awarded the *Croix de Guerre* by the French for his work with Intelligence during

World War II, since his late teens he had enjoyed a playboy's existence, living almost exclusively for the pursuit of pleasure and excitement: racehorses, safaris, fast cars and, most of all, beautiful women, of whom there had allegedly been five thousand. In 1949, he had married the glamorous film star, Rita Hayworth, who had left him just months later, declaring, 'Once a cheating rat, always a cheating rat!'

In Paris, 'chaperoned' by a kindly but jealous Elsa Maxwell, who had hoped to have Maria to herself for a while, Maria and Aly met the Duke and Duchess of Windsor at the Hôtel Continental, dined at Maxim's, shopped in the fashionable rue St-Honoré Faubourg, and attended race meetings at Enghien and Longchamps – a champion jockey, Aly had ridden over one hundred winners. Maria soon made it clear that she was not in the least interested in horses, cracking, 'Any animal that walks and shits at the same time has *got* to be stupid.' Together, they gave the appearance of a strange couple: Maria, in her picture hats and stiletto heels standing a good six feet tall – linking arms in the most amusing fashion with this short, exotic-featured man who belied his forty-six years. It was of course Aly's *power* that attracted her – the fact that he was so wealthy that he had but to snap his fingers or stare fixedly at a woman across a crowded room, and she was his for the taking. 'Aly dances with a woman slowly and rapturously as though it is the last time he will ever hold her in his arms,' Elsa Maxwell observed, adding, 'When he tells a woman he loves her, he sincerely means it for a moment. The trouble is that a moment passes so quickly.' Therefore, whilst Maria tried to forget about opera and how bored she was becoming with her sixty-year-old husband, Aly Khan – reputed to be phenomenally endowed and an experienced practitioner of *Imsák*, an Egyptian technique enabling a man to make love for hours without climax – brought her all the joys of a *real* lover for the first time in her life.

All too soon, Maria's idyll ended and she flew to Rome, where on 26 June she sang *Lucia* on the radio, before returning to Milan and an inquisitive Meneghini, who tried and failed to learn more about her 'exploits' in Paris. Early in July he accompanied her to Cologne, where she opened the recently built Openhaus with La

Scala's production of *La Sonnambula*. 'This outdated opera would be incapable of survival without the vocal and dramatic miracle of this towering artiste,' declared the *Kölnische Rundschau*. The critic continued: 'One has heard or read often enough that as a singer, Callas is something extraordinary – now we have experienced her with our own eyes and ears, and find her legendary fame confirmed in the most complete fashion.'

Whilst she had been in Paris with Elsa Maxwell, Meneghini had decided to surprise Maria by commissioning a portrait of her from the young Florentine painter, Silvano Caselli, then very much in vogue. In recent years Caselli had painted Gide, Colette, Thomas Mann and Toscanini, but Maria had especially admired his beautiful portrait of Anna Magnani. She did however take some persuading to allow Caselli into her home, declaring, 'I *hate* being stared at. It makes me feel like I've been shoved inside a goldfish bowl!' Then, when she finally consented to the twelve one-hour sessions, she instructed the artist to paint her in a floral dress – only to pose in a cream skirt and halter-top, the straps of which she constantly lowered and raised, deliberately flirting with the young man, but solely to incur Meneghini's wrath. Some years later, one of the photographs taken during the Caselli sittings appeared in Michael Scott's biography of Maria, with the caption, 'The influence of Visconti, perhaps? Or maybe even Dali. Is she about to disrobe?' But when a perplexed Caselli asked Maria how he could possibly paint her in a floral dress when she was not wearing one, all she did was bark, 'Use your imagination!' The portrait, measuring 4 by 3 feet, was completed quickly and hung on the living room at Via Buanarroti, but Maria often told friends that she had never really liked it. 'My husband *told* me that it was a gift,' she once said, 'but in reality it was just another investment, as indeed was I.'

It was at around this time that Maria learned of her mother's most recent machinations. According to Jackie Callas, Litza had given the interview with *Time* magazine, hoping for some kind of response from her 'errant' daughter – a ridiculous attempt at reconciliation which of course had been guaranteed to fail. Subsequently, she had spoken to the Italian magazine, *Oggi*, about her aspirations for her other daughter: Jackie, at thirty-nine and seemingly without a mind of her own, had now set off on a secondary career as an operatic soprano. 'She was like some desperate general,' Jackie remembered, 'who, though aware that the war is lost, is yet unable to surrender, and who tries desperately to bolster his men with tales of a dream weapon that will save the day. With such a tale she had got me, her ragged army, to this point but now the ruse was exposed, the great new weapon of war lay revealed as a damp squib.'

At the end of 1956 – whilst Maria had been in America – in order for Jackie to enter an under-35s singing competition in Vercelli, near Milan, Litza had doctored her passport. Jackie had quickly been eliminated from the contest, but this had not dampened her mother's enthusiasm and in the spring of 1957 she had organised a concert at Athens' Parnassos Hall, where Jackie had sung a nerve-racking programme, largely of Verdi and Puccini. Although the concert had only been moderately successful, news of it had reached Maria in Milan, who had not taken too kindly to being referred to by the Italian press as the *elder* of the Callas sisters. And though she had sworn never to speak to her mother again, Maria had telephoned Jackie's apartment – only to be told that she and Litza had left for New York, where Litza claimed to have contacts who would recognise Jackie's potential and launch her on an international career.

Physically, vocally and mentally, Maria was exhausted. Since returning from Cologne she had recorded two complete operas for EMI with Tulliio Serafin – Puccini's *Turandot* and *Manon Lescaut* – the former the most taxing work she attempted in her later years, and a role she loathed. Singing the part of Liu, at Walter Legge's insistence, was his wife Elisabeth Schwarzkopf, one of the few sopranos Maria truly liked – no doubt because most of her output had been in German, eliminating rivalry. In her 1982 autobiography, *On And Off The Record*, Schwarzkopf speaks lovingly of Maria even though their friendship was terminated before Maria's death, with considerable acrimony, and refers to an incident during a break from the *Turandot* sessions which took place at the Biffi Scala when the pair suddenly began belting out top notes to see who could sing the highest. Schwarzkopf was concerned that Maria might have been overdoing things, as were Meneghini and her new doctor, Arnaldo Sameraro. All three strongly advised her to rest up before that year's Edinburgh Festival, at which she would be singing *La Sonnambula*. This she refused to do. For some time she had been hoping to sing in Greece, and now that her 'parasites' were safely across the Atlantic, she arranged for two concerts to take place at the huge Herodes Atticus Theatre in Athens, for 31 July and 5 August.

The Meneghinis arrived in Athens on 29 July, just two days after the completion of *Manon Lescaut*, and to tremendous hostility from the local press, who for almost a year had been reporting Litza's half-crazed, mostly fictitious accounts of the sacrifices she had made for her daughter, only to be treated like dirt, then ignored. A great deal was written, too, about the large fee Maria was being paid for her concerts, at a time when Greece was in a period of severe hardship – an argument which was supported by the Greek Opposition Party in a ferocious attack on the Karamanlis government. Sick and tired – literally, having bellowed herself hoarse – of being badgered by reporters and political activists, she called the management of the Herodes Atticus and cancelled the 31 July concert – an instruction which was deliberately carried out just thirty minutes before the performance was due to begin, when most of the audience were in their seats.

Maria would have cancelled the second concert, too, but urged by her husband and Antonino Votto, who was conducting the Athens Festival Orchestra – and by a telephone call from Elsa Maxwell, who advised her quite rightly that backing out would only earn her an even more spiteful press than she had already – she decided to face whatever fate had in store for her. Needless to say, as she stepped on to the stage – having been escorted to the theatre by two armed policemen, who remained in the wings throughout the performance, ready to whisk her away to her waiting car in the event of trouble – there were more hisses and boos than she had ever encountered from the Tebaldiani at La Scala.

Maria struggled valiantly through her first aria, 'D'amor sull' ali rosee', from *Il Trovatore*, and the audience were still very restless during her second – 'Pace, pace,' from *Il Forza del Destino*. However, such was her cast-iron will to succeed, coupled with the ferociousness of her singing during 'Ai vostri giochi', Ophelia's Mad Scene from Thomas's *Hamlet*, that a hush fell over the arena, broken only by the *bravos* as she finished the piece and the lights dimmed. Indeed, such was the enthusiasm of this politically swayed throng that Maria was forced to sing the aria again, before launching into an emotive 'Liebestod' – in Italian, as usual, and being performed for the last time ever – before concluding the recital with Lucia's 'Regnava nel silenzio'.

In Athens, after her concert, Maria and Meneghini had a violent quarrel over her decision to donate her entire fee towards founding a scholarship for young Greek singers from poor backgrounds. She also seems to have welcomed a reconciliation with her sister, who had recently returned from New York – leaving her mother there – having failed in her mission to secure backing for her singing career. Jackie was currently living outside Athens, where most of her time was taken up caring for Milton Emberikos, who was dying from cancer of the jaw. Meneghini, however, 'advised' Maria that her sister would probably be seeking handouts – Jackie had not even been invited to the concert.

When Maria returned to Milan, she was clearly on the verge of anorexia – pitifully thin, as can be seen from photographs taken at the time, and so shaky on her feet that her doctor warned her, melodramatically perhaps, that she was in danger of going over the edge completely unless she slowed down and cancelled all her engagements for the foreseeable future. This of course would have rewarded the press with a field-day after the 'let-downs' in Athens and Vienna, so she opted for a compromise – changing her doctor! Then, in the middle of August, she and Meneghini swapped a warm, sunny Milan for a wet, miserable Edinburgh where she was to open the Festival's opera season with another revival of Visconti's *La Sonnambula*. It was not a pleasant trip. Maria disliked the King's Theatre intensely – the stage was not big enough to accommodate all of La Piccola Scala's scenery, there was no orchestra pit, and backstage conditions were nothing short of lamentable. shrugging her shoulders, however, she told Robert Ponsonby, the Festival's director, 'Ah, well. I've sung in worse places. I'll just have to make the best of it!'

'La Divina ... not in her most divine voice,' was Andrew Porter's opinion of the 19 August première. Writing for *High Fidelity*, he continued, 'The première had uneasy moments, and by the third performance, almost every sustained note around F threatened to crack and collapse: "Ah, non credea" was a painful experience for everyone in the theatre.' Some of Maria's critics suggested that perhaps Porter was being a little too harsh, particularly when the performance was later released on a pirated recording, allowing the applause to speak for itself and the listener to form his own opinion as to the quality of Maria's singing, which though slightly faltering on account of her dramatic on-stage movements, rarely falls short of perfection. Quite simply, Maria had reached the very pinnacle of her profession, and as some of these critics were getting a little tired of dragging out the same superlatives time after time, they concentrated instead on magnifying the flaws in her voice, albeit tiny and mostly inconsequential – knowing only too well that despite their barbed, ill-informed remarks, Callas was still the most important diva of this century.

When Maria had signed the Edinburgh contract with Antonio Ghiringhelli, it had been for just the first four performances of *La Sonnambula* – the fifth was to be sung by the young soprano, Renata Scotto. However, both Ghiringhelli and the Festival's management *assumed* that Maria would be singing this one too since the first four concerts had been so successful. She very quickly announced that she would not, adding that inasmuch as she hated being taken advantage of, she would *never* step into the shoes of another singer unless that singer was indisposed. This latter comment was omitted from her statement to the press, and over the coming weeks the newspapers made a meal of Maria's 'vocal demonstrations, foibles and tantrums', as one put it. Absolutely no one mentioned the fact that she had felt dreadfully ill throughout her entire stay in Edinburgh, or that she should not have undertaken the project in the first place. Most of the press fabrications could also have been stopped, had Antonio Ghiringhelli made a public statement and put the record straight. No doubt thinking that his silence would repay Maria for all the headaches he claimed she had given him, he refused.

And yet, Maria again succeeded only in making a rod for her own back the minute she returned to Milan. She had been contracted to sing Lady Macbeth and Lucia in the San Francisco Opera's forthcoming season, beginning on 13 September, but at the end of August Meneghini telephoned the director, Kurt Adler, and informed him that Maria's health was so delicate, she might not make the trip. This was followed a few days later by a call from Maria herself, who told Adler that if she did find herself unable to sing, she would 'clear October' so that he could make alternative arrangements for her to sing then – this way, she said, she would not be failing her American fans. What she did *not* do was cancel Elsa Maxwell's party in Venice – a move which would damage her reputation almost irreparably, whilst bringing her face to face with the greatest but most damaging love of her life.

10

Svegliate La Gioia!

Hissing from the gallery is a part of the scene, a hazard of the battlefield. Opera *is* a battlefield, this must be accepted!

Elsa Maxwell later reflected that her party for Maria was the most exciting and successful she had ever organised. Raging on for several days and nights, it began at the Lido, then by way of several glitzy nightclubs including Florian's and Harry's Bar – it was here, accompanied by Maxwell at the piano that she sang a sultry, impromptu *Stormy Weather* – the guests transferred to Aristotle Onassis's yacht, moored at the entrance to Venice's Grand Canal. for the time being, however, Onassis was regarded by Maria as just another wealthy acquaintance, another cog in the wheel of Elsa Maxwell's social machinery which momentarily took her mind off her problems.

These problems became more pressing as soon as she returned to Milan. Following the so-called 'Edinburgh scandal', even some of her closest friends – including Wally Toscanini – refused to have anything to do with her, and Antonio Ghiringhelli still would not issue that vindicating public statement. Worse still, someone from La Scala – Maria suspected Mario del Monaco – dispatched a folder of photographs to Kurt Adler of the San Francisco Opera, of a giggly, radiant-looking Maria having the time of her life at the Maxwell party. Adler had already been outraged to read Maxwell's admission in her column, 'I have had many presents in my life, but I've never had a star give up a performance in an opera because she felt she was breaking her word to a friend.' Adler immediately cancelled Maria's contract, replacing her with Leonie Rysanek (for Lady Macbeth) and Leyler Gencer (for Lucia). He then referred the matter to the AGMA (American Guild of Musical Artists), an all-powerful body with sufficient clout to prevent Maria from singing in the United States, should she lose her case. Adler was confident that she would, particularly when on 5 November she and her husband arrived in New York for the conclusion of the Bagarozy case, another legal battle she was expected to lose.

In fact, Maria's greatest worry was barely touched upon by the press, and on 17 November an out-of-court settlement was reached when she paid Bagarozy an undisclosed amount – thought to be in the region of just $30,000. The following year, Maria's former agent would die suddenly and she would tell a reporter, 'Well, I only hope he saved some of *my* money to pay for his funeral.'

Four evenings later, Maria appeared at a benefit concert fêting the recently formed Dallas Civic Opera – the brainchild of her pal Lawrence Kelly, who had split from Carol Fox of the Chicago Opera to form his own company with Nicola Rescigno, still Maria's preferred conductor. The 'Callas Boys' turned out in droves, some wearing 'Dallas For Callas' lapel badges, and fifty or so of these young men cheered her as she entered the theatre. She sang arias by Mozart, Bellini and Verdi, and after the interval appeared in a lace-edged, black velvet sheath-dress to sing 'Al dolce guidami' – the Tower Scene from *Anna Bolena*. Towards the end of this, she dramatically approached the footlights – one critic recorded that he actually expected her to leap into the orchestra pit! – and proclaimed, pointing accusingly but at no one in particular up in one of the galleries, 'Manca solo a compire il delitto d'Anna il sange ... e versato sarà!' (Only Anna's blood is lacking to complete the crime ... and it will be shed). Maria had made her point. But, would anyone listen?

When Maria returned to Milan – having recuperated for just five days at her newly acquired retreat at Sirmione, on the shores of Lake Garda – she flung herself into the final rehearsals for *Un Ballo in Maschera*. Ten years after Amelia had been denied her, she was to open La Scala's new season with the role. The backstage tension was virtually unbearable, much of it instigated by Antonio Ghiringhelli, who had barely a civil word to say to her. Giuseppe di Stefano tried to lighten the proceedings by pulling faces at him behind his back and by generally playing the fool, but this only upset Maria more – renowned as she was for her lack of humour whilst working, she spent most of her free time between rehearsals with her 'sensible' friends Gianandrea Gavazzeni, for whom she could do no wrong, and Giulietta Simionato, who was singing Ulrica. The press, too, were sympathetic and had albeit temporarily shelved their smear campaign. 'She was in fine voice and sang superbly,' declared Ernest de Weerth, in *Opera News*, adding, 'Callas is never dull … her personality is without doubt the most imposing on the opera stage. Others may have more beautiful voices, but at the moment there is only *one* Callas.'

This uneasy truce did not last long. On New Year's Eve, nine days after the final *Un Ballo in Maschera*, Maria sang 'Casta Diva' on the television, offering her admirers a taster of the new production of *Norma* which was scheduled to open at Rome's Opera House in a gala performance on 2 January. Immediately afterwards, she and Franco Corelli – who would be singing Pollione – headed for the nearest bar, ostensibly for one drink to herald the festive season. Here they were joined by several of Corelli's friends, who invited them to a party at the Circolo degli Sacchi, then one of Rome's most fashionable night-clubs.

Maria was having such fun, dancing to Bill Haley records and surrounded by half a dozen of her boys, that she purposely disregarded Meneghini's 10pm curfew. It was well after three in the morning when Corelli got her back to the Hotel Quirinale, where she and Meneghini had a suite. Maria was inebriated, but over the last few hours, for the first time in her life she had felt truly *alive* and wanted.

The next morning, disaster struck when, as a result of inhaling a great deal of smoke in the packed night-club, she had a sore throat

Maria's Chicago *Lucia* (November 1954, with Guiseppe di Stefano)
earned her a huge gay following. She said of her Callas Boys,
'To them I'm the Bette Davis of opera, and that pleases me no end!'
(*Courtesy S. Mathers*)

Maria's arrivals and departures were a feast for the press, who were never able to gauge her moods. Here, arriving for her Covent Garden *Norma* (1957) she looks radiant. (*Courtesy of the Mander and Mitchenson Theatre Collection*)

June 1956. Enjoying a break from Meneghini at Gracie Fields' home, the Canzone del Mare, on Capri. (*Courtesy S. Mathers*)

1957, at the Martini Club in Brussels. (*Courtesy S. Mathers*)

1958, the Covent Garden *La Traviata*. 'There is no other singer in the field of Italian opera today who can work this sort of poetic magic' – Peter Heyworth, one of her favourite critics. (*Courtesy of the Mander and Mitchenson Theatre Collection*)

'Remind me to come back here after they've demolished this place,'
Maria said, as she was leaving Bilbao's Coliseo Albia, the theatre she
detested, in September 1959. (*Courtesy S. Mathers*)

October 1959. Singing 'Si mi chiamano Mimi', from *La Bohème*, at London's Hackney Empire. (*Courtesy of the Mander and Mitchenson Theatre Collection*)

August 1961. Maria's favourite *Medea*, at the ancient amphitheatre of Epidaurus. Jason was sung by Jon Vickers. (*Courtesy of the Mander and Mitchenson Theatre Collection*)

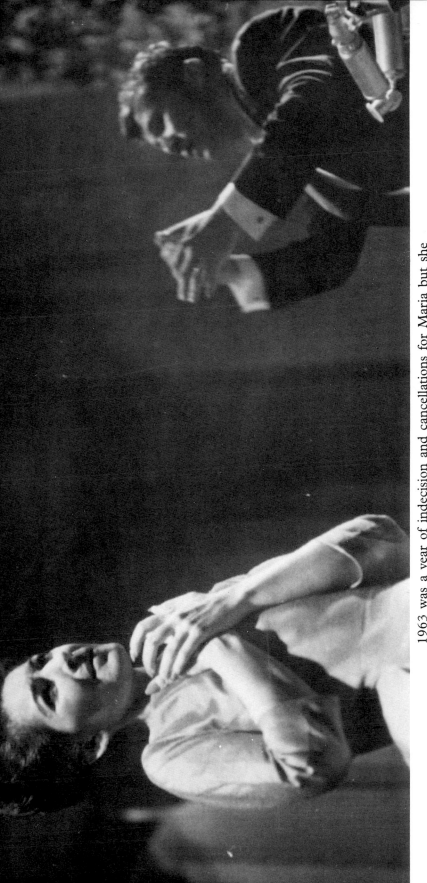

1963 was a year of indecision and cancellations for Maria but she triumphed in Paris in June. Singing her most requested encore, 'O mio babbino caro', with Georges Prêtre conducting. (*Courtesy of the Mander and Mitchenson Theatre Collection*)

Maria's final appearance on the operatic stage, July 1965, *Tosca*, Covent Garden. With her is Renato Cioni of whom she said, 'He's *so* beautiful . . . the perfect father for my children.' (*Courtesy of the Mander and Mitchenson Theatre Collection*)

September 1965, Paris. With Maurice Chevalier for the great chanteuse Barbara's première at the Bobino Music Hall. (*Courtesy S. Mathers*)

Casta diva . . . (*Courtesy S. Mathers*)

and could hardly speak. There was of course no sympathy from the dreary Meneghini, who told Maria that her indisposition was her own fault for behaving like a child. Antonio Ghiringhelli merely hit the roof when Maria told him that he would have to find a replacement for the *Norma* première. Fedora Barbieri, who should have been singing Adalgisa, had been laid low with the flu and Ghiringhelli had brought in the lesser-known Miriam Pirazzini, but no one had ever thought of engaging an understudy for Callas, for what the theatrical world were already hailing as the showbusiness event of the year, with a guest-list comprising a veritable *Who's Who* of Italian society – headed by President and Mrs Gronchi, Anna Magnani, Sophia Loren and Gina Lollobrigida.

The performance took place with Maria beginning well enough – this much may be discerned from the pirated recording, which was broadcast live on the radio – though as the first act progressed, it was obvious that her voice was weakening by the minute, and that she was in some pain. Those closest to the stage, too, observed the look of anguish on her face each time she attempted a high note, and how she was struggling not to stumble as she ambled aimlessly about the stage. Then, as she was taking her curtain call at the end of the act, someone yelled, 'You've cost us a million lire – get back to Milan!'

Franco Corelli helped Maria back to her dressing-room where, if she did not feel bad enough already, she was subjected to more sprays and potions, and more chiding from her husband and Elsa Maxwell. Maria had already told Corelli that she felt too ill to continue, and an eavesdropping soprano from the chorus quickly conveyed the news to Antonio Ghiringhelli. It was then that pandemonium erupted, with La Scala's Superintendent – in charge of the proceedings in Rome – out-yelling everyone by making it perfectly clear to Maria what would happen if she walked out on a performance being attended by the Italian president.

'Ghiringhelli was very upset,' Maria later recalled. 'He told me that it would be bad for the theatre if I didn't sing Act Two. I told him to look after his goddam theatre, and I would look after my voice.' In fact, whilst Ghiringhelli was giving Maria a hard time, President Gronchi was already leaving the building. Meneghini had sent him a personal apology on behalf of Maria.

Maria herself left the theatre by way of an underground passage which connected to the Hotel Quirinale, supported by Meneghini and Elsa Maxwell. This was just as well, for a mob of two hundred irate spectators – astonishingly, some of them were armed with eggs and tomatoes, which means that they must have taken them into the theatre – had surrounded her car. 'Rome had not had such a fiery evening of music since Nero's famous violin recital,' quipped her biographer, George Jellinek. Minutes later, some of them burst into the hotel foyer, demanding to see her. What is interesting, yet at the same time appalling, is that many of these troublemakers, who stayed outside the hotel most of the night, baying for Maria's blood, were well-to-do, middle-aged couples who should have known better.

Some of the newspaper reports the next day were so atrocious and vicious – fuelled by the unbridled spite of Antonio Ghiringhelli – that it is no small wonder Maria did not sue them. Criticising one's artistic abilities was one thing, even when the writer was being *paid* to do so – the gratuitous application of personal insults and libellous remarks was however entirely different. Although the word 'lesbian' was not actually used in any of these columns, such a thing was implied by one journalist, who wrote of 'Callas's dangerous friendship' with Maxwell. Another lost little time in informing his readers of Maria's 'fondness for homosexuals and champagne', referring of course to her evening at the Circolo degli Sacchi. Other comments focused on her infamous temper and colourful vocabulary – whilst virtually nothing was mentioned about her illness.

Maria was championed by the ever-faithful Franco Corelli and by Giulietta Simionato, who had visited her on New Year's Day. In the Circolo degli Sacchi, her 'honour' was defended by a handful of her 'boys', who began brawling with several drunken government officials who had voted for Maria to be publicly denounced and banned from the Italian stage – 'for personal insults to President Gronchi and the people of Italy', even though Mrs Gronchi had personally called on Maria to offer her condolences, and to assure her that neither she nor her husband had been in the least offended. The young men were arrested and thrown into prison, though the next morning they were released when Maria paid their bail. These same admirers volunteered their services a few days later when Maria returned to Milan – they helped the household staff to clear away the several tons of farmyard manure which had been dumped in her driveway, and to wipe off the human excrement which had been used to daub filthy slogans on her windows and doors.

Maria, meanwhile, received an order issued by the Prefecture of Rome, banning her from singing the three remaining *Norma*s – scheduled for the following week, by which time of course there was every possibility of her having recovered – and ordering her to forfeit her fees. She was replaced by Anita Cerquetti, a hefty, twenty-six-year-old soprano. Cerquetti's career would last but another three years before she retired, and Maria would hate her with a fervour second to none, particularly when word got back to her that Cerquetti had accused Maria of putting a curse on her. Some years later, when the soprano had almost died whilst having an inflamed appendix removed, she responded, 'It's a pity she didn't expire whilst she was in Rome. And in any case, with the size of that belly how in God's name did they manage to find her appendix?'

What is strange is that, although Maria refused to take action against several very nasty journalists who certainly *deserved* to be taught a lesson, she did sue the Rome Opera for loss of fees, in a case which would drag on for another ten years. In the end, Antonio Ghiringhelli was ordered by the court not just to pay the money he owed her, plus her legal costs – but to offer a public apology which, to Maria, was worth all the money in the world.

Maria retreated to Sirmione, where she rested in preparation for her next trip to the United States, which was to begin with a benefit concert in Chicago for the Alliance Française, a safe proposition now that Eddie Bagarozy was off her back. She was also looking forward to a second season at the Met, singing *Tosca, Lucia* and *La Traviata* – providing, of course, she could exonerate herself before the AGMA. She had recently begun negotiating a recording contract with Pathé Marconi, EMI's French counterpart, so on 16

January –en route for Chicago – she spent just six hours in Paris being fêted like a queen. The Rome scandal was not even mentioned until Maria herself volunteered a statement, in near-perfect French, saying, 'If *any* good came out of the fiasco in Rome, it taught me who my *real* friends are!'

Maria, Meneghini and Toy, her poodle, were met at Orly airport by the head of Pathé-Marconi and a press delegation and, after posing for photographs and answering the usual perfunctory questions, they were escorted to Maxim's, where the *plat du jour* was *selle d'agneau à la Callas*, which was eaten whilst the management broke with tradition and allowed a radio onto the premises ... so that everyone could listen to the von Karajan *Trovatore*, which was being previewed on *France-Inter*.

The Chicago concert was a triumph, raising $22,000 for its cause – and earning Maria $10,000, not one cent of which Meneghini would allow her to hand back to the charity. 'There are beautiful voices in the world,' observed Claudia Cassidy, 'but Callas takes a beautiful voice and goes on from there.' There was just one detractor, this time, when Roger Dettmer wrote in *Chicago American*, 'Her voice was recurrently strident, unsteady and out of tune. It seems to have aged ten years in one.' Two days later, she flew to New York for a fifteen-minute appearance on Ed Murrow's television chat-show, *Person To Person*. This was unrevealing. Murrow was completely out of his depth attempting to discuss opera, and the by now Italianate Maria spoke such disjointed English that she did not always make sense. There was a slight touch of humour, however, when she repeated her earlier comment, regarding her fluency in several languages, 'But I always *count* in English!'

On 27 January, the hearing with AGMA took place in the organisation's offices on the corner of Broadway and 60th Street. Armed with a sheaf of medical evidence, and her tiny poodle, she pleaded her case for two hours before the twenty judges, and emerged with no more than an official ticking-off for the so-called 'San-Fan-Fiasco', having satisfied them that whilst legally bound to Kurt Adler's contract, she had not actually worked elsewhere.

'Her interpretation of the part was far and away the finest I have encountered at the Metropolitan or anywhere else in all the years I have been listening to opera,' was how the *New Yorker*'s Winthrop Sargeant summed up Maria's first *Traviata*, on 6 February, adding, 'Hers is not a pure, innocent voice (pure, innocent voices are a dime a dozen), but a fiery conveyance for female passion, and it is used with amazing skill to underline each shifting mood of this extremely subtle role.' It *was* a stupendous interpretation which earned her a twenty-minute standing ovation and twelve solo curtain-calls. Maria, on the other hand, whilst naturally appreciating such adulation, was far from happy with the way Rudolf Bing had misorganised the production. The tenor Daniele Barioni was only capable of singing consistently off-pitch, she declared, and demanded that he be disposed of – by which means, she added, she did not care. Bing obliged, and for the second performance, four evenings later, he brought in Giuseppe Campora. What *really* incensed her, however, was the fact that the acutely insensitive Bing had refused to give her a new production of *La Traviata* – telling her that she would have to make do with the one he had commissioned from Tyrone Guthrie, for Renata Tebaldi.

There was also the inevitable drama, this time instigated by Elsa Maxwell, who wrote defensively in one of her columns, 'Why should a woman capable of noble expression in the classic arts be tortured by a destiny that makes her happiness almost impossible? Her mother, I believe without question, has been the cause of this situation.' During this particular trip to New York, Maria was escorted virtually everywhere by her father – George was celebrating his new-found freedom, now that he and the troublesome Litza were divorced. Having read Maxwell's piece and seen photographs of her ex-husband hob-nobbing with the celebrities at one of Maria's backstage parties, Litza sent word to her daughter that she too was thinking of turning up at the Met. Maria took this threat much more seriously than those from the Tebaldiani and other detractors who had vowed to disrupt her remaining performances, telling Bing, 'If that fucking woman comes within a hundred yards of this theatre, I'll be on the next flight to Milan!' Bing reacted sarcastically to this, stationing a guard in the foyer – armed with a photograph of the offending mother – and hiring ten plainclothes policemen who were positioned in the aisles, close to the stage, like bouncers at a modern-day rock concert.

Maria's first *Lucia*, on 13 February, according to the *New York Times'* Harold Schonberg 'made most present day Lucias sound like amateurs', though her *Tosca* of 28 February – conducted once more by Mitropoulos, with George London repeating his remarkable Scarpia, though Maria dismissed Richard Tucker's Cavaradossi as 'almost but not quite professional' – was slightly marred by the booing from one of the galleries. To this the Callas Boys at the front of the house responded with deafening shrieks of approval, throwing flowers and sticks of 'Victory Red' lipstick ... one of which she used to sign programmes, after the performance.

The Meneghinis returned to Milan at the beginning of March, by way of Brussels. Here, as in Paris, Maria spent a few hours being courted by theatre managers and the press, and even managed a lightning trip to Maria Malibran's chateau and grave at Ixelles. On 24 March, she gave her first concert in Spain, at Madrid's huge Cinema Monumental, and three days later she sang the first of two *Traviata*s in Lisbon with the dashing Spanish tenor, Alfredo Kraus, then at the start of his career.

The first of these performances was taped by EMI and released on a set of albums later that year. Such was its intensity that it inspired the American dramatist Terence McNally to write *The Lisbon Traviata*, a work which touchingly displays Maria's considerable importance to the gay community, whose fan-base today is just as powerful as her so-called 'conventional' one ... a fact which, despite the protestations of self-styled moralists, remains unalterable. The play tells the story of two young men who have built relationships around their memories of Maria – one, unable to find physical fulfilment, seeks love and solace within her music, whilst the other, who has found a lasting relationship, nevertheless uses her music to maintain emotional stability.

After Maria died, McNally wrote affectionately, 'I came to love Callas, in my teens, as a blind man must come to love someone, with all my other senses engaged. Her voice was the face, and I came to love every feature of it. It is *still* the best way to know Callas, and now it is the only way.' In 1993, too, inspired by McNally, Maria's beautiful rendition of 'D'amor sull'alli rosee' from *Il Trovatore* was used as the soundtrack for the Oscar-nominated Cuban film, *Strawberry And Chocolate*, a tale of unrequited gay love set against a climate of political oppression.

On 26 February, Maria appeared on *Hy Gardner Calling*, one of America's top television chat-shows. Gardner, who was also a columnist with the New York *Herald Tribune*, had lunched with the Meneghinis two weeks previously, and had observed in his column, 'I came to lunch expecting to meet a cold, tempestuous but talented female ogre, but found instead a warm, sincere, handsome and down-to-earth human being, a real live doll!' The programme was broadcast in split-screen, with Maria and her father sitting in her hotel suite, and with Gardner addressing her from the safety of the television studio. It was an exhilarating experience for Maria, but an ordeal for Gardner, who could scarcely get a word in edgeways – in almost *all* her taped interviews, Maria is so highly charged that it is often impossible to determine what she is saying without playing through the tape several times. In addition she also had an annoying habit of barging in with her reply halfway through the question. 'I wish I could be a human being sometimes. I would avoid certain situations,' was part of her babble when Gardner asked her to explain what had happened in Rome – whereupon he placed his fate well and truly in her hands, in the days where broadcasting had no safety cut-off facility, by responding, 'Well, a lot of stories have painted you as being *exactly* that – not a human being.' He proceeded to get himself in even deeper by adding hurriedly, 'Gosh, after I first met you I realised that you were, and I felt very sorry that at one time I described you as The Dizzy Dame of Opera Singers, because I don't think you're dizzy at all. I think you've got your feet right on the ground.' To which Maria replied, caustically, 'Thank you, Mr Gardner. That's very wonderful of you to say so. That's *all* I want!'

Meneghini, who was not seen in the interview, was brought into the conversation several times – at around this time, if his nagging got on her nerves, she would introduce him to complete strangers who did not know differently as 'my father'. Now, however, she was full of praise for him. Admitting, as she had many times, that she had fallen in love with him within five minutes of setting eyes on him, she added, 'I just loved the way he smiled. It was as though God had sent him to me.' Gardner then asked, in a roundabout way, the one question that every Callas interviewer had wanted to ask since 1949, but had never dared: '*National* magazine quoted you as saying, "I am happier when I am in bed with my dog and my husband is asleep in another room." Madame Callas, do you think that married people should sleep in twin beds, or double beds?' Maria laughed at this and replied, 'Well, *I* love double beds!' Some years later, however, when Gardner wanted to interview her again, she refused, saying, 'Are you joking, with the kind of questions he asked? I'm still waiting to spit in that son-of-a-bitch's eye for the last trial he put me through, without going through it all again.'

For Maria, meanwhile, there was little stability, emotional or otherwise, at La Scala on 9 April 1958, when she sang the first of five performances of *Anna Bolena*. Antonio Ghiringhelli had not wished to engage her at all – he was of course 'convinced' to do so by her assured success with the box-office – and he claimed too that he had encountered severe problems trying to get anyone to work with her. Subsequently, throughout the entire La Scala season he refused to speak to her. The faithful friends – Gavazzeni, Simionato and Cesare Siepi – stood by her, and whilst rehearsals were tense, they were certainly better than Maria had anticipated.

In the Piazza Scala, several hundred anti-Callas demonstrators had gathered, some carrying banners, and most of them screaming obscenities at the 200-strong contingent of armed police who had been drafted in, in the event of trouble. Maria herself was jeered as she approached the stage door, and several of her 'boys' were knocked to the ground trying to defend her. Within the theatre, the audience were almost as bad throughout the first two scenes. Then, in Scene Three – the second time she had used the scene for personal protest – where Anna is arrested and dispatched to the Tower, the character and the actress became as one when Maria/Anna broke free of her captors and rushed to the footlights to vociferously pronounce, 'Giudici! … ad Anna! … Ah! segrata è la mia sorte!' (Judges! … For Anna! … Ah! my fate is sealed!). From then on she could do no wrong, and at the end of the performance she took five curtain-calls.

Maria knew by now, of course, that her days at La Scala were numbered. The audiences, in spite of the hecklers who were but a part of the 'battlefield' deal – 'It is when there is *no* hissing that I will worry,' Maria once said – may have wanted her to go on for ever, but deep down inside they too must have known that as far as this particular theatre was concerned, she was rapidly losing heart. Even so, she decided to give Antonio Ghiringhelli the benefit of the doubt. She returned to the arena on 19 May to sing a new, exceptionally demanding role: Imogene, in Bellini's almost forgotten *Il Pirata*.

Although this time Maria was working only with friends – Votto, Corelli and Bastianini – the rehearsals were such an ordeal that, more than once she came close to walking out of the production. Once again, the perpetrator of unpleasantness was Antonio Ghiringhelli, who made a point of fussing over the rest of the cast, whilst muttering insults to Maria under his breath. She was also suffering from painful haemorrhoids, and on 24 May, the day before her third *Pirata*, she went into hospital for an operation, the after-effects of which were as unpleasant as the malady itself. Even so, she sang sublimely, and ultimately exacted her revenge on Ghiringhelli – albeit gaining a Pyrrhic victory – on 31 May, at the end of the fifth and final performance of *Il Pirata*.

The opera concludes with Imogene – whose pirate-lover Gualtiero (Corelli) has been sentenced to death – fantasising about the scaffold. She sings, 'O sole, ti vela di tenebre oscure! ... Là vedete! Il palco funesto!' (O Sun, cast quickly a darkness! ... Behold! The fated scaffold!) When Maria pronounced this last line – in Italian *palco* may mean *scaffold* or *theatre-box* – she advanced menacingly towards Ghiringhelli, and pointed accusingly at him ... and La Scala's Superintendent was so incensed that, whilst Maria was taking her curtain-calls – these had gone on for thirty minutes after the première – he signalled for the technicians to bring down the safety-curtain, abruptly cutting her off from the audience. It was a final, as will be seen, almost lasting insult ... after twenty-one roles and 157 performances in almost exactly eight years.

When asked backstage if she would ever sing again at the theatre she had often called her second home, Maria shrugged her shoulders and told reporters, 'Who knows what I might do, should they change the administration?' Ghiringhelli, for his part, gave a clear indication that even without him, the theatre would never *want* her back, responding, 'Prima donnas come and go, but La Scala remains standing!'

Ghiringhelli's smug expression changed to one of disbelief, however, when through an upstairs window he observed the scene within the Piazzo Scala as Maria made the most famous exit of her career. Because of the crowds, Maria's chauffeur had been forced to park her car at the far end of the square, and reaching it necessitated a lengthy but beatifying, flower-strewn walk through a dense sea of admirers who screamed out her name, whilst fighting past the police cordon to touch her and personally tell her goodbye – many people truly believed that this was the end, that she would never sing again, and the photographs of her, choking back the tears whilst surrounded by her adored Callas Boys, are nothing short of heartbreaking. 'We were watching an exact re-enactment of the abdication of Garbo's Queen Christina,' remarked one onlooker, 'and though her heart was broken and her nerves were in shreds, Callas loved every minute of it. We all knew that she'd be back. No woman on earth could have given up so much *love!*'

When Maria arrived at the Savoy Hotel, early in June, she was asked what she was most looking forward to during her stay in London. She replied, candidly, 'A decent cup of tea, and not having shit thrown at the windows.' She was in a foul mood when a call was put through to her suite from Noël Goodwin of the *Observer*, who politely requested an interview. Slamming down the receiver, she told the Savoy's receptionist who asked her if she had been accidentally cut off, 'All men are assholes, but male journalists more especially so!' Goodwin forgave her the indiscretion. Correctly coming to the conclusion that most of her troubles lay rooted in the psychological insecurities of her early years, he wrote in his column, 'Buried inside the slim and hugely successful singer is a fat little girl still desperately compensating for an unhappy childhood: and the fruit of this compensation has been the metamorphosis of an unloved child into the greatest prima donna of today.'

Maria was in the British capital to sing *La Traviata* at Covent Garden, but prior to this on 10 June she appeared at a royal gala celebrating the venue's centenary. The concert boasted a full bill including Joan Sutherland, Margot Fonteyn and Jon Vickers, but it was Maria who stole the show, earning eight curtain-calls with her last ever performance of 'Qui la voce' from *Il Puritani*. She also raised a few eyebrows by refusing to curtsy to the Queen – who, having paused to chat with the other artistes on the bill, merely walked past Maria, rewarding her with an enforced smile. The following week, Maria made her British television debut on Granada's *Chelsea At Eight*, broadcast from the stage of the Chelsea Empire. She sang 'Vissi d'arte' and 'Una voce poco fa', and the event resulted in a sudden escalation in the sales of her records.

Many critics did not respond well to Maria's porcelain-doll Violetta which, though this was not an actual revival of Visconti's *La Traviata*, nevertheless had Maria singing the last scenes in the subdued tones of a dying woman. 'The death scene was almost horrific,' wrote Harold Rosenthal in *Opera*. 'The last "E strano" was uttered in an unearthly voice, and as Violetta rose to greet what she thought was a new life, a glaze came over her eyes, and she literally became a standing corpse.'

On 2 July, the Meneghinis returned to their villa at Sirmione, where Maria rested briefly whilst preparing her most gruelling schedule so far – a ten-concert tour of the United States, two performances each of *La Traviata* and *Medea* in Dallas and, preceding these events, the recording of two new albums for EMI which, now that she was no longer associated with La Scala, would have to be cut in London. She had also signed a contract with the New York Met for an even more punishing workload: an incredible twenty-six performances of *Tosca*, *Macbeth* and her own choice of *Lucia* or *Traviata*, to take place between January and March 1959. Maria had opted for the latter.

The albums were *Callas Portrays Verdi Heroines* and *Maria Callas: Mad Scenes*, and they were recorded in just five days at the end of September 1958. The former contained arias from *Don Carlos*, *Macbeth*, *Ernani* and *Nabucco*. Maria was still pressing Walter Legge to allow her to record these roles in their entirety. The previous year, Legge had persuaded EMI to abandon their plans to record *Medea* and, to prove a point, Maria had ignored the terms of her contract and accepted a one-off deal with Ricordi. The recording of *Medea* had sold well, and EMI had subsequently purchased the rights from them and released it on their own label. Walter Legge, however, would not budge and replied, 'Still too obscure' ... to which Maria responded, 'And *you* still have no goddam *guts*!' The second album consisted of arias from the similarly fated *Anna Bolena*, *Il Pirata* and Thomas's *Hamlet*.

The Meneghinis arrived in New York on 7 October, where they were met at Idlewild airport and driven straight to the Met for a lunch meeting with Rudolf Bing. Here, Maria expressed her concern over mixing the roles of Violetta and Lady Macbeth – a murderous test for any voice – denouncing Bing for making what she considered, quite correctly, a reprehensible request. Bing told her that she was worrying over nothing. Firstly, she was currently mixing the equally heavy Medea with Violetta, in Dallas, and she had already agreed to return to Dallas at the end of 1959 to sing Medea and Lucia. Secondly, Bing added that he would be prepared to allow her eight days to lighten her voice down from Lady Macbeth to Violetta, and four days to step it back up again. What Bing would *not* agree to was Maria's request that the central role of Macbeth should be sung by someone other than Leonard Warren, whom she could not abide, or that the outdated, rickety sets for *La Traviata* should be replaced before they fell on top of somebody. Even so, she told Bing that she would consider his proposals – though secretly she had no intention of giving way – and the next morning she and Meneghini flew to Birmingham, Alabama, where the tour was scheduled to begin at the Municipal Auditorium, on 11 October.

Maria's tour had been organised by her new American agent, Sol Hurok, whom she had engaged following an investigation of his credentials. In the wake of the Bagarozy fiasco, she trusted no one. An elderly, brash, Russian-born naturalised American, Horuk was used to fiery-tempered female entertainers, having arranged hugely successful tours for Joséphine Baker and Mistinguett. What Maria did not know, and what Hurok made no effort to tell her, is that only a short time before, Litza had contacted him, begging him to audition Jackie ... and that he had come close to doing just this, assured by colleagues that, although the elder Callas was nowhere near as talented as Maria and never would be, her name would probably prove a draw, as a 'curiosity' item.

Aside from her actual performances, Maria hated touring. Most of the cities she was visiting were off the regular international opera circuit; the hotels she stayed in were not up to her standards; and she was forced to travel everywhere by train because the airlines would not allow her to take a dog on the planes. The warmth of her audiences, of course, more than made up for these inconveniences. Each evening, Maria was escorted on to the platform by Nicola Rescigno, and she always left weighed down by the huge bouquets from the camp-followers who devotedly trailed after her from one end of the country to the other, and even up into Canada, some having parted with their life-savings for the privilege.

The same critics who had recently covered the fan-crazed tours of Elvis Presley, Pat Boone and Johnny Ray were not interested in having their columns complicated by operatic jargon. 'She can look like a pixie or a devil. She can croon like an angel, or she can wail like a banshee,' proclaimed the *Atlanta Constitution*'s Dick Gray, whereas J Dorsey Callaghan of the *Detroit Free Press* accurately pinpointed one major cause for 'dissension' in the past: 'The voice did not come up to *all* expectations, but only because these expectations have been so *immensely* enlarged.'

On 31 October, Maria sang the first of her two *Traviata*s at the 3,500-seater Dallas Civic Opera House. The production was directed by Franco Zeffirelli and, just as Visconti had brought forward his story for La Scala, so Zeffirelli opted for a revolutionary change in the scenario which Maria initially disapproved of. The curtain rose on the stricken Violetta, lying on her death-bed – looking healthier than Maria usually permitted – and the story was told in flashback. One week later, in the same theatre, she sang Medea in a scintillating production directed by Alexis Minotis, one of Greece's leading theatre directors who was married to the distinguished actress, Katina Paxinou.

Like Visconti and Zeffirelli, Minotis was capable of getting

Maria to do absolutely anything. She also got along remarkably well with Teresa Berganza, the pretty young Spanish soprano who was singing the role of Neris, and because of her tremendous respect and admiration for these two, there was less tension behind the scenes, apart from one or two sharp exchanges with Jon Vickers, who was singing Jason. Neither could Minotis placate Maria or prevent the angry outburst which erupted when, on the eve of the première, a telegram arrived from Rudolf Bing. The previous week, Bing's telegram wishing her luck for *La Traviata* had ended, coldly, 'Why Dallas?' – a clear indication of his jealousy that she had become a heroine in that city, where she could do no wrong. Subsequently, she had written a letter to Bing – in *Italian*, just like she had purposely insulted her parents by using this language to inform them of her marriage – explaining why she did not wish to sing *La Traviata* at the Met. Her basic grievance was that, although this was a new production, its première had taken place already – with Renata Tebaldi – and that Maria had been asked to sing Violetta *only* because her rival had refused to sing the role in the 1959 season.

'Tebaldi has refused to sing *Traviata*, although she was committed to do so,' Maria wrote. 'And you, for the sake of peace, have accepted this. It is therefore logical that I should not perform this role either, since Tebaldi has dared to impose the aforesaid cancellation.' Bing had responded at once by sending a letter by courier, in which he had explained that, if need be, he would be willing to replace *La Traviata* with *Lucia*. Unfortunately, the rest of the letter had been extremely sarcastic and off-hand, and had contained the biting comment, 'Your attitude sounds more like the Maria Callas of whom I have been warned than the Maria Callas that I know, like and respect.' Maria had immediately seen red, and as she had failed to reply, this second telegram comprised a *command* – she was to inform the Met of her decision by ten the next morning, or else. Dismissing what she termed Bing's 'Prussian tactics', Maria ignored the instruction, and the next afternoon a *third* telegram arrived from Bing ... informing her that her contract with the Met had been terminated.

At once, the world's press – using banner headlines such as

BING FIRES CALLAS – began vying for the most sensational interview: Maria, screaming and cursing, and calling the director of the Met every filthy name she could conjure up –and Bing, his comments lacking the expletives but wickedly sarcastic, retaliating in the words of one journalist, 'like a spitting cat on heat'. Bing had lost no time at all in replacing Maria with Leonie Rysanek, the Austrian soprano who had stepped into her shoes in San Francisco. Rysanek would not cope well with this most demanding role, and some years later Bing admitted that for the first and only time in his long career he had been compelled to hire a claqueur to encourage the applause – by yelling, 'Brava, Callas!' Bing told the *Daily Telegraph*:

> Madame Callas is one of the world's outstanding artists, but after her histrionic off-stage performances here and in other opera houses, the Metropolitan is relieved that our association with her is at an end. Furthermore I will not engage in any public argument with Madame Callas since I am well aware that she has considerably greater competence and experience at that kind of thing than I have. She also told me not so very long ago that it was her intention to give up her singing career. Her attitude together with other things that have happened elsewhere in her recent career are designed to accomplish that end.

An irate Maria, in a statement which had been 'cleaned up' considerably, told the same journalist:

> I'm afraid certain statements by Mr Bing have caused what little door there was left open to be shut. He has made certain statements that I, or for that matter any artists, do not deserve. I have already had lots of offers. In the very near future I will be in New York to sing, so I say to Mr Bing that opera *can* be done outside the Met. He has put himself in a stupid, idiotic, ridiculous situation and it is up to him to get himself out of it. The whole world, including me, is watching to see *how* he will get himself out of it – nicely or badly. As for those stinking

*Traviata*s he wanted me to do – they were lousy performances, and everybody knows it. They are not art, *I* do art, and that's the only thing I'm interested in!

She then added, as a somewhat lame afterthought,

What I'm trying to say is that unless I can do justice to a role, in a *good* production, then I would rather not present it to the public. Many artists can be difficult, nervous or irritable. I'm not one of them!

In fact, when she gave this statement on 6 November, Maria had received no offers at all, though some were forthcoming once the news of her dismissal from the Met had been circulated. The first telegram came from David Webster of Covent Garden, declaring simply, 'Come – Come!' Webster told the press, 'We have never had the slightest trouble with Madame Callas. She is one of the most conscientious artists I have ever met, and we will be delighted to have her back for a sixth season.' Webster's invitation was swiftly followed by others from Paris, Philadelphia, and the very pantheon of the New York entertainment scene, Carnegie Hall. There were even offers from several Las Vegas casinos and nightclubs, and a hotel complex in Miami Beach, which she wisely declined.

Maria, meanwhile, continued with her tour. After record-breaking concerts in Cleveland, Detroit and Washington – for which she was paid upwards of $10,000 a performance, *plus* a percentage of the box-office receipts – on 26 November she sang at San Francisco's War Memorial Theatre, where the audience was almost exclusively gay. Here, for the first and only time – to Meneghini's horror – she played to her 'boys' almost like a vamp – clad in a white satin gown, and using her long, shocking-pink stole as a prop which alternately drove them from tears to mass hysteria. She even encouraged several young men to jump up on to the stage and kiss her. The scenario in Los Angeles, three evenings later, was much in the same vein, though after it, Maria's coquetry vanished as quickly as it had appeared. Technically, the tour was not scheduled to end until 11 January, but for the moment she resigned herself to returning to

Italy, to a sedentary life with her unattractive, grumbling husband, and wholly uncertain of her future now that engagements were thin on the ground.

11

Questo Odiato Veglio!

I didn't want to marry an impresario – had this been so,
I would at least have married a professional one.

On 19 December 1958, two weeks after her thirty-fifth birthday,
Maria made her Paris debut at the Opera House, in what she called
her 'monster recital' – a gala performance benefiting the Légion
d'Honneur, to which just about every personality who happened to
be in Paris at the time had been invited: the French president and
most of his Cabinet, the ambassadors of Great Britain, the Soviet
Union and Italy, the Secretary General of NATO, Charlie Chaplin,
Jean Cocteau and Jean Marais, Brigitte Bardot, Juliette Grèco,
Gérard Philipe, the Duke and Duchess of Windsor, Prince Aly
Khan – and Aristotle Onassis and his wife, Tina. The Paris Opera
had offered Maria an unprecedented $5,000 for the concert, which
was televised and broadcast throughout most of Europe – *she* and
not Meneghini asked for double this amount, and promptly
donated it to the charity, incensing her penny-pinching husband.

Maria made the most stunning entrance, seemingly gliding
down the staircase in a gorgeous Biki creation, with the now obligatory stole draped over her shoulders and wearing $3 million worth
of rented diamonds. She began with a somewhat tremulous 'Casta
diva' which was reflected in the applause, though as the first half

progressed, so did the audience's enthusiasm – after the 'Miserere' from *Il Trovatore*, sung with the Opera's leading tenor, Albert Lance, they became so wild that the manager feared a riot. The second half of the programme comprised the whole of Act II of *Tosca*, with Albert Lance and Tito Gobbi. 'Let it not be said that the spectators, near or far, did not get their money's worth,' wrote the *Saturday Review*'s Everett Helm, defending the absurdly inflated ticket prices of which *France-Soir* commented, 'The only people who could truly have afforded to see Callas, last night, were the ones who got in free anyway!'

In New York, the Meneghinis had been invited to dine with Prince Aly Khan, and Maria's husband – who knew absolutely nothing of her earlier tryst with the handsome playboy, whom he could not stand, and denounced as 'that smarmy Arab' – advised her that she might be best meeting him on her own. Maria would have loved nothing more than a rekindling of the flame with the man Mistinguett had once boasted to be 'hung like one of his stallions'. Aly, however, who could never settle down with one woman for any length of time, had only been interested in a platonic friendship. Subsequently, when he had called Maria on the morning of her Paris concert to ask her to supper, she had put the phone down on him. Only minutes before, she had received a huge bunch of red roses and a good-luck card, inscribed in Greek, from Aristotle Onassis.

Since the Elsa Maxwell party, Maria had not given the shipping tycoon much thought, and she did not know what to make of this most recent gesture. However, when an identical bunch of flowers arrived at her lunch table, followed by a *third* bouquet as she was leaving for the Opera House, she realised that Onassis was making a play for her right under her husband's nose. This became even more obvious at the sumptuous party after her recital, for as her 'celebrity fans' formed a line to congratulate her, the wiry little Greek pushed his way to the front of the queue. Many years later, Meneghini would talk about this party in his memoirs: 'For me, as organiser, it constituted a personal vindication, but I didn't know that it was to be, alas, the final great testament of my total devotion to Maria before she betrayed me.' Meneghini was of course by this time allowing bitterness to cloud his memory of long-past events, for in December 1958 Maria had yet to fall into Onassis' clutches – she merely thanked him for sending her so many flowers, told him how flattered she had been, then resumed her task of meeting the *haute société* of Paris.

During the first week of January 1959, the Meneghinis flew to New York, then on to St Louis, where Maria completed the tour that had been arranged by Sol Hurok. On 24 January, she sang three arias in a gala concert at Philadelphia's Academy of Music, under the baton of Eugene Ormandy. Three evenings later, conducted by Nicola Rescigno, she gave the first of two concert-performances of *Il Pirata* at New York's Carnegie Hall (the other was on 29 January, in Washington), for the American Opera Society. Wearing a floor-length white gown, surmounted by a 12-foot scarlet silk stole, she created a vision of loveliness then and now unsurpassed on the opera stage – particularly during the 18-minute finale. As she began singing 'E giorno, o sera? Son io nelle mie stanze ... o son sepolta?' (Is it day, or night? Am I in my apartments ... or in the tomb?), the other singers left the stage and, save for the musicians' and EXIT lights, and the single spotlight which picked out Maria, the great concert hall was plunged into darkness, creating an atmosphere more tense and exciting than would have been possible, had she been performing with the sets, effects and costumes. 'With only her beautiful, expressive face and her arms visible, she looked like a Piaf and sang like an angel,' remarked one critic. And at the end of the performance, such was the hysteria of the Callas Boys – who had already begun charging down the aisles towards the stage, as the lights came on again and she was pronouncing her final, 'Là ... vedete il palco funesto!' – that in order to curtail the seemingly endless curtain-calls and, according to the theatre manager, 'to prevent someone from having a heart attack', an attendant came out to dismantle the prompter's box, after which the spectators began leaving, knowing that the show was now well and truly over.

The next day, Maria was officially honoured by Robert Wagner, the Mayor of New York, in a citation which read, 'To the esteemed daughter of this city, whose glorious voice and superb artistry have contributed to the pleasure of music-lovers everywhere.' Such praise was appreciated by Maria, naturally, though it did not compensate for the barrenness of the next few months – a period during which, barring the recording of *Lucia di Lammermoor* in London with Tullio Serafin, saw Maria plunging into some of the deepest depressions of her life. Then, quite suddenly, she pulled herself together by telling herself that unless she did something about the lamentable state she was in – brought on by a combination of self-pity and acute neurasthenia, added to which was a lack of confidence in her own abilities – she would very quickly lose heart altogether, and so would her public.

With tremendous cunning, Maria used her tenth wedding anniversary as a means of catapulting herself back into the limelight. Those closest to her had known for some time – effectively, since she had slimmed – that she was no longer amorously interested in her husband, who if he had not become impotent soon after marrying her, certainly was now. Also, although she had rarely cheated on him, her most recent lovers had been young, handsome and virile, caring more for the woman than for the name MARIA CALLAS in large imaginary letters above the bed, and for furthering their own selfish aims. Even so, although she was now in the enviable position of being able to choose the cream of the crop, she did not have it in her heart to hurt Meneghini by leaving him, much as it is now known that she wanted to. Therefore, for her wedding anniversary, she orchestrated the entire scenario which took place at Maxim's, in Paris, on 21 April 1959 … engaging third parties to inform friends and colleagues all over the world who otherwise would have overlooked the occasion, so that when she and Meneghini entered the famous eaterie, they were showered with flowers and toasted with champagne. Then, after she had read out the dozens of blazingly sycophantic telegrams – including the archetypal 'May all your troubles be little ones', which hurt her feelings considerably because she had always wanted children – she continued this ridiculous charade by announcing, 'I cannot sing unless my husband is with me. I may be the voice, but he is the soul.' Just how much Meneghini actually meant to her would, of course, be fully revealed over the coming months.

As a contrived publicity stunt, the Maxim's party brought in huge dividends. Maria had already been engaged to sing *Medea* at Covent Garden – the first time the opera had been staged in London for over ninety years – but now offers poured in from all over Europe, and with fabulous fees. The Covent Garden engagement, however, did present Maria with an inadvertent dilemma, for the production was the one staged by Alexis Minotis in Dallas, and Lawrence Kelly had struck up a deal with David Webster – in exchange for Kelly's *Medea* with Maria, Webster would send him his *Lucia di Lammermoor*, produced by Franco Zeffirelli with Joan Sutherland singing the central role. The problem was, Kelly did not want Sutherland, but Maria.

Having learned that the young Australian soprano was about to 'purloin' one of her most celebrated roles, Maria had flown to London in the February to sit in on Sutherland's dress-rehearsal, sandwiched between Walter Legge and Elisabeth Schwarzkopf, who later remarked unfairly how stunned Maria had been by the evidence before her that, whilst *her* voice was on the wane, Sutherland's was in its ascendancy. Neither is it true that Maria knew, at this stage, that she would be 'usurping' Sutherland in Dallas. What is true, however, is that although Maria was outwardly civil towards the younger singer when they met in her dressing-room, she told reporters, 'That woman has put my work in the bel canto repertoire *back* by a hundred years. Her voice is good, granted, but I have seen more dramatic movement in a lump of wood.' Joan Sutherland would, of course, make *Lucia* synonymous with her name, but in spite of her astonishing talent for interpreting the most testing coloratura roles with almost uncanny ease, Maria would always deride her for doing nothing about her size, as she had, and for not trying to improve on her occasionally muddy diction. She would also resent Sutherland for having a handsome conductor husband in Richard Bonynge, a Svengali figure who, unlike Meneghini, was neither grasping nor old enough to be her father.

Meanwhile, for Maria the whole of May was taken up with the first leg of her European tour, which began in Madrid and progressed like a tidal wave through Germany. Sandwiched between engagements was a party in Venice, organised in her honour by the Contessa Castelbarco. This event would change her whole life, for amongst the guests, and not just by chance, were Aristotle Onassis and his beautiful young wife, Tina – the shipping heiress, Athina Livanos.

It is not difficult to ascertain Onassis's fascination for Maria Callas. She was young, beautiful, successful – but above all, she was the most famous Greek in the world, in his opinion, after himself. What she saw in him is another matter entirely. Some eighteen years Maria's senior, Onassis was a vulgar, uneducated, unattractive individual – everything, in fact, that Meneghini was not. He was, however, tremendously exciting – 'A rampant heterosexual, the spirit and virility of an Aly Khan inside the body of an ape', was how he was once described by a fellow countrywoman, Melina Mercouri. At the Castelbarco party, Onassis invited the Meneghinis to cruise with him on his 1640-ton yacht, the *Christina*, though for the moment Maria politely refused the offer, explaining that she was about to begin her Covent Garden season. This did not deter Onassis in his pursuit of the woman he wanted more than any other on earth: the next morning one of his aides called Covent Garden and demanded forty of the best seats in the house for the *Medea* première on 17 June. These were sent out to Onassis's guests, including the Churchills, Lord Harewood (who as director of the Opera House did not need to be invited!), Princess Marina and her daughter Princess Alexandra, Cecil Beaton, Margot Fonteyn, the actors Gary Cooper and Douglas Fairbanks Jnr, and of course, Elsa Maxwell. According to Maxwell's secretary, Onassis had telephoned her that afternoon to announce, as crudely as only he could, 'My greatest ambition, my dear Maxwell, is to fuck Callas. And *you* shall help me!'

The London *Medea* was sensational. Onassis, rushing from a pre-performance, Callas-less reception in Covent Garden's Crush Bar, escorted Lady Churchill to her seat only minutes before the curtain rose and, admitting to those about him that he detested opera and often fell asleep whilst Tina was playing Callas recordings, he chatted loudly until Maria made her appearance – enveloped in a dark, voluminous cloak which enabled the audience to see only her eyes, huge and terrifying. Vocally, she was in terrific form, as the *Saturday Review*'s Irving Kolodin observed, 'She appears to have profited from a period of relative idleness, for the sound was fresh, responsive and endlessly expressive in her veiled, *chalumeau* manner.' Lord Harewood remembered, 'The performance was mesmeric. There was a kind of fury about her, a demonic Greek power I'd seen before but never with quite such intensity. It was as if a torrent of fury was being unleashed.' Onassis, of course, was totally uninterested in the Callas *voice*, and after the performance, with Elsa Maxwell in tow as 'personal adviser', he threw a party expressly aimed at wooing her. 'Mr and Mrs Aristotle Onassis have the pleasure to invite you to a party in honour of Maria Callas which is to be held at the Dorchester Hotel at 23.15', read the invitations, and the guests were whisked off to the bash in a fleet of limousines. The vast ballroom was filled with shocking-pink roses, and the orchestra played a selection of Maria's favourite tunes, everything from Gershwin to Gardel, whilst Onassis ignored his upper-crust coterie to devote himself entirely to Maria, who sailed into the room just after midnight, swathed in furs and with a miserable-looking Meneghini trailing behind.

During the first half hour of the party, Maria was in a foul mood. According to Meneghini, she had not wanted to be there in the first place, and during the interval of *Medea* there had been a nasty altercation with a royal aide who had brought a message to her dressing-room, telling her that Princess Marina wanted to see her in her box. Maria had snarled, 'If she wants to see me, she can come to my dressing-room the same as everybody else!' There had also been on-stage problems with Fiorenza Cossotto, the young mezzo soprano interpreting the role of Neris. Cossotto had sung with Maria in 1957, in the Milan and Edinburgh *Sonnambulas* when an overzealous admirer had told her, 'Keep it up, and you'll end up *surpassing* Callas!'

Cossotto had not forgotten this, and during rehearsals at Covent Garden she had tried her utmost to upstage Maria. Sir John Tooley, who had joined the company in 1955, and who later became General Director, remembered one particular episode when he and several others, including the dancer Robert Helpmann, were watching from the gallery: 'One of the group commented on

Callas's amazing stillness as she lay on the couch during Neris's aria, to have his attention drawn by Helpmann to the position of Miss Cossotto's left foot, firmly on Maria's dress!' After this incident, Maria had told her latest rival, whom she believed inferior to 'real' rivals such as Tebaldi because, in her own words, 'she was third-rate', 'Do that again, fat woman, and I'll kick your ass so hard you'll end up in the orchestra!' Cossotto, however, had exacted her revenge. During the première, after her aria, she had stepped out of character to bow and acknowledge the applause – infuriating Maria, who *never* did such things. This time she was told, in the wings, 'If I were you, dear, I'd be careful what I ate tonight at the party. You stepped out of your character. I'm still *in* mine!' Needless to say, the mezzo had not showed up at the Dorchester, and Maria's mood changed abruptly once the party was in full swing. She was surprised to find her host such pleasant company, so much so that when Onassis now begged her to join him and several close friends on his yacht, she told him that she would seriously think about it – but only after she had finished at Covent Garden.

The crunch came a few weeks later, when Maria gave two concerts – one, her Dutch debut at the Holland Festival, in Amsterdam, the other in Brussels – and requested that her fees for these be paid directly to her, and not into the Meneghini-Callas account. She had received several calls from Tina Onassis urging her to take a trip on the *Christina*, which suggests that Tina was not yet aware of her husband's intentions – and several more from Onassis himself, promising her excitement such as she had not experienced in her life, should she accept. It seems likely that she too may not have guessed the tycoon's ulterior motive, particularly as there were to be more than a dozen distinguished guests on the yacht besides herself and Meneghini. Even so, she took some persuading. She had no engagements until mid-September, so it was not that she did not have time on her hands. However, following the adverse criticism of her upper register, she had contacted her old teacher, Elvira di Hidalgo, still resident in Turkey, with a view to taking a course of 'refresher' lessons. Now, it was her husband, in an action which he would rue for the rest of his life, who joined forces with Maria's doctor in advising her that the sea air would benefit her health – and that someone else paying for the excursion would benefit his pocket, as he freely admitted at the time – well aware that he would probably feel out of place away from his own friends, and of the fact that he had always suffered terribly from seasickness.

Informing Onassis that she and Meneghini would meet the rest of the company 'at Prince Rainier's place' in Monte Carlo, Maria contacted Madame Biki and ordered a forty-piece wardrobe for the three-week cruise – dresses, evening gowns, slacks, swimwear and nightdresses – and asked for the bill to be sent to her husband. She also packed the score for a new role she was hoping to revive: Alaide in Bellini's long-forgotten *La Straniera*.

On 21 July 1959, the Meneghinis flew to Nice, then on to Monte Carlo by taxi, where they checked in to the Hôtel de Paris. A few hours later they were introduced to their sailing companions: Sir Winston and Lady Churchill, with their daughter Diana, their dog Toby, and Churchill's personal physician Lord Moran; Giovanni Agnelli, the head of Fiat, and his wife, and a sixty-strong crew of Onassis lackeys – stewards, waiters, valets, chefs, masseurs, a croupier, seamstresses and cabin boys. Elsa Maxwell was also in Monte Carlo, staying with Prince Rainier and Princess Grace, but afraid of giving the game away – the fact that she had supplied Onassis with a list of 'Callas do's and don'ts' and stood to receive a sizeable cheque, should the yearned-for seduction take place. She sent her apologies to Maria by way of a letter which, some years later, Meneghini delighted in making public.

Praising Onassis as 'that marvellous and intelligent master of the house', and informing Maria that she was in fact taking Greta Garbo's place on the cruise because Onassis now considered the legendary film star too old to bed, Maxwell's letter concluded:

I never cared for Garbo, but I *loved* you. From this moment on, enjoy every moment of your life. *Take* (this is a delicate art) everything. *Give* (not a delicate art, but a very important one) all that you can bring yourself to give, for this is the way to true happiness which you must discover in the wilderness. I no longer wish to see you. The world will say – is *already* saying, in fact – that you only wanted to use me. This I deny categorically. The little I have done, I did with my eyes wide open, and with my heart and soul. You are already one of the greats, and you will only become greater.

When Maria read Maxwell's 'goodbye', she immediately flew into a panic and rang the woman she called her 'surrogate mother' – but who for years had rather hoped for more than the conventional mother-daughter relationship, in spite of the forty-year age gap – and begged her not to desert her. The next day they met, did a little shopping, and in the evening dined with Onassis' sister, Artemis, before heading off to a night club, where Maria waltzed and jived for over two hours – leaving her husband sitting at the table with a woman whose language he could not converse in, and with Elsa Maxwell, who he later denounced as 'that maliciously slobbering old harridan, that foul-faced bird of ill omen'.

The cruise began the next day, with everyone getting along fine on this massive, floating palace with every conceivable luxury. Maria spent much of her time with Tina Onassis, whilst Meneghini became violently ill after just a few hours at sea. Onassis himself played cards with Sir Winston Churchill, now 83, and feeble. The first stop was Portofino, then Capri, where Maria spent a day with Gracie Fields and the writer Grahame Greene, who also lived on the island – she even laughed when Gracie told her of Onassis's last visit to her restaurant complex, the Canzone del Mare, with Greta Garbo ... when one of her friends had described the pair as 'the Ice Maiden and her pet chimp'.

From then on, for Meneghini the trip began turning into a nightmare. 'Many of the couples split up and found other partners,' he said afterwards, 'The women, and also the men, often sunbathed totally nude and fooled around in broad daylight. I had the impression of finding myself in a pigpen. But one of the things that made the strongest impression on me was seeing Onassis naked. He didn't seem to be a man, but a gorilla. He was very hairy. Maria looked at him and laughed.'

The next day, whilst heading for Smyrna (now Izmir), Onassis's birthplace on the Turkish coast, the *Christina* ran into a fierce storm which sent everyone scurrying below deck. Meneghini, already confined to his cabin, now only found his condition aggravated by Maria, who refused to allow him to switch on the air-conditioning, declaring that this would affect her vocal cords when she began going through the Bellini score. In fact, she never got around to unpacking it, for whilst Tina Onassis fussed over her stricken, bilious guests – and Meneghini in particular – her husband entertained Maria in his quarters by telling her his life-story.

The son of a wealthy Greek tobacco merchant, Onassis had fled to Athens with his family when the Turks had brutally recaptured Smyrna from the Greeks in 1922, slaughtering several of his relatives. Initially, like Maria's family, the 16-year-old had hoped to emigrate to the United States, but he had sailed for Argentina instead, with just a few hundred dollars to his name. Here, he had begun working as a switchboard operator, and after saving his money and living on next to nothing, he had started his own small cigarette factory. A few years later had come the great depression, and the temporary slump in the shipping trade which had enabled him to buy, at rock-bottom prices, several cargo boats.

Such was Onassis' instinct for spotting a bargain and moving quickly – aided by the most extraordinary luck – that by the age of twenty-five he had made his first million. In 1954 there had been a hitch when, during Eisenhower's administration, he had been arrested and indicted on charges of defrauding the United States government by tax-dodging. To avoid trial, he had paid officials $7 million. Then in 1956, already one of the world's richest men, he had hit the jackpot – raking in over $150 million, simply because his entire fleet of oil tankers had been available during the Suez crisis. On top of this, shortly before deciding that Maria Callas should be another of his assets, Onassis had ploughed $25 million into Olympic Airlines, earning his company a monopoly on domestic flights inside Greece.

At the time of his 'make-or-break' cruise with Maria, Onassis is reputed to have been worth in excess of $500 million – and by the time he had finished telling her about himself, not least of all about his sexual conquests which had begun when he had been just thirteen, the pair had become lovers. That same evening, he called Elsa

Maxwell and announced that 'it' had taken place.

The *Christina* docked at Smyrna on 4 August, and Onassis spent much of the day escorting his company on a tour of his home town. In the evening, leaving the Churchills, Maria and Tina behind, he treated his male guests to an enlightening trip to Smyrna's red-light district and its seedy bars, cheerfully pointing out some of the now aged doxies with whom he had sown his wild oats as a youth. Two days later, the next port of call was Mount Athos, a sacred promontory for the Greek Orthodox Church on the Macedonian coast occupied by a community of 3,000 Basilian monks. Here, in full view of their travelling companions, Maria and Onassis were received by the elderly Patriarch Athenagoras and, in a ceremony spoken entirely in Greek, made to kneel and be ordained with his blessing. Tina Onassis and Meneghini were shocked to the core, for although the ceremony was ostensibly to pay homage to what the Patriarch described as 'the world's greatest singer and this new Ulysses, the greatest seaman of the modern world' – and perhaps persuade them to cough up a few million *drachma* in appreciation – these wronged spouses were in effect watching something entirely different. 'It almost seemed as if he were performing a marriage rite,' Meneghini remembered, adding, 'Maria remained profoundly troubled afterward. I could see it in her eyes, which were luminous and wild.'

The next evening, in Athens, Onassis threw a party aboard the *Christina* which raged until the early hours of the morning, and when Meneghini complained of feeling tired – hoping that his wife would descend to their cabin – she told him sharply, in front of everyone, 'Get to fucking bed!' The next morning when he awoke, Maria was not there, though minutes later when he bumped into the man who henceforth would be referred to only as The Greek, Onassis delighted in telling him, in minute anatomical detail, what had transpired between himself and Maria in his private quarters.

The row which followed between Maria and Meneghini was heard by everyone on the yacht, and contained enough expletives to warrant Lady Churchill remarking to a steward, 'That lady needs to have her mouth washed out with bleach!' In her blind fury, Maria flung every accusation at her hapless husband, though

Meneghini ought to have seen this coming – branding him her 'jailer and loathsome guardian', and 'an odious, ill-educated old buffoon who doesn't even have the sense to dress properly and comb his balding head'. And if this was not enough to be going on with, less than an hour later Meneghini received a call on the *Christina* informing him that his elderly mother had suffered a heart attack and was close to death.

Throughout the day, Maria and Meneghini avoided one another – she even refused to sit at the same table as him for meals – and when Sir Winston Churchill attempted to lighten the tense, explosive atmosphere by asking, 'Madame Callas, would you honour me by singing my favourite aria?', she turned on him and snarled, 'No, I will not!' Later, when one of Churchill's aides explained how upset the old man had been, and asked, 'Don't you think you ought to at least send a message to his cabin?', Maria responded, 'Fine. Just tell him that he's a boring, incontinent old fart!'

The drama only grew worse when, that same evening, there was another party and Meneghini refused to leave his cabin, declaring that he had suffered enough insults whilst aboard the *Christina* to last him a lifetime. Yet he was still sufficiently confident that Maria's one night of passion with Onassis had been her way of getting the frustrations of the last months out of her system, and that once they returned to Milan, life would return to normal. During the early days of the cruise, Meneghini had even condoned Maria for spending so much time with their host. 'She seemed more vivacious than I had ever seen her, and she danced continuously, always with Onassis,' he recalled. 'I was almost happy about it. Maria was still a young girl, I thought whilst observing them. She was letting herself go. It would do her good.' Then he had explained how, in the early hours of the morning, his cabin door had opened to reveal a semi-naked woman whom he had assumed to be Maria – only to realise, once he had taken her in his arms, that it had been Tina Onassis, who sobbed that she had just found her husband in bed with Maria.

The *Christina* returned to Monte Carlo on 13 August, from where the Meneghinis were driven – by an Onassis chauffeur – to Nice airport to catch the afternoon flight to Milan. 'Between us, for the entire trip, there was a glacial silence,' Meneghini recalled. Clasped about Maria's wrist was the platinum bracelet which Onassis had given her, inscribed TMWL – 'To Maria With Love' – though to be fair, he had presented similar bracelets to Gracie Fields and Greta Garbo, with no hint of romance.

The ensuing events were nothing short of bizarre. No sooner had Maria entered the house on the Via Buonarrati than she suggested to her husband that he might be better staying in Sirmione, where he would be closer to his ailing mother. This he did, yet whilst they were apart she rang him constantly, and two days later begged him to return ... playing the dutiful housewife when he walked in, relieving him of his coat and briefcase, she poured him a drink and told him to put his feet up whilst she cooked their evening meal. This of course was Callas at her most Machiavellian, for no sooner had he finished eating than she told him, point-blank, that she had decided to leave him for Onassis, although she wanted their separation to be a civil, dignified affair. She then added that she had taken the liberty of inviting her lover to the house to discuss the matter further!

Onassis arrived, as if on cue, only minutes later, determined to cause as much trouble and humiliation for Meneghini as possible, and of course the ensuing discussion solved nothing. 'I went to bed destroyed, leaving them downstairs together,' Meneghini wrote in his memoirs, 'and at six the next morning, without disturbing anyone, I left my home. As I closed the door behind me, I was in tears.' Meneghini went straight to his mother's house in Zevio, then drove to Sirmione, where he hoped for at least a little peace to reflect upon his dilemma. This was not to be. The next evening, 17 August, Maria and Onassis barged into the villa, both roaring drunk, and Stavros, the chauffeur, recalled what happened next as Maria offered her lover a guided tour of the property.

Between them, they'd quaffed an entire bottle of whisky during the drive from Milan. Madame Callas showed him each room in the house, with Meneghini trailing after them like a frightened servant. Mr Onassis found fault with everything he saw – the furniture, the drapes, the wallpaper. Then they went outside, and he pointed to the lake and said, 'I've pissed bigger puddles.' Then Meneghini asked him what *he* could possibly offer his wife, besides a great deal of money and a good time. At this, Mr Onassis unbuttoned his flies and took out the biggest member I'd ever seen in my life. '*This*,' he said, 'is what I can offer your wife.'

According to Meneghini, the vulgarity continued back inside the house. 'I insulted *him*, calling him all the epithets he deserved,' he remembered, adding that he had become so angry that both Maria and Onassis had burst into tears, the latter confessing, 'Yes, I am a disgrace. I'm a murderer, a thief, and I'm no good. I'm the most revolting person on earth, but I'll never give up Maria and I'll take her away from whomever it's necessary, using whatever means, sending people, things, contracts and all conventions to hell. Then he had asked, "How many million do you want for Maria? Five … ten?" ' Upon this, Maria and Onassis had left.

A few days later, several of Onassis' personal assistants went to Sirmione to collect Maria's clothes – and the highly personal letters from Elsa Maxwell, which she had decided to destroy. She then offered Meneghini the supreme, final insult by returning the Cignaroli portrait of the Madonna he had given her at the time of her debuts in Verona, along with a note which read, 'You're going to need all the luck, now!'

Maria shut herself away from the press at her house in Milan, whilst Onassis flew to Venice, where the *Christina* was moored at the mouth of the Grand Canal. On board were Tina and her children, who had been told the truth about 'Aunt Maria'. For the time being, however, it was 'business as usual' for the two women in Onassis's life. Elsa Maxwell had organised a party for Tina on the yacht, and she now persuaded her that, as *she* had done absolutely nothing to be ashamed of, this should still take place. Tina danced the night away with her handsome escort, Count Brando d'Adda, and the paparazzi agreed that she had never looked lovelier. After the party, she left for Paris with her children and a few days later, Onassis joined them at her father's house in the Avenue Foch. From here he issued a statement dismissing any involvement with

Maria or rift in his marriage as 'ridiculous', adding, 'But if Madame Callas is *still* unhappy when I set off on another cruise in a few days' time, I shall ask her to join me. As for romance, they call me a sailor – and sailors and sopranos don't generally go together.'

Maria, meanwhile, had ended her feud with Antonio Ghiringhelli when the pair had met, purely by chance, whilst she had been lunching with Franco Corelli, and both had been surprised to find themselves getting along so well. Ghiringhelli would later opine that Aristotle Onassis was entirely responsible for teaching the world's greatest soprano not just how to smile, but how not to make life hell for those around her. Maria told the tetchy Superintendent that she had missed 'the old place', and he had replied that La Scala had not been the same without her, a statement which of course could have been interpreted two ways. Subsequently, a verbal agreement had been reached, uncomplicated by a rapacious husband: there was no question of Maria participating in La Scala's new season because this had already been finalised, but she would return to record *La Gioconda* with Antonino Votto. Such was the enthusiasm on both sides that the rehearsals began at once. Maria drove herself to La Scala each day. she had sold the now 'unlucky' green Alfa Romeo given to her by Meneghini, and had bought a brand new Mercedes. By 10 December the recording had been completed.

Maria's visits to La Scala were a feast for the press, who made a big point of reminding their readers that, inasmuch as *La Gioconda* had brought Maria and Meneghini together, so it was now being interwoven into the break-up of their marriage – though she persistently denied that she and Onassis were lovers. He, on the other hand, returned to Venice to make the final preparations for the new cruise and told reporters, 'How can I *not* be flattered if a woman of Callas's class falls in love with someone like me?' Meneghini then invited the press into his lounge at Sirmione and for the first time, opened his heart:

The break between Maria Callas and myself is now final and irrevocable. The personages in this drama are well-defined. They are Maria, Medea, myself who can be a hard one, and Mr

Onassis, a multi-millionaire who wants to give lustre to his oil-tankers with the name of a great actress. To be nearer her, I abandoned my career as an industrialist. Her voice grew and grew before my eyes. Then I fell in love with my masterpiece and married her. But I was unable to change her character, though perhaps the fault is mine for deluding myself with hopes of eternal love. I gambled everything on her. But I am no longer bitter – just sad. Who knows, maybe I shall now find peace again.

The press also tracked down Maria's mother, in New York. Some time before, Litza had appeared on a television chat-show with Jolie Gabor, the mother of actresses Eva and Zsa Zsa who owned a jewellery shop in the city. The subject had been famous daughters and their Svengali mothers, and Jolie had subsequently offered Litza a job. 'Maria will never be happy,' Litza told a reporter from the *Daily Mail*. 'I *know*. Battista Meneghini is a marvellous man. He was a father and mother to Maria – something she would not let me be. My daughter is just tired of him, but she will never marry Mr Onassis. Maria is interested only in her career, not in a happy marriage.' In another statement to Hy Gardner, she expostulated, 'I was Maria's first victim. Now it's Meneghini's turn. Onassis will be the third.'

On 12 September 1959, two days after Litza's statement – which Maria dismissed as 'the ravings of an old lunatic' – she and Onassis once more set sail on the *Christina*, accompanied by his sister Artemis, her husband, and a crew of forty-six. Onassis had collected Maria personally from her Milan home in his private plane, and Harry Weaver of the *Daily Mail* was the lucky journalist invited aboard the yacht to view Maria's cabin, which had been redecorated in shocking-pink and filled with thousands of blood-red gladioli – though he did not get to meet Maria. Earlier that week, Weaver had listened to rumours of a new twist in the Meneghini-Callas-Onassis scandal – that a third man was involved, reputed to be Franco Corelli or Prince Aly Khan, whom Onassis had respectively dismissed as 'that tenor faggot' and 'the horse-fucker'. Onassis now found this amusing, telling the journalist,

'The only *third man* I know is the music from Grahame Greene's film – ha, ha!'

12

In Mine Ear Hope's Knell is Ringing

The press were writing so frequently that I had lost my voice, I got to the point of believing it myself. I thought, they all say it so it *must* be true.

It was as if she was living on borrowed time: Maria Callas, a legend in her own lifetime and one of the greatest entertainers of this century, was now hopelessly in love with a man, who as far removed from the proverbial knight in shining armour as any man could be, had at least taught her that there was such a thing as life outside one's career and beyond self-absorption. There had been talk of an Onassis-backed feature film, possibly of *Medea*, and a stint with the Monte Carlo Opera, in which Onassis had controlling interest. Sadly, it was only talk, and Maria, who had previously fought tooth and nail to achieve her ambitions, did not see much point in pressing too hard now – preferring to fling herself with almost reckless abandon into this new, exciting existence, at the expense of all she had striven for in the last twenty years and, it has to be said, to the detriment of her voice, which henceforth would become her worst enemy.

On 17 September, the *Christina* docked in Athens, and Maria very reluctantly flew to Bilbao, in Spain, for a concert. The reticence came from the fact that the evening had been organised by

Meneghini, and for the first time in twelve years he was not going to be there to guide, console, or as had been the case most recently, to be Maria's whipping-boy. When asked by a reporter if she was looking forward to entertaining her Spanish fans, she merely pulled a face and gruffed, 'I never wanted to do this silly little engagement in the first place. Please don't ask!' The reporter rushed to the nearest radio station, blurted out his anecdote, and Maria walked on to the stage to an absolute silence. The applause after each aria was hardly encouraging, she took no curtain-call, and next morning her photograph appeared on the front page of a local newspaper with the caption: Do Not Bother Coming Back Again, Callas Told. Spain Will Not Miss You.

On 22 September, the *Christina* arrived in Monte Carlo, and Maria flew to Rome, from where she was to catch the early evening flight to London for a concert at the Royal Festival Hall. Breezing into the airport lounge, wrapped in a white fur coat beneath which she was dripping with diamonds, she told the waiting reporters, 'I am completely penniless, and in a very delicate state. Mine is not an enviable situation. I'm having to fight for my living, and I need money very badly.' Then, after posing for photographs, she added, 'As for my friendship with Mr Onassis, I only wish that it could be more than just friendship. I could do with a little love in these difficult days. Other than that, I have nothing more to say. My lawyers have told me to keep my mouth shut, except when I am singing, of course.'

Some of the reporters who interviewed Maria in Rome boarded the plane with her, though with her fondness for making up stories or for stretching the truth – often towards the point of absurdity, a supreme example being her recently dictated 'autobiography' to *Oggi*'s Anita Pensotti – by the time she reached London, the story of her plight had been more than slightly amended and the black rings under her eyes, which had wrought pity amongst those seeing her off in Rome, had mysteriously disappeared during a visit to the washroom on the plane.

Maria was met off the plane by Sandor Gorlinsky, her British agent, and the pair were escorted to the Rolls-Royce supplied by the Savoy – only to find that the chauffeur had gone walkabout –

but rather than throw a fit, as most of those present expected or even hoped she would, whilst Gorlinsky set off in search of the driver, Maria climbed into the back of the car, sprawled her legs somewhat ingloriously across her suitcases, and for the delight of the two hundred passengers and the airport staff who had deserted their posts, she gave an impromptu press conference:

Myself? I came here to work, dear, because now I have to work for my *living*!

My husband? No, there is not the faintest possibility of a reconciliation.

Mr Onassis? Why do people keep asking us if we're in love? I keep saying No. Mr Onassis keeps saying No. He and Tina, his lovely wife, are just two very dear friends who are at the moment trying to help me.

My money? Quite simply, I will not say that I'm broke, but I do have severe financial problems, and that is all I have to say about that particular matter.

Issuing a statement which almost cost him his job, and Maria's friendship, Sandor Gorlinsky – on his way back to her car, having located her chauffeur – refuted this latter comment by telling a reporter, 'The question of Madame Callas's financial position is relative. She does not like the word "broke", but whilst some people are broke when they get down to their last pound, others feel insecure with £50,000 because to them it's chicken-feed.'

The concert at the Royal Festival Hall on 23 September was a great success, and as if making a conscientious statement with regard to her fictitious financial dilemma, Maria left her jewels in the Savoy's safe and sang in a simple, one-carat diamond necklace. The highlights of the evening were her superb renditions of 'Tu che le vanità', and the sleepwalking scene from *Macbeth* – such was the enthusiasm for the latter that Covent Garden's David Webster asked her, after the performance, if she would consider singing Lady Macbeth in his 1960 season. Maria told him that she would think about it, though she had already decided not to take on any major commitments for the near future. 'I'm too tired,' she told

Sandor Gorlinsky.

Maria should have stayed on in London to appear in a television variety show, in the days when there was no such thing as pre-recording, but early the next morning there was a furious row over the telephone with Meneghini over property settlement, and their respective outbursts to the press. 'She began insulting me, and I stood up to her for once,' he recalled. 'She told me, "Be careful, Titta, or I'll turn up at Sirmione one day with a revolver!" "Fine," I yelled back at her, "and when you do, I'll be waiting with a machine-gun!" '

Maria left for Milan that afternoon, and the television show was rescheduled for 3 October, when she sang 'L'altra notte' and 'Si, mi chiamano Mimi' under the baton of Sir Malcolm Sargent. Because the producers refused to submit to the expense of sending out tickets again, there was no audience – just 'canned' applause added by a technician. On 23 October she sang at Berlin's Titania Palast, and a few days later she flew to New York, en route for Kansas City and a concert at Loew's Midland Theatre. Maria had hoped to slip into the country unobserved, but she had made the mistake of discussing her itinerary with Elsa Maxwell. There were wild scenes at Idlewild Airport, and even wilder behaviour from Maria as she was mobbed not by fans, but more reporters and photographers than she had seen in her life, making it impossible for her to cross the tarmac to her waiting car. Not surprisingly she cracked, screaming, 'Lay off me, for Christ sakes!' then, turning on a photographer who exploded a flash-bulb in her face, she spat out, 'Get that thing away from me, or I'll shove it down your fucking throat!'

In Kansas City on 28 October there was more drama when the proceedings were interrupted for forty minutes owing to a bomb scare, thought to have been aimed at ex-President Harry S. Truman, who was in the audience, and to have had nothing to do with Callas detractors. Lawrence Kelly, now representing her in America, had received a call stating that the device, planted somewhere in the orchestra pit, had been timed to explode at 9:30, and Maria was informed just before her performance that the theatre would have to be evacuated. She insisted upon going on stage before this happened to sing the first item on her programme –

'Non mi dir' from Mozart's *Don Giovanni* – just to let the audience see her before Kelly made his announcement. Afterwards she said, 'I *had* to let them see me, otherwise someone would have said, "Ah, that's Callas for you, always cancelling!" '

By this time, Meneghini had filed for legal separation, and although he was hoping to force Maria to return to Brescia for the hearing – this would have meant cancelling at least one of her Dallas *Lucia*s, adding to the dilemma of two performances of *Il Barbiere di Siviglia* which had already been cancelled – Maria's lawyer petitioned the court, and the hearing was postponed until 14 November. The strain of the last weeks was, however, in evidence on 6 November when Maria, already risking credibility by refusing to wear Joan Sutherland's blood-spattered dress – 'The drama should be in the music and in the mind,' she told Lawrence Kelly – sang Zeffirelli's *Lucia*, for she lost control of her voice during the Mad Scene and missed a usually effortless E flat. There was a tremendous intake of breath from the audience, and though after the performance she barged into Laurence Kelly's office and belted out five consecutive, perfect E flats, terrified of taking the risk she omitted them from her performance of 8 November. 'Even so,' concluded the *Dallas Morning News*, 'it was a finer Mad Scene than New York ever heard in her Metropolitan Opera days.' Maria was unconvinced – she never sang the role again.

Six days later, representatives of the world's press congregated in and around the tiny courthouse in Brescia for the Meneghini-Callas hearing. Public sympathy was initially on the side of the 'wronged' husband, who was cheered as he entered the building. A few days before, he had showed reporters some of the letters and cards he had received from well-wishers, telling him that he was doing the right thing in divorcing an adulteress – the press did not see, of course, those letters accusing Meneghini of manipulating, money-grabbing, and of being a 'dirty old man', though the latter accusation was untrue and therefore unjustified. He had also pointed to Tea, one of their poodles which had been left at Sirmione – the other, Toy, was with Maria – and cracked, 'Mark my word, if everything we own has to be split down the middle, we'll have to divide this poodle. Knowing Maria, she will get the front end and

I'll be left with the tail!' By contrast, as Maria stepped out of her car there was a dignified silence. 'She looked serene, like a queen attending the funeral of a child,' wrote one journalist.

The settlement, preceded by a lengthy attempt at reconciliation by the magistrate which neither party was remotely interested in, took six hours to achieve. Maria was allowed to keep the house in Milan, her jewellery and her car, plus half her antiques, porcelain collection, most of her paintings and both her poodles. Meneghini retained the property in Sirmione. But if he had entered the court-house with a view to exposing the names of the several men with whom Maria had been sexually involved over the last few years – not just Onassis, but 'several opera singers and a playboy' – the magistrate, Cesare Andreotti, persuaded him to avoid more trouble and doubtless more court action by persuading him to scrawl 'sepa-ration by mutual consent' across the relevant documents. Under Italian law there was no such thing as divorce, in those days, though Maria could have obtained a divorce from her husband, had she wished, for despite her Italian marriage she had retained American citizenship.

The next day, Onassis's chauffeur drove Maria to the airport, where she boarded the plane for New York, en route for Dallas and the two *Medea*s which represented her final engagements under Meneghini's jurisdiction. 'Battista said that it would have been pointless our living together, unless he had complete power over me,' she told Peter Dragadze of *Life* magazine, an admission which was almost true, adding, 'He put the screws on all the theatres for more money, and said it was *I* who insisted', – which was wholly fictitious, for towards the end of their association, largely on account of Meneghini, but influenced by Elsa Maxwell and acquaintances such as Piaf and Dietrich, and most recently by Maurice Chevalier, Maria had come to realise her true value in pounds and dollars. When Dragadze cautiously pointed this out, she added, 'Yes, that's true, but naturally I wanted to be paid what I felt was my worth, and I never penny-pinched if an important performance or theatre was at stake. I know people say I'm stingy, but I call it careful. My fear has always been to live my old age or to die in poverty.'

On 25 November 1959, four days after Maria's second *Medea*, Tina Onassis sued her husband for divorce and issued a lengthy press statement which concluded that, since his vast wealth had brought happiness to neither of them, her sole concern was not in wrenching more money out of him, but to be left in peace to bring up her children. The divorce papers were served to Onassis on the *Christina*, moored in Monte Carlo, and though Maria was on the yacht, she stayed well out of sight, having been tipped off by Elsa Maxwell that Tina had cited her as co-respondent. In fact, no such thing happened. Until finding her in a 'compromising position' with her husband, Tina had regarded Maria as a dear friend, and her surviving friends have exonerated Maria of deliberately falling for Onassis, maintaining that owing to her naivety she had in all probability been unable to resist his ebullient charms, as had hundreds of other women in the past – dozens of them whilst he had been married to Tina. Most of Onassis's entourage had looked upon Maria as the latest in a never-ending line of money- and power-inspired flings. It has also been suggested that Tina would have divorced Onassis in any case, and that owing to his intense dislike of opera everyone assumed he would soon tire of Maria and drop her for someone else – which, of course, is what did happen.

Having spent three weeks in Meneghini's company, Tina was also convinced that Maria had perhaps suffered enough already, which may explain why she cited a 'Mrs J.R.' as the other woman who had had a 'land and sea' affair with her husband. The J.R. was exposed by the press as Jeanne Rhinelander, a Riviera socialite with whom the Onassises had stayed several times at her house in Grasse – the last time had been during the summer of 1954, when Tina had unexpectedly returned from a shopping trip to find the pair having sex. Rhinelander willingly admitted that the affair *had* taken place, since which time she and Tina had met several times, still as friends, so the press knew that she had been cited as a scapegoat to prevent an even greater scandal. But if Rhinelander was interested in 'setting the record straight', she was to be disappointed, for there was no concrete evidence that the Onassis-Callas romance had progressed beyond the still-alleged flirtation aboard the *Christina*. The yacht's crew had all been vetted and briefed, and paid handsome salaries to ensure discretion, and the mere fact that the Churchills had been present during the first cruise convinced some reporters – stupidly perhaps – that nothing untoward could have taken place. As for the second, more intimate excursion, Onassis himself had freely admitted that he had been taking Maria for a holiday so that she could recover from the breakdown of her marriage. Finally, everyone knew that Meneghini had been a greedy, possessive individual, far too old in years and ideals to tame the spirit of a temperamental, pretty young woman who had fought all her life against humiliation and oppression, and that with or without Onassis, her union with her husband had been doomed for some time.

Now, the couple became shining examples of discretion. Hours after receiving his divorce papers, Onassis had Maria secreted into Monte Carlo's Grand Hotel, and he ensured that the press saw him leaving the palace alone, after dining with Prince Rainier and Princess Grace. That same night, adding credence to Tina's accusation and to draw attention away from Maria, he took Jeanne Rhinelander to the casino. Then, the next day he issued his own statement, to the effect that he had been surprised by his wife's quite unexpected action – adding that he would now do his utmost to effect a reconciliation. This he began doing, and in a bizarre twist which certainly confused the media, whilst he plied Tina with telephone calls and baskets of flowers, Maria returned to Milan – where on her thirty-sixth birthday she was seen entering the Biffi Scala with Meneghini, sparking off more rumours that they would soon be together again. Such a thing, of course, had no chance of ever happening. 'I've made up my mind,' she told a journalist who interrupted her lunch, mindless of her husband's embarrassment. 'There will be no turning back, now.'

On her actual birthday, Maria received two important telephone calls. The first was from Rudolf Bing of the New York Met, apologising for his past indiscretions, and inviting her back again on her own terms, now that she was shot of the troublesome Meneghini. Maria knew, of course, that scandal only bred demand, and was aware that Bing was probably only after her so that he could inflate ticket prices. Placing commerce ahead of artistry, she accepted his apology and told him that she would sing at the Met – but not yet. The second call was from Antonio Ghiringhelli, inviting her – entirely without malice or sarcasm – to Renata Tebaldi's comeback at La Scala. After an absence of some five years, the great soprano was to open the new season with *Tosca*. With equal sincerity, Maria returned the invitation, having scribbled across the bottom of the card, 'Now that Renata Tebaldi is returning to La Scala, public attention should be focused on what is for all of us an important occasion, without direct or indirect interference from me. I hope you will understand, and understand also that I only wish her luck.' It was a wise decision, for Maria was right – the media would have been more interested in *her* personal life than this major point of Tebaldi's career. All the same, it would take Maria's rival another nine years to read what she had said about her.

Maria's first Christmas aboard the *Christina* saw her feeling very disorientated. His children, Alexander and Christina – aged ten and eight respectively – visited only briefly, but soon made it apparent that they would never accept her as their 'stepmother', and Onassis spent much of the festive season on the telephone to Tina. When Maria developed trouble with her sinuses and pains in her right jaw, a condition which was aggravated by singing, he told her, 'Stop yodelling, then.' He had already stopped her from wearing her spectacles in public, although he could hardly see without his, and he had even taken to buying her undergarments and advising her on how to wear her hair. Far worse than this, however, was Maria's exclusion from Onassis's cruise across the Atlantic – because the Churchills had been invited, and he did not wish for a 'repeat performance' of the first cruise, when Maria had spent much of her time screaming at her husband. Her friend Franco Zeffirelli, in whom Maria often confided, maintained that the irregularity of their relationship was Onassis's way of humiliating her, adding, 'Although he had used her fame as a means of increasing his social status, there were occasions when Onassis would decide that it was "improper" for him to be seen with his mistress.'

Maria retreated to the Via Buonarrati, where for several weeks she succumbed to a state of severe depression, dwelling on a future which had never seemed more uncertain. The first thing she observed upon entering the house was the large space on the living room wall – Meneghini had audaciously returned Maria's portrait to Silvano Caselli, and asked for his money back! Exactly how much the painter reimbursed Meneghini is not known: shortly afterwards it was sold to a local businessman, who some years later donated it to the Associazone Maria Callas, who exhibited it in theatres and museums around the world. On 29 January 1996 it was destroyed in the fire which gutted Venice's La Fenice, after which Caselli executed the work again – depicting the famous theatre being consumed by flames in the background.

Meanwhile, when Onassis returned from his latest adventure, aglow with the tidings that Tina had decided to drop her original New York divorce suit, in favour of a 'quickie' divorce from a court in Alabama, he and Maria resumed their relationship. Yet no sooner had she resettled into this renewed pattern of confused well-being – enjoying complete sexual freedom for perhaps the first time ever, yet aware that her career was being forced into taking a back-seat, with no engagements at all for the foreseeable future – than her personal life was delivered another savage blow by the publication of her mother's ghost-written memoirs. *My Daughter, Maria Callas* is now generally regarded as a cheap kiss-and-tell, penned by an old woman who was more interested in revenge for her daughter's alleged ingratitude than she was in speaking the truth. In 1960, however, it attracted the same response as Litza's earlier 'confessions' for *Time* magazine – in other words, few critics were interested in hearing Maria's side of the story, and those who knew it were not in any hurry to offer sympathy, particularly when Litza demanded that all her interviews be conducted in a shabby hotel room in a poor district of New York.

Litza's book was hurtful not just towards Maria, but also towards her husband and other daughter, who strongly criticised Litza for portraying herself as the one who had held the family together, whilst George Callas had done virtually nothing to support them. But the worst part of the book, Jackie concluded, was Litza's pleading of poverty and her famous daughter's stead-fast refusal to help her out. 'I knew full well that my mother was living a reasonably comfortable life and that she was much fêted in the Greek-American community,' Jackie said.

Neither was Litza's book a resounding success. Because Maria had refused to rise to the occasion by entering into a public fracas with her mother – Fleet, the American publisher, had counted on this for publicity – this unimportant, unwarranted exercise in revenge and spite was soon deservedly forgotten.

On 12 May 1960, Maria was shattered by the news of the death in a car-crash of her friend and former lover, Prince Aly Khan, at the age of forty-eight. Yet she had little time for grief when, a few weeks later, the Onassis divorce became absolute. At the beginning of July she flew to London to record an album of arias by Verdi and Rossini. The sessions took place at Watford Town Hall and Kingsway Hall, and were conducted by one of her least favourite musicians, Antonio Tonini. Listening to these recordings today, one is hard put to comprehend why Maria refused EMI permission to release them. Technically and vocally she is in great form. The sessions were abandoned, however, after she had completed just three arias, setting an unfortunate precedent which resulted in her admirers having to wait until after her death to hear some of her finest work.

Maria *was* in poor form a few days later, however – again, the problem lay with badly infected sinuses and a repetition of the migraines she had suffered some years before – when she was forced to cancel a concert in Ostend. Onassis, entirely ignorant of the fact that she *needed* to sing, and that for one as dedicated to her art as she, money could occasionally be a secondary factor, told her, 'I don't know why you keep on torturing yourself like this, when you could so easily retire.'

Now that Onassis was a free man, Maria began living with him openly, as his mistress, aboard the *Christina*. It did not take her long to recover from her latest indisposition, though she may have been casting caution to the winds by spending most of her nights dancing at Monte Carlo's latest night-club, the Maono which, despite its Hawaiian decor and Polynesian-sounding name, was an amalgamation of the couple's names. It was here, on 10 August, that in order to get a persistent journalist off her back, she smiled sweetly and announced, 'Yes, dear, of *course* Ari and I are going to be married!'

... forcing Onassis to declare to the same man the next day, 'She was joking, you fool!'

Onassis's and Maria's friends, Prince Rainier and Princes Grace – both devout Catholics – did not see the funny side of Maria's remark, and the pair were privately told to 'cool it or kindly misbehave beyond the boundaries of the principality'. Therefore in the middle of August they set off on a 'pilgrimage' to Greece, where Maria was to sing two performances of *Norma* with Mirto Picchi and Tullio Serafin in the massive, fourth century BC theatre at Epidaurus, on the North-East Peloponnese – the first time this pantheon of Greek drama had staged an opera, and Maria's first opera performance in her homeland since 1945 when she had been billed Maria Calogeropoulo. She said at the time that the performances, her first stage appearances in nine months, had only been arranged to serve as 'polished, experimental rehearsals' for the recording of *Norma* she was going to make for EMI at the beginning of September – not with Picchi, but with her pal Franco Corelli – and this goes to show, of course, how much she was worried about the increasingly apparent flaws in her voice. However, it was unfair of Picchi to recount to Sergio Segalini, not without a tinge of jealousy now that he was about to be displaced, that the 'first signs of wear' had already been detectable in their 1957 recording of *Medea*.

Onassis gave instructions for the *Christina* to be moored at Glyfada, so as to be close to the theatre. Maria, however, would not stay on the yacht and she was supplied with an apartment only yards from the venue. Here, she was reunited with her father, who was spending his summer holidays with Jackie, still nursing Milton Emberikos, and still no nearer to being reconciled with her sister. In Epidaurus, George and Onassis met for the first time, getting on like the proverbial house on fire – drinking *ouzo* aboard the *Christina* until the early hours of the morning and, according to Maria, swapping stories about the women they had seduced.

Epidaurus was in a remote part of the country, some sixty miles from Athens, an ordeal for the 17,000 spectators who made their way there from all over Greece, for the first night had to be cancelled thirty minutes before the performance, owing to torrential rain. After Maria's death, perhaps by way of an apology for what he had said about her singing, Mirto Picchi recalled how she had walked into his dressing-room, looking rejected, to lay her head against his shoulder. Picchi added, 'She wasn't anything like a tigress, that night, just a feeble woman with no one to turn to in a difficult moment.'

This first performance, which was rescheduled to 24 August, was one of the most memorable Maria ever gave. The proceedings had to be halted for fifteen minutes when she entered the stage – this time there were no political activists, just a healthy, heartrending standing ovation which caused her to burst into tears. The enthusiasm continued throughout the performance, reaching fever-pitch when she sang 'Mira, O Norma' with Kiki Morfoniou, a Greek mezzo-soprano virtually unknown outside her country. At the end of the evening, the tears flowed freely when, eschewing the traditional bouquet, Maria was awarded the supreme honour: a crown of laurel leaves. Four evenings later, after her second *Norma* she donated her $10,000 fee towards the Callas Scholarship Fund for impoverished singers, she was decorated with one of Greece's most prestigious honours, the Medal of Merit.

'I'll be back next year, I promise!' she shouted to her fans, as she was boarding the *Christina*.

For her La Scala comeback on 7 December 1960, after an absence of more than two years, Maria had chosen another forgotten work – Donizetti's *Poliuto* – last performed in Milan two decades before with Gigli and Maria Caniglia – in which she would be singing the non-central role of Paolina, opposite Franco Corelli. It should have been a splendid showcase for her talents, produced by Visconti, with sets by Nicola Benois, based on the designs of the 18th century architect Pietro Gonzaga, who had worked at La Scala before being appointed head set-designer at the imperial theatres in St Petersburg.

Discussing her role with Visconti, Maria had found herself casting aside her fears of singing once more in a major theatre. Being with him soothed her frayed nerves and gave her the self-confidence which, over the last year, had been in decidedly short supply. Visconti, however, was having monumental problems with the

Italian censor. His production of Giovanni Testori's stage play, *L'Arialda* had been denounced obscene and banned, and he had been forced to make what he considered to be unnecessary cuts in his film, *Rocco And His Brothers*, described by one critic as 'an epic of pathos, brutality, murder and collective rape'. Therefore, at the end of his tether, on 16 November he telegraphed an apology to Maria, explaining why he felt compelled to abandon the *Poliuto* project, having sworn never to work again in the Italian state-subsidised theatre, adding, 'It is painful to me, above all because it prevents me from working with you, which is the work that gives me the greatest satisfaction. Although I apologise to you, dear Maria, I am nevertheless sure that you will understand my state of mind and approve of my decision.' Maria wrote back at once: she had been counting the hours until she could begin working with him again, but what upset her most of all was the fact that he was being tormented so. She further criticised the way in which the censors could be allowed to interfere with art, whilst the media were constantly being allowed to get away with messing up people's lives. Her letter ended, portentously, 'Dearest Luchino, I doubt if you and I will *ever* be free of troubles.'

Visconti was replaced at the eleventh hour by Herbert Graf, a producer with whom Maria did not get along. There were further problems when Onassis informed her that he would be personally organising the guest-list, assisted by Elsa Maxwell, who had been flown in especially from New York. If her nerves were not already shot to pieces, they soon would be when she realised that she would be singing in front of Prince Rainier and Princess Grace, the Begum Aga Khan, Marlene Dietrich, just about every major celebrity in Italy, some of the most distinguished and feared critics in the world, and a critical audience of 3,000, some of whom had paid an outrageous $2,000 for tickets from touts. Consolation came from the fact that, as Paolina was far less challenging than any of the 'new' roles she had sung in the past, she was at least certain that there would be no wayward E flats in this one. What she did *not* count on was that the opera would be generally regarded as a vehicle for Franco Corelli, with herself in supporting role, though most of the critics were sympathetic to a degree. Peter Heyworth of the

New York Times knew *exactly* why Maria sounded a little tremulous, and why she sang the four remaining 'Poliutos' better than this one, declaring, 'She is a highly wrought singer, and the feverish excitement that surrounded the evening probably took its toll.' Harold Rosenthal of *Opera*, however, heard only 'an artificial performance by Callas, imitating Callas being Paolina', whilst *High Fidelity*'s H.C. Robbins London thought it best to go straight for the jugular, pronouncing, 'Callas is not what she once was ... In the last act, the critics in the press-box winced, and there was an audible hiss of sympathy from the audience when she flattened – and flattened like a ton of bricks – in several high notes. It was a memorable comeback, but not a flawless one.'

Although this was by no means the end of the road, as many so-called Callas experts have professed, Maria's confidence in her pioneering abilities was shattered. 'When you are working well, life can be sublime. But when you are not, it can be torture,' she said a few weeks later, adding, 'I was very pleased with the first two *Poliuto*s but by the third, I just thought I would die. It went beautifully, but there had been too much tension and one started to pay the price. This is *too* much to ask of an artist, when all *I* ask is the chance to give what I can.'

Henceforth, there would be no more exciting forages into the neglected repertoires of the great bel canto composers.

13

O, Rendeteme La Speme

If you love music truly, you can only feel humble before its infinite potentialities in serving it – perhaps at the cost of never knowing any lasting, consistent happiness.

The Christmas of 1960 was the most miserable of Maria's life, though she tried desperately not to let her emotions surface. She tried her utmost to befriend Onassis's children, stressing that in no way was it her intention to replace their mother – with whom, incredibly, she was still on reasonably friendly terms – but her efforts were in vain. The youngsters blamed her for driving Tina away – *never* their father – and proceeded to make life as difficult as possible for Maria. Because the *Christina* was a large craft, avoiding her was comparatively easy, but if she did speak to them, always with affection, they stuck their tongues out or completely ignored her. She took great pains choosing suitable presents which were left unopened, but the last straw came when Onassis gave his son a motor-boat. Alexander would wait until Maria was rehearsing the arias she planned recording for EMI that spring – then he would rev up his engine and encircle the yacht dozens of times, making as much noise as he could. Christina would then disgust Maria by entering her state room, sticking her fingers down her throat and vomiting on the carpet. 'When I first met Ari's children they seemed such little angels,' Maria later told Roger Normand, 'but only too soon I realised they were obnoxious, evil little demons. Ari would say sometimes that perhaps the odd spanking would not have gone amiss. I only wanted to wring their necks!'

In January 1961, Maria received a visit from Sandor Gorlinsky, now her exclusive representative, with an offer from Rudolf Bing of the New York Met to sing Bellini's little known *Beatrice di Tenda*. By coincidence, Antonio Ghiringhelli offered her the same role but in a better package – with Franco Corelli as her co-star, and with Tullio Serafin conducting. Covent Garden, it is now known, had offered her no fewer than *five* productions: *Don Carlos*, *Il Trovatore*, *Der Rosenkavalier*, *Macbeth* and *Salome*, with David Webster begging Maria, 'Take any one – or all five!' A few days later, she received a telephone call from the film director, Carl Foreman, offering her a huge fee – and apparently not for the first time – to appear opposite Gregory Peck in the film he was about to begin shooting, *The Guns Of Navarone*. She was offered too the lead in the film version of Hans Habe's *The Primadonna*, and whilst she was pondering over this, Lawrence Kelly of Dallas invited her to sing in his new production of Gluck's *Orfeo ed Eurydice*. After consulting Onassis, she turned down every single one of these offers.

Maria was similarly wary about the agreement she had made (but not signed) with the *Sunday Times* at the end of 1960 to serialise her 'memoirs', as she had three years previously with *Oggi*, but minus the fabrications. The journalist chosen to interview her was Derek Prouse, and Maria herself decided upon the location – Monte Carlo's Grand Hotel – though she forgot to tell the establishment that the meeting was going to take place. Subsequently, when Prouse arrived one afternoon in February, the hotel staff declared that she was not there, and it was only after he had thrown a very Callas-like tantrum with the receptionist that a call was put through to her suite, and she remembered their appointment!

'One encounters a friendly, bespectacled American girl mixing a whisky and soda,' was Prouse's first impression of Maria as he was ushered into her suite – and with a man she took to on impulse, yet who admitted to being petrified of her, she was more open than ever before. 'In this present phase of my life,' she told him, 'I am in the process of rediscovering myself, trying to dissociate myself from the spurious image of me which other people have tried to impose. I've always fought to be a normal human being, but I've been unfortunate in having people around me who have done everything to prevent me from being that.'

Maria then spoke of her techniques and methods of tackling new roles, her intense shyness, and her hopeless, seemingly incurable lack of confidence: 'One so easily becomes fearful of not being up to what is expected of one. This is a thing which had made me much misunderstood. When I get angry, sometimes it is rarely with people directly, but with myself. In a way, this is my defence: one is discontented, and takes out on other people what one has against oneself.'

Of her problems with the press, she avowed, 'Certain newspapers and certain people have created a picture of me as a woman who thrives on wild scenes. When I go for a walk I don't want to be constantly aware of Callas the singer. Callas? Yes, she sang and she's fine, but please leave her to walk along the street like a normal human being. We need that atmosphere of relaxation for our singing, for our mental stability.'

She also defended her relationships with the great opera houses, saying, 'I've had good relationships in most theatres I've worked in. It's a pity that good relationships are never the ones to make the headlines.'

She was however dismissive of 'modern' opera singers: 'Unfortunately, opera has gone from bad to worse. I come from the old routine where we rehearsed a lot. Nowadays, many artists don't care to rehearse. They just want to arrive shortly before the performance, get their money, do the job and get on to the next place. It's a way of earning quick money, but when money comes in, art goes out.'

Finally, she stressed the importance of the prima donna, telling Prouse, 'The position of prima donna in a company carries great responsibility. It should signify discipline. *We* have to set an example. *We* have to be punctual at rehearsals, then the chorus respects us and works with more pleasure!'

Derek Prouse walked out of Maria's suite that afternoon,

shaking only slightly less than when he had entered it, yet enriched by having met his idol in the not-so-terrifying flesh. In the lobby he scribbled on his pad, 'One's final impression is of a lonely woman, immensely spirited and utterly dedicated to her musical world: alternately gay and wretched, relentlessly determined to impose her own conceptions of her work, even though fully aware that the perfection which alone could satisfy her is "not of this world".'

Shortly after her interview with Derek Prouse, Maria went to Paris to record her first album for Pathé-Marconi. The director, Michel Glotz, had recently introduced her to the conductor Georges Prêtre, with whom there had been an immediate rapport. 'He was a man of my own heart,' she told Roger Normand. 'With Georges I could curse to my heart's content, and he never so much as batted an eyelid. Most of my conductors only wanted to take me to dinner after we'd finished working. This one, a Black Belt, wanted me to take judo lessons!'

Callas à Paris, recorded intermittently over a two-week period, was an innovation, a kick in the teeth for those critics who were only too eager to write Maria off. It featured eleven arias from French operas, sung in French: *Alceste, Carmen, Samson and Delilah, Romeo and Juliet, Mignon* and *Le Cid* traditionally were roles associated with the mezzo-soprano – and, thrown in for good measure, was a sublime 'J'ai perdu mon Eurydice' from Gluck's *Orphée et Eurydice*.

Whilst she was in Paris, Maria decided that it was time to put down new roots, and with hardly any deliberation at all she settled on an apartment at 44 Avenue Foch, in the fashionable area known as L'Étoile. The idea to rent in this part of the city came from Onassis, whose own apartment was at Number 88 – not that she spent much time there once the place had been redecorated and furnished, for as soon as the Pathé-Marconi recording sessions were over she rejoined Onassis on the *Christina*. The couple set off on another cruise, returning at the end of May for Maria to sing in a concert at London's St James's Palace, accompanied at the piano by Sir Malcolm Sargent, in aid of the Edwina Mountbatten Fund. Then, yet another cruise. But, was all this pleasure-seeking really to the detriment of her vocal abilities, as has been frequently suggested? Maria clearly did not think so, as she explained to Derek Prouse, 'I prepare much more in the mind instead of grinding away endlessly at exercises to achieve something that a few minutes' work, in the right spirit of mind, can bring about effortlessly.'

In August 1961, as she had promised, Maria returned to Epidaurus for two performances of *Medea* – the brainchild of Alexis Minotis, who was now able to realise a dream by transferring his Dallas production of Cherubini's opera to this sacred temple of ancient Greek drama. Maria was unbelievably relaxed with the cast. She loved working with Jon Vickers, who again sang the role of Jason, and she had tremendous respect for Kiki Morfoniou. She also broke with tradition by allowing selected friends to sit in on some of the rehearsals, and this time there was no interference from Onassis, who was attending a business meeting in Alexandria – one which had been deliberately timed to coincide with the 6 August première, for he was becoming increasingly intolerant of having to stand in the shadow of Maria's sun.

The first Epidaurus *Medea* gave Maria the largest audience of her career. The 17,000 tickets for the event had sold out in just two days, mindless of the fact that the venue was miles from the nearest civilization, and an estimated 10,000 additional spectators gathered in the hills around the amphitheatre to hear her, in a superlative performance which was, of course, governed by the location: *Medea* is set in Corinth, in the Epidaurus district. Maria herself had chosen her guests of honour, which included the Greek Prime Minister and almost his entire Cabinet, Prince Rainier and most of Monaco's *haute société*, Antonio Ghiringhelli and David Webster, Melina Mercouri, Elsa Maxwell and George Callas. 'Seldom in recent years has Callas been in such excellent form,' declared Trudy Goth of *Opera News*, adding, 'Few singers with steadier top notes could approach her for dramatic impact, musicianship (style and phrasing), the unfailingly right coloration of voice and body movement that she brings to the role, having made it so much her own.' And at the end of the performance, Maria took seventeen curtain-calls.

Jackie Callas had not been invited to the première of *Medea*, though Maria had wanted her there, because someone had told her that her mother was going to be in Athens for the summer holidays. When she discovered this not to be true, and when Onassis cabled to say that he would be arriving in Glyfada in time for the second *Medea* of 13 August, she asked her sister – whom she had not seen for nine years – to dine with her at a plush society restaurant, close to which the *Christina* would be moored.

Jackie was naturally very apprehensive about meeting Maria after such a lengthy, enforced separation, and particularly in front of so many eminent people – although Onassis would not be in the restaurant, several important business associates would be there and so too would Elsa Maxwell. Also, although she had read all the newspaper articles about her sister and seen the accompanying photographs, Jackie was still shocked by the change in her appearance. 'Her hands were long and she used them with a sense of drama,' she remembered in her memoirs, 'and I suddenly realised that I didn't know this woman at all. Here I was standing and waiting to be introduced to a total stranger. The Maria I had last seen, the Maria I knew, was fat and awkward, ill-tempered and greedy. Here was this vision of refined elegance.'

Initially, the reconciliation went well. After the meal, Maria took Jackie aboard the *Christina*, where she was introduced to Onassis and given a guided tour of the yacht which, according to Jackie, Maria said she was starting to tire of, with its ever-attendant lackeys and chronic lack of privacy. A few evenings later, Jackie accompanied George Callas to the second *Medea*, the $10,000 fee for which Maria had again donated to the Callas Scholarship. She recalled, 'She acted with her whole being. Even the sandals on her feet seemed to project the role.'

The rot set in the next day, however, at a luncheon party at the Glyfyda home of Onassis's sister, Artemis, when one of the guests asked Jackie why she had suddenly abandoned her own singing career, particularly as she was reputed to have such a good voice. Before Jackie could answer for herself, Maria shouted across the table, 'Singing is for *young* people. It needs years of study, not the braying of a donkey. You a *voice*! Do you want me to start breaking dishes?' Although Maria apologised for this outburst soon afterwards, but only after the other guests were gone, Jackie instinctively knew that henceforth they would remain little more than strangers. 'I felt sorry for her,' she said. 'She was so wrapped up in her daily worries, no one except she and Onassis existed.'

In November 1961, Onassis accompanied Maria to London, where she was to record an album of arias by Bellini, Rossini and Donizetti. During her stay in the British capital she was pestered by reporters who wanted to know how she felt about Tina Onassis's recent marriage to the Duke of Marlborough's son, the Marquess of Blandford – and she was far from satisfied with the recording sessions, allowing only one of the six arias, 'Sorgete' from *Il Pirata*, to be released in her lifetime. At the end of the month she returned to Milan, where she was to sing the Minotis production of *Medea* – supported by a formidable cast which again included Jon Vickers singing Jason, along with her friend Giulietta Simionato and the great Bulgarian bass, Nicolai Ghiaurov.

The *Medea* première took place on 11 December (this year, the main feature was Verdi's *La Battaglia di Legnano*, with Franco Corelli), with all the usual hissing and booing from the galleries without which, at La Scala in particular, no Callas performance would have been complete. Vocally, Maria was not at her best, though in such a dramatic, active role, the odd off-key note was only to be expected. 'What if her voice *is* a bit frayed and wobbly at times?' posed Trudy Goth of *Opera News*. 'It *still* retains all the lyric intensity, the emotional inflections and nuances, the dramatic projection that no singer of her time can equal.'

There were also moments during the performance when, much to the delight of the Callas Boys, the actress and the character became as one. In the first act aria, 'Del tuoi figli la madre', when Medea is begging Jason to return to her as her husband, she pronounces of herself, 'Tu lo sai quanto un giorno t'amo, crudel!' (You know how much she once loved you, cruel man), the last word, which is repeated several times, was on this occasion spat out with all the venom she possessed at the whistlers in one of the galleries. A moment later, when she sang the line, 'Ho dato tutto a te!' (I give up everything for you) – she raced up to the footlights and shook her fists at them. 'It was my polite way of saying, "Fuck the lot of you!" ' she told Roger Normand.

What the press and public did not know was that Maria ploughed through two of her three *Medeas* in abject agony, on account of her sinuses which became so badly affected that on 15 December, five days before her final performance, she booked herself into a clinic for an operation which, without anaesthetic, was even more painful than the condition itself. She was further distressed when Onassis called to say that he was too busy to visit her, fuelling rumours already circulating with the press that they were on the verge of splitting up – rumours which were exacerbated by Onassis, boasting to gossipy friends such as Elsa Maxwell, that wooing and conquering Callas had been infinitely more thrilling than the prospect of having to spend the rest of his life with her – and with Maria fervently praying for those things she wanted more than anything in the world: a marriage licence and a baby.

These rumours were temporarily scotched when the couple spent Christmas in Monte Carlo, this time without the Onassis children, though they only resurfaced when Onassis failed to turn up at Maria's 27 February 1962 concert at London's Festival Hall, an event which was most unfairly butchered by the critics. Wearing an unusual black tube-skirt and pink top – 'looking every inch the serpent of old Nile,' commented the *Daily Mail*'s Charles Reid – she opened with Weber's 'Ocean, thou mighty monster', which she had not performed in public for twelve years. 'Most of her notes above the stave had so pronounced a wobble that one could count the number of beats to the bar,' Reid continued, adding, 'But no matter. The audience roared approval.' This was proved to be but a repetition of the press condemnation which had followed Maria's Edinburgh Festival *Sonnambula*, for the critics were again made to look foolish when the performance appeared on a pirated album: though Maria does sound slightly tremulous during the opening aria and the subsequent 'Pleurez mes yeux' from Massenet's *Le Cid*, the remainder of the recital lacks none of the familiar Callas sparkle.

Maria's *chevalier-servant*, replacing Onassis during this trip to London, was Panaghis Vergottis, a sixty-nine-year-old shipowner friend of his whom she had first met at the Dorchester party in

1959. Tall and aristocratic, well-mannered and educated, he was a direct contrast to the vulgar, worldly Onassis, but much more importantly, Vergottis was passionate about opera. He also had a great fondness for the ladies, for though he had never married, Vergottis is reputed to have had at least fifty mistresses in the thirty years that he had been a multi-millionaire, most of this time living in a suite at the Ritz. The first time Maria visited this, she was astonished by its air of impersonality – there were no ornaments, photographs and personal effects, and Vergottis told her that his most prized possession, an oriental carpet given to him by a friend some years before, was lying in the bottom of the hotel's store-room, still wrapped in the polythene it had been delivered in. One cannot be certain if Vergottis was ever at any time Maria's lover – though some friends have maintained that with her fondness for 'men of a certain age', anything would have been possible. What she actually said, some years later, after their acrimonious split, was, 'I had the great joy of considering Panaghis more than my father. I was very happy with our relationship. He knew that and he considered me *his* greatest joy. He was very proud to travel around and participate in my glory – and I am not trying to be funny.'

After her performance, Vergottis escorted Maria to the supper-party held in her honour at the Savoy, where the invited press were surprised to find her refusing a platter of food – only to walk around the room, picking titbits from the plates of the other guests, a trait she had acquired during her first cruise aboard the *Christina* when she had leaned over Clementine Churchill's shoulder and filched her fillet steak, cooing, 'Well, dear, it'll only make you fat!' At midnight, she entered the Savoy's weekly 'Twist' competition – against Margot Fonteyn – and won. The next day, she lunched at the hotel with Lord and Lady Harewood, Walter Legge, Sandor Gorlinsky, and Olga Franklyn of the *Daily Mail* who asked her, point blank, 'Madame Callas, do you ever fear that you are losing your magnificent voice, as the critics are saying?' Her mouth full of food, Maria turned on her and snarled, 'I *never* discuss what people are saying or writing about me. Besides, my reviews are *so* lousy of late that I don't have to bother reading them to know what people are saying! Drink your wine dear, and shut up!' The next morning,

Franklyn observed in her column, 'Miss Callas, in my opinion, need never worry about her *voice*. Her *personality* will see her through.'

Maria was not the only famous soprano visiting London that week, for her rival-of-sorts, Joan Sutherland, was currently rehearsing Franco Zeffirelli's acclaimed production of Handel's *Alcina* – a role with which she had already delighted audiences in Dallas and Venice – at Covent Garden. Comparisons between the two were of course only inevitable, particularly considering the comments the pair had made about each other – Sutherland unable to praise Maria enough, whilst Maria offered such quips as, 'Sutherland at Covent Garden? *That* should please the canary-fanciers!' The *Sunday Times'* J.W. Lambert, who had amused Maria by calling her a 'blacksmith', and her voice 'an anvil which she uses expertly to mould her nuances and phrases,' aptly summed them up.

> When Callas sings, shooting stars blaze across the storm-racked sky, fireworks hiss and roar and send cascading lights down over the astonished earth. When Sutherland sings, sunlight glitters, now gentle, now diamond-sharp, upon the morning-fresh cascades of Elysian fountains.

Antonio Ghiringhelli inadvertently fanned the flames of dissension by calling Maria, whilst she was in London, and proposing that she and Sutherland should sing together in the production of Meyerbeer's *Les Huguenots*, which was to be the highlight of that year's Milan Fair. 'No dice,' was the firm reply.

On 12 March, Maria and Georges Prêtre flew to Munich to begin a four-date tour of Germany which almost ended in disaster when she cracked a contact lens and this became lodged in the corner of her eye, causing an infection. She had taken to wearing them because of Onassis's taunts of 'four-eyes' each time she put on her forbidden spectacles – absolutely essential when she was at the piano or reading scores. George Prêtre immediately took her to a clinic, where a doctor told her that she had been lucky not to have suffered permanent damage by trying to get the lens out without medical assistance. The contact lenses were thrown away, and

Maria went back to wearing spectacles – though she usually carried them around in her hand when she was with Onassis, putting them on only when he was not looking.

In Munich, Maria met Fritz Wunderlich, then one of the leading lights with the Bavarian State Opera, and regarded as *the* German-speaking Mozart and *lieder*-interpreter of his day. Maria told the young tenor that she had always admired his Tamino, and likewise he confessed that he had always wanted to work with her. But here lay the problem. Wunderlich, fiercely proud of his Palatinate dialect, hardly ever sang in Italian, and Maria loathed the German language. 'It reminds me of the rough time the Nazis gave us in Athens during the war,' she once told an accompanist friend (Robert Sutherland) who tried to get her interested in *lieder*. Four years later, she would be distressed to hear the news of Wunderlich's death, at just thirty-five, following a fall. 'If only he might have compromised, just the once,' she said tearfully, though she could of course have asked herself the same question.

In April 1962, and very reluctantly, Maria recorded three arias for EMI in London, including a definitive version of 'Ocean, thou mighty monster'. Her friends, including Lord Harewood, had tried desperately not to let her see the reviews, albeit biased, of the Festival Hall concert, but Walter Legge now showed her a newspaper clipping. Distressed by the way in which the Weber aria had been denounced, quite unnecessarily, she told Legge that she would not give permission for the new recording to be issued, adding, 'And you might as well dispose of the others, too.' Again, these beautiful pieces were consigned to the vault.

On 26 April, whilst Maria was in London – as if she did not already feel bad enough – she received word of another of her mother's attempts to gain public sympathy, at the expense of her daughter's reputation. Having spent the morning shopping in downtown New York for meaningful little gifts for friends, and for relatives who could not abide her, Litza had scribbled a note for Maria and another for the press before swallowing a large number of barbiturates, and she had been admitted to the Roosevelt Hospital. When Maria was told by a hospital spokesman that Litza had confessed to calling an ambulance *before* taking the tablets, she bawled down the telephone, 'I've half a mind to sue you for not letting the evil old bitch die!' She then insisted that her mother be seen by the hospital's resident psychiatrist, and if possible be committed to an asylum without delay!

Litza was indeed examined, but allowed to go home when she told the psychiatrist that Maria was coming to New York in the middle of May, and that she had promised to look after her. This was of course only wishful thinking, and Maria told Roger Normand, 'The only time I'll ever want to see my fucking mother is when she's lying in her box, and then it'll be to make sure she's dead!'

The visit to the city of her birth was brief. Maria participated in a gala concert at the Madison Square Garden on 19 May, staged to celebrate President Kennedy's forty-fifth birthday. The show remains infamous because during it Marilyn Monroe – by this time such a mental and physical wreck on account of her personal dramas and addiction to pills that she was not expected to turn up, and when she did she was announced as 'the late Marilyn Monroe' – sang a sexy, giggly *Happy Birthday, Mr President*. Maria sang two arias from *Carmen* – the 'Habañera' and the 'Séguedille' to 18,000 people, her largest ever *paying* audience. When many years later it emerged that Monroe and Kennedy had been having an affair at the time, people tended to forget that there had been others on the bill besides Marilyn, and only this is seen in the documentaries, which is a shame. Afterwards Maria was introduced to Kennedy and his wife, Jackie. She told a friend, ironically perhaps, 'He's very handsome, in a rugged sort of way – but there's something about *her* that I definitely don't like.'

14

E un Serto Ebb'Io di Spine

'Professionally, the world of Maria Callas has become a lonely world of a woman looking for her voice, and seeking perfection in her art. She has everything else in a way and only her art remains a challenge.'

During the summer of 1962, Maria's voice began deteriorating so rapidly that the critics, and Maria herself, came to the conclusion that if her magnificent career was not already over, it soon would be. The major source of her problem, however, lay not with her vocal cords, but with the recurring sinus infection which had begun affecting her right jaw, preventing her resonance chambers from working correctly and also affecting her hearing – in short, she was striving too hard to attain her top notes, and going off-key because she could not hear them. This was very evident at La Scala on 23 May – in what would be her penultimate appearance in the theatre she often referred to as 'my second home' – just four days after she had sung so beautifully in the Kennedy concert, whilst she was making her entrance as Medea. During her opening line 'Io? Medea!' (I? Medea!), her voice broke down completely and there was a storm of disapproval from the galleries which immediately filled her with terror.

Maria later said that it had been the most harrowing evening of her life, yet with Herculean strength and nerve she soldiered on to the end of the performance making few noticeable mistakes – and if some critics remarked on her 'sudden nasal qualities', by the skin of her teeth, she was *still* the Great Callas. 'Dramatically, she left no doubt who remains the outstanding figure on the operatic stage,' declared *Opera News*. This was certainly true, though even the least critical of the experts, her friend Lord Harewood, could see that there was something radically wrong. However, he waited until after Maria's death before saying what it was – more's the pity, for other friends have said that it would have helped her to have known a few home truths. Writing in the *Evening Standard* in November 1989, he observed:

> It was evident that her voice had deteriorated markedly. It had become very ragged. Being at sea with Onassis in his boat can't have helped, and she took rather less care of herself that she ought to have done. Too many parties, that sort of thing. The audience booed, and you felt that this wonderful career was coming to an end. But I thought that she still had great power, a tremendous grandeur about everything she did. In spite of everything, she never lost that.

Shortly after her second *Medea*, Maria had another operation to remove the pus from her sinuses, and hopefully alleviate some of the excruciating pain. The operation was a success, and so as not to overtire herself she spent the next five months as a virtual recluse, in seclusion aboard the *Christina*, seeing only her closest friends and emerging only to host the odd reception or party. On 25 September she attended Edith Piaf's final gala performance in Paris – a concert from the top of the Eiffel Tower for the première of the film, *The Longest Day*. The concert was preceded by a banquet in the Palais de Chaillot gardens, where Maria was photographed with the Shah of Iran, Queen Sophia of Greece ... and another Greek, Piaf's devilishly handsome fiancé, Théo Sarapo. Two evenings later, Piaf and Sarapo were opening a new season at the Olympia, and Maria was naturally invited. Unfortunately, Maurice Chevalier's one-man show at the Théatre des Champs-Elysées was opening that same evening, so Maria decided whom to see by tossing a coin. Chevalier won.

On 4 November, Maria and George Prêtre flew to London, where she was that week's 'surprise' guest in Lew Grade's Sunday night television show, *Golden Hour*, broadcast live from the stage of Covent Garden. She sang 'Tu che le vanita' from *Don Carlos* and the 'Habañera' and 'Séguedille' from Bizet's *Carmen* in a production which, according to Covent Garden's General Director Sir John Tooley, was a trial from start to finish. 'The combination of her nerves and the tenor's tummy upset almost wrecked the show,' he remembered, adding, 'With some ingenuity and by several strokes of good fortune the show went on, but for the only time in my life I welcomed commercial breaks, which were moved around to fill awkward moments as we endeavoured to get our performers on.'

There had also been a minor drama, the subject of which was displayed by 'before' and 'after' shots in several newspapers the next day, at a time when such things were considered by journalists to be more in the public's interest than Maria's voice. This was when the pendant she was wearing fell off during her first aria. She gave absolutely no indication that she knew she had lost it, yet with what can only be described as intuitive stagecraft, in spite of her myopia, it had been retrieved and replaced by the end of the performance with no effect on continuity.

This television appearance brought Maria a flood of offers from around the world to sing *Carmen*, which she wisely turned down. Although most of the critics were of the opinion that she was over her vocal crisis, Maria knew that they had based their assumptions on just three arias, and that singing a complete opera in costume would be another matter entirely. Also, soon after the London show she was hospitalised with severe abdominal pains – the surgeon who examined her diagnosed a hernia near her appendix, and after operating on her successfully warned her that she could suffer a relapse unless she refrained from singing full-voice for at least two months because of the damage the hernia had done to her stomach muscles – as essential a part of her singing apparatus as her vocal cords.

1963 dawned with yet more antagonism from Maria's mother. This year, Litza was to celebrate her sixtieth birthday and, according to American law, she was no longer elegible for the $250 welfare payment she had been getting each month – no great problem, for Litza simply declared herself destitute and took advantage of another regulation which stipulated that the children of 'down-and-outs' were responsible for supporting them. Initially, Maria was all for ignoring the writ served against her US earnings, but when her lawyer warned her that this would only result in a repetition of the Bagarozy case – in other words, she would be arrested the moment she set foot on American soil *and* have to face Litza in the dock – she capitulated.

To Maria's delight, the New York court fixed a monthly subsistence payment of just $200, $50 a month less than Litza had been getting from the state. Also, one of the conditions for her getting any money at all was that she should refrain from any kind of work – including 'personal appearances on radio, television and any medium likely to promote any relationship to Maria Callas, for which undertaking, after a probationary period of six months, the aforementioned Miss Callas will increase this allowance'. The allowance was of course never increased, because Litza was wholly incapable of keeping her vendetta against her daughter to herself. Not long afterwards, when the editor of the Italian magazine *Gente* asked Maria if she had anything to add in the way of defence after Litza's latest 'exclusive', she replied caustically, 'Only that my mother represents the very worst kind of cancer.'

Having begun badly, 1963 continued as a year of indecision and cancellations. Maria had arranged to sing in a new production of *Il Trovatore* at Covent Garden, to be directed by Visconti, and the première had been set for 28 February. She had also been contracted to sing *La Traviata* at the Paris Opera in April, and Antonio Ghiringhelli had proposed two roles: Countess Almaviva in Mozart's *Le Nozze di Figaro*, and the title-role in Monteverdi's *L'Incoronazione di Poppea*. She cancelled everything but the London *Trovatore*, which was postponed until later in the year and *then* cancelled.

Maria did appear in six concerts: Berlin, Düsseldorf, Stuttgart, London, Paris and Copenhagen – between 17 May and 9 June. With the exception of Paris, she sang an identical programme each evening of bel canto arias, supplemented with Musetta's 'Quando m'en vo' from *La Bohème* and, from Puccini's *Gianni Schicchi*, the aria which henceforth would be regarded as her 'theme-song' and used mostly as a curtain-call, 'O mio babbino caro'. Oddly, again apart from her Paris concert, she did not sing any of the lovely French arias – from *Faust, Iphigénie en Tauride, Manon, Werther* and *Les Pêcheurs de Perles* – which she had recently recorded with Georges Prêtre. This would be her last album produced by Walter Legge, who was to retire from his post with EMI early the next summer. By all accounts, discussions had also taken place with Legge for a recording of Verdi's *Requiem Mass* with Maria, Elisabeth Schwarzkopf and Nicolai Ghiaurov, to be conducted by Carlos Maria Guilini. Maria's part in the recording was, however, now given to Christa Ludwig, as a result of which she is said never to have spoken to Legge – or his wife – again.

The tour was a resounding success, with each venue selling out only hours after the box-offices opened. Vocally, she had improved considerably, though she was by no means the Callas of old, which the critics now declared – correctly perhaps – had more to do with her sylph-like figure than lack of rehearsal and abstention from the concert platform. 'The flirtation with the mezzo repertory seems to have abandoned, and we are now back with the soprano roles,' wrote *Opera's* Harold Rosenthal, adding, 'But the breath control is less perfect than it was. One only feels that this slim little figure just cannot meet all the demands the singer puts on the voice.'

Maria returned to the *Christina*, and an idle summer. During a cruise around the Ionian Sea, she and Onassis spent several days on Ithaca, the mythical birthplace of Odysseus which, he told her, he had always wanted to own, along with its 60,000 inhabitants. Such a goal, of course, could only ever have been achieved in his sailor's dreams, though soon afterwards he did settle for what he considered to be the next best thing when the 350-acre island of Skorpios, ten miles north of Ithaca, was put on the market. The tycoon spent just a few hours walking amongst its olive groves, declared that he would build a replica of the Cretan Palace of Knossos on its summit, then signed the papers.

At around the time of Onassis's latest extravagance, Meneghini applied to the court in Brescia to have the terms of their separation order revoked, so that Maria alone would be held responsible for the break-up of their marriage. He had made a similar plea at the beginning of the year, claiming that his wife's 'adulterous behaviour' had blackened the Meneghini name. It had been rejected, and so was this one. Not to be outdone, Meneghini invited the press to Sirmione and informed them that Onassis had 'dumped' Maria and was having an affair with Jackie Kennedy's sister, Princess Lee Radziwill, whose husband, Stanislas, was one of the tycoon's closest friends. This was not true. Although the Radziwills had spent a great deal of time aboard the *Christina* of late, Onassis was still very much in love with Maria, though since wooing her completely away from Meneghini he had not remained faithful to her, nor she to him. In America, however, press reports of the Onassis-Radziwill 'romance' were taken very seriously – particularly when the rumour began circulating that Lee was about to divorce her husband, marry Onassis, and make him the brother-in-law of the President. Jack Kennedy's brother, Robert, about to embark on a crucial political campaign, publicly voiced his opinion, telling Congress, 'We don't want any Greeks in the White House, especially one who has been accused of defrauding the American government out of millions of dollars.' Kennedy then sent a personal message to Lee Radziwill, advising her that if she knew what was good for her, she would leave the *Christina* at once and return to Washington. This she did, but for reasons which were purely personal: Jackie had given birth to a premature baby, Patrick, who had died the next day, and Lee flew to her bedside to comfort her. A few days later, she rejoined her husband and Onassis, and as soon as the latter heard how ill and depressed Jackie was – mindless of Maria's protests, and those of the Kennedys – he invited her to join him for a cruise around the Greek Islands when she was well enough to travel. Jackie shocked her family by accepting, whilst Onassis offered a lame excuse to the press that his reasons for inviting Jackie aboard the *Christina* were entirely platonic. He added that, in any case, she would be well chaperoned not just by the Radziwills, but by a host of society friends including Frank Roosevelt, the American Under-Secretary of Commerce.

Few swallowed the story – particularly when, as soon as Jackie arrived in Athens, Maria left in a huff for Paris.

Over the next two weeks, sulking in her Avenue Foch apartment, and not without reason, Maria studied the newspaper and television reports of the cruise. With America's First Lady as Onassis's special guest, no expense had been spared: eight varieties of caviar, a Swedish masseur and two hairdressers, and an orchestra should she feel like dancing. Maria was most upset when she saw film footage of the yacht's visits to some of the places where Onassis had taken her, four years previously, including Smyrna. When the couple were photographed dancing cheek-to-cheek, however, it was President Kennedy's turn to be incensed, so much so that he called his wife and demanded that she return to Washington. When this instruction was ignored, and when Maria saw pictures of her 'rival' wearing the $500,000 diamond and ruby necklace Onassis had given her as a parting gift on the final day of the cruise, she truly believed that she had lost him.

The cruise ended in the middle of October, when Maria and Onassis were reunited in Monte Carlo. Four weeks later, he left for a business conference in Hamburg and it was here, on 22 November 1963, that he learned of Jack Kennedy's assassination. Without even bothering to call Maria, he flew straight to Washington to help console the grieving widow. Onassis not only participated in the wake, deeply offending some members of the dead president's clan – upon Jackie's insistence he stayed in a suite at the White House and advised her how to add the 'finishing touches' to the funeral, the event which elevated the Kennedys to royal family status more than anything the President had done in his two years and ten months in office. The black 'royal' veils worn by Jackie, the gun-carriage use to convey his casket, the burial at Arlington's National Cemetery for the dead of the American wars (as opposed to the Kennedy plot in Boston), the Eternal Flame copied from that under the Arc de Triomphe, the erection of the JFK Memorial Library in Boston, and even the re-naming of New York's Idlewild airport were all joint-stage-managed by Jackie and Onassis, taking advantage of the country's profound sorrow and state of shock.

Maria, on the eve of her fortieth birthday and lonelier than ever, now turned to the only solace she had ever been allowed to rely on – her career. 'If I don't have my work, what do I do from morning till night?' she had asked Derek Prouse, as if peering into the near future. 'I've always been active in my life, and I have no children. Now, more or less, I haven't even got a family. What do I do if I don't have my career? I can't just play cards or gossip. I'm not the type.'

Maria flung herself back into her work with a vengeance. She had decided, virtually on the spur of the moment, to record a second album of Verdi heroines, *and* to complete the albums she had attempted to record in London with Antonio Tonini. Therefore, having flatly refused to have anything to do with this conductor, and as Georges Prêtre was tied up with other engagements, Nicola Rescigno was summoned from Chicago. The first session took place in Paris on 4 December – between this date and 24 April 1964 she would record twenty-seven arias from works as diverse as Verdi's *Aroldo* and *Attila* to Donizetti's *Lucretia Borgia*, of which only two were not released during her lifetime.

Maria's saving grace, at the beginning of 1964, was a call from Franco Zeffirelli, ostensibly enquiring about her health. Zeffirelli was at Covent Garden, directing *Rigoletto*, and he later confessed that he would never have got around to speaking about work, had he not detected a note of despair within her voice indicative that all was not well in her relationship with Onassis, something he had suspected during a recent visit to the *Christina* when it had been moored in Venice. 'Maria's desperate adoration of Onassis only brought out the worst in him', Zeffirelli would recall. 'He treated her as badly as he could. There was no limit to his sadism. He persistently humiliated her in front of their friends, and showed absolutely no sign of asking her to marry him.'

Now, all Zeffirelli had to do was *suggest* that maybe a comeback was all Maria needed to shrug off her depression, and that it had always been a dream of his to direct her in *Tosca*, opposite Tito Gobbi's definitive Scarpia. Without hesitation, Maria told him that she would do it, but only if the production could take place within the next few weeks. It took David Webster of Covent Garden just five minutes to agree that it would, providing Maria agreed to accept his choice of conductor. He came up with a nervous young Italian, Carlo Felice Cillario, who later confessed that Maria had been so worried about his possible reluctance to work with her on account of her 'capricious' behaviour that, before meeting him, she had 'ensured safe passage' by sending him a letter which had concluded, 'Please do not believe the rumours that I am a monster and a terrible woman. I am only interested in one thing: making music well. That is the one goal that I have.'

The next day, Franco Zeffirelli flew to Paris for an emotional reunion with his friend. Maria told him that, in anticipation of a big break, she had been rehearsing solidly each day for weeks, and even showed him photographs of her sitting at the piano. 'I let her go on for a while,' he recalled, 'then I examined her hands. Her nails were long and immaculately painted. She hadn't touched that piano for weeks'. Maria's excuse, once she had been 'sprung', was that she had *meant* to rehearse, but that she had been too preoccupied with putting her personal life in order to dwell too much on her work.

This was of course true. Formerly, Maria had been so obsessed with her career that everything not directly connected to it, not least of all personal happiness, had been remorselessly shunted aside. Now, her sole concern was hanging onto a man who, time and time again, had proved himself entirely undeserving of her affection. Zeffirelli was also able to draw comparisons between Onassis and Scarpia, Tosca's protagonist. 'I explained how I saw the relationship between Tosca and Scarpia as the key to the dramatic structure of the opera,' he said. 'Far from hating Scarpia, Tosca is mysteriously attracted to his power and cruelty. In the end she kills him not merely to save her lover, but to save herself from herself. I stopped myself from saying it was not unlike her own feelings for Onassis. Then I asked her what her reactions would be to a man like that, and she nodded. She had seen exactly who Scarpia was.'

The rehearsals were initially relaxed, and for once were interrupted not by tantrums, but by raucous laughter from Tito Gobbi, who amused Maria with his dry sense of humour and made her feel alive again, particularly when he told her what he had devised for

Scarpia's murder scene: Tosca was to be grabbed by the wrists, bent backwards over the table and almost raped before escaping to kill him. It was no secret that in *his* lovemaking, Onassis enjoyed agression, and Maria once admitted, albeit jokingly, that she would have loved to have seen the expression on his face, had she suddenly drawn a dagger! And yet, Maria added her own cold, calculating twist to the tale, supporting the fact that Tosca's revenge was no mere impulsive action – breaking free of this foul man, she pours herself a glass of water, gulps it down and, as Scarpia comes for her from behind, she turns suddenly and plunges the blade into his heart. A masterpiece!

As the 21 January première of *Tosca* drew nearer, almost five years since she had sung an opera on the London stage, so Maria began falling apart. The tickets for the six performances had all been sold in record time, with some fans queuing for forty-eight hours in sub-zero temperatures for the cheapest seats. Franco Zeffirelli and Tito Gobbi never stopped reminding her that, vocally, she was at her most supreme – also that her Cavaradossi, Renato Cioni, was the handsomest tenor she had ever worked with. Maria was not sure what to believe about her voice, though she certainly fell for the young tenor in a big way. Cioni, however, did not feel the same way about her, and once more she found herself leaning on an older man for moral and spiritual support – though Gobbi was only ten years her senior. Many years later he wrote in his memoirs, 'To a creature of Maria's sensibility, it must have been sheer torture. There are few more appalling ordeals than making a stage comeback when you are headline news. Mercilessly caught in the crossfire of public searchlights, you hang there suspended for all to observe and criticise.'

Maria's nerves became so bad that her doctor prescribed tranquillisers, once the production reached the costumes stage, in order to get her to sing. She was in such a state during one of the dress-rehearsals that when her wig brushed against one of the lighted candlesticks and began smouldering, she never noticed until Tito Gobbi doused her head with water. Later, when her retractable dagger failed to work, she continued 'stabbing' him until blood began seeping through his shirt and he had to gently restrain her.

Her problems were largely psychosomatic. By now an acute hypochondriac, she spent so much time dwelling on imaginary ailments – laryngitis, influenza, rheumatism, chest and back pains – that she actually developed some of the symptoms, and three hours before the première she was almost completely hoarse and virtually unable to move. Then, as soon as Franco Zeffirelli escorted her from her dressing-room to the wings, her fears and inhibitions just as quickly vanished . . . until the next time.

No one could honestly fault this *Tosca*, which ended with a twelve-minute standing ovation and forty minutes of curtain-calls. 'She was past her best, but still better than anyone else', said Sir John Tooley, and Harold Rosenthal, often one of her severest critics, declared that the three performances he saw were Maria's best since her 1957 *Traviata*s. On 9 February, Act Two was filmed and broadcast by the BBC as part of its *Golden Hour* series when those of Maria's fans – and detractors – who had only listened to her were able to marvel at the intensity of her acting and understand why audiences were apparently willing to tolerate her occasionally 'faulty' vocalising – the fact that it is far from easy to hit a top C when one is charging from one side of the stage to the other. They were also able to see the tortured expression on her face when she delivered 'Vissi d'arte', the aria which, by this time, said a great deal more about Maria Callas than the character she was portraying on the stage, a performance which was so utterly riveting that after she had finished singing, such was the emotion that, for a few seconds, there was no applause, as the audience had been stunned into silence.

One person not over-enamoured by Maria's singing, however, was the conductor Herbert von Karajan, who in Covent Garden's Crush Bar during the interval was unable to keep his comments to himself. Callas was but a shadow of her former self, he declared – more so, for if that night's effort was anything to go by, she might just as well throw in the towel and go back to being the captain's plaything. Karajan's wife, an occasional friend of Maria's, knew nothing of his outburst when she went backstage to congratulate Maria in her dressing-room after the performance, but Maria did and she was livid. The door was slammed in Frau von Karajan's face, though not before she had told her, through gritted teeth, 'And please tell your husband to go and boil his head!' The repercussions of this remark would be far-reaching.

Meanwhile, there were further problems with Maria's family which ostensibly began with her sister Jackie's trip to Italy during the spring of 1964. Milton Emberikos had died the previous June, leaving her very little cash, though she had been allowed to keep the apartment he had bought her many years before. Jackie had subsequently sold this and moved to a small flat. Taking some of the leftover money, she had decided to go on a holiday with friends of her music teacher's at Crema, near Milan. By a strange coincidence, which Maria had refused to believe was any such thing, these people had known Meneghini, now living as a virtual recluse in Sirmione, and the next day, Jackie had been invited to the villa. According to her, the first thing she had seen upon entering the building had been Maria's coat, hanging from a peg, and the whole place had smacked heavily of her presence. 'Her room was as it had been when she had last occupied it,' Jackie recalled. 'Such clothes as she had abandoned still hung in the closet. It was as if the place were ready for her to step back into at any moment should she choose to do so.'

Maria learned of her sister's rendezvous with her estranged husband only hours after it had taken place, and jumped to the very wrong conclusion that the two were conspiring towards a reconciliation which might prove financially beneficial to them both: Meneghini to regrasp the management reins now that her career had taken off again, and her sister some kind of payout now that she was reputedly down on her luck. Not only did Maria swear never to speak to either of them again, she also put the Milan house on the open market, telling friends, 'I had to sell the place. Every time I entered it, I kept seeing his miserable face. I wanted to remove every trace of him from my life.'

No sooner had she cooled down than Maria received a cable from America. Some months before, George had contracted pneumonia, from which he had never really recovered, and though he had intended spending his twilight years in Athens with Jackie, he had returned to New York for the medical treatment to which he was entitled as part of his pension rights. What hurt Maria was the fact that no one bothered informing her about her father's illness until he had been admitted to Lenox Hill Hospital – by which time he had married his longtime mistress, Alexandra Papajohn. The fact that Alexandra's family had been the ones to cable her with the news about his condition only made matters much worse – Maria cabled back at once, emphasising that though she was so very obviously concerned about her father, she was nevertheless disgusted with him for not involving her in his wedding plans. 'First my mother and sister, then my husband, and now my father,' she told a friend. 'Finally I can say I have no family, and for that I thank God. I only hope that if any of them die before me, *I* will never be criticised. I never *asked* to be related to such greedy, selfish people.'

15

Ritorna Vincitor!

I don't know if I would consider marriage again even if I
were free to do so. Once you're married the man takes
you for granted and I don't want to be told what to do!

In April 1964, Maria was practically begged to sing *Anna Bolena* in
La Scala's Moscow production of Donizetti's opera, scheduled to
take place that August. However, when Antonio Ghiringhelli told
her that she was not being considered for La Scala's 1964-5 season,
she refused to travel with the company to Russia. Subsequently,
Anna Bolena itself was dropped – quite simply because Ghiringelli
was unable to find another soprano capable of tackling such a
hugely demanding role. Maria, meanwhile, devoted herself to her
latest project: eight *Norma*s with Franco Corelli at the Paris Opera,
to be conducted by Georges Prêtre and directed by Franco Zeffirelli.

'One of the things that mystified me was how Maria believed she
could spend months with Onassis, completely drop the habit of
singing, and return to perform as though she had never been away,'
Covent Garden's Sir John Tooley observed, adding, 'That was of
course not possible, and every performance became a first night, a
greater and greater ordeal.' The 22 May première of Maria's first
ever opera on a French stage, however, saw her more relaxed than

usual – Onassis was not present, so she did not feel quite so pres-
surised as she would have done had he been 'organising' the guest-
list. Zeffirelli's production was almost allegorical: a forest setting
whose colours changed seasonally for each of the four acts, with
Maria seeming to materialise from the sets, a vision of loveliness
draped in gorgeous pastel voiles. Janet Flanner, the infamous
'Genet' of the *New Yorker* – a contemporary of the then recently
deceased Elsa Maxwell so beloved by the French that they had
awarded her the *Légion d'Honneur* – was, naturally enough, sitting
in the audience, for she had been present at every major Parisian
première since 1925. Maria was extremely flattered to meet the
legendary scribe after her performance, though she did not appreciate some of Flanner's comments once they reached the printed
page:

No one among the melomaniacal Friday-night gallery gods
who booed her peak peacock cries could have been ignorant
that the once fabulous Callas voice no longer reliably functions above an F or a G in her esthetically thinned body, so
their booing sounded particularly uncouth. This writer first
heard Callas in 1948, singing *Turandot* in Naples. We had been
warned in advance that she was fat, young, unknown and
temperamental, with a great and gorgeous, still inexperienced
voice – which all turned out to be true. Today, even without its
upper reaches, she has been truly sensational as a belated
operatic newcomer in Paris.

By this time, of course, no two Callas performances were remotely
the same, and this was reflected in the reviews which ranged from
the astutely sycophantic to the downright scathing. 'I feel sorry for
anyone who, after ninety-nine perfect notes forming one sublime
paragraph, then falls all spoiled by a single horrid, or fairly horrid
sound,' commented Andrew Porter of *Music Times* . . . adding as an
afterthought, 'But she *is* the greatest musician on the stage today.'
Similarly, the anonymous scribe from *Le Figaro* defended her with,

'Does anybody really *care* for a few sour fractions of a second, compared with those tremendous half-hours where Callas's genius shines in its purest state? I think not!'

It was during the fourth *Norma*, on 6 June, that Maria reached crisis-point with her nerves. Onassis, who thus far had been too busy with business commitments to meddle in Maria's new venture, decided to turn the evening into a gala affair by inviting fifty of European society's leading luminaries, including the Begum Aga Khan, Princess Grace, Marlene Dietrich, Yves St Laurent, Charlie Chaplin, Rudolf Bing, most of the French Cabinet, and representatives from the French, Italian, American and Greek embassies. When Maria was told who she would be singing to she became so agitated that a doctor had to inject her with a tranquilliser from her dressing-room to the wings, from which she had to be carried to the edge of the stage.

During the first three *Norma*s there had been a resurrection of the rivalry between Maria and Fiorenzo Cossotto, the young mezzo who had infuriated her five years previously during the Covent Garden *Medea*s. Cossotto was singing the role of Adalgisa, and by this time had amassed a sizeable fanbase which now joined forces with the other anti-Callas factions in the galleries – applauding wildly each time Cossotto had appeared on the stage, only to greet Maria with boos and jeers. With astonishing nerve, Maria had put paid to this nonsense, after their duet, 'Mira, O Norma', by taking Cossotto by the hand and leading her to the front of the stage – encouraging the public to acknowledge her rival, she had actually turned the tables in her own favour and the applause had gone on for several minutes. Now, however, as her shattered nerves began affecting her voice, she let slip a succession of extremely strident, wobbly top notes and, during the final scene of the last act, broke completely on what should have been a lengthy high C. This was the cue that her detractors had been waiting for. Initially, there was a stark silence, before a woman yelled from the orchestra stalls, 'Why don't you piss off back to your dressing-room, Célise,' – referring to Elyane Célise, a popular French operetta star of the thirties, renowned for singing beautifully but, towards the end of her life, for going off-key at the end of her arias in the most spectacular fashion. Trying to ignore this, Maria bravely approached the edge of the stage and mouthed to Georges Prêtre, 'Encore!' She began the recitative once more, and this time the note was spot-on: at the end of the performance she received the standing ovation she so richly deserved ... whilst Fiorenza Cossotto was making a hasty exit from the theatre.

Unfortunately, the matter did not end there, for as soon as the house lights came on, pandemonium broke out amongst the rival factions in the audience. The Callas Boys, in one of the galleries, began scrapping with a troop of off-duty Légionnaires who had broken into a chorus of 'Non, je ne regrette rien' as Maria was leaving the stage. Way below, in the stalls, a battle raged amongst a contingency of pensioners, one of whom was stretchered out of the theatre with a suspected fractured skull after being hit over the head with a pair of opera-glasses. Yves St Laurent had his spectacles whipped off and flung into the orchestra pit. The fighting continued for thirty minutes, and was only brought under control when the manager of the Opera House summoned the *Garde Républicaine* ... resulting in twelve broken bones, four gashed heads, and thirty-five arrests for public disorder.

In the midst of this mêlée, Onassis escorted Maria's guests backstage. She was especially pleased to see Rudolf Bing, though more than a little concerned that she might have blown her chance of ever securing another contract with the Met which, she hoped, was Bing's reason for being there. Bing had never heard a major singer 'break' in public before. 'I went backstage to her dressing-room, and I didn't know whether to refer to this episode or not,' he recalled. 'It's like a woman wearing a very low-cut dress. You're not sure whether it's rude to look or not to look. I decided not to mention it, and she never mentioned it, either.'

The next day, Maria and Bing lunched at one of Paris's trendiest restaurants, the Pré Catalan in the Bois de Boulogne, with Michel Glotz, her French agent. Initially, Bing asked Maria if she would sing *La Traviata*, which she had actually planned to record the following spring with Carlo Bergonzi – on her own terms, of course – but she was terrified of singing a role which would have to be rehearsed from scratch, so an alternative deal was finalised for two

*Tosca*s at the Met, for March 1965.

The final *Norma* took place on 24 June. Franco Corelli had sung Pollione in just two of the productions, but he returned to Paris for the backstage party, and the next afternoon escorted Maria to the Salle Wagram where, in what was tantamount to a 'jam' session, they recorded duets from *Polluto*, *Il Puritani*, *Un Ballo In Maschera*, *Don Carlos*, *Il Pirata* and *Aida*. Technically most of these pieces were perfect, but Maria was again dissatisfied with her contribution. The master tapes, with the exception of *Pur ti riveggo*, the beautiful 'Nile Duet' from *Aida*, which was released in 1990, are said to have been destroyed. Furthermore, her long-awaited studio recording of *Macbeth*, again with Carlo Bergonzi, which was to have begun on 25 August, was also cancelled, as was her recording of Massenet's *Werther* with Nicolai Gedda, and an album of sacred songs.

In the July, after a short break aboard the *Christina*, Maria was willing to return to the Salle Wagram to record a mezzo role, that of 'Carmen', with Nicolai Gedda singing the role of Don José. The sessions were hampered by violent thunderstorms which rattled the roof of the famous theatre – the quintet from Act Two required fourteen takes to get it right, and Maria's nerves were once again shot to pieces by Onassis's presence. Though she could not see him, she knew that he was sitting somewhere in the darkened auditorium.

Maria and Onassis spent what was left of the summer cruising the Mediterranean, stopping off every now and then at Skorpios and the nearby island of Levkás. It was during a stop-off at the latter that Maria gave the most curious performance of her later years. This was the week of the Levkás Folk Festival, and when an old woman in the crowd asked her if she would sing a snatch from her favourite aria, 'Casta Diva', Maria smiled and responded, 'I can think of nothing which would give me greater pleasure!' She then unceremoniously climbed onto the stage, after scowling at Onassis for trying to talk her out of it, looking very much like the tourist in her sleeveless checked dress and sandals, clutching her handbag, she sang the requested aria to the delight of 10,000 people who seemed to materialise out of thin air. Then, instead of getting down from the stage, she sang several more arias before moving onto a repertoire she thought she had forgotten of Greek folk-songs and sea-shanties ... after which she was escorted back to the *Christina* by almost the entire island population.

A frequent guest on the Onassis yacht during the summer of 1964 was Panaghis Vergottis who, knowing how much it distressed Maria in these days to discuss her work – particularly in front of Onassis – fed her with all kinds of ideas about becoming a businesswoman. 'I am perfectly happy to hide away on a small island when I'm not working,' she told *Life*'s Peter Dragadze, who interviewed her at the beginning of September. 'Now I am fascinated by the stock market and love to discuss shares, bonds and investments – perhaps that's my greatest personal interest.'

The business deal she was interested in now involved the purchase of *Artemission II,* a 28,000-ton tanker nearing completion in a Spanish shipyard. The asking price was £1,400,000 – a fifth to be paid on delivery, and the remainder on an eight-year mortgage. Onassis managed to knock this down to £1.200,000, and between them, Maria and Onassis accepted Vergottis's suggestion that their friend should form a Liberia-based company to manage the ship – this would be known as Overseas Bulk Carriers Corporation – and that Maria should have a 51 per cent controlling interest: this would be effected by her buying twenty-five of the hundred shares, and with Onassis giving her twenty-six of his fifty shares, with the other twenty-four shares being shared out amongst his nephews. Maria loved the name: the boat was named after Artemis, the Greek goddess of chastity and hunting. 'I may not be chaste any more,' she quipped, 'But I certainly know a lot about hunting and about being unable to catch anything worth holding onto!' The deal, which cost Maria £60,000 – one-tenth of the amount she would be required to pay for twenty-five shares – was soon settled, and on 31 October the trio celebrated with a small dinner party at Maxim's in Paris, where Maria was officially congratulated on becoming a shipowner – a move she would one day bitterly regret.

In Paris, on 3 December – the eve of her forty-first birthday – Maria recorded *Tosca* for EMI, with Tito Gobbi and Carlo Bergonzi. Then, after the Christmas break she began rehearsing the same role for the Paris Opera – the Zeffirelli production once more, with Georges Prêtre and Nicolai Rescigno alternately conducting the eight performances. The première took place on 19 February, with Renato Cioni again singing Cavaradossi.

Despite his indifference, Maria was aching to have an affair with the ethereal-looking young tenor, confiding in Roger Normand, 'He's *so* beautiful it hurts not to have him. And so strong – the perfect father for my children. But even if Cioni were interested, how would I get away with it?' Earlier, she had told Peter Dragadze of *Life* magazine, 'I'm in a stinking situation because of the Italian divorce law. I have no real freedom because Battista watches me continually. I dare not be photographed alone with one good friend because he would say I was flaunting a relationship. I dare not be seen in public in Paris with the same man for three nights running. If I marry tomorrow and have a child – and like all women I want lots of children – I could go to prison for two years according to Italian law.'

The Zeffirelli *Tosca* formed part of the Paris Opera's exchange programme with Covent Garden – his 'Norma' was to be transferred to London later in the year, and David Webster was hoping that Maria would be appearing in it. Such was her reception in Paris that a ninth performance was added to the run, on 13 March – something of a risk, for just six days later Maria was scheduled to sing the first of her two *Tosca*s at the New York Met.

At the end of February 1964, Maria spoke freely of some of her inhibitions in an interview with *France Inter* radio's Micheline Banzet:

In the beginning, I never suffered from stagefright. When you are young, you think you are owed the world, so I feared nothing. I couldn't have cared less. Now things are different. The audience's slightest reaction affects you. At times you feel enormous, bigger even than the theatre. Then at other times you feel tiny, ashamed, terrified. All you want to do is run away. It's hard, you know, being famous whilst at the same time retaining the humility of a little schoolgirl.

Maria flew to New York on 14 March, uncertain of her reception, having been forewarned that her *father* had threatened to sell his story to the press. During the Paris *Norma*s she had received a bill from the Lenox Hill Hospital for George's treatment – $5,000, which, as he was over retirement age and allegedly without means, Maria was legally obliged to pay. In her anger she had initially told the hospital's administrator, 'If he can't afford to pay you should get him to donate his body for medical research – or send my mother out onto the streets.' A few days before leaving Paris, however, she had telephoned her New York lawyer and left a message with his secretary, asking him to settle the bill. This he had done at once, and though George Callas would never have anything to do with his daughter again, unlike his wife he was not spiteful – the press never got their exclusive.

This was supreme acting, unforgettable acting,' declared the *New York Times* Harold Schonberg, after Maria's first appearance at the Met in seven years – for which she was paid $14,000 – though he was much less enthusiastic about her singing, concluding, 'Miss Callas is operating these days with only the remnants of a voice. Her top, always insecure, is merely a desperate lunge at high notes ... her tones are shrill, squeezed, and off-centre.' *Time* magazine, commenting on the three-minute ovation she received after pronouncing her first, 'Mario! Mario!' – during which, incredibly, she stayed in character – could only add, 'But *Tosca* is *not* a play. The singing's the thing – and even Callas could not make it otherwise.' Any problems Maria may have been experiencing with her voice – bearing in mind that both these publications were by now firmly ensconced within the anti-Callas faction – had been rectified by the second performance of 25 March. The *New York Herald Tribune*'s Alan Rich, describing the event as 'one of the most remarkable achievements in my memory', was like Franco Zeffirelli able to observe the artist and the character she was portraying as one. Rich continued:

What she did with her voice in the first act was an extension of the totally delightful girlish conception she had devised. What she did with it in the second act was even more remarkable, because it stripped this old-fashioned melodrama down to human proportions. Her 'Vissi d'arte', soft and floating, became what it is supposed to be: a prayer from a frightened, confused, trapped human being. The whole act, in fact, was a stunning study in humanity.

Maria's fans had strung a banner across the façade of the opera house: WELCOME HOME CALLAS. The performance had over-run by more than an hour on account of the thunderous applause, not just after each scene, but following the recitatives, and there had been sixteen curtain-calls for her and Franco Corelli . . . and, in the privacy of her dressing-room, a lukewarm but important for the media handshake from Jackie Kennedy, who had been sitting in the front row. And yet, Maria was more frightened of this adulation than she had been of failing, telling reporters, 'If I fall flat on my face, that much I can handle inordinately well. Being hailed a magnificent success, however, only raises the public's expectations of me, so that in my next performance I am expected to be no less than perfect. And who in this world is such a thing?'

On 14 May 1965, the first of Maria's five Paris *Norma*s, she was in a dreadful state. Her blood-pressure was dangerously low, she had psychosomatic pharyngitis, severe period pains, and her nerves were so bad that she had to be injected with a tranquilliser to get her out of bed. One hour before the performance, when she was starting to feel a little better, there was a telephone call from her husband's lawyer: Meneghini wished to inform her that he was still proceeding with his appeal regarding their separation order, and this time he would be citing Maria as an adulteress and supplying the court with the names of her lovers. Normally, Maria would have given the caller short shrift, but on this occasion she went to pieces. Her friend Giulietta Simionato, who was singing the role of Adalgisa, and at the age of fifty-six, appearing on a Paris stage for the first time, soothed her as best she could, though the manager of the opera house took the unusual step of addressing the audience through the tannoy a few minutes before curtain-up: 'Madame Callas is not feeling well this evening, but she will sing, and therefore begs you to please be understanding.

During this first performance, Maria had little to worry about. Simionato escorted her to the wings, and the hysterical applause as she stepped onto the stage was sufficient to set her up for the rest of the evening. Vocally, she was near-perfect, even though at times she had some difficulty staying on her feet. The journalist Jacques Bourgeouis who had followed Edith Piaf's 'suicide' tour of 1960, when the little singer had been so ill that she had had to be carried on and off the stage every evening, drew inevitable comparisons between the two, writing in *Arts*, 'The fact that in such a state of health she was able to perform the most arduous role in the international repertoire demonstrates a rare professional conscience. That she managed, with obviously diminished means, to transform this performance into a personal triumph such as she herself has rarely known, seems a true miracle.'

The second *Norma* was an even bigger triumph, but this time one of mind over matter. During the afternoon, Maria collapsed in her Avenue Foch apartment, and to combat her low blood-pressure she was given a coramine injection and ordered to rest on account of the drug's side-effects: nausea, fainting, and severe headaches. This she flatly refused to do. 'I *had* to sing,' she told the press at the end of the evening, another triumph. 'But not for my sake, you must understand. This has been my friend Simionato's Paris debut, and I didn't want to spoil things for her. She's supported me through thick and thin for as long as I can remember.'

Simionato was, however, contracted only for the first two of the five *Norma*s, and on 21 May she was duly replaced by the hated Fiorenza Cossotto, who like before seemed to deliberately antagonise Maria, much to the delight of her fans, many of whom supported *her*, it is alleged, because they were anti-Maria and *had* to support someone and give Maria her 'come-uppance'. This was La Scala and the Tebaldiani repeating itself, only this time Maria was rapidly losing heart, and the willpower to fight back.

During that afternoon's snatched rehearsal, the atmosphere had been austere, but the two women had been civil towards each other, and had blended well in their duet, 'Mira, O Norma'. This changed alarmingly when they were facing the public. Taking advantage of Maria's delicate health and state of mind, Cossotto purposely upstaged her by holding on to the final note for several seconds longer than Maria was able to, making it appear that Maria had run short of breath, and effectively stealing the applause. After the performance, Zeffirelli told her that, should such a thing happen again, she would be fired. Cossotto knew, of course, that he would be unable to find another Adalgisa at such short notice, and such was Maria's humiliation, the next evening after the duet, that she came close to hitting the offending mezzo. Her nerve finally snapped during the last *Norma*, on 29 May, when the guests of honour included the Shah of Persia. All day long, Maria's doctor had been begging her to cancel – he was even prepared to furnish her with a medical certificate to show to the press and minimise any scandal. Unable to forget that other *Norma* in Rome, Maria would not, and the last straw came in the duet with Cossotto, whose moment of glory occurred when she completely drowned Maria during their duet, getting her so worked up that Maria collapsed on her way back to the dressing-room.

This time there were no complaints from the audience when they were told that the rest of the evening had been cancelled, and many of those detractors who had booed were left feeling decidedly guilty. One hour later, supported by her doctor and a paramedic, and still wearing her stage make-up, Maria was escorted through a crowd of sad-faced fans to her car. Weakly, she told them, 'I'm so sorry about this. But I'll be back to earn your forgiveness, I promise.' Later she issued a formal statement to the press: 'Maria Callas will not be content until she has returned to the Opéra de Paris to erase the memory of her failure and collapse there on Saturday night.' Sadly, this was one promise she would be unable to keep.

By and large, the media were sympathetic. On the eve of the *Norma* première she had sung several arias on French television's cult series, *Les Grands Interprètes*, and sung them well, telling the interviewer Bernard Gavoty afterwards, 'My voice never gives me any trouble when I'm alone. It's only when I'm in a packed theatre that I start to panic and lose some of my high notes.' It was therefore inevitable that at least one publication should pick up on this – in this instance, the *Daily Mail* – running the headline, 'Callas:

Was It Panic? Was It Illness? Was It Jealousy?'

'The world's most celebrated opera singer is sailing the Mediterranean aboard the world's most famous luxury yacht in the company of a devoted friend who is also a millionaire,' Robin Smyth's editorial began, before asking, 'Could any woman ask for more? Unfortunately, yes.' Everything about Smyth's demeanour infuriated Maria: his accusation that she had *deserted* the Rome *Norma* of 1957, his praise of Fiorenza Cossotto's ability to 'securely grasp' the high notes which Maria could only 'snatch at'. She was most offended by his description of Cossotto's voice as 'pure dependable gold' and his repetition of an audience member's quip, 'Their duet was more like Clay-Liston than Callas-Cossotto,' referring to the world heavyweight boxing championship of the previous year, prior to which both contenders had engaged in several very nasty public slanging matches. 'How nice it would have been to invite *that* particular journalist to take a cruise on Aristo's yacht,' she told Roger Normand, 'and throw the bastard over the side when we got out to sea!'

The next morning, Maria flew to Monte Carlo, where she joined Onassis. There was just over a month to go before her next London season – four *Tosca*s at Covent Garden, the last of which was to be a charity gala before Queen Elizabeth – and she was absolutely shattered. Yet no sooner had the *Christina* set off for Skorpios than she was informed that the court in Brescia had transferred Meneghini's long-running application – for the words 'exonerated of all blame' to be added to their separation order, thus entitling him to a greater portion of Maria's earnings, by Italian law – to the Public Prosecutor's office in Milan, and that a decision had been reached. Both parties were held equally responsible for the breakdown of their marriage – Meneghini, for the rapacious manner in which he had handled the financial aspects of Maria's career, and for harming her reputation by offering several quite vitriolic statements to the press – and Maria, for her obvious adultery with Onassis and for her 'flirtatious and irresponsible liaisons' with several other unnamed men.

The *Tosca* première had been set for Friday 2 July, and tickets for Maria's three public performances went on sale two weeks prior to this, when it was revealed that over one thousand fans had spent *four* days and nights queuing on the pavement. On the Saturday before the première, photographs of Maria appeared in the newspapers, snapped at the annual Rothschild Ball, in Paris: she looked radiant, and the brief editorials accredited her with saying that her brief cruise had done her a power of good, and that she was looking forward to her trip to London.

The flight from Paris had been booked, as had her usual suite at the Savoy, and Maria should have arrived in London some time during the afternoon of Monday 28 June. When she was found to be not on the plane, Covent Garden's David Webster naturally became concerned. When, however, after innumerable calls that day and throughout the whole of the next he was unable to track her down – the Avenue Foch telephone had been left off the hook – Webster's concern became blind panic. Then, on the Wednesday evening, forty-eight hours before the première, Maria called him and explained her predicament: she was suffering from very low blood-pressure, and her doctor had forbidden her to travel, at least for the time being. She then dropped the bombshell – following her doctor's explicit orders, she would only be able to sing *one* of the four performances. When Webster then declared that she would have to supply him with a medical certificate detailing the exact nature of her illness, to strengthen her point, Maria passed the receiver to her doctor who, she said, had been ministering to her day and night over the last week. Webster had no option but to believe what he was told, and of course the press were alerted. They had a field-day, particularly when Maria decided that this single performance should be the one before the Queen.

When the *Evening Standard*'s Sydney Edwards telephoned Maria's French agent to enquire about her health, he was told that she had suffered a relapse. 'Presumably it was not that drastic,' Edwards concluded, 'because Callas could still decide not to disappoint the Queen.' David Webster, meanwhile, had less than forty-eight hours to find a suitable replacement Tosca, rehearse her with Renato Cioni and Tito Gobbi, *and* fit her with costumes. He settled for an Australian soprano, Maria Collier, who was good, but certainly no Callas, even if Cioni later confessed that she had been a delight to work with after Maria, and Gobbi boasted to the press in a sudden surge of over-enthusiasm, 'I'm going to make her the greatest Tosca in the world!' When Maria read this in the newspaper, she called Gobbi and remonstrated, 'And you, my dear Tito, are the biggest *shit* in the world!'

Franco Zeffirelli later said that he should have known, taking into account Maria's increasingly neurotic behaviour, that there would be trouble with her London *Tosca*s. He added, 'As soon as she arrived in London, I knew this would be the end. That's why I called all my friends and told them to come to Covent Garden by whatever means, that I was certain this would be the last chance to see Callas. And I was right.'

For Maria, the final struggle was about to commence – an almost schizophrenic battle between the fun-loving socialite and the once-meticulous, hard-working opera star, between her conscience and her most formidable enemy – The Voice. At Covent Garden on 5 July, Maria sang well, though not inordinately so. There was little or no straining to reach and hold on to those controversial top notes, but they were delivered mechnically, almost without warmth. There was no over-exertion in the dramatics department, no obvious on-stage histrionics, as expected, against those colleagues who had spoken disrespectfully about her to the press. There *was* a standing ovation, but one which meant absolutely nothing to her because this was a royal gala, *un grand spectacle*, where the better part of the audience were there to be seen, where the galleries were bereft of Maria's true fans and those all-important Callas Boys who had made it all worthwhile.

'She got through it respectably, and the audience was generous with applause, but that was it,' was how Franco Zeffirelli summed up Maria's final appearance on the legitimate opera stage, adding, 'Without any great crisis, no cracked notes or sudden temper, neither collapse nor glorious performance. It was on a downbeat, fading note that Maria surrendered the stage at last.'

16

Hanno Confin le Lagrime

We are all vulnerable. I am extremely so and naturally
have tried not to show it for my own self-preservation.

In August 1965, Maria flew to London, where she eschewed her
usual suite at the Savoy for a room at the Ritz so that she could be
closer to Panaghis Vergottis, whose brother had recently died. 'We
were together most of the time,' she later confessed, adding defensively, 'but I never went up to his room because it stank of cigar
smoke, and of course he was never allowed to smoke in mine, *or* get
up to any mischief.' Whilst she was in London she also saw a lot of
Franco Zeffirelli. The eminent director, still smarting over the
Covent Garden *Tosca*s, was nevertheless keener than ever to work
with her again. 'I was not prepared to let the greatest stage talent I
had ever known slip through my fingers so easily,' he said, confi-
dently boasting, 'if I could film Shakespeare, why not opera, and
why not Callas in *Tosca*?'

Maria was enthusiastic about the idea, and invited Zeffirelli to
join her and Onassis aboard the *Christina*, moored at Skorpios,
where they would be able to discuss the matter further, in amicable
surroundings. She no longer negotiated deals and contracts, she
added, unless Onassis was present. Earlier in the year, Zeffirelli had
spent some time in Dublin trying to persuade Elizabeth Taylor and

Richard Burton to appear in his film version of *The Taming of the Shrew*, but he later claimed that even their marital upsets had been nothing like what he had seen on Onassis's yacht.

When Zeffirelli arrived at Skorpios in mid-September, Onassis had already taken the liberty of inviting Anthony Havelock-Allan and Lord Brabourne of the government-backed film company, British Home Entertainments, and during their first business meeting Maria effected a complete volte-face by announcing that *Onassis* had insisted that she make the film, when all *she* wanted to do was cruise around the world and take things easy. She added, however, that she would be perfectly willing to undertake the project for a fee of $500,000, together with 50 per cent of the box office ... terms which were readily agreed by Havelock-Allan, Brabourne and Zeffirelli, though for the time being Onassis hedged.

The last time Zeffirelli had met the couple, Onassis – the opera-*hater* – had denounced Maria's voice as 'a whistle that no longer works'. Now, he complicated matters by interjecting, 'Save your voice for when you go on stage, darling, because that's when you're going to need it!' 'Maria fell silent, whilst we shuffled with embarassment,' the director recalled. 'It was to this that the great love affair had descended. We were all suddenly frightened for her. One had heard rumours of how these Greek tycoons treated their unwanted women, stories of violence and even murder.'

Onassis did beat Maria regularly. She confessed this to Roger Normand and even showed him some of the bruises. On numerous occasions, she added, she had found the courage to hit him back – once over the head with a wine bottle, knocking him unconscious – but that making up afterwards had always been heavenly. Some years later Onassis's secretary, Kiki Moutsatsos, also spoke of how she had witnessed some quite severe beatings.

It is not known if Onassis actually resorted to physical violence during Zeffirelli's visit, though his behaviour *was* beastly. Several times during dinner, Maria is said to have indicated the priceless table settings, or to have pointed to the servants hovering in attendance of her every need, declaring, 'Why should I work when I have all this?' The conversation had then become heated when

Havelock-Allan, David Lean's longtime producer, announced that Herbert von Karajan had moved in on the negotiations by purchasing the film rights for *Tosca* from Ricordi, the Milan-based company that owned the copyright on all Puccini's operas, and that it was now his intention to produce it for Beta, the Munich film company. Initially, Zeffirelli had been willing to undertake a joint production, to which Maria had resorted, 'Two prima donnas in one show are *too* many.' Karajan, for his part, had snarled, 'Me, work with that foul Greek bitch? I'd rather commit suicide!' Onassis, however, whose 'language' most of the time was hard cash, had offered to 'buy out' von Karajan – 'As if the conductor of the Vienna State Opera were a rival shipping magnate,' Zeffirelli observed – after which there had been a ferocious quarrel between Maria and Onassis, in Greek, one which had resulted in her fleeing from the dining-room in tears, whilst Onassis had continued drinking with the other guests as if nothing had happened.

Some years later, Zeffirelli recalled how, when he had tiptoed into Maria's suite after leaving the table, she had flung herself into his arms and sobbed her heart out. He added, 'She started to talk through the racking sobs, telling me how Ari was the first to make her feel like a woman, the first really to make love to her, and how afraid she was of losing him, telling me, "I'm quite simply at his mercy!" So, I comforted her as best I could.'

The next morning, Onassis told the director that he was wholly in support of Maria filming *Tosca*, and that he would give him $10,000 'development' money – in effect, but a fraction of the pre-production costs. 'It was a sign of how he viewed the project,' Zeffirelli said. 'By giving so little he could *appear* to be promoting Maria, while actually ensuring that nothing happened.'

Such was Zeffirelli's burning ambition to work with Maria again, however, that he began working on the pre-production, engaging a script writer and set designer, and organising a suitable location. Early in September, Maria and Tito Gobbi filmed a screen test in Rome, in colour, with which everyone was delighted, and a few days later part of the soundtrack was recorded, featuring the entire Covent Garden cast – including Renato Cioni, of whom Maria boasted, 'He may not be the world's best tenor, but with those looks he'll sure as hell set the screen alight!' There were also clandestine meetings with William Wyler, Maria's favourite film director, and with her alter-ego, Audrey Hepburn, who passed on a few 'tricks of the trade'. She even discussed make-up techniques with Alberto di Rossi, at that time one of Europe's leading exponents of the art.

Herbert von Karajan, however, proved a tough nut to crack: when he refused to sell Zeffirelli the rights to the film, the project had to be cancelled. Maria then telephoned the director and asked for her money back – of course it had already been spent – and when Zeffirelli told her not to worry, that it had been Onassis's money and that to such a man $10,000 was little more than petty cash, she screamed at him, 'It was *my* money. He made me pay it out of the little I have left. Give me my money back, or else!'

'It was the other Maria,' Zeffirelli concluded, 'the woman who hoarded cash, who resented paying her father's hospital bills, who loved shopping at Woolworths. My attempts to help her and save her for her art had ended in acrimony and estrangement.' He told a press conference at the time, however, 'This had been the saddest experience of my career. On all sides there are people who claim they are losers in this deal. I say the big loser is the public which had been robbed of seeing the greatest operatic performance of our time.'

Maria swore never to speak to Franco Zeffirelli again, and for a few years – until she had broken free of Onassis – she was as good as her word. In her current state of neurosis, however, she cancelled *all* her engagements for the near future: several *Medea*s and *Traviata*s which had been scheduled for Paris in the spring, and with dire consequences, her Covent Garden *Norma*s which were but weeks away. For the chairman of the Royal Opera House, Lord Drogheda, this was the last straw. His annual report for 1964/5, prepared *before* Maria's illness, declared that the company anticipated debts of £230,000 by the spring, and Maria had only further aggravated the dilemma. On 17 November, therefore, Lord Drogheda felt obliged to issue a statement to the press:

Maria Callas's withdrawal from three performances of *Tosca* in

July and six proposed performances of Norma next month reduced our box-office receipts by £30,000. Not only did we have to refund large sums of money for Tosca, but we lost our subsidy at 17s 6d for each £1 takings. Subsequently Miss Callas's low blood-pressure has put Covent Garden another £56,250 in the red.

The aborted *Tosca* film also led to the most appallingly filthy exchange between Maria and Panaghis Vergottis, who had supported the project from the off. The previous February, when the two had dined tête-à-tête at Maxim's, Vergottis had expressed his concern over her £60,000 investment with his company. *Artemission II* had recently developed engine trouble, and even Vergottis was convinced that they had purchased a 'jinx' ship, so much so that he had urged Maria to convert her twenty-five shares to a loan, for which she would be paid 6.5 per cent interest. Maria had agreed to this but now, when Vergottis accused Onassis of sabotaging the *Tosca* project by being tight-fisted, Maria took her lover's side and, hoping to make up for the money he or she had given to Franco Zeffirelli she demanded that the loan be reconverted to shares. Vergottis refused, and when Maria vented her fury over the telephone using some of the worst language he had ever heard, before threatening to sue him, Vergottis admonished, 'Appear in the witness box, and you will *both* be faced with a great deal of scandal, in the court *and* in the press.' He then added that, as far as he was now concerned, their friendship was over, and hung up.

It now seems very likely that, given her tendency for spouting off, only to later regret what she had said and take whatever steps were required to make amends, Maria would have apologised to Vergottis, and the mess they had created between them would have been sorted out. Onassis, however, only made matters much worse when he bumped into Vergottis at Claridge's. Both men swore at each other, Vergottis threatened to smash Onassis's face in with a whisky decanter, and the latter publicly accused him of blackmail and declared that, regardless of what came out in court, he and Maria *would* sue him. The ball was set rolling that same day, though it would take some time for the matter to reach the High Court.

At around this time, Onassis also ended his friendship with Prince Rainier and Princess Grace of Monaco, in whose sides it would appear he had been a particularly painful thorn for years – not simply because the royal pair frowned on his adultery with Maria, which effectively was none of their business, but because for more than a decade he had been treating the principality as if he owned it, referring to it publicly as 'my head office'. The fact is, Onassis *did* have a controlling interest in the State of Monaco, the organisation in control of the principality's major activities, a situation which changed at the end of 1965 when Prince Rainier released half a million shares on to the market and refused to allow Onassis to buy any of them. In addition the tycoon was paid $10 million for the shares he did own, and privately told not to darken the Rainiers' doorstep again.

The rupture with Monaco naturally affected Maria, for though she was told by Princess Grace, 'Drop in for tea any time you're passing,' it was but a token gesture, and as with Vergottis, who had *dared* criticise her man, so she took his side once more, venting some very cutting remarks about Princess Grace. She called Roger Normand in Paris and told him, 'Who is she, anyway, but a glorified fucking starlet who married into money?' Even so, as her circle of intimate friends diminished further, so too her relationship with Onassis slowly but surely began disintegrating. Therefore, in the wake of what now seemed the inevitable, Maria began taking steps to ensure her independence.

On 28 March 1966, decked out in her latest Biki creation, dark glasses and picture hat, and looking every inch the rich tourist, Maria marched into the American Embassy in Paris, handed in her passport and signed the necessary documents relinquishing her American citizenship. On 6 April, she issued a formal statement to the press: 'After seven years of struggling with divorce proceedings, my lawyers have now found that in taking up my Greek nationality once more, my marriage will become null and void in the whole world apart from Italy.' Her lawyers' finding was in fact based on a little-known statute of 1946 which decreed that any Greek marriage conducted outside the Orthodox Church was non-existent.

If Maria was hoping, however, that such drastic action might persuade Onassis to propose marriage, she was sorely disappointed, for whilst she continued to wear her heart on her sleeve and lived in hope, in spite of his calling Vergottis's bluff, Onassis churned out the same response whenever questioned about Maria: 'Callas and myself are very good friends. That's all I have to say regarding the matter.' Jackie Callas, some years later, put into words what everyone but Maria was thinking then: 'Clearly she worshipped Onassis, and just as clearly he was toying with her. He had wanted the lustre of possessing the world's most famous singer – now that her performing days were clearly over, he had lost interest.'

Even so, Maria clung precociously to her precognitive dream – the fact that all *would* turn out well in the end, providing she willed it to be so. During the spring of 1966, this dream almost became a reality when, after treating her for a stomach upset which he claimed could have been linked to an early menopause, her doctor informed her that she was two months pregnant. 'More than anything in the world, I've always wanted a child,' she had said. 'So much that, if it were so, I would give up my career tomorrow and regret absolutely nothing.' Initially, she kept the news from Onassis – he was away on business, and she wanted to tell him her good news face to face – so she confided only in her closest friends, who by this time could almost be counted on the fingers of one hand. She even went out and bought the layette – choosing white, so that it would not matter what sex the baby was, though she was convinced that Onassis would be hoping for another son.

In fact, Onassis did not want a child, period, and Maria later repeated his reaction to Roger Normand: 'If you're expecting to hold on to me, get your bastard flushed down the sluice!' Such was Maria's obsession with this by now odious man that, rather than displease him, she booked into a clinic at once and had not just an abortion, but a hysterectomy so that she would not slip up again. The downward spiral in their relationship, and Maria's long, painful trip to Calvary had begun in earnest.

A few weeks later, devastated by what she had done, and deeply ashamed that she had allowed herself to be manipulated by a man whom she had trusted and loved unreservedly, Maria moved out of the rented apartment on Avenue Foch to a much larger one on the second floor of Avenue Georges-Mandel. It is not known how much she paid for her new home, other than that she purchased it with her own money, and in cash. And, whilst the decor of her house in Milan had been astonishingly tacky, Georges-Mandel was furnished only in the best possible taste now that there was no man to boss her around. 'I'm starting out again, from scratch,' she told Roger Normand, who with her maid, Bruna, accompanied her to the auction rooms at Drouot. 'And what's more, I don't give a damn. This will be my last home, and henceforth I'm out to please only myself. Nobody's ever really cared for me, have they? All they've always been interested in is what they could get out of Callas the meal-ticket, Callas the key to high society. Becoming independent and having my own roof over my head is my way of saying, 'Fuck the lot of you!'

The furniture which Roger helped her to choose was mostly Louis Quinze and Regency, original works by Renoir, Fragonard, Bassano and Marie Laurencin graced the living room walls, some of the carpets and rugs were by Gesmar, and the huge white and rose mirrored bathroom was by Georges Grandpierre, one of France's most distinguished contemporary interior designers – and one of Maria's biggest fans. 'Like my great friend Piaf, Maria would spend hours in her bathroom,' Roger said. 'Actually, it was more like a salon than a washroom, with massive plush armchairs you could get lost in and a matching sofa, a record-player and refrigerator, desk, drinks cabinet and two telephones, and flowers absolutely everywhere. During the last years of her life, Maria conducted most of her business and held court in her bathroom.'

For almost a year, Maria concentrated her energies on turning Georges-Mandel into what was almost a mausoleum in the centre of Paris. She was still not in the best of health, however, as was evident on 17 April 1967 when she and Onassis arrived in London for the lawsuit against Panaghis Vergottis: thick make-up scarcely concealed the bags under her eyes, and her legs and ankles were swollen through water-retention. Even so, her smile was radiant as she took her place in the courtroom, where she was introduced to the presiding judge, Mr Justice Roskill, as Maria Calegoropoulos – hammering home the point that she was now a *respectable* Greek citizen, no matter what anyone said, and unmarried – though throughout the proceedings she was persistently addressed as Madame or Miss Callas. This air of 'respectability' was, however, hard to believe for many: having left the choice of her outfit for the occasion to Madame Biki's judgement, she turned up in a *scarlet* dress, complemented by a white toque. A similar outfit had been commissioned by Gloria Magnus, the Capri-based Cockney socialite and restauratrice whom Maria had met during one her trips to see Gracie Fields – a notorious man-eater whom one journalist had described as 'coming free with every course', and at least one Italian newspaper drew comparisons between the two.

The case was an ordeal for Maria, who over the next ten days would have far too much of her dirty washing laundered in the glaring spotlight of the world's media – and for the seventy-seven-year-old Vergottis, who was by the this time so ill that his doctor had to be constantly present. Only Onassis was in his element, cracking jokes with reporters during the recesses, living out a very public adventure at the expense of a once-dear friend, and, the woman who was supposed to be the greatest love of his life. In his and Maria's defence, Sir Milner Holland QC, told the court how Onassis had introduced Maria to Vergottis in the summer of 1959, and that the latter had become 'extremely friendly' with her – bringing a smirk to Onassis's face, and much mumbling amongst the gathering of press. The purchase of *Artemission II* was then discussed, and a document describing Maria's £60,000 investment as unsecured loan – dated 17 November 1965 but not presented to Maria until the following January – was produced as evidence, as were receipts signed by Vergottis to the effect that she had since received two interest payments. Maria's 'vulgar remarks' to Vergottis, made over the telephone, were then discussed, and a copy of a letter produced which proved that she had since attempted to apologise for her behaviour.

It did not take long, however, for Vergotti's defence, Peter Bristow QC, to begin digging about the Callas-Onassis relationship. Having asked the tycoon if he and Maria had parted from their respective partners *after* meeting each other, to be told, 'Yes, sir. Nothing to do with out meeting. Just coincidence', Bristow now asked Onassis if he regarded Maria as being in a position equivalent to being his wife, should she be free. Maria shuddered visibly as he replied, 'No. If that were the case I have no problem of marrying her – neither has she any problem of marrying me.' She fought back the tears, however, when Bristow asked Onassis if he felt any obligation towards her other than those of mere friendship, for the response was a smug, 'None whatsoever.'

This battle of wits and words between Bristow and Onassis continued the next day when under cross-examination the latter dismissed Vergottis's declaration – that Maria's investment had been a loan, and not a subscription for shares – as 'an Aesop's myth'. And once more, Peter Bristow began dishing the dirt when he asked Onassis if there had been a breach between himself and Maria during the *Tosca* film negotiations with Zeffirelli. Onassis pleased her by denying that there had – only to admit to the court that they had had a row over the telephone, when Maria had been at the Ritz with Vergottis, comforting him over the death of his brother. When asked if he had prevented Maria from making the film, Onassis retorted, 'Madame Callas is not a vehicle for me to drive. She has her own brakes and her own brains.' Even so, Bristow pressed, 'But have you any *influences* on her? – to which came the snarl, 'I did not stop her, and would not assume the *responsibility* of stopping her!' Maria, when her time came to be interrogated, stated that whilst her feelings for Vergottis had been those a daughter might nurture for a father – her reasons, she said, for 'affectionately pestering' him into allowing her to invest her money with his company – she had another kind of relationship with Onassis because he was a younger man. Then she added coldly, positively glaring at Justice Roskill, 'But *not* the one Mr Bristow might have accused us of by implication.'

As if to prove the point, that evening Maria went to a performance of *La Traviata* at Covent Garden. The event was of course stage-managed with precision – although the visit was supposed to be a strict secret so as to avoid courting publicity, her arrival was deliberately leaked one hour before she arrived, and as she stepped out of the Savoy's limousine looking downright gorgeous, three hundred of her faithful Callas Boys rushed her, chanting her name whilst she signed autographs. For Maria it was her third costume change in less than twelve hours. That morning she had turned up at court in a lilac outfit and the same white toque as before, but for the afternoon session she had worn a vivid orange coat and matching hat. She now refused to discuss the court case with the attendant press, telling them instead, 'The next time you see me here, dears, I'll be the one on the stage!'

The next day, when Maria was grilled by Peter Bristow, she was not as patient as Onassis had been when discussing their relationship. Having repeated her earlier statement, 'Mr Vergottis was a father to me,' she rounded on Bristow – who, having attempted to question her about Meneghini and her friendship with 'these two Greeks' remonstrated, 'These questions *have* to be asked, Madame Callas!' – yelling across the courtroom, 'No, they do *not*! We are here because of twenty-five shares for which I paid, *not* because of my relationship with another man!' Bristow then asked her if she was still married to Meneghini, to which she reacted only slightly less vociferously, 'Under the Italian law I am very still married to him. *That* is a problem, for an American divorce would not be valid in Italy.' When asked if she therefore still regarded herself as a single woman, her patience truly tried she snapped, 'In *Italy*, no. *Elsewhere*, yes!' She then raised a ripple of amusement amongst the public gallery – effectively putting Bristow in his place for intimating that she had only told the truth when it had suited her, whereas Vergottis' evidence had been consistent – by keeping a straight face whilst telling him, 'I am here to answer *all* questions. Ask anything you want, but please speak *louder*, dear. I'm short-sighted and cannot see what you're saying!'

The case ended on 28 April. Justice Roskill, in his summing up, declared that the ages of those involved in the case – Maria, 44, and Onassis and Vergottis 61 and 77 respectively – was of some relevance, adding:

The events of the autumn of 1965 have given rise to a bitter breach between them which the allegations made on either side can have done nothing to heal but much to excerbate. Indeed, this case has many of the elements of a Sophoclean tragedy ... The final determination depends upon a single question of personal credibility. Who is telling the truth – Mr Onassis, Madame Callas, or Mr Vergottis? ... There is no escape – one could wish there were – from the fact that, by one side or the other, perjury has been committed. If the defence is right there can be no doubt that Mr Onassis and Madame Callas have put their heads together to frame Mr Vergottis. But if the plaintiffs are right there can be no doubt that Mr Vergottis has deliberately broken a bargain with the plaintiffs and lied, more than once, in order to escape the consequences of the breach. There is no halfway house to this case, and the task of deciding where the truth lies is as distasteful to a judge as any judicial task.

Even so, Justice Roskill's conclusion was a simple one: Maria and Onassis *had* been duped by their former friend, and judgement was awarded in their favour, together with costs estimated to be in the region of £25,000. Vergottis launched a successful appeal, which was eventually heard at the House of Lords on 31 October 1968. This time he was not so lucky. Maria repeated what she had told Justice Roskill in April 1967 – 'I am a woman who works for a living, but who may be coming to an age when it might be no longer possible to do so,' – and after the judge had taken this into consideration, bearing in mind that she was at least semi-retired, she and Onassis won the case.

For Maria and Onassis, the Vergottis episode clearly marked the beginning of the end. In August 1967, Onassis tried to buy off the author Willi Frischauer, who had been commissioned to write an unauthorised, warts-and-all biography of him. Frischauer, however, returned the somewhat paltry $50,000 cheque, insisted upon meeting his subject, and the pair became instant friends. Onassis told the author that his book would be *the* definitive Onassis biography, but that it would be worked on only in the most luxurious surroundings – in other words, during a cruise on the *Christina*. Frischauer spent *so* much time with Onassis, however, who almost completely ignored Maria when he was around, that after only a few days she flew back to Paris.

The tense atmosphere intensified in September, the day after Onassis's return to Paris, when Maria telephoned his Avenue Foch apartment only to be told that he had left implicit instructions not to be disturbed because he was dining with a mysterious guest. Maria instinctively assumed that this could only have been Jackie Kennedy, and that the secrecy was linked to the tight security surrounding America's former First Lady. She knew that since the murder of her husband, Jackie had increasingly felt alienated from her family, a feeling she herself knew only too well and sympathised with. Neither does she seem to have minded the fact the Onassis had appointed himself Jackie's personal adviser, simply because Onassis had never given her the impression that he might have been two-timing her. He was still swamping her with expensive gifts and flowers – combining the two, the day after Jackie left Paris, by arriving at Georges-Mandel with a huge bunch of pink roses, secured with a $20,000 bracelet.

Indeed, Maria was convinced that their relationship had taken a turn for the better when, on 14 November, Onassis escorted her to Régine's night-club, one of the most fashionable in Paris. For some reason – it is thought that Onassis, terrified of Maria finding out what he was really up to, had tipped off the press – they were approached by a young reporter form the Italian magazine, *Oggi*, who asked them if the rumours circulating that they were about to be married were true. For once, Maria was dumbstruck, though her escort more than made up for this by growling, 'You are too late. We're *already* married!'

The next day, photographs of the 'happy couple' were splashed across newspapers worldwide, whilst Onassis's London spokesman telephoned as many editors as would speak to him and demanded a retraction. This never happened, and it quickly emerged that the 'ceremony' had taken place somewhere in Mexico. 'Mr Onassis is Greek Orthodox,' declared the *Evening Standard*'s Sam White. 'The marriage, therefore, cannot be recognised as legal in Greece. There is, however a possibility that the couple will remarry in church.'

What most of these newspapers omitted to report was that Maria was *still* legally married to one Battista Meneghini, though he of course brooked no delay in letting the press know his opinion on the matter. 'This story is complete and utter rubbish,' he told one publication. 'Onassis is using Maria the way he had always used her – only this time he must be hiding something *really* big up his sleeve. Time alone will tell.'

He was of course absolutely right, though even Meneghini with his alleged army of spies and overworked imagination could not have known what was just around the corner.

17

Solitaria . . . a Sospirar

I thought that when I met a man I loved, that I didn't need to sing. The most important thing in a woman is to have a man of her own, to make him happy.

1968 would prove the most distressing of Maria's life, yet on the other side of the Atlantic, the other woman in Onassis's life, Jackie Kennedy, was feeling just as miserable as the new year dawned. The common factor for both women, of course, was an almost crippling loneliness. Maria possessed wealth, a beautiful home, and her usually delicate health was better that it had been for some time. However, there were few close friends to turn to, and certainly no confidante to help shoulder the increasing burden of neurasthenia which at times suffocated her, and more that once made her seriously consider taking her own life.

Jackie, on the other hand, was stifled with affection – but only from a distance. Since the murder of her husband, the American public had placed her on a golden pedestal: the emobodiment of all that was graceful in a widow, a good devout Catholic, and above all an impeccable mother who in their eyes could do no wrong. Away from the media spotlight and public glare, however, and aside from her mother and children, she had almost no one. She certainly did not feel comfortable amongst the Kennedys, save for when she was with Bobby, Jack's brother who, since that dreadful day in November 1963, had been her closest friend and ally – so close, in fact, that during her first year of widowhood he had spent more time with her than he had with his own wife and children.

Since Jack Kennedy's death, Jackie had rarely been short of a male escort: Frank Sinatra, Lord Harlech, Leonard Bernstein and J.K. Galbraith had all accompanied her to society functions, yet such was the American media's respect for this woman that there had not been so much as a whiff of scandal, and on each occasion Jackie had been returned to the quaint respectability of her huge Fifth Avenue apartment overlooking Central Park. All this began changing, however, during the spring of 1968 when Onassis – having already boasted to friends, 'The Kennedy woman is going to be the ultimate trophy. It'll be like sticking a hot knife into butter!' – persuaded her to break the news to Bobby Kennedy that they were thinking of getting married. This resulted in Kennedy practically *ordering* Jackie to have nothing more to do with the man he openly referred to as 'that damn Greek crook'.

Kennedy was of course also thinking of his own reputation as well as that of his sister-in-law. Having been elected Senator for New York in 1965, he now caused a conflict of public opinion by announcing that he would be standing for President – his supporters hailing him as an idealistic reformer who identified with the struggling, under-privileged minorities, whilst his opponents branded him a publicity-seeking opportunist. But as Bobby had helped Jackie to come to terms with her grief, so she gave him her word that she would support him throughout his campaign. Out of gratitude for this, he therefore promised her that, providing she 'steered clear of marriage-talk' until he had secured his Democratic nomination, he would *consider* giving the couple his blessing. Secretly, of course, he was hoping that in the meantime Jackie would see Onassis for what he really was, and send him packing.

This never happened, and in May 1968 Jackie joined Onassis aboard the *Christina* for a Caribbean cruise, whilst Maria retreated to Georges-Mandel to observe the event through the eyes of the media. 'I sometimes wish I were dead,' she told Roger Normand one day, and probably meant it – she had reverted to a diet of sleeping pills and anti-depressants, she was eating little, and smoking ten cigarettes a day, an excessive number for a woman who claimed she was allergic to smoke, and loathed the habit in others, refusing to allow even her most intimate friends – Onassis included – to light up in her presence. And yet, when the cruise was over, the errant tycoon returned to Paris, where he and Maria took up their affair as if nothing had happened. Then, on 5 June, only minutes after winning the Californian primary, Bobby Kennedy was shot in a Los Angeles hotel by a twenty-four-year-old Jordanian immigrant named Sirhan Sirhan. The next day he died, and Onassis lost no time in flying to be by Jackie's side: Bobby's murder is said to have affected her almost as much as that of her husband, and she was desperately worried about Bobby's widow, Ethel, who was carrying her eleventh child.

A few days after Bobby's funeral, now that there was effectively no one to object, Onassis and Jackie set the date for their wedding – 20 October 1968 – but this was not made public for two reasons: firstly, the bride-to-be wished to consult with Cardinal Cushing, who had conducted her first marriage ceremony – and secondly, Onassis *said* that he wanted to break the news gently to Maria. In fact, no such thing happened. Over the next two months Onassis commuted regularly between the *Christina* and wherever Jackie happened to be. He met his future parents-in-law, and attempted to win over Jackie's children, Caroline and John-John, by spoiling them rotten. He visited the family's matriarch, Rose Kennedy, who immediately announced that she could not stand him, and finally he 'entered negotiations' with Edward, Rose's only surviving son. Edward would later surprise everyone by pleading clemency for Sirhan Sirhan, who instead of going to the gas chamber had his sentence commuted to life imprisonment. Edward Kennedy disliked Onassis, but he did not detest him the way Bobby had, and he reluctantly gave Jackie his blessing. Christina Onassis, on the other hand, who escorted her father on most of these trips, did not take too kindly to her new family – now seventeen and opinionated, she loathed Jackie as much as she had Maria, and never missed out on an opportunity to tell her so, often most unpleasantly.

As for Maria, she had to work out for herself what was happening. At the beginning of August, to assuage her loneliness, she asked her old friend Lawrence Kelly of the Chicago Opera to join her on the *Christina*, yet no sooner had Kelly unpacked his bags than a call came through from Onassis: he was on his way back to the yacht where he was expecting an important guest, therefore would Maria mind going back to Paris and waiting for him there? Maria stayed put until Onassis arrived, then she did what some of her friends had been advising her to do for months – she told him to his face that she was leaving him, and that she would not be coming back.

Lawrence Kelly accompanied her to Paris, where in order to comfort her he began discussing the comeback he was sure she would never make – not because of vocal problems, which in any case could be rectified by coaching, but because her self-confidence had hit absolute rock-bottom. 'I won't do a tour right now,' she told her friend. 'I'll just *pretend* that I'm touring!'

From Paris, the pair flew to New York, from whence the 'tour' zig-zagged across America. For no other reason than that she could not bear to be alone, and mindless of the possible scandal, she shared Kelly's bed. In Cuernavaca, she slipped on the wet tiles of her bathroom and sustained two cracked ribs, and whilst she was recuperating, room-service delivered a copy of *Newsweek* with the breakfast tray. On the front page was a photograph of Jackie and Edward Kennedy leaving for their trip on the *Christina*, where they would be discussing Jackie's pre-wedding contract with Onassis. In Los Angeles, Maria switched on the television to watch *The Merv Griffin Show*. One of the guests was Doris Lilly, the acid-tongued gossip columnist from the *New York Post* who predicted that Onassis and Jackie would be married by the end of the year. The public did not take kindly to this: Lilly was spat at and booed as she was leaving the studio, and over the next few weeks she received sackloads of poison-pen letters for *daring* to suggest that this pretty young woman, considered *so* perfect by Rose Kennedy that she had referred to her once with the utmost respect as 'The Madonna', would ever sink so low as to become involved with a man of Aristotle Onassis's reputation.

From Los Angeles, Maria and Kelly flew to Dallas, where they spent a few days at the house of her friend, John Ardoin, then the music-critic of the *Morning News*, but who later became what many regard as *the* authority on Callas's recorded legacy, publishing two full-length studies and writing innumerable articles and papers. At the end of September, still with Kelly, she flew to New York: her old rival Renata Tebaldi, now ensconced with the Met, was about to open in a new production of *Adriana Lecouvreur*, and Rudolf Bing had invited Maria to share his box. Mischieviously, perhaps, she turned up sheathed in black velvet and dripping jewels – earning a standing ovation from the audience as she took her seat. Tebaldi, upon hearing the commotion from her dressing-room, took it that Bing's favourite soprano, Zinka Milanov, had entered the theatre as was her wont on first nights – the entire staff of the Met had been sworn to secrecy concerning Maria's visit.

After the performance, Bing rushed backstage to inform Tebaldi that 'an old friend' wished to spend a few minutes alone with her. The soprano was however instantly suspicious – that afternoon she had perused the guest-list and decided who she would or would not see. Then, as she was about to give Bing a piece of her mind for tricking her into meeting what she assumed must only have been a reporter, she observed Maria's tall, imposing figure at the end of the corridor. Twenty-three years on, Tebaldi explained to the music critic, Mel Cooper, what had happened next:

> For a moment it was difficult. And then I thought about the state her life had reached, the problems with her voice – Onassis, already with Jacqueline Kennedy. Perhaps she saw my thoughts in her face, that I had sympathy. But I just *stood* there. Suddenly she flew down the corridor and threw her arms around me. She told me over and over how wonderful the performance was and how glad she was for me and for how things were working out in my career. And I knew that she meant it – she *really* was happy for me. There was some change in her, something different. It was like meeting an old school-friend . . .

For several minutes, the two women clung to each other, sobbing.

Then, as they dried their eyes, the wily Bing – who by this time had 'briefed' Tebaldi's co-star, Franco Corelli – ushered in the press, and photographs of the sincere, smiling trio, with himself skulking in the background, were wired across the world.

Renata Tebaldi and Maria would remain firm friends for the rest of Maria's life and, whenever she was in Paris, Tebaldi would be expected to stay at Georges-Mandel. Rudolf Bing, however, failed in what some thought had been an attempt to woo Callas back to the Met. She told him, 'I shall always be grateful to you, dear, for effecting my reunion with Renata, but I do not feel that I will ever be able to sing for you again, much as I would like to.'

Towards the end of 1967, Maria had given an unusually relaxed interview to the American opera buff, Edward Downes – a non-pushy man for whom she had a tremendous admiration and who only brought out the best in her. She always regretted that this interview – broadcast during the intermissions of two New York Met radio performances – was not filmed. Now, however, she did consent to film *The Callas Conversations*, a two-part interview for the BBC with her friend Lord Harewood, but whereas she had appeared mildly flirtatious with Downes, she seemed on her guard with Harewood, who was unable to get a word in edgeways much of the time. There was one light-hearted moment – when Maria's poodle dashed into the room and began howling whilst she was demonstrating a top C – but sadly, this incident, one of several which might have given viewers a little more insight into what made this century's greatest diva 'tick', had ended up on the cutting-room floor.

'The respect shown to the subject by the almost stationary camera suggests an interview *of* instead of *by* royalty,' declared the *Daily Telegraph*'s Sean Day-Lewis. 'The brocaded Callas sits there, in her well-cushioned Paris apartment, looking marvellous with those well-placed eyes and face bones, talking with superb articulation and saying unbelievably little.'

In this respect, comparisons must be made between the 'Downes' Callas and the Callas of Lord Harewood. To the former, she had spoken freely of her weight-loss, the press attacks, her dislike of *Tosca* and of 'Vissi d'arte' in particular, which she declared only hindered the flow of the second act. To him she had blurted out, without pausing for breath, 'Decisions come from myself – I talk with myself frequently, every now and then I withdraw to myself and I calculate to myself – *this* happened and *that* happened, why this should happen, why did I do that and why *should* I do that, and why don't I do it better and why don't I have enough willpower, and you reason to yourself. Doesn't it happen to *you*?'

To Lord Harewood, Maria spoke of her formative years with di Hidalgo and Serafin, the intense preparation that had gone into every role. She enthused the characters she had loved: Norma, Medea, Traviata – and dismissed Carmen as 'going against her principles'. The film would have been considerably more interesting, had the questions, or at least some of them, been more confrontational: the family squabbles and artistic rivalries, the friendship with Onassis, and Maria's apparent retirement from the opera stage were all steered well clear of, and if Lord Harewood seemed to be working his way towards overstepping the mark, Maria very quickly changed course. Indeed, there were moments when she found it near-impossible to conceal her arrogance and indignation – though one must, of course, make allowances for her feelings at the time, and the delicate state she was in.

On 17 October 1968, Maria was relaxing in her bath when a call was put through to her, from Lawrence Kelly in Dallas. That afternoon, on the television news, a statement had been read out on behalf of Mrs Hugh D Auchincloss, Jackie Kennedy's mother, and Kelly thought Maria might appreciate hearing the news from someone who genuinely cared about her, before the press came banging on her door. Although no date had been set, and the location was not known, Jackie and Onassis were to be married within the week.

Maria was not as upset as most people had anticipated – at least this was the impression she gave – just surprised that the wedding had been arranged so quickly, for she had not taken Doris Lilly's prediction seriously. She even joked with Roger Normand, telling him, 'Ari's probably gotten Jackie in the family way. My God, what an ugly little bastard that one will be!' Over the telephone, she told the editor of *France-Soir*, 'I bear Jacqueline Kennedy no ill-will, and I have taken the news of their impending marriage in my stride. I'm sure they will be well-suited to each other.' Later that evening, her comments to an American reporter were somewhat less endearing: 'Jackie has done well to give her children a new grandfather. Ari is as beautiful as Croesus.' She was referring to the 6th century BC King of Lydia, in Asia Minor, fabled for his greed and wealth, and a man so hideous that any subject who did not bow to him and tell him that he was the handsomest man in the world was immediately put to death!

Three days after Mrs Auchincloss's announcement, Onassis and Jackie Kennedy were married in a simple Greek Orthodox ceremony at Skorpios's tiny, white-walled chapel. The thirty-nine-year-old bride, wearing a white Valentino mini-skirt, was given away by her stepfather, Hugh, who had done the same thing when she had married Jack Kennedy, when her own father had been too drunk to attend the ceremony. Maria was in Paris, attending a party celebrating the 75th anniversary of Maxim's, but if she tried desperately not to let her true feelings show, her performance was unconvincing – several times during the evening she emerged from the ladies' room, her eyes red through crying.

The marriage, after the idyllic first few weeks on Skorpios – where Onassis's personal security was so stringent that virtually no reporters were awarded a glimpse of the couple, and at least two photographers were beaten up by bodyguards – was little more than a farce, and certainly no love-match. When he married Jackie, Onassis was reputed to be worth in excess of $220 million, and if the 100-clause pre-nuptial contract, mostly in Jackie's favour, was anything to go by, she had certainly ensured that she would not lose out, should the marriage fail. Besides an annual six-figure allowance, Jackie had demanded substantial allowances for her already extremely well provided-for children, separate bedrooms should she deem this necessary, and no obligation whatsoever to bear Onassis children.

The greatest part of the American public, the ones who had worshipped her, now regarded Jackie as a joke and an insult to Jack Kennedy's memory – which was also just starting to become blighted as stories of his womanising began to come to light. Hate-mail arrived at Jackie's New York apartment by the sackful, whilst the American media, with one fell swoop, knocked her off her pedestal. In their eyes, Onassis had rarely been less than repulsive, and for many of them Jackie was little better for taking up with him in the first place. It was generally concluded that she had only married him for his money, and until she could prove otherwise, she was regarded as little more than a 'gold-digger' and a 'courtesan', two of the politest terms used to describe her. Jackie did not prove otherwise. Taking advantage of Onassis's seemingly limitless wealth, she set off on a series of shopping binges which were almost unprecedented amongst American society, running up quite astronomical bills, for purchases which she could well have done without. Unable to make up her mind which of the six shades in a particular Valentino range best suited her complexion, she would take them all, at $10,000. On one occasion she spent $25,000 on lingerie, yet reproached Onassis as wasteful for doling out $100 bills for her children – who disliked him slightly less than his son and daughter loathed her – to buy sweets and Coca-Cola. On another occasion during a fifteen-minute 'blitz' on a New York department store, when the assistant informed her that the bill was $150,000, she shrugged her shoulders like she always did and retorted, 'Fine. charge it to Mr Onassis!' It has been estimated that during their seven years of marriage, Jackie spent over $50 million of her husband's money on herself, and that he lavished *fifty* times this amount on her . . . ostensibly to keep her happy whilst he was entertaining the other women in his life.

Maria, meanwhile, received literally thousands of letters, cards and telegrams from her fans – and just a few from caring friends such as Visconti, Princess Grace, Maurice Chevalier and Marlene Dietrich – urging her to continue with her career and put Onassis, the sole perpetrator of her misery and the reason why her career had ground to a halt, firmly behind her. Offers were forthcoming, not just for opera, but for stage and screen. Tennessee Williams, having witnessed the mass hysteria of Maria's 1958 San Francisco 'gay' concert, saw in her a replacement for his favourite 'camp' icon, Tallulah Bankhead, the outrageous star who had died at the end of

1968. Maria and Tallulah had met several times, most noticeably when she had attended one of the performances of 'Crazy October' in November 1958, in which Tallulah had co-starred with the British actress, Estelle Winwood. After the performance Maria, Tallulah, Winwood, Williams and the actor Montgomery Clift had had a 'girls' night out' in downtown Detroit, where Maria and Clift had discovered a shared predilection for leaving their own meals untouched, much preferring to swipe the tastiest morsels of food from the plates of the other diners. Now, Williams offered Maria *two* parts. The first was Flora Goforth in the screen version of his *The Milk Train Doesn't Stop Here Anymore* created on the New York stage with Tallulah in 1964, with Tab Hunter as co-star. Hunter had agreed to appear in the film, and Maria thought very seriously about the role of the dying, has-been music-hall star who is spending her last days on the Italian Riviera, dictating her memoirs and having an affair with a opportunist gigolo nick-named 'Angel of Death' because of his tendency for preying on the emotions of sick, vulnerable women. Tallulah had dismissed Flora as 'a promiscuous, pill-ravaged rip born in a Georgia swamp', and though she came very close to accepting the part, Maria turned it down after deciding that some parts of the script were a little too close to the truth. For exactly the same reason she rejected the lead in the film adaptation of Williams' *Boom*, joking with him, 'You'd better give *that* one to Elizabeth Taylor!' . . . which he did. Other rejections included the part of Sarah in John Huston's *The Bible*, which went to Ava Gardner, and within hours of his arrival at Georges-Mandel with the contract she backed out of Visconti's new production of *La Traviata*, with Franco Corelli, which would have been staged at the Paris Opera during the spring of 1969.

Once more, Maria was addicted to tranquillisers, and she had also begun drinking heavily – though thankfully this latter phase was short-lived, ending abruptly when one morning, feeling very much the worse for wear, she received a telephone call from the Italian film-producer, Franco Rossellini, whom she had first met in Rome at the time of her split from Meneghini. Back then, Rossellini had been keen to film one of her opera performances, though he had not got around to telling her which one before she silenced him with a resounding, 'No, thank you!' Now, the producer informed her that his friend, the controversial director Pier Paolo Pasolini, was looking for an actress to portray a Medea which was neither operatic nor Euripidean, but one of his own adaptation – which like everything else Pasolini did would be sure to be 'off-beat'. Maria told Rossellini that she would think about it, then hung up.

Maria had never been a fervent admirer of Pasolini, the Bologna-born, self-professed champion of, in his own words, 'homosexuals, delinquents, paupers and communists'. One year her senior, he had been brought up in Frioul, where he had taken up a teaching position and joined the local Communist party – only to be ousted from both when his anti-Communist enemies had 'outed' his homosexuality in a local newspaper, forcing him to flee to Rome, where he had sought solace amongst down-and-outs in the seediest section of the city's red-light district. Here he had begun writing novels and poems, giving full vent to his furtive sexual imagination and frequently falling victim to obscenity charges. His first full-length book, *Ragazzi di Vita*, had been published in 1955 when Maria had purchased a copy to see what all the fuss had been about. She had been disgusted by this violent world of thieves, rent-boys and murderers, even more so because the work had been penned by a man who declared himself a devout Catholic – the gay characters in Pasolini's early tomes were mostly stereotyped, effeminate, unpleasant victims – and she had burned the book before finishing it. She had been equally shocked by one of his most recent films, *Theorem*, wherein the British actor Terence Stamp, passing through a provincial town, had in turn seduced the mother, the daughter, the maid, the son and the father of a middle-class family before indifferently continuing his travels. Even more revolting, from Maria's point of view, was the subject-matter of *Porcine*, about to be released, for in this one the objects of the hero's sexual desires were not the women in his lives, but the pigs! His earlier epic, however, *The Gospel According to St Matthew*, which Maria saw for the first time after Pasolini had proposed *Medea*, moved her to tears and it was on the strength of this that she decided to work with him. She called Franco Rossellini and told him, 'If Signor Pasolini can make *my* film half as good as that one, I'll do it!' Rossellini assured her that this would be the case. Neither the terms of her contract nor Maria's fee were discussed, and a meeting with Pasolini was arranged.

Before this took place, Maria received a visit from an agitated Luchino Visconti. Having heard on the grapevine about the *Medea* project, her friend urged her not to work with a man whose ideals – openly promiscuous homosexuality, and liberal expression of his Marxist opinions – would almost certainly distress her at a time when she was searching desperately for peace of mind. It was even proposed that, with Onassis and Meneghini both out of the way, she should make a film with him. Visconti suggested *Macbeth*, an idea which might have suited her once, but not now. Maria turned him down with a not so gentle rebuff, adding, 'In your film I would have to become Lady Macbeth, whereas I already *am* Medea!'

Maria was nervous about meeting Pasolini – Visconti was not the only one of her friends with hardly a good word to say about him, though she was looking forward to a clean break, an opportunity to work with a man who, regardless of reputation, had absolutely no links with her past. Bruno Rosi, a young Venetian journalist who many years later mounted a Callas-Pasolini exhibition of photographs and memorabilia on this period of their careers, said, 'Medea was supposed to be Callas's way of saying to Onassis: the end of our love affair has not destroyed me. I'm still alive!'

In Pasolini, Maria was surprised to find a gentle, sensitive man – a man who, like herself, had suffered the slings and arrows of misfortune, albeit mostly self-inflicted. The director was also having problems with his lover, Ninetto Davoli, so in essence Maria could not have arrived in his life at a more appropriate moment. In short, these two vastly contrasting icons needed each other. What surprised everyone, however, was the fact that the impossible happened – knowing that there could never be anything physical between them did not prevent Maria from falling in love with Pasolini, but unlike her one-sided attractions for Visconti, Cioni, Corelli and Zeffirelli, this one was reciprocated. Over the course of the next year Maria would spend more time alone with Pasolini that she had with any man. He would dedicate ten quite beautiful poems to her, including one – Verba – which began, 'Quest' ombra caduta su di te, che io sento,' (This shadow that has fallen over you, which I feel). He also said of her at the time, 'Maria was so defenceless against love that you just wanted to protect her. Perhaps she felt her self-imposed exile from the stage was something unforgivable and painful, so she dedicated herself to love with a determined and anxious mind.'

Medea began shooting during the first week of June 1969 in Goreme, a remote part of Turkey which perfectly suited the violence and mysticism of the scenario. There is a particularly gruesome scene near the beginning of the film where a youth is sacrificed, hacked to pieces and shared out amongst the peasants, who smear bits of him onto their crops to make them grow. 'Give life to the seed and be reborn with the seed,' Medea pronounces. In another scene, she calmly butchers another beautiful young man who has helped her to steal the Golden Fleece, then tosses his head out of her cart onto the desert sand. And as with all Pasolini films, homoeroticism abounds with an endless catalogue of close-ups of hirsute torsos and thighs – at least twenty of these young men are said to have slept with Pasolini during the auditions for the cast, and as many more whilst the film was being shot.

Maria's love-scenes with Jason, however, are unconvincing, perhaps because she disliked Giuseppe Gentile, the actor playing him. 'He had a beard,' she told Roger Normand, 'and I have always hated men with beards.' She did however love posing for Pasolini, and some of her profiles are quite staggering – one in particular where she is sleeping, then suddenly opens her huge, lovely eyes. Her dialogue too leaves much to be desired. Pasolini was rarely interested in synchronisation, and some of the dialogue is pronounced in English, then over-dubbed by Maria into Italian, taking away a great deal of the film's essential continuity – which is further disrupted by the inclusion of several scenes more than once. Her acting, however, is stylish and gives a clear indication to those of her fans who never saw her what she must have been like on the stage – her expressions of anxiety and woe reflect what she was no doubt feeling after the split from Onassis. Even when making love to Jason, very un-Callas-like in a transparent gown, she is indifferent to pleasure and only smiles when, towards the end of the film, she is plotting her revenge. 'Nothing is possible any more,' she screams at him, as the final credits roll.

As far from the opera world as she could possibly get, Maria was more relaxed than she had ever been in her professional life. There were no tantrums, no problems with her nerves, no insomnia, and she got along with everyone – even Giuseppe Gentile – insisting that she should only be addressed by her first name. She was naturally hounded by reporters, several of whom bribed the costumes departments to allow them to dress up as extras to enable them to get close to her – she even joked with one young man, telling him, 'Take off your shirt, and I'll arrange to have you sacrificed!' She was patient with these people because for once the questions centred around her first non-singing role and not her private life. Only once was Onassis's name brought up, and this was when *she* passed a veiled comment to a reporter from the *Daily Telegraph* 'Medea was a demi-goddess whose downfall came about when she put all her trust in one man.'

After six weeks in this torrid wasteland, shooting moved to Aleppo in Syria, then to Pisa, and finally to the outskirts of Rome – and it was only here, as the project was drawing to a close, that the old Maria returned and she grew tetchy and irritable. To a certain extent, she was helped by Pasolini, who invited her to 'assist' him with the film's editing and soundtrack – the latter little more than a noisy fusion of Greek Orthodox music and wailing. Then in the September, totally out of the blue, she received a telephone call from Onassis, who with apparent sincerity – not to mention incalculable nerve – told her how much he was missing her. For ten minutes, the pair reflected on old times – neither his new wife nor Maria's career entered the conversation, save that he was looking forward to seeing the film and her portrayal of the role which had brought them together. Then, before hanging up, Onassis asked her if she would consider going to dinner with him. Maria replied that she would think about it. The next day, as with the Covent Garden *Medea* of 1959, the flowers and gifts started up again, including a tiny poodle which Maria baptised Djedda.

After featuring in Argentina's Mar del Plata Film Festival at the end of 1969, *Medea* was premièred at the Paris Opera on 28 January 1970 in the presence of the president's wife, Madame Pompidou. The invited audience applauded wildly – not on account of their having enjoyed the film or even understood most of it, it is said, but because Maria and Pasolini were there. The critics, as they had been with her opera and concert performances, were divided in their opinion. Most of them, accurately forecasting that the venture would prove a commercial failure, agreed that Maria *looked* the part. 'She is the possessor of what I imagine as the perfect Indo-European face in which the obstinacy of the past and the impetuousness of the future – Asian serenity, and European ruthlessness, if you like – coexist so uneasily,' concluded the (unamed) film critic of the *Observer*. When it came to acting *material*, however, Pasolini was accused of not giving her enough to do, and making his Medea far too passive, a far cry from the monster Maria had created on the opera platform. 'It was a heroic *bore*,' declared the *Evening Standard*, 'and is it not disturbing to find oneself wishing that the enchantress of Colchis would get on with dispatching her children and let us all go home?'

Maria was naturally upset by some of these adverse comments, but took some consolation from the fact that most of them were directed at Pasolini and not herself. Also, her spirits had been lifted, a few days before the première, when she had finally agreed to see Onassis – inviting him to a small dinner party at Georges-Mandel where, though he had tried to act neutrally in front of her other guests, he had found several minutes to convey to Maria that he was missing her the way she was him, and that his marriage to Jackie Kennedy was proving a huge, costly mistake. Over the next few weeks, Maria and Onassis began meeting again on a regular basis, and eventually they saw little point in hiding the fact that they had resumed their relationship. Whether or not Onassis considered making this more solid by divorcing Jackie is not known, though according to several of her friends, Maria expected him to. Such dreams were therefore dashed when, on 21 May, the pair were photographed at Maxim's. Jackie learned of the event only hours afterwards, long before the pictures appeared in the press, and rather than argue with her husband she booked a seat on the next plane to Paris, then insisted that he take *her* to Maxim's the very next evening. They sat at the same table, and even partook of the same menu that Onassis had eaten with Maria.

To Maria's naive way of thinking, Onassis – in whom she had confided her innermost secrets and feelings over that same table – had betrayed her by cheating on her with his own wife. Three days later, at 6.45 on the morning of 25 May, she was rushed to the Hôpital Americain de Neuilly, just outside Paris. Two hours later, the first of the news-flashes was broadcast on *RTL* radio: 'Maria Callas has been admitted to hospital following a suicide attempt. She is known to have swallowed a quantity of barbiturates, but her condition is not thought to be serious.'

Minutes later, the press gathered outside the hospital, where no official statement was given – and outside Georges-Mandel, where Maria's maid only made matters worse by telling reporters, 'Madame has simply gone to the hospital for her regular check-up.' Bruna had overlooked the fact that outpatients usually travelled to the hospital under their own steam, not via ambulance with flashing sirens, and never before 9am. Neither had an earlier comment gone unnoticed when, in the February, Maria had told the *Observer*'s Kenneth Harris why Norma had always been her favourite role: 'When *she* finds herself in a terrible crisis of love, she chooses death rather than hurt the man she loves, even though he has betrayed her.' Another theory was that Maria *had* overdosed, but only accidentally – she was being prescribed so many pills that some of her friends believed that it would only be a question of time before such a thing happened.

Maria stayed in the hospital just ten hours – long enough to have her stomach pumped, and for the news to leak out to a journalist from the weekly magazine, *Noir et Blanc*, that it had been a genuine suicide attempt. Maria's lawyer prevented other sections of the media from reporting this – not a difficult process under France's draconian privacy laws – but the editor of *Noir et Blanc* stuck his neck out and printed his story. Maria sued both him and RTL and later in the year was awarded a somewhat paltry 20,000 francs in damages, plus costs.

If Maria *had* attempted to take her life because Onassis, having raised her expectations, had only duped her again, he certainly did not rush to her side now, as he had when Jackie had lost Kennedy's baby. Her anchor throughout this distressing episode was Pasolini, who when the initial hubbub had died down took her for a holiday to Trigonissi, a private island in the Aegean owned by the Emberikos family. For almost four weeks, they conducted themselves like any other tourists, swimming and skuba diving – two sports at which Maria excelled – taking long walks on the beach with Djedda, her poodle, and sharing the same bed in a minuscule cottage overlooking the sea. After the first week, Maria invited Nadia Stancioff to join them and even contemplated writing her memoirs – then decided against this because, unlike her detractors and some critics, she was convinced that her story was by no means over. Shortly before making *Medea* she had recorded six arias from *Il Corsaro, Attila, I Lombardi* and *I Vespri Siciliani* with Nicola Rescigno, in Paris. 'Everyone in the studio was enraptured,' she had told *Elle* magazine, 'but as usual I had to demolish it, track by track.' And though she had subsequently withdrawn her permission for EMI to release all but two of these, this in itself was an indication that she was more satisfied with her voice than she had been for some time. Added to this, of course, was the fact that she was still only forty-six, an age where, vocally, she should have been in her prime.

One person *did* find out about Maria's 'intimate evenings' with Pasolini – Onassis, who was quite unable to share her with another man, albeit one who would never be less than a calculating, voracious homosexual. On 15 August, Maria's name-day, the tycoon's helicopter landed on Trigonissi for what was to be a lightning trip, though ostensibly long enough for him to let the world know that so far as Callas was concerned, she was still his for the taking. Onassis had arranged everything: a sumptuous lunch, gifts for all guests and for Maria's 'birthday' a pair of antique $100,000 earrings – and, of course, a photographer who snapped the two of them kissing passionately under a beach umbrella. Only weeks before, Maria had been captured in a similar clinch with Pasolini, but the captions attached to this by the press had been unflattering, as had the biting comment from Onassis, 'Callas has spent half of her life running around after queers. What she's always needed was a *real* man!' A few days later, Pasolini returned to his troublesome lover, Ninetto Davoli, Maria to her life of near-solitude at Georges-Mandel, and Onassis to his wife . . . but the lives of all three had been strangely touched by that sojourn in the Aegean.

18

Ha Forse Alcuno Cura Di Me?

I've never stopped learning. Do you know what that means? It's a lifetime job!

At the end of November 1970, Maria flew to New York for a non-singing appearance on David Frost's television show. Her friend Montserrat Caballé was in town, and Maria at once sought her out. 'We spent the whole afternoon together,' she told me. 'For some reason, Maria was terrified of meeting him. 'I desperately need to be understood,' she said, 'and it's so difficult trying to make people see what I'm really like when they have a preconceived image of me before I even enter the studio. No matter what kind of questions that man asks, the public will never believe the answers that I give! And then there'll be all those tiresome compliments!' Maria hated such things. She knew that like any other human being she made mistakes, so when people came up to her and said, "Madame Callas, you were *wonderful*," she would cringe.'

Effectively, Frost's questions were largely routine, and Maria managed to stay calm throughout the interview – though she did say afterwards that she would never wish to appear on the programme again.

Whilst she was in New York, Maria heard of the celebrations in Italy following parliamentary approval of a Bill legalising divorce.

This had been passed following a bitter, five-year struggle between the Christian Democrat Party and the Vatican. Even so, the country's divorce laws would remain amongst the most stringent in Europe – couples would have to be legally separated for five years before being granted a divorce – and there was fierce opposition from the largely Roman Catholic population. Maria was delighted, for she could now be rid of her troublesome husband for good, and she rang her French lawyer and told him to commence proceedings.

A few days later, Maria spoke to the press, who naturally wanted to know if, when she became free, she would marry again. The response was a very definite, 'No' ... which did not prevent her from being subjected to a particularly arduous grilling about her personal life which she could have done without. Her mother had recently returned to Athens, and though Maria's monthly allowance would continue – and go considerably further on account of a healthy interest rate – Litza still expected more, and shortly before sailing from New York she had once more pleaded poverty with the press who were still firmly on her side, years after the damning *Time* exposé. On top of this, Maria had received another 'begging' letter from her sister Jackie, who now also had a legal obligation to look after her parents – who, though living in the same neighbourhood, would never set eyes on Maria again. 'Any letters that I receive from my so-called family go straight into the bin, unopened,' Maria had confessed earlier. Now at her press conference she several times deliberated before replying to some of the questions, and twice flared up and came very close to walking out – though by the end of the interview, the press had more than exacted their pound of flesh:

- 'No, I did *not* try to kill myself! I'm too full of life. The French newspapers have given me some guarantees that they will never print anything about my private life again. If they do, I shall sue them again. Make no mistake of that!'
- 'Yes, Mr Onassis *is* my best friend. He is, he was, and he will always be so! And why should it be considered *unusual* for us to see each other since his marriage? We have worked

together on several business deals, and when two people have been together as we have, there are many things that *tie* you together. Mr Onassis knows that he will always find cheerfulness, honesty and mutual friendship when he sees me.'

* 'Scandal? *What* scandal? Any scandal only comes about because I have not met Mr Onassis's wife. *That* is not wished on the other side, dear, and frankly I don't understand why she doesn't come into my life. If we *did* meet, it would certainly stop all the gossip in your newspapers!'

* 'My mother and my husband? I haven't spoken to them for years, and nor do I wish to! *He* has a bad case of the blah-blahs. He has told lies and tried to take credit for everything in my success. Also, he is not as rich as he says he is. And no, dear, I have *nothing* to say to you about my mother!'

Maria spent a very lonely Christmas at Georges-Mandel that year – ringing friends who could not or did not wish to see her, because by this time she was so obsessed with playing her own old recordings and pirated tapes that even some of those closest to her found her a bore. She also suffered several domestic mishaps: tripping over a coffee table, twice walking into a closed door she thought was open, and slipping again in the bathroom. At first she attributed her 'giddiness' to the potentially lethal cocktail of tranquillisers and anti-depressants she had been prescribed – still unable to cope or to sleep, she had simply upped the dosage – until a friend admonished her that maybe all she needed was an eye-test.

This only made matters worse. Maria became paranoid that she might be going blind. She had been booked to give two weeks of master-classes at Philadelphia's Curtis Institute for the February of 1971, but she left Paris a few days early so that she could see an eye-specialist in New York. Ironically, her own fears were confirmed, for she was diagnosed as suffering from incipient glaucoma and almost certainly would have lost her sight had it not been for the emergency treatment she received.

Even so, she was in good spirits when agreeing to a 'question-time' at New York's prestigious Julliard School on 3 February, an event which was attended by not just the press but most of the city's opera fraternity – who were warned, before she walked on to the platform, 'Anyone asking questions about Miss Callas's personal life will be immediately escorted from the building!' In fact, she was astonishingly forthright and began by dismissing as 'rubbish' the theory held by some that her voice had deteriorated since she had lost weight. 'First you *must* have the voice. Then and *only* then you must look for the appearance. What is outside is *not* inside! If you're fat outside, your diaphragm does not necessarily work well *inside*!'

She also defended herself against those critics who had accused her of sacrificing vocal excellence for dramatic content: 'In opera, drama comes *first*, ahead of music. If you're angry, there is no voice that can be beautiful *and* efficient. When you get angry you *shriek*! Otherwise it's boring, it's just oratorio!'

Regarding her 'former' vocal problems, she was now profoundly optimistic: 'Yes, I developed some bad vocal habits, so I retired to start again. Now I am ready. I've never stopped learning and I'm planning to announce, probably soon this year, my plans for singing again. I've never *asked* for anything. I've *been* asked! I know how to wait, and I'm always ready when the chance comes!'

And, much to everyone's surprise, she did speak candidly about love: 'Love is sometimes like a sickness. To make a love-affair or a marriage work takes all our attention. Women are not *pals* enough with men, so we must make ourselves indispensable. After all, we have the greatest weapon in our hands by just *being* women! In *bed* isn't enough. After one or two years it's all the rest – the lying and the not lying. I hate lying, but sometimes you have to tell a white lie. And sometimes you have to tell the truth, even if all hell breaks loose!'

The master-classes in Philadelphia, however, never took place, solely because Maria was dissatisfied with the students the Curtis Institute had selected for her to teach. She had the courtesy to audition each one, but after dismissing them as 'a talentless bunch of no-hopers', she returned to Paris, and several more months of crippling loneliness. On the evening of 3 March she received an unexpected visit from her lawyer: Meneghini's lawyer, the former cabinet minister Guiseppe Trabucchi, had officially opposed Italy's new divorce law as 'Unconstitutional', and as a result of his having referred the matter to Rome's Constitutional Court, Maria's was one of hundreds of divorce hearings that had been temporarily suspended. 'Fucking old idiot,' she told Roger Normand. 'Even *he* can't change the law!'

Normand was one of the few friends to really spend time with her these days, and on rare outings the pair would dine at a little restaurant just off the Place Blanche – or stroll around the local cemetery. Once, heavily disguised, she watched workmen filling in a grave and remarked, 'Just imagine how awful it must be, being shoved down there to be eaten by worms. When my time comes I want burning. God, I wish it could be soon!'

Montserrat Caballé, on the other hand, remembers seeing a very light-hearted, even giggly Maria when she visited Georges-Mandel, though she did detect an element of despair and loneliness not too far beneath the surface. 'I was about to sing 'Norma' at the Théâtre des Champs-Elysées,' she told me. 'Then Maria called, on the afternoon of the première, and invited my husband and me to dine at her apartment that same evening. I told her that it was out of the question – I was singing that evening. She said, 'No, you're not. The orchestra and chorus have gone on strike. I had a call from the director this morning!' Because Maria had been invited to the première, and because the director considered her more important than his Norma, he had told her before me, and she spent the entire evening trying to cheer *me* up!'

Because of the events on Trigonissi, Pasolini rarely risked having anything to do with Maria: he rang Georges-Mandel once and Onassis answered the telephone, letting forth such a torrent of filth that the placid little Italian was terrified of dropping by again. As for Onassis, he too was going through emotional turmoil. In the July his daughter Christina – even to Onassis's face, Maria referred to her as 'that odious little creature' – married Joseph Bolker, an American real-estate tycoon more than twice her age, and Onassis immediately cut her out of his will – rescinding this action the following year, when Christina and Bolker divorced. Then in the September he learned that his ex-wife Tina, recently divorced from the Marquess of Blandford, was about to be married – to his arch-rival Stavros Niarchos, who had formerly been married to Onassis's sister, Eugenia, and accused by him of involvement in her death in 1969 ... an autopsy had revealed a large quantity of barbiturates and severe physical injuries, but though Niarchos had been taken into custody, all charges had been dropped. Later, Onassis would further accuse Niarchos of 'paying off' the authorities, forgetting that had this been true, he himself had done exactly the same thing when arrested in the United States for tax-evasion. However, the fact that his beloved children now had such a man as their step-father would haunt Onassis for the rest of his days.

Maria was largely indifferent towards her lover's woes, however, for after the Curtis Institute 'fiasco' she had been approached by Peter Menin of the Juilliard School of Music and invited to give a series of master-classes. Initially, she was extremely demanding, telling friends, 'I've had to spit blood to get where I am today. If they want me, they'll have to pay!' Exactly how much she was offered for the twenty-three twice-weekly classes which ran between 11 October 1971 and 16 March 1972 is not known, but it is said to have been a lot. On top of this, all her other demands were met without quibble: first-class travel and a suite at New York's Plaza Hotel, a personal maid and chauffeured limousine, and the services of Alberta Maziello, a top singing coach ... for not only did Maria's voice have to be in top form so that she could pass on her consummate skills to others, she had to convince the world, the critics, but most of all herself that she was still The Great Callas, all this *and* having the nerve to walk on to a stage and face an audience again. She also told Peter Menin that the 1,000-strong audience would have to pay 'opera prices' to *hear* her teach. Then, when he agreed to these conditions, with uncustomary generosity Maria waived her fee.

Maria was not renowned for her confidence in young singers. Too many of them, she had told Edward Downes, now expected to *start* at the top by making their debuts in the big houses. '*Our* experience was obtained by starting off in little theatres and coming up the hard way, which is not something that people *like* to do, but it makes you or breaks you,' she had said. 'Then, by the time you reach La Scala and the Metropolitan you are already a mature singer, because *they* do not have any space for amateurs.'

The Juilliard master-classes were attended by largely celebrity audiences: Maria was photographed with Lillian Gish, Ben Gazzara, Tito Gobbi, Placido Domingo and Franco Zeffirelli, looking very un-Callas-like in a black Balenciaga trouser-suit, horn-rimmed glasses, and with her long hair untied and spread over her shoulders. All the classes were taped and subsequently released on commercial recordings, and in 1987 these were edited into fluent English by her friend John Ardoin, and transcribed into a best-selling book. For those sitting in the hall who were not fully conversant in musical jargon in its entirety, however, the sessions must have been hard going, even though these spectators were witnessing an historical event – for much of the time Maria comes across as a talking glossary, and her curious accent frequently adds to the confusion. For the twenty-five young singers who had the immense privilege of being 'knocked into shape' by her, of course, these may have been arguably the greatest moments of their careers – even for the few, including John Woods and Shirley Verrett, who made it to the international circuit.

Maria proved an authoritative, occasional strict teacher, setting a good example for discipline by striding on to the stage at *exactly* 5.30 as detailed in the programme, and summoning each of her students like a forceful but kindly schoolma'am. A baritone about to deliver 'Il lacerato spirito' from Verdi's *Simon Boccanegra* was told, 'This aria is sung by a man in great anguish. But grief does not mean moaning. He has dignity, so make sure you sing with authority and dramatic warmth.' When another baritone, a timid young Korean, began the Prologue from *I Pagliacci*, she stopped him and instructed him to open his throat: 'You have a big voice there. Let it out! I don't care if you crack on the top note, but hit hard. Caruso cracked many times!' A tenor, before tackling 'Vesti la giubba' from the same work, was forewarned, 'Let's have no sobbing, here! Gigli did, but I must say that I disliked it. He cried *too* much in his singing. You can convey the heartbreak of Canio being betrayed without sobs!'

Maria told a soprano who was about to sing part of Beethoven's 'Ah! Perfido' – ironically perhaps, in the light of recent events –

that the work focused on strong feelings, adding, 'A woman deserted by her lover cries to heaven to punish him, then begs the gods to take her life instead. In short, she doesn't know her own mind.' Another soprano was allowed to sing a bland 'Caro nome', from Verdi's *Rigoletto*, all the way through before Maria tapped her pen on the table and admonished, 'Miss Benson, Gilda's a passionate girl, you know, and you must convey to the audience all her palpitating emotion before you even *begin* to sing. The very act of breathing is an emotion!' Then, Miss Benson was shown how the aria should have been sung, whilst Maria urged the soprano to try and keep up with her, which of course she was unable to do. The opera-critic Alan Blyth, sitting in the audience, remembered the shiver that ran through the auditorium, and concluded, 'There is the inevitable sad thought that that particular kind of magic cannot be transferred to even the most talented of students.'

During the first week of March, on the eve of her penultimate master-class, Maria was summoned before the Metropolitan Opera's board. Some months before. In Paris, she had been made Honorary President of the Gala de l'Union des Artistes – now she was offered the position of the Met's Artistic Director. Naturally she was very flattered, and over the course of the next few days she seriously thought of accepting. Then, having convinced herself how much she owed the public to continue serving them from the *artist's* side of the footlights, she politely refused.

After her final master-class, on 16 March 1972, Maria addressed her students and the audience with a speech which was a poignant as it was sincere:

For thanks, the only thing I want for you all is that you sing properly, that you apply whatever knowledge I've given you to your scores. That's the only thing I can say for the moment. Each and every one of you – it doesn't stop here. It has to keep on going because you're supposed to follow up what we have done. What [whether] I keep on singing doesn't make any difference. You are the younger generation and you *must* apply. That's the only thanks that I really do want. Keep on going, and the proper way – not with fireworks, not with an easy applause, but with the expression of the words, the diction, and with your real feeling, whatever it is. This is what I want to say, and I'm not good at words. So, that's that!

A legendary star who had now sadly fallen by the wayside was the tenor, Giuseppe di Stefano, who had last partnered Maria in 1957 at La Scala. Aged just fifty, di Stefano was a typical example of what may happen to the human voice if stretched beyond the limits of endurance – in short, his career as one of the greatest lyric tenors of this century was over because he had sung too much, too quickly, with unrestrained, almost superhuman power so that not much was left to sing with. Therefore, when he and Maria met again in March 1972 after one of her Juilliard master-classes and, putting all their quarrels behind them decided to form a musical partnership, it was regarded by many as tantamount to two blind people trying to help each other across a very busy road. 'Poor Maria,' declared one friend, who insisted upon remaining anonymous for this book, 'she considered herself so washed up by this time that she allowed herself to latch onto a man who couldn't sing two out of three notes in tune. Not only this, she fell in love with him and even rang his wife to tell her what they were doing because she felt so ashamed!'

Maria and di Stefano spent several weeks of that summer in San Remo, rehearsing ten arias for a proposed album with Philips – she had slammed the phone down on EMI's Michel Glotz because he had criticised her choice of partner, hence the change of label. And in spite of the excitement brought about by this project and the couple's so-called 'autumnal love' – both had apparently been fighting against this happening for two decades – it was also quite an anxious time. Di Stefano's teenage daughter was slowly dying of cancer, and Maria received word from her sister in Athens that her eighty-six-year-old father, who over the last few years had suffered recurring bouts of pneumonia, was very ill. She even thought about going to see him, then decided that such action might be unwise: the last thing she needed at this make-or-break stage of her career was adverse publicity, and now that her mother was back on home territory Maria was certain that she would make sure that the Greek press had a field-day.

There was another reason why Maria did not wish to return to Greece, certainly not at the moment. Although, throughout her whole life she had remained staunchly a-political, now that she was effectively a Greek citizen, she felt it her duty to speak out against Colonel George Papadopoulos' military regime, which had ousted the monarchy in 1967. She called the actress and political activist, Melina Mercouri, later to become Greece's Minister of Culture, and told her, 'No matter what happens, I'll never come back whilst the Colonels are running the show. And, God forbid that I should die whilst they are, I'm making arrangements that my ashes will be buried in Paris. Greece holds nothing for me at the moment. We'd enough of that sort of thing under the Germans.'

On 28 November, Maria and di Stefano arrived in London, where two days later they began working on the new album at Philips' studio in St Giles, Cripplegate. Certain conductors disapproved of her working with a man who in their eyes, could no longer sing – whereas they believed that she *was* capable of making a successful comeback with a minimum of tuition – and the sessions were eventually conducted by Antonio de Almeida. Their first effort, 'Una parola, o Adina' from Donizetti's *L'Elisir d'Amore*, was abandoned halfway through, but five more arias were completed before the sessions ended on 20 December, including a passable 'Pur ti riveggo' from *Aida*, but one which was by no means as good as the unreleased June 1964 version with Corelli. And needless to say, though di Stefano was content with *his* efforts, most of which were unbelievably dire, Maria flatly refused to allow any of the arias to be released.

On 4 December 1972 – Maria's forty-ninth birthday – she received a call from Jackie in Athens to say that her father had died. Maria did not feel that she owed it to her sister, or anyone, to explain why she would not be attending the funeral, though the French press completely accepted her brief, tearful statement, 'Le spectacle doit continuer!' In Athens, a seemingly sympathetic Jackie told a reporter at the graveside that Maria had been unable to leave Paris on account of recording commitments, and that the Callas family were fully supportive of her decision. She gave the impression that she had joined the Callas detractors some years later, however, by observing in her memoirs, 'I said she was heart-broken over the death of her father but [that] as a professional she knew she had to carry on. When one remembers all the contracts she had broken in the past, when one thought of all the opera houses she had walked out of, I wondered why they didn't just laugh in my face!'

A few weeks later, on 22 January 1973, Maria was rocked – albeit indirectly – by another tragedy when Onassis's twenty-four-year old son, Alexander, crashed one of his father's private planes during a test-run from Athens. For more years than she cared to remember, Maria had been attempting to befriend Onassis's children, always to no avail, but if she had given up on Christina, she had nurtured a soft spot for Alexander – even though he had frequently made her life a misery for no other reason than he held her responsible for the break-up of his parents' marriage. Alexander was not killed outright in the crash – he suffered irreparable brain damage and was kept on a life-support machine long enough for his family to gather at his bedside.

Onassis was inconsolable. Alexander's handsome face had been smashed beyond recognition, yet even whilst Alexander had been fighting for his life his hysterical father had begged the doctors to perform plastic surgery on the boy. Such a thing had of course not been possible ... so Onassis demanded that his face be repaired now, after death, and initially refused to allow his son to be buried until his 'killer' had been found and brought to justice. To his grief-inspired way of thinking, as with the death of his sister Eugenia, it had to be *someone's* fault, and he accused everyone from Stavros Niarchos to the American government of sabotaging the plane. It was only after several independent investigations concluded that it *had* been an accident that Onassis had Alexander laid to rest next to the tiny chapel on Skorpios.

The tragedy clearly marked the beginning of Onassis's downfall. For several months he completely lost interest in business affairs, and his holdings slumped from an estimated $1 billion to less than half of this amount. Jackie, who over the last few years had been more preoccupied with spending his fortune than actually caring for the man himself, now attempted the role of the doting wife, though she was of course too late. Onassis and Alexander had not been close, but he had regarded his son as an anchor for the future, an assurance that his own name and pioneering reputation would live on. With Alexander gone, his daughter became his focus for survival, whilst Jackie was not undeservedly shunted to one aside and ordered to curb her spending. 'The Gold Digger doesn't understand him,' Maria later told her friend and accompanist, Robert Sutherland, of whom more later. 'He's married a national monument. She was never right for him. She tried to change his whole way of life. It's typical that she redecorates everything – even the yacht. That's a big mistake. It's like taking away his past. I never did that – I wouldn't have dared!'

Maria left Onassis to grieve, and flung herself into her work, and her latest love affair. The recordings with di Stefano having been consigned to the vaults, and terrified of singing in public for fear of being branded a failure, or worse, she announced that she would like to 'do something' from the other side of the footlights, but insisted that it should not be another series of master-classes. She was immediately contacted by Stefano Vernizzi, the Artistic Director of Turin's Téatro Regio. The building had been gutted by fire in 1936, but was scheduled to re-open on 10 April 1973 with a gala production of *I Vespri Siciliani*.

More than anything in the world, Vernizzi would have liked Maria to sing Elena, but he knew she would not accept so, after engaging Raina Kabaivanska for the role, he asked Maria to direct the production. She agreed, but on one condition – that Vernizzi appoint di Stefano as co-director. This caused a furious quarrel between Maria and one of her closest friends, Gianandrea Gavazzeni, who was to conduct. Gavazzeni flatly refused to work in the same production as di Stefano, and the baton was passed to Vittorio Gui, who was almost ninety. When Gui was taken ill during rehearsals, Vernizzi was left no choice but to take up the baton himself.

The première of *I Vespri Sicilian* went well, but in the newspapers the next day the critics were undivided in their opinions: Callas would never make the grade as a director. Maria defended herself, as only she could, by launching a blistering attack on the current operatic climate. From her hotel suite in Turin, she told a reporter from the Associated Press, 'Today, the values are all wrong. Directors *think* they make the opera, but opera is a dead corpse without the singers. Some have brains and sensibilities. Others just sing and act like fools and are much too interested in the material- istic fruits of wealth. They have nothing to talk about except their beautiful homes, jewels and furs. They are good anywhere but on the stage.'

'But what about the *big* stars of comntemporary opera?' the reporter posed. 'Isn't Joan Sutherland *great*?' To which Maria could but scoff, 'Sutherland? A beautiful instrument, yes. She *said* she had followed my path. The trouble is, she did not. I used embell- ishments for expression. *She* uses them for fireworks, dear!'

Had Maria taken the advice of sincere, knowledgeable friends such as Zefferelli, Corelli, Lawrence Kelly and even Renata Tebaldi, she would have ended her professional relationship with Giuseppe di Stefano there and then – if not her amorous one as well – and concentrated on her own career. Antonio Ghirighelli, Covent Garden's John Tooley and Lawrence Kelly all suggested a brief concert tour – nothing too heavy to begin with – of 'showpieces': 'O mio babbino caro', 'D'amor sull'ali rosee', 'Quando m'en vo', and so on. Such was her obsession with di Stefano, however, that she turned down every worthwhile offer that came her way, and on 20 May the pair set off for Osaka, in Japan, to hold a master-class for the winners of the third Madame Butterfly Competition. They were met at Tokyo airport by a delegation headed by the soprano Nobue Kobayashi who, completely ignoring di Stefano, flung her arms around Maria – one foot taller than she was and sporting an eye-catching 'Butterfly' hairstyle.

At the end of May, Maria returned to Georges-Mandel where she was again inundated with offers for a concert tour, this time with the orchestra of her choice. She selected Georges Prêtre, and was close to signing the contract when di Stefano announced that he too wanted to tour – 'Maurice Chevalier-style', singing on a series of huge, bare stages with just a piano for accompaniment. Sandor Gorlinsky, however, was unable to find many theatres willing to take on the faded star, so di Stefano insisted that he and Maria continue their enterprise – not that it had amounted to much thus far – and he suggested that they tour the world together. In fact, although the two singers were paid a joint fee for each engagement, to be split at Maria's discretion, the actual contract only had her name printed on it, and contained a clause to the effect that the tenor was to be her support act.

At the end of June, Maria received a telephone call from Gracie Fields, inviting her to spend a few days at the Canzone del Mare complex, on Capri. Maria would have loved a holiday, but she was terrified of leaving di Stefano in case being away from him made her change her mind about the tour. 'Every morning, when I awake I have an urge to call Gorlinsky and tell him I can't go through with it,' she told her friend, 'Then after my first cup of coffee I'm raring to go and I think of those thousands of fans who queue all night for tickets and who have never stopped loving me. What else can I do?'

A few days before their conversation, one of Gracie's guests on Capri had been the veteran pianist, Ivor Newton, who had toured with her during the last war – some years prior to this, he had accompanied many legendary stars, inlcuding Tetrazzini, Melba and Gigli. When Maria said that she had assumed Newton to be dead by now, Gracie quipped with typical Lancashire humour, 'Well, love, he does look as if he's got one foot in the grave, but so long as he doesn't drop off his perch, there's plenty of magic left in them there fingers!'

Maria called Sandor Gorlinsky at once, and with a little string-pulling Newton was engaged, but on one condition: as he was in his eighties and in poor health, none of the theatres would insure him unless he had a stand-in. Newton himself proposed a young Scot named Robert Sutherland. Soon afterwards the first concert was set for 22 October at London's Royal Festival Hall, whilst in the middle of August Newton and Sutherland flew to Paris to be introduced to di Stefano and Maria.

According to Sutherland, Maria's first question when she walked into the room – looking 'noticeably long-legged and positive' – was, 'Sutherland? Are you Australian?' Di Stefano he described as 'a black-eyed Sicilian with immediate glamour and appeal'. Then only moments after their meeting, an alarm sounded in Maria's antique pendant watch and she disappeared into her bedroom to put in the drops she had been prescribed to use at two-hourly intervals by the New York specialist . . . and shortly after this interruption, di Stefano announced that he and Maria were waiting for the chauffeur to arrive, to drive them to San Remo and that, moreover, they did not know when they would be coming back!

Maria and Sutherland became immediate friends, but she disliked Ivor Newton. 'He's too foisty,' she told Roger Normand, 'and Gracie Fields was wrong. He's got both feet in the grave! The youngster's okay, though. A lovely kid who thinks that when I'm speaking I've got the voice of a man. He must know some funny men, hah!'

The actual rehearsals for the tour did not begin until early in September, but they were soon halted when Maria received a call from a London newspaper – Renata Tebaldi, who had not appeared in the British capital since the mid-fifties, was to give a concert at the Royal Albert Hall with Franco Corelli on 9 October, an event which was being promoted by *Maria's* agent, Sandor Gorlinsky! Such a deal was, of course, tantamount to treason, to Maria's way of thinking. Her own London concert, plus another scheduled for November, were already over-subscribed and as the Tebaldi/Corelli tickets were moving slower than anticipated the press jumped to the obvious conclusion: 'The [Tebaldi] recital bears all the signs of having been hastily arranged,' concluded *The Times* Diary. 'We are thus witnessing the revival of one of the great and legendary operatic rivalries.'

Maria was initially unconsolable, flinging herself weeping onto Robert Sutherland's shoulder – before calling Gorlinsky to tell him exactly what she thought of him. She even threatened to fire him, but soon relented, telling the pianist, 'No other agent gets us so much money, so I'll have to keep him!' Even so, she cancelled her first London concert: Tebaldi's voice may have been only recently described as 'hard and thin', but she was terrified of facing the competition which would only lead to the inevitable comparisons from the critics.

The Callas-di Stefano tour, which opened in Hamburg on 25 October 1973, has been almost unanimously declared a tragic climax to one of the most magnificent careers of this century. This of course is only partly true, a fact which was underlined by Harold Schonberg, one of Maria's sincerest critics. 'It would be silly to pretend that Miss Callas has much voice left,' he observed in the *New York Times*, adding much more importantly, 'but unlike the tenor, she remains an artist ... and everybody washed her with oceans of love. She, at least, deserved the tribute.' One immediately thinks of those final, heartrending performances from Garland and Piaf who, though perhaps vocally past their best and in Piaf's case literally dying on her feet, could do absolutely no wrong. They, like Maria, only had to be *there*.

Basically, Maria's and di Stefano's repertoire throughout the tour would remain unchanged: a handful of arias from *Cavalleria Rusticana*, *Werther*, *Carmen*, and *La Gioconda*, several Sicilian songs from di Stefano, and duets from *I Vespri Siciliani*, *Faust* and *L'Elisir d'Amore*. The actual programme, astonishingly, was sometimes not decided until the pair were on stage.

The Hamburg concert was held up for ten minutes. Elizabeth Taylor was in town: she had asked for complimentary tickets, but Maria had refused, predicting that if Taylor turned up at the theatre she would only end up stealing her thunder. This almost happened, for Taylor had purchased an entire row of seats and she entered the auditorium in a blaze of popping flashbulbs. Maria, however, was too nervous to be angry and this showed in her voice, though her reception here and everywhere else on the tour circuit was utterly hysterical. It was as if her fans, and the Callas Boys in particular, knew that they would never see her again.

A whole new generation fell under Maria's spell as the tour progressed through Germany: Berlin, Düsseldorf, Munich, Frankfurt and Mannheim – with di Stefano's voice getting progressively worse. Ivor Newton, finding it virtually impossible to cope with his unexpected changes of key and tempo, sought help from Robert Sutherland – the young man not only turned the pages of the music, he had to mouth the words to the arias to di Stefano, so that he would not forget them. Between engagements, too, the accompanists frequently found themselves caught in the crossfire between the volatile pair, who despite an allegedly passionate relationship fought like cat and dog most of the time, bringing out the worst in each other ... and endless complaints from hotel guests about the noise and their language. A few years later, Robert Sutherland described one of these tirades as a never-to-be-forgotten experience. 'I've never seen anger expressed in such a way,' he recalled. 'The words she used seemed superfluous. It was the intensity of the expression, the enormous eyes black with rage and the electric tension in her physical being. I trembled at the keyboard and di Stefano stood stock-still with his mouth open. The tension in Maria's hands had curled her long fingers so that they looked like the talons of an eagle.'

More than once, also, Maria told Sandor Gorlinsky that Newton would have to be relieved of his post – he was so frail, she was convinced he would drop dead on the stage. Gorlinsky refused: if Maria wanted her pianist dismissed, he declared, she would have to dismiss him herself and risk the wrath of her detractors, the ones who still accused her of being heartless towards her similarly elderly husband and parents! Against her wishes, Newton stayed.

The next stop on the road, on 20 November, was Madrid where the concert was attended by Princess Sofia of Greece. For the occasion, Madame Biki had created a floating red chiffon dress, which Maria complemented by eschewing her diamonds for a simple Greek Orthodox cross. Afterwards, instead of curtsying to the young princess, she ignored protocol by kissing her on both cheeks ... and by speaking to her in Greek about the 'lamentable' political dilemmas of Spain and Greece, who were both in the hands of dictators. 'It won't last much longer,' she whispered, 'just you wait and see!' She was certainly right as far as Spain was concerned: two years later, upon the death of Franco and the restoration of the monarchy, the 'pretender' Juan Carlos and Sofia would be crowned king and queen.

Two days later, Maria and di Stefano arrived in London for two concerts at the Royal Festival Hall – the second one taking place on 2 December, which everyone including the tenor wrongly assumed (according to Maria) was her fiftieth birthday. At the end of the evening, di Stefano led the audience in a roof-raising 'Happy Birthday', and all Maria could do was stand there, with tears streaming down her face. 'At fifty, as glamorous, yet refined, as ever,' observed one critic. Tickets for the two concerts had been sold for over £100 on the black market because, according to the racketeers, it was widely rumoured that after London, Callas would never sing again.

The histrionics between Maria and di Stefano continued in Paris, and in Amsterdam. Here, at the famous Concertgebouw, they even tore at each other whilst they were on stage – smiling radiantly at the screaming mass of fans, whilst mouthing obscenities from the corners of their mouths.

The pair then went their separate ways for the Christmas break – di Stefano to his family in Milan, and Maria to another period of crippling depression at Georges-Mandel. She had always loathed public holidays, but this one especially, telling Robert Sutherland, 'You're forced to buy presents and be happy and merry when maybe you don't feel like it.' It was also a terrible wrench to have been dragged away from the tour when it had taken her so long to find the courage to sing again, though it helped that the first recital of the new year was not in front of a paying audience, but for the patients of a Milanese hospital.

Then, in Stuttgart on 23 January 1974, thirty minutes before the concert was due to begin, di Stefano devleloped a sore throat and was unable to sing. The audience became so rowdy when the announcement was made that Maria insisted upon leading him on to the stage so that he could apologise in person. She then sang 'O mio babbino caro', and would have continued alone – after all, she knew only to well that everyone was only interested in *her* – and Sutherland had already taken up the music for 'Suicidio', when a middle-aged man *smoking a pipe* lumbered up to the front of the stage and began insulting her in Italian. Maria decided that enough was enough, and the audience were given their money back.

Ten days later, Maria, di Stefano and Robert Sutherland flew to New York for the American section of the tour – Ivor Newton, unable to cope with the strain, had finally thrown in the towel. The party had rented a large apartment on the tenth floor of the Stanhope Hotel, where visitors and reporters would often be ushered in to find four television sets blaring out at the same time, full-blast, and with Maria and di Stefano screaming at each other over the din. Her nerves were so frayed by this time that she was swallowing as many as fifty pills in any one day, and being seen by a doctor, Louis Parrish, who was actually registered as a psychiatrist. Her only pleasure was derived from the thrice-daily telephone calls from Onassis, whose mental turmoil matched hers, and whose framed photograph stood on the table next to her bed.

At her New York press-conference, Maria persistently patted her poddle, Djedda, and hugged her frail, 85-year-old American impresario, Sol Hurok, who each day would send her two dozen red roses. She squared up to several critics who, she knew, would be following her around the tour-circuit, daggers drawn, telling them, 'I make a habit of not reading critics. I always found out the best critic is the public that comes, pays and enjoys it. Also, I happen to be the best critic of myself.' And when asked by an impertinent, T-shirted reporter if it was true that her voice had deteriorated, as was rumoured by the musical experts, Maria stayed calm and levelled with him, '*Nobody* can sing as well as in the old days, dear. It would be foolish to expect it. At twenty or thirty, whatever age you are, you have the strength of an athlete – less experience but great possibilities. It is the same with us opera stars. You are born an artist or you are not. And you *stay* an artist, dear, even if your voice is less of a fireworks. The artist is *always* there!'

Maria was in an awesome mood on 3 February, when interviewed by Mike Wallace on CBS Television's *Sixy Minutes*. She had been forewarned that Wallace was frequently abrupt with his guests, if not downright aggressive, and remembering her earlier ordeal with Hy Gardner she was taking no chances. Therefore, when Wallace assumed a judgmental tone and began, 'You took up with Onassis . . .' Maria snarled, 'What's wrong with that?' 'Maria Callas devoured the fearsome Mike Wallace like a starving lioness digesting a nervous Christian,' one newspaper declared. And as Maria was leaving the studio, she was heard to mutter, 'I hope the goddam son-of-a-bitch drops dead!'

'When such an artist as Miss Callas returns, there is bound to be disappointment,' proclaimed the *Philadelphia Enquirer*, after Maria's and di Stefano's opening concert in the city on 11 February.

'There is much to admire in the way she managed as much singing as she did, but the impression remained – her voice is probably something to be recalled from recordings of the fifties.' The fans clearly did not agree – more than two hundred of them trailed after her to the next stop on the road, and what should have been *the* concert of this series: New York's Carnegie Hall.

According to Robert Sutherland, on the morning of the New York concert Maria was in excellent voice, but furious that the event was to be in aid of the Metropolitan Opera, scathing by yelling, 'What did the Met ever do for me? They didn't even give me a new production!' As the day progressed, she grew more and more tetchy, working herself up so much that by the end of the afternoon she had lost her voice. Dr Parrish, assuring her that the problem was probably only psychosomatic – she was in fact exhausted through lack of sleep, even though she was said to be *trebling* her dosage of sleeping pills – did everything he possibly could to get her voice back, but to no avail. It was the tour manager – aptly named Mario de Maria – who had the invidious task of announcing, ninety minutes before it was due to begin, that the concert had been postponed until 5 March.

Pandemonium ensued. A large part of the audience, who had paid up to $100 for tickets, were already outside the theatre, hoping to catch a glimpse of Maria as she arrived, and as more fans turned up they became so disruptive that mounted police had to be brought in to disperse them. Robert Sutherland was sent out to monitor the situation, and was told by one fan, 'It may be a cancellation, but it's the biggest theatrical event of the season so far!' this resulted in a personal plea from Sol Horuk and Dr Parrish, who both addressed the angry mob, who had by now begun ripping down Maria's posters and trampling them underfoot. Hurok, unable to make himself heard, waved Maria's medical certificate upon which were printed the words: SEVERE RESPIRATORY INFECTION. Then Parrish read out a statement, 'Miss Callas pleaded with me to let her do the concert, but her throat is so inflamed that she can hardly speak, let alone sing.' Then he added tremulously, 'Neither can we be certain that Miss Callas will be able to fulfil her engagement in Toronto next week', ... to which a woman in the crowd yelled, 'She did the same thing in London. She's not sick at all, and if I get my hands on her, I'll kill her!'

The Toronto concert of 21 February *did* take place, and it was followed three days later by the pair's longest recital thus far, in Washington, where they were on stage for just over two hours – forty minutes of this taken up by applause and curtain-calls. They then turned their attention towards Boston – 'Kennedy country', as Maria called it – for a concert on 27 February without her partner, who was suffering from laryngitis. Maria took advantage of this by increasing her programme from four to six arias, and a concert-pianist friend, Vasso Divetzi, kindly stepped in to play whilst Maria was off the stage – though the fans were of course interested in hearing no one but Callas. Richard Dyer of *The Nation*, confessing that Maria had made him cry, added, 'It moved me mostly because it was such a human triumph . . . Callas has long commanded our attention, our respect, our gratitude, our awe. Now in her struggle and in her exhaustion she asks and earns, at cost to herself, and to us, what she had never before seemed to need – our love.'

The ordeal continued. In Chicago, Maria learned that she had been booked into a hotel which did not allow dogs. This did not deter her, however, and as she and her party were entering the foyer, Mario de Maria attempted to shove Djedda inside a holdall, telling her, 'We must do this, Madame Callas. Dogs are against the rules.' In front of scores of onlookers she levelled, at the top of her voice, 'Don't talk to *me* about rules, dear. Wherever I stay I *make* the goddam rules!'

The Chicago concert was regarded by the mass of Callas Boys as the very epitome of 'camp'. Halfway through the duet from *Don Carlos*, di Stefano's voice suddenly gave up on him, and he told the audience that he was suffering from a cold and that he had only done the concert in the first place for Maria, who now threw open her arms – according to one critic, 'in a fashion which owed more to Bankhead than Bernhardt – and pronounced, 'Not for *me*! Let's say *we're* doing it for our Chicago public!'

The delirium continued when Maria announced 'Vissi d'arte', and someone in the gallery yelled, 'Thank you, Maria!' Smiling ruefully, she responded, 'You're welcome, but I can't promise how

I'm going to sing it!' Several times during the aria, she went off-key, yet still she could do no wrong, and the aria received a seven-minute standing ovation.

Three days later, with the by now superfluous di Stefano, Maria returned to New York for the postponed concert at Carnegie Hall. Yet even whilst she was getting ready in her suite at the Stanhope there was the most dreadful set-back: a call was put through, informing her that Sol Hurok had died that afternoon.

Everyone expected Maria to cancel the concert, and for once she had a valid enough reason. On top of this she was terrified that something bad would happen if she went on stage because she was convinced that someone had put a jinx on her. Eventually, di Stefano escorted her to the microphone, and once the applause had settled down she announced that tonight she would be singing for Sol Hurok alone. The atmosphere was electric. Then, at the end of the evening – bearing in mind that the whole thing had been organised to benefit the Met – she launched into a near-incomprehensible attack on the way opera houses were being mismanaged, which left some members of the audience in no doubt whatsoever why her entourage included a psychiatrist. An hour later, when she left the theatre, she was still feeling wretched, but still managed the sincerest of smiles – tossing one of Sol Hurok's last red roses to a fan, followed by another, then the whole bunch.

Later, at Maria's hotel, any number of celebrities cluttered the foyer when she arrived, hoping to be snapped with her by the ever-present contingent of photographers, as had happened through-out the tour. This time they were to be disappointed. Montserrat Caballé, who was staying in the same hotel, told me how after sending everyone away, Maria had turned to her and said, 'But I insist on having my photograph taken with *you*. Most of my so-called friends and colleagues only ever wanted to be photographed with me for their own publicity. And you have never done that because you're one of the few people that have ever really loved and respected me. I want you to know how much I appreciate that.'

The tour continued: Detroit, Dallas, Miami Beach, Columbus, Long Island, then back to New York on 14 April, where she was asked to pre-record an interview for CBS Television's 'Today' show, to be broadcast the next morning, the day she and di Stefano were to give a second concert at Carnegie Hall. She immediately balked when she read the name Wallace on the contract, relenting only when a studio aide assured her that this was not the horrendous Mike, but a kindly lady named *Barbara* Wallace. Even so, the questions were almost as abrupt as before, almost all of them centring around her relationship with Onassis – who, having been forwarded a tape of one of her duets with di Stefano, had told her over the telephone, 'Maybe I should come over there and partner you. Even I can bark better than him!' During the interview with Barbara Wallace, Maria stayed calm, though she was very much on her guard. Insisting that she and Onassis were still the very best of friends, she defended her single status: 'There are no chains for love. But why should I marry again? Give me one good reason *why* I should marry? I'm well off!' There was however a veiled threat against Jackie Onassis when Maria was asked if she had any ill-feelings towards her. Shrugging her shoulders, she replied, 'Not at all. Why should I? Of course, if she treats Mr Onassis very badly, then I might be *very* angry . . .'

After the Carnegie Hall concert, a more relaxed than usual Maria went to supper with Renata Tebaldi. The concerts, she explained to her friend, were now getting better because she was vocally more sure of herself, and because her partner had missed some of them. Indeed, di Stefano was again laid low with laryngitis, and when he suggested that their 28 March Montreal concert should be postponed, as opposed to Maria 'slogging on with her one-woman show', she rang Sandor Gorlinsky in London and demanded that he recall the tenor – only to be warned that, with a temperament as volatile as her own, di Stefano would not only end their relationship, he would probably sue her. Maria realised the predicament she was in: she could no longer cope with this man, yet she knew she would never withstand the rigours of the tour without him. She was however greatly relieved when on 13 May, after Cincinnati, Seattle, Portland, Vancouver, Los Angeles and San Franscisco, the American tour ended with the postponed concert in Montreal, where the party was augmented, and no doubt complicated, by the arrival of another Maria – di Stefano's wife.

Maria returned to Paris utterly exhausted, and quite clearly on the verge of a complete breakdown ... yet seemingly full of plans for the future. Almost all of these included di Stefano: recordings, more concerts, operas. On the eve of the fateful recital in Stuttgart she had announced that there would be a new production of *Carmen* – this would take place in Dallas the following year with herself and di Stefano directing as well as singing. Now, however, she had changed her mind. The opera was to be 'something by Verdi', and there was no longer talk of directing or of sharing the bill with di Stefano. 'I want a *great* conductor, a *good* colleague, and above all a *good* producer, she told the *Evening Standard*, adding, 'Producers forget the singers nowadays. They don't leave room for them with so much staging, so much movement going on. I haven't seen [the new] *Vespri Siciliani* at the Met, but I hear there are staircases moving up and down, and nothing about Sicily.' But were the rumours true that she had fallen out with her pal, Lawrence Kelly? Kelly himself set the record straight on this, declaring, 'Absolute bullshit! Callas and I always got on well. We're honest with the music. She never makes a fuss about small problems, unlike some of our Italian friends who can be a pain in the ass!'

Maria was also thinking about living with di Stefano, telling friends that after a suitable period of mourning for his recently deceased daughter, he would break the news gently to his wife that he was leaving her. During the summer of 1963, she and Onassis had visited Arkoudhi, a 1,100-acre island nature reserve near Skorpios, owned by the wealthy Dendrinos family. Here, intoxicated by the scent of the jasmine, they had shared a meal with the island's one inhabitant, a shepherd. Now, the last of the Dendrinos had died, and the family trustees had put the island on the market. 'I must have it,' she told Onassis over the telephone. 'It's one of the most beautiful places I've seen!' The asking price was quite steep – allegedly around $750,000 – but Maria's lawyer contacted the trustees, and her bid was registered.

Maria rested for an entire month before beginning rehearsals for the third and final leg of her tour with di Stefano: two concerts in Korea, and seven in a country she had never wanted to visit in the past because of its wartime atrocities – Japan. 'And yet most of *those* people are now dead,' she told Roger Normand, 'so what's the point in bearing grudges?' There had been talk of several concerts aboard the cruise-ship *Renaissance*, during the first two weeks of September when the vessel was scheduled to visit Malta, Turkey, Israel and Greece with 220 passengers who had forked out an average of £1,500 each for the privilege. 'If fans can afford £100 for tickets on the black market *and* travel halfway across the world,' proclaimed the organisers, 'then surely they'll pay our prices to hear Callas on a sun-flooded, breeze-embraced, floating luxury palace!' Upon reading this in a newspaper, however, Maria had promptly cancelled the engagements; declaring that such an undertaking would smack too heavily of her days on the *Christina*.

At around this time, Maria began dictating her memoirs to Roger Normand – or at least snippets of her life which she felt she could share with the world: the 'twisted' years with her mother and sister, her constant straying from the marital bed on account of her husband's impotence, her all-consuming desire to have a child, and her schoolgirl-like crushes on heart-throb actors such as Cary Grant and Gérard Philipe. Roger, who had been introduced to Maria by the French socialite Marie-Louise Courtois at one of Marlene Dietrich's parties, was or had been an intimate friend of a great many stars, including Chevalier, Garbo, Piaf, Mistinguett, and the controversial actresses Alice Sapritch and Arletty, between whom she was once placed at dinner. Roger said, 'Maria loathed them on sight, and they spent the entire evening trying to shock her, constantly leaning across her to discuss, as loudly as they could, all they knew about men's private parts, which was considerable. Then, seeing that they were having no effect, Alice nudged her and said, 'Maria, don't you know *anything* about pricks?' To which she retorted, in a rare burst of Callas humour, 'No dear, only that I'm sitting between two.'

Roger's godmother was the chanteuse Lucienne Boyer, whose most famous song was *Parlez-moi d'amour*. Chez Roger, during the summer of 1974, Lucienne persuaded Maria to sing the song, and taped it – her very last recording, which she sings beautifully. And until recently, when Roger left Paris, a large photograph of the trio hung on the wall of his sitting room in Pigalle. The Callas anecdotes and recollections, however, along with those of his other famous friends, are included in a huge tome entitled *Le Ring*, which is in this author's possession and will not be published until after Roger's death.

One morning, Roger breezed into Georges-Mandel with a copy of a filmscript which he and Maria had discussed over the telephone. *Love, Love, Sarah!* told the warts-and-all story of the legendary actress, Sarah Bernhardt, who had died in the year of Maria's birth, and Maria was so enthusiastic about the project that she was even prepared to cancel her tour of the Far East to devote more time to it. She had discussed it with Zeffirelli and Visconti, by this time confined to a wheelchair, and a compromise had been reached wherein Zeffirelli would direct, with Visconti keeping a producer's watchful eye from a covered invalid carriage.

The script for the film was divided into three tableaux: 'Henri, Prince de Ligne', 'La Dame aux Camelias', and 'Damala' – referring to Sarah's first lover and the father of her son, her most famous play, and her Greek husband. 'The Divine Sarah and I had so much in common,' Maria told Roger. 'She fell in love with every single one of her leading men, only to discover that the ones who weren't as old as Adam were homosexual. She played on the stage many of the roles that I sang: Traviata, Fedora, Ernani, Tosca. And she married a Greek, which is something I *would* have done, were it not for Little Miss You-Know-Who! All I'm worried about now is that they don't want to cut my leg off, or worse still expect me to sing. I'll do the film, but I absolutely forbid that I should be asked to sing!'

Maria rang Sander Gorlinsky in London and told him about the film, and a few days later Roger Normand flew from Paris to negotiate the contract. This presented certain problems. Because Sarah Bernhardt had been French, Maria insisted that the film be shot in a studio near Versailles, but as she was no longer on speaking terms with Michel Glotz, her French agent, she did not wish him to be involved. Similarly, since Sander Gorlinsky was reluctant to encroach on another agent's territory, he told Roger that he would only handle the contract if Maria agreed to make the film in England. This she refused to consider, and Roger explained what had happened when he returned to Georges-Mandel to collect the script: 'There was no angry outburst, none of the famous Callas histrionics. She picked up the phone and very calmly told her British agent what she thought of him, saying, 'You are the most stupid, selfish and arrogant man I have ever known. All you've thought about in your entire association with me is lining your own pocket, and you know fuck-all about art and never have. When I return from Japan I want you out of my life – period!'

In the Far East, Maria felt as if she was under less pressure. Di Stefano too – both were in better form, vocally, than they had been in Europe and America, and there were few arguments. She had also received word from the Dendrinos trustees that, with just a few days to go before the bidding closed for Arkoudhi – and with no offers topping hers – the island was as good as hers. Meanwhile, Hiroshima, on 7 November, was a painful experience and despite the adulation, the carpet of flowers on the stage after the performance and the plaudits in the newspapers, Maria later confessed that the tears she had shed had been for those who had perished there in 1945. Her pain was doubled by a call informing her that Onassis had been taken to hospital, though for the time being none of his aides appeared to know what was wrong with him.

Then, two evenings later – 11 November 1974 – in Sapporo, Japan, Maria sang on the stage for the last time in her life.

19

Vissi D'arte, Vissi D'amore . . . .

If you love music truly you can only feel humble before
its infinite potentialities and recognise its infinite potentialities in serving it – perhaps at the cost of never knowing any lasting, consistent happiness.

Shortly before going on stage in Seoul on 8 October 1974, Maria
had been in her dressing-room when a bolt of pain shot through
her abdomen – another hernia which had resulted in slight inter-
nal bleeding, though she had refused to enter a Korean or Japanese
hospital, or to even think of cancelling the tour and returning to
Paris. She had also received another call from the Dendrinos
trustees: this time with disappointing news: Arkoudhi had been
sold – at the very last moment she had been outbid by a German
political economist named Wolfgang Muller, who said in a press-
statement, 'I waited until the last minute because I want to keep the
island for idealists and nature buffs.' Maria's reaction to this had
been a scathing, 'What the hell did he think *I* was going to do with
it – turn it into a zoo?'

In Japan too, the thrice-daily calls from Onassis had continued,
though by now they were desperate cries for help. His daughter,
Christina, had recently been rushed into hospital after a suicide
attempt. 'Two more sleeping pills, and she would have been dead,'

he told Maria. Outwardly, she was sympathetic, but she later told a friend, 'Only *two*? I wished I'd have known. I would have given her two of mine.' Genuinely distressing was the call explaining that Onassis's ex-wife, Tina, had been found dead in a Paris hotel room, and that he was certain she had taken her own life on account of all the complications and traumas in her personal life. Like her rival, Maria, Tina had always been sensitive and highly-strung. An autopsy proved otherwise – death had been caused by oedema (tissue-swelling) of the lung.

When she had settled in at Georges-Mandel, Maria received another call from Onassis explaining his 'mysterious' illness. He told her that he had been diagnosed as suffering from myasthenia gravis, a rare but non-terminal illness characterised by the loss of muscle power, mostly in the face and neck. He even joked that sometimes, when he was in a business meeting, an aide had to tape his eyelids open so that he could see. Onassis also informed Maria that he had hired a private detective to follow Jackie, who like himself had had a number of affairs since her marriage, though hers had been considerably more discreet – and that as soon as substantial evidence came to light he would be commencing divorce proceedings. Maria was far from optimistic, and of course if her various outbursts in recent interviews were anything to go by, so long as there was a man by her side she does seem to have resigned herself to staying single.

Whatever action Onassis was planning against Jackie, however, was suddenly shelved in January 1975 when in a clandestine, step-by-step retrenchment of his empire – having failed to sell his oil tankers to consolidate his holdings – Onassis put Skorpios on the market and began negotiating with the Greek government over the sale of one of his most personal but disastrous undertakings of recent years, Olympic Airways. The document relinquishing this, to which he had added a codicil stating that in addition to the cash price he should also retain his helicopters and private jet, was signed on 15 January. Then three weeks later, during a visit to Athens, Onassis collapsed and was rushed into hospital, where a liver specialist diagnosed gallstones, and urged him to fly to Paris for an operation. This took place at the American Hospital at

Neuilly on 10 February, but complications set in and the next day Maria received a call informing her that the greatest love of her life, the man whom she had always regarded as indestructible, was dying.

Here was one drama that Maria had no intention of dealing with on home ground. The mother of Vasso Devetzi, the concert-pianist who had replaced the stricken di Stefano at times during the tour of the United States, was a patient in the same wing as Onassis, and Vasso was able to inform Maria of Jackie Onassis's movements. Therefore, on the afternoon of Sunday 9 March, Maria went to see him for the last time. He was hooked up to a respirator and barely recognised her. The next afternoon, Maria flew to Palm Beach where she had rented a house on Golf View Road. It was here, six days later, that she received the news of Onassis's death.

For forty-eight hours, Maria truly wanted to die. The doctors at the hospital had told her, bluntly, to expect only the worst – that this was one situation that Onassis's vast wealth would not get him out of – and now her great solace was her faith, which she had always combined with an astute realism. 'When I pray, I don't ask God for favours,' she had told Robert Sutherland. 'The only thing I ask for is the strength to deal with what He sends, good or bad.' Now, however, it was as if even God had deserted her and in a drug-induced haze she saw ahead of her only blackness, and misery. As if Onassis's loss was not enough, two days later Maria received a telegram informing her that her great friend Visconti had died in his sleep, aged sixty-nine, the same age as Onassis.

In the last five years, Visconti had suffered two strokes, and though confined to a wheelchair for the last six months of his life, he had refused to heed the advice of his doctors – eating, drinking, and above all smoking far too heavily. The last time Maria had seen him she had been shocked by his gaunt appearance, but his lion's courage whilst facing the inevitable had moved her, and it was reflecting upon this that gave her the strength to continue with her own struggles. Over the next few days she received further encouragement from the hundreds of cards and letters of condolence which arrived at Golf View Road, and from the endless telephone calls. She was neither exaggerating nor acting with malevolence towards Jackie Onassis when she issued the briefest of statements to the press, '*I'm* the widow, now.'

The widow, however, was compelled to mourn privately, for the 'enemy camp' – Jackie and Christina – had made it perfectly clear that her presence would not be required at Onassis's funeral, on Skorpios. Christina was of course now head of the Onassis empire. Two weeks before his death, her father had summoned her and her fiancé – Peter Goulandris, the thirty-year-old heir to another huge shipping fortune – to his sickbed and made them promise to marry. 'I hope she's very happy,' Maria had said, sarcastically, adding, 'the poor man doesn't know what he's letting himself in for. That girl's so selfish, she'll end up destroying everything she touches.'

For two more weeks, Maria deliberated about buying the house in Palm Beach and completely relocating to the United States. For the time being Milan, Rome, Paris and probably London too had given up on her – at least they were waiting for her to prove herself elsewhere before committing themselves to expensive productions which, given her reputation, she might cancel at the last minute. In America, however, there was still hope. She had dicussed the role of Cassandra in Berlioz's *Les Troyens* with the Met, and there was the season in Dallas. Then she received a call from Lawrence Kelly's assistant, and more dreadful news. Her great friend was dying from cancer and, no longer able to speak, had asked to see her. Maria turned him down gently, hoping that he would understand that she had suffered too much already. She told Kelly's assistant, 'Tell him I'll pray for him, night and day. More than that I cannot do.' And suddenly, for her, America no longer seemed like a good idea.

Her saving grace, or so she was allegedly led to to believe, was again to be Giuseppe di Stefano, though had she not been in such a feeble state of mind, Maria might have questioned her motives for returning to Paris as soon as she did. Although the pair had been hammered by many critics during their tour, most of these had agreed that by the time she and di Stefano had reached Japan, they had almost returned to their old vocal form. Indeed, whilst there they had been offered a new production of *Tosca*, which neither of them had been much interested in at the time. Now, di Stefano gave Maria the good news. They had been offered four *Tosca*s . . . three to take place in Yokohama in November, to be followed by a gala performance in Tokyo on 6 December. Maria's friend Giuseppe Modesti had already been engaged to sing Scarpia, and the New Japan Philharmonic Orchestra would be conducted by Alberto Ventura. Maria pretended to be delighted, and over the next three months took the project very seriously. Then someone informed her that she had not been di Stefano's original choice for *Tosca*, but the Spanish soprano Montserrat Caballé. Both the tenor and Madame Caballé have denied this, but Maria believed the story at the time, and dropped out of the production at once. She told Roger Normand, 'All I now have to do is get shot of the man.' This she did soon afterwards. At the end of the year, when di Stefano and Caballé returned from Japan, Maria and he were no longer lovers, and barely friends.

Over the next few months, friends old and new dropped in at the 'mausoleum' on Avenue Georges-Mandel: Leonard Berstein, Marlene Dietrich, Vasso Devetzi, and Covent Garden's John Tooley. Few of them, however, were able to cope with spending the whole evening listening to her current fad – her own Berlin *Lucia* – or watching old John Wayne movies. Like Piaf and Marlene in the later years, Maria had become *une créature de minuit*, running up astronomical phone bills by chatting to friends, acquaintances and the occasional comparative stranger until two or three in the morning and rarely getting up before noon. At the end of October, she received a call from Pasolini – his first since Onassis's death. Her friend would be arriving in Paris in a few weeks' time, and would she have dinner with him? Maria agreed, but the rendezvous was not to be. On 1 November 1975, after a sexual encounter with a rent-boy, he was found repeatedly stabbed on the beach road at Ostia – though whether the killing itself was sexually or politically motivated has never been determined.

Maria pretended to feel surprised by the circumstances surrounding Pasolini's brutal death, and even tried to convince one journalist that she had been unaware of his homosexuality – desperately trying to forget the occasion when, during the planning stage of *Medea*, she had actually walked in on the director whilst he had been 'auditioning' a young man for a bit-part in the film. In reality, however, she like many others knew only too well that Pasolini had been flirting with danger for most of his adult life, and that it had been a question of time before something bad happened to him.

Pasolini's death, however, coming so soon after all the others, seemed to be the last straw. Maria had even been affected by the demise of Joséphine Baker, only days after opening in a new season at the Bobino in April. Although she had never really liked the black *meneuse de revue*, she had admired her fight against racial oppression, and in July 1969 she had helped Princess Grace organise Joséphine's Red Cross gala in Monte Carlo to raise money for their survival after she and her 'Rainbow Tribe' of twelve children had been evicted from their château in the Midi. It was on this occasion that Maria had posed for her only photograph with Anna Magnani, a short time before the great actress's death.

'Maria had become a living corpse,' Roger Normand said. 'A still-beautiful, desirable woman. But it was all shell. Her entire life had become a parody, a masque, a fight between Maria the woman and Callas, the mighty star. She even conversed in two voices, the one constantly attacking the other. Maria, the sad creature who had loved and lost Onassis. Callas, the bitch who had made her life a misery. And sandwiched between were all the characters she'd played and become. She had always been obsessed with death, but now she said it could never come soon enough. Her only desire was that her relatives – her mother and sister in Greece – should die before her. She also changed her mind about singing again, saying that she wanted to give just one more concert before she died. That's when we began discussing the Théâtre des Champs-Elysées.'

Maria had attended Maurice Chevalier's farewell concert at the Théâtre des Champs-Elysées, opposite Marlene Dietrich's apartment on Avenue Montaigne, on 21 October 1968, and it was here that she originally planned her comeback with a programme of bel canto arias during the spring of 1976. She changed her mind about this, however, when after numerous telephone calls and visits from Covent Garden's John Tooley she elected to sing Santuzza, opposite Placido Domingo, in a new production of *Cavalleria Rusticana*. 'She agreed that this role would suit her well vocally, and that she would gain immeasurably from working with an artist of Domingo's stature,' Tooley later said. In fact, it was the overzealousness of Covent Garden and the Parisian theatre, where Maria continued rehearsing for her London season, which proved their undoing and the world's loss. According to the French tabloid, *France-Dimanche*, an employee from Covent Garden contacted them to divulge what was happening on the Avenue Montaigne – money is alleged to have changed hands and a reporter sneaked into the theatre took several photographs which appeared in the publication the following week, together with the blatant statement that this was the picture of a woman who could no longer sing. The Covent Garden productions were cancelled immediately, and Maria retreated further into her shell. There would be no more.

Early in September, Montserrat Caballé spoke to her friend, on the telephone:

I was about to open in Tosca at Covent Garden, in a revival of the Zeffirelli production, and the director had asked me to make the same movements on stage as she had. When I told Maria about this on the fifth, she was furious. She rang the director at once and told him that he was stupid – for one thing, she said, she was much taller than me and her arms were longer. For another, she added, I should be allowed to sing Tosca my way, and not be made to imitate her! The next day, however, when I rang her back to thank her, she sounded very down, very tired. We only spoke for five minutes. 'You are going to sing a wonderful Tosca,' she said. 'But *please* wear my earrings, this time!' A few years before, when I was making my Norma debut at La Scala, she had sent me the beautiful silver earrings she had worn for *her* first Norma, with a card wishing me luck. I had worn them until the evening of the première, but then I had taken them off. I admired her so much, it would have been like sacrilege. And now, whilst she was on the telephone, I reached for them and put them on, and we arranged to meet at the end of the month. She needed someone to talk to, and I loved her so very much. that was the last time we spoke.

★

The end came very quickly, as Maria would have wished. At 2:15pm on 16 September 1977, two gendarmes from the commissariat in the 16me arrondissement were summoned to the apartment at Georges-Mandel. When they arrived some ten minutes later, Maria was lying on her bed. Her eyes were closed and her hands crossed palms-upwards across her lap. Her long hair was spread across the pillows, and sitting on either side of the bed were Bruna, the maid, and still wearing his uniform and white gloves, Ferrucio the butler. Also present was a doctor, who only minutes before had certified Maria dead. There then followed a swift but full investigation to determine whether she had died of natural causes, whether she had taken her own life, or indeed if there had been foul play.

In her statement, an extremely distraught Bruna declared that Maria had collapsed in her bathroom at around 1:00pm. There had been a loud thump, Maria had called for help, and Bruna had managed with a struggle to get her into her bedroom and onto the bed, and she had been sufficiently coherent to demand a strong cup of coffee. After propping her against her pillows and helping her to drink this, Bruna had next called Maria's doctor, only to be told that he was out on a call. Accordingly, she had then telephoned the American Hospital at Neuilly, claiming in her statement that the number had been engaged. Why she had not simply sent for an ambulance, Bruna did not say, though it does seem likely that once she realised that Maria was dying, she became so hysterical that she did not know what she was doing. In the end, someone had contacted Ferruccio's doctor – thirty minutes after Maria's collapse – and by the time he had arrived it had been too late to do anything but notify the police.

The case was quickly closed, and there was no post-mortem. Two doctors signed the certificate to the effect that Maria had died of *un accident cardiaque*, and at once there were whispers amongst the Callas coterie of a cover-up. Although absolutely no one even suspected foul play, few ruled out suicide, particularly as Maria had for so long given the impression that there was little left to live for now that she had become so terribly lonely. Montserrat Caballé remains certain that Maria took her own life. She told me, 'I believed it then, and my suspicions were confirmed a few years later when I was singing in a concert tribute to Maria at the Paris Opera. It was confirmed in the programme that she had committed suicide.' Roger Normand backed up the theory, saying, 'Here, in France, you *can* libel the dead, and our laws on such things are so draconian that nobody would risk saying that Maria had died by her own hand unless it was true. And during her last months, she often spoke about killing herself.'

Michel Glotz, on the other hand, argued against the suicide theory, telling the press that only recently he and Maria had been discussing plans for new recordings and a television comeback. Then, several years later in a taped statement for a British radio programme, he confessed that at the time of her death he and Maria had still not been on speaking terms following their row over the tour with di Stefano. After the débâcle with the photographer from *France-Dimanche* she had told friends, including Roger Normand, 'That's it. I shall never sing again.' This time, it would appear, she had meant it. 'Glotz was simply trying to protect Maria's memory,' Roger said. 'And rightly so by telling the world that she had still been interested in continuing with her career.'

Maria's would-be partner, Placido Domingo, offered yet another theory. It is the theory that we, who loved her, would most like to believe and which is not at all unlikely:

> I believe that Maria permitted herself to die of sadness. One really can die, if one wishes, even without suicide, by just abandoning life. It's as simple as that.

The tributes were legion. 'We have lost one of the truly great artists of all time. The world will be a poorer place without her,' read part of the official statement from Covent Garden. 'She was one of the shining lights of this century, carrying the art of singing to heights where she reigns forever,' declared the Paris Opera's Rolf Liebermann, adding, '*Goddesses* never die!' and Maria's old protagonist Rudolf Bing, paying tribute to her infamous temperament, could only conclude, 'We will not see her like again.'

So far as the press were concerned, Maria's death was not

permitted to hog the column inches entirely. The conductor, Leopold Stokowski, died during the same week, and on the same day as Maria the rock-star Marc Bolan was killed in a car crash. 'Two great stars, vastly different, yet linked by the grief of their respective admirers,' ran one tabloid headline, alongside photographs of a lurex-clad Bolan and Maria's Violetta. And critics who had often passed judgement over the years now only had good things to say about her, though only a few got it exactly right and did not come across as condescending.

The Times praised her for being, 'The most colourful, exciting and traditionally powerful prima donna of the mid-twentieth century.' The *Guardian* simply called her 'divine' and added her name to a short list of operatic luminaries – Ferrier, Wunderlich and Björling – who had attained mythical stature by dying prematurely. Alan Blyth wrote in the *Daily Telegraph*, 'Only a person as genuinely vulnerable and at the same time as perceptive as she was could have been such a creative singer and reached to the heart of each of her heroines.' Perhaps the most heartfelt tribute of all, however, came from Lady Rachel Ellenborough, who had met the Meneghinis in Milan in 1950 when Maria had been overweight, then bumped into Maria again many years later in Monte Carlo – 'thin as a rake and beautiful, a vital woman being killed off by the boredom of the jet-set morons.' Writing a long article for the *Sunday Telegraph*, Lady Ellenborough praised not just Maria's obvious musical genius, but her ability to have fun and make people laugh with her brilliant send-ups and stories which she mimicked in any number of Italian dialects:

> Maria Callas could have filled any theatre on her own had she not been able to sing a note. She had the most intense sense of humour, a mixture of Maria Lloyd, Rosa Lewis (for the racy anecdotes), with a dash of Gertrude Lawrence. All one can do is sigh – and play her records. There have been more perfect voices, of course, but who having seen Maria Callas in any role can ever really believe in anyone else? That sort of magic is evanescent, vanishing when the magician has gone. But magic does not come all that often, does it?

Epilogue

For four days, Maria lay in state on her beautiful 18th century bed at Georges-Mandel, whilst friends, colleagues and carefully selected fans filed in and out of the room. 'Her face does not have a single wrinkle. She has the appearance that she is merely reposing,' Michel Glotz told the press, who were not allowed in. Word had leaked out that one of the tabloids was offering a huge reward for anyone who photographed the death-bed, and no one had been more disturbed than Maria to see pictures of Edith Piaf laid in her coffin and, just weeks before, Elvis Presley.

Maria's funeral, on 20 September, was almost a repetition of the way she had been compelled to live most of her life: relatives and former friends, now enemies, she would not have wanted were there, the solemnity of the occasion marred by the clicking of hundreds of shutters, and a final insult when a journalist shoved the coffin aside so that a photographer could get a close-up of Princess Grace, who with Jackie Callas, Bruna and Ferrucio led the mourners into the Greek Orthodox Church in Paris in the aptly named Rue Georges-Bizet. Behind were the Gorlinskys, Franco Rossellini, Vasso Devetzi, and representatives of the world's governments, embassies and opera houses. Most important of all were the two thousand white-faced fans, many of whom had to stand out in the street to listen to the service, conducted by Melittios Carabinis, the Greek Archbishop of France, Spain and Portugal, being relayed to them via loudspeakers. There then followed a private cremation, after which Maria's ashed were placed in a vault in Père Lachaise, resting place of the famous: Oscar Wilde, Colette, Piaf, Victor Hugo and Chopin, all of whom she had admired.

Simultaneously, at the Greek Orthodox Church in Rome, Nadia Stancioff and Maria's great friend Guilietta Simionato organised a mass, and in London's Bayswater, another had been organised by Franco Zeffirelli and John Tooley. Here, four hundred admirers wept as the loudspeakers blasted out Maria singing her credo, 'Vissi d'arte' . . . and the final irony was that, after the aria finished, the people would not stop cheering until they had been given an encore. Other services were held in Milan, New York. And in Moscow where her only brief visits had been to judge a Tchaikovsky piano competition, there was a two-minute silence.

In death, Maria was treated as shabbily by some as she had been in life. Meneghini almost came across as sincere when he told the press, upon hearing of his ex-wife's death, 'I am destroyed. I would have preferred to die myself, I am in despair!' . . . until he burst the bubble by boasting, 'Of course, it was *me* who created her, until she was taken away from me by that Onassis!' No one bothered telling Litza, who only found out what had happened when it appeared on the early evening news.

Jackie Callas was summoned to Paris, though initially she was reluctant to go. 'Maria had never wanted me with her,' she later confessed, 'and now I was to go at the behest of the dead Maria, for I was her sister.' Indeed, for as long as she cared to remember Jackie had been scraping together the most frugal existence, and she had to borrow the fare from a friend. At Georges-Mandel, too Jackie had run into an argument over the funeral arrangements – the fact that Maria was to be cremated, something which was not usually permitted in the Greek Orthodox religion, unless a special dispensation had been acquired. 'Were they frightened a post-mortem might reveal Maria's addiction to all those pills?' Jackie asked in her memoirs. 'Were they trying to avoid a scandal? If so, then perhaps it was for the best, though I found it hard to accept the idea of my sister being burned.'

There next began the squabbling over Maria's fortune, estimated to be in excess of $12 million dollars, a figure which the experts expected to double, through record sales, by the end of the century. In April 1977 she had drafted a document, leaving everything to Bruna and Ferrucio, but she had not signed this and the fact that another will could not be found baffled her lawyers and once more had everyone speculating as to how she had died. If it had been suicide, one posed, then would she not have signed a will, if only to prevent her detested relatives from getting their hands on her money? To which another pointed out that even if suicide had been proved, with or without a will they certainly would not have been allowed to claim on the insurance policies, which amounted to over $1 million. Then there was a third, very plausible theory, presented by Jackie, who declared that a woman as superstitious as her sister would not have 'tempted fate' by signing a will, as this would have been a recognition that she had been about to die.

According to French law, the contents of Maria's apartment could not be removed until a statutory period of forty days had elapsed: this was to ensure that all claimants to the estate had an equal chance. Jackie therefore returned to Athens, assuming that as she and her mother were Maria's only relatives now that she was divorced, they would inherit everything. Meneghini, however, who claimed that he had been unable to attend Maria's funeral due to 'extreme distress', arrived in Paris on 26 October, and only minutes after the end of the forty-day deadline petitioned the courts with a will which Maria had signed in 1954, leaving everything to him. His claim also added a clause to the effect that, inasmuch as Maria had been married to him then, so in the eyes of the Catholic church she had still been his wife at the time of her death. On the strength of this document, however, Meneghini was legally entitled to seal Georges-Mandel, with the exception of the servants' quarters, and this he did at once.

Meneghini's actions brought a speedy reaction from Litza, in Athens, who told the press, 'Maria never had time to prepare her will because she died so suddenly. But she had already made it quite clear to all lawyers concerned that my daughter and I were in effect the sole heirs.' This was of course untrue – Maria had never spoken of her relatives to her Paris coterie, and it had come as a shock to many when Jackie had turned up for the funeral. Also, Litza could not resist a final gibe by telling journalists that *Maria* had been her eldest daughter, and concluded her statement with yet another fabrication: 'But I have appointed the very best lawyer in France, and will have what is rightfully ours.'

In fact, as Litza was still living on state benefits, and as Maria's monthly allowance had now stopped, neither she nor Jackie could afford even the cheapest lawyer – a problem which was solved by Maria's pianist friend, Vasso Devetzi, who suggested that the best course of action, rather than fighting Meneghini, would be to settle out of court and agree a fifty-fifty split of Maria's estate. Both parties also agreed that Bruna and Ferruccio should be well recompensed for their loyalty towards Maria, and they were awarded an estimated $250,000 each. Bruna retired to Italy, but Maria's former butler committed 'high treason' by going to work for Christina Onassis.

Jackie Callas later confessed how much she had regretted Vasso Devetzi's mishandling of her affairs. It is now known that the pianist, whose career had been curtailed by arthritis, had been sponging off Maria for years, and she now told Jackie that Maria's greatest wish was that some of her money should go towards founding a scholarship for young singers, in addition to the one which existed already in Athens. Over the course of the next few years, without questioning the woman's honesty – the fact that she had done so much to help in the fight against Meneghini, *and* handled most of the arrangements for Maria's funeral proved that she could be trusted, Jackie maintained – Jackie and Litza would hand over more than $1 million for a foundation which would never materialise, until Vasso Divetzi was exposed by the Greek courts as an opportunist and a fraud.

The auction of Maria's possessions took place at the George V on 4 June 1978, and raised $800,000. This did not include her fabulous collection of jewellery, over which Meneghini and Jackie had come to another amicable agreement: the pieces he had bought would revert to him, whilst the family would receive those given to Maria by Onassis. A few days later, the everyday items were auctioned:

kitchen equipment, linen and bedding, the washing machine, dish-washer and vacuum cleaners, and all the worthless bric-a-brac that Maria had collected over the years.

Towards the end of the year, Litza insisted upon relocating to Paris. 'If she could get to where Maria was still worshipped, then a new life could be hers,' Jackie observed. 'Maria had been the queen of Paris society, she said: now that same society would eagerly welcome the Queen Mother.'

On 26 December, Maria's ashes were reported to have been stolen from the columbarium at Père Lachaise, yet within hours of this being announced on the radio, they had been found in another part of the cemetery. Litza immediately accused Meneghini of the theft, but in an official statement a representative from the City of Paris declared that Maria's ashes had not been in the vault in the first place, adding, 'The urn containing the remains of Mme Callas was removed from the Sepulchre in January 1978 at the request of her family.'

The mystery has never been solved, and on 3 June 1979, Maria's ashes were returned to Athens, at the request of the Greek govern-ment, to be scattered across the Aegean. Here, there was to be the ultimate irony. Neither Litza nor Meneghini were present and though the waters were calm when the Greek Navy destroyer set out from the port of Piraeus, no sooner had it left the harbour than a fierce storm began brewing. As Vasso Devetzi and the Minister of Culture fought open-mouthed to catch their breath in the wind, whilst wrestling with the lid of the urn, Maria's ashes blew back into everyone's faces. 'I looked around at the illustrious party and realised that we were all swallowing Maria's remains,' Jackie recalled. 'We were helplessly eating my sister. The greatest diva of the century was being consumed by those who had thought to placate her spirit.'

The retainers, good and bad, are almost all gone. Meneghini died alone, in Verona on 20 January 1981, aged eighty-five. Litza died on 20 August 1982, embittered and complaining until the end. She was buried in a new grave in Athens, but a few years later Jackie had her disinterred and placed underneath George Callas: 'So that she could now know for eternity the role she ought better to have fulfilled during life.' Vassi Devetzi died in November 1987. The fortune she had embezzled from the Callas family was never recovered, and her last wishes – that her ashes be scattered near Maria's final resting place – were refused by the Greek government.

Gone too are many of the colleagues, the friends and foes: her old teacher di Hidalgo, Princess Grace, Jackie and Christina Onassis, Carol Fox, Walter Legge, Stignani, Rossi-Lemeni, del Monaco, Christoff, Karajan, Bernstein. And Tito Gobbi, who probably summed up Maria Callas more touchingly than anyone else:

She shone for all too brief a while in the world of opera, like a vivid flame attracting the attention of the whole world, and she had a strange magic which was all her own. I always thought she was immortal – and she is.

Maria Callas: Concert Appearances

1938
11 April, Parnassos Hall, Athens.
Weber: *Der Freischütz*: 'Leise, Leise'.
Gounod: *La Reine de Saba*: aria unknown.
Psaroudas: song: 'Two nights'.
Puccini: *Tosca*: unknown duet with Zanni Kambani.
Piano accompaniment: Stefanos Valtetsiotis.

1939
22 May, Parnassos Hall, Athens.
Weber: *Oberon*: 'Ocean! thou mighty monster'.
Offenbach: *Les Contes d'Hoffmann*: 'Belle Nuit, O nuit d'amour', duet with Anita Bourdakou.
Verdi: *Aida*: 'Ritorna Vincitor'.
Psaroudas: song: 'I will not forget you'.
Verdi: *Aida*: 'O, terra addio'. Duet with Zanni Kambani.
Piano accompaniment: Stefanos Valtetsiotis.

23 May, Parnassos Hall, Athens.
Weber: *Oberon*: 'Ocean! thou mighty monster'.
Massenet: *Thaïs*: 'Dis-moi que je suis belle'.
Piano accompaniment: Stefanos Valtetsiotis.

25 June, Parnassos Hall, Athens.
Verdi: *Un Ballo In Maschera*: Act Three, the role of Amelia.
Mascagni: *Cavalleria Rusticana*: Scene Two, the role of Santuzza.
Piano accompaniment: Elli Necolaidou.

1940
23 February, Odeon Concert Hall, Athens.
Bellini: *Norma*: 'Mira, O Norma', duet with Arda Mandikian.
Piano accompaniment: Gerassimos Coundouris.

1942
Palace Theatre, Salonika.
Command performance for Italian troops comprising Rossini arias. No other details.

1943
28 February, Sporting Cinema, Nea Smerni, Athens.
Benefit concert. No other details.

21 July, Costa Moussouri Summer Theatre, Athens.
Callas's first solo recital.
Handel: *Atalanta*: 'Care selve'.
Rossini: *La Cenerentola*: 'Nacqui all'affanno'.
Cilea: *Adriana Lecouvreur*: 'Poveri fiori'.
verdi: *Il Trovatore*: 'Tracea la notte'.
Lavda: song: *They are marrying my love*.
Palantio: song: *Kimitri*.
Piano accompaniment: A. Paredis.

September, White Tower Theatre, Salonika.
Solo recital command performance for Italian troops comprising works by Schubert, Brahms and Rossini.

26 September, Olympia Theatre, Athens.
Beethoven: *Fidelio*: 'Abscheulicher!'
Massenet: *Thaïs*: 'Dis-moit que je suis belle'.
Verdi: *Aida*: 'Ritorna Vincitor'.
Mozart: 'Mass In C Minor'.
Turina: song: *Canzone spagnola*.
Lavda: song: *They are marrying my love*.
Piano accompaniment: Costas Cydoniatis.

12 December, Cotopouli-Rex Theatre, Athens.
Benefit concert.
Beethoven: *Fidelio*: 'Abscheulicher!'
Rossini: *Semiramide*: 'Bel raggio'.
Verdi: *Il Trovatore*: 'Tracea la notte'.
Turina: song: *Canzone spagnola*.

Piano accompaniment. L. Androutsopoulos.

1944
22 May, Olympia Theatre, Athens.
Benefit concert.
Bellini: *Norma*: 'Casta diva'.

October, White Tower Theatre, Salonika.
Command performance for Italian troops. No other details.

1945
20 March, Olympia Theatre, Athens.
Benefit concert for British troops. All songs.
Anonymous: *Willow, willow*.
Ronald: *Love, I have won you*.
Vaughan Williams: *On Wenlock Edge*.
Nimey and Jornay: *Think not strange*.
Conductor: Totis Caralevanos.

3 August, Cotopouli-Rex Theatre, Athens.
Farewell recital.
Mozart: *Don Giovanni*: 'Non mir Dir'.
Rossini: *Semiramide*: 'Bel raggio'.
Verdi: *Aida*: 'Ritorna vincitor'.
Verdi: *Il Trovatore*: 'Tracea la notte'.
Weber: *Oberon*: 'Ocean! thou mighty monster'.
Plus several Greek and Spanish songs by Lavda andTurina. Piano accompaniment, Alice Lycoudi.

1949
9 July, Téatro Colón, Buenos Aires.
Bellini: *Norma*: 'Casta diva', Puccini: *Turandot*: Act 3.
Callas, del Monaco, Rossi-Lemeni, Arizmendt.
Conductor: Serafin.

18 September, Church of San Pietro, Perugia.
Stradella: *San Giovanni Battista* (Oratorio).
Callas, Siepi, Corsi, Pirazzini, Berdini.
Conductor: Santini.

31 October, Arena, Verona.
Bellini: *Norma*: 'Casta diva', *I Puritani*: 'Qui la voce'.
Wagner: *Tristan Und Isolde*: 'Liebestod'.

Meyerbeer: *Dinorah*: 'Ombra leggiera'.
Verdi: *La Traviata*: 'Ah! fors'e lui'.
Conductor: possibly Serafin.

1951
21 April, Téatro Verdi, Trieste.
Bellini: *Norma*: 'Casta diva', *I Puritani*: 'Qui la voce'.
Verdi: *Aida*: 'O patria mia', *La Traviata*: 'Ah, forse'è lui'.
Conductor: La Rosa Parodi.

11 June, Grand Hotel, Florence.
Bellini: *Norma*: 'Casta diva'.
Meyerbeer: *Dinorah*: 'Ombra leggiera'.
Verdi: *Aida*: 'O patria mia'. Proch: *Variations*.
Verdi: *La Traviata*.
Piano: Bartoletti.

14 September, Municipal Theatre, Rio de Janeiro.
Verdi: *La Traviata*: 'Ah, fors'è lui', *Aida*: 'O patria mia'.
Conductor: possibly Votto.

20(?) September, Municipal Theatre, Rio de Janeiro.
Verdi: *La Traviata*: 'Sempre libera'.
Conductor: possibly Tullio Serafin. This is the famous 'benefit' concert which began Callas's rivalry with Renate Tebaldi.

1952
8 February, Circolo della Stampa, Milan.
Verdi: *La Traviata*: 'Ah, forsé lui'.
Rest of programme not known. Pianist: Tonini.

17 November, Italian Embassy, London.
Callas gave a private recital of Bellini and Puccini arias. No other details.

1953
? May, Auditorio di Palazzo Pio, Rome.
Verdi: *Il Trovatore*: 'D'amor sull'ali rosee'.
Verdi: *La Forza del Destino*: 'Pace, pace'.
Meyerbeer: *Dinorah*: 'Ombra leggiera'.
Conductor: de Fabritiis.

1956
17 December, Italian Embassy, Washington.

Verdi: *Il Trovatore*: 'D'amor sull'ali rosee'.
Bellini: *Norma*: 'Casta diva'.
Verdi: *La Traviata*: 'Ah, fors'è lui', Puccini: *Tosca*: 'Vissi d'arte'.
Donizetti: *Lucia di Lammermoor*: 'Regnava nel silenzio'.
Piano accompaniment: Schaefer.

1957
15 January, Civic Opera House, Chicago.
Bellini: *La Sonnambula*: 'Ah, non credea'.
Meyerbeer: *Dinorah*: 'Ombra leggiera'.
Puccini: *Turandot*: 'In questa reggia', Bellini: *Norma*: 'Casta diva'.
Verdi: *Il Trovatore*: 'D'amor sull'ali rosee'.
Donizetti: *Lucia di Lammermoor*: 'Il dolce suono'.
Conductor: Cleva.

19 June, Tonhalle, Zurich.
Verdi: *La Traviata*: 'Ah, fors'è lui'.
Donizetti: *Lucia di Lammermoor*: 'Ardon gli incensi'.
Conductor: Moralt.

5 August, Herodes Atticus Theatre, Athens.
Verdi: *Il Trovatore*: 'D'amor sull'ali rosee'.
Verdi: *La Forza del Destino*: 'Pace, pace'.
Thomas: *Hamlet*: 'Ai vostri giochi'.
Wagner: *Trisan und Isolde*: 'Liebestod' (sung in Italian).
Bellini: *Lucia di Lammermoor*: 'Regnava nel silenzio'.
Conductor: Votto.

21 November, Civic Opera House, Dallas.
Mozart: *Die Entführung aus dem Serail*: 'Tutte le torture'.
Bellini: *I Puritani*: 'Qui la voce'.
Verdi: *Macbeth*: 'Vieni t'affretta'. *La Traviata*: 'Ah, fors'è lui'.
Donizetti: *Anna Bolena*: 'Al dolce guidami'.
Conductor: Rescigno.

1958
22 January, Civic Opera House, Chicago.
Mozart: *Don Giovanni*: 'Non mi dir'.
Verdi: *Macbeth*: 'Vieni t'affreta'.
Rossini: *Il Barbiere di Siviglia*: 'Una voce poco fa'.
Boito: *Mefistofele*: 'L'altra notte'.
Thomas: *Hamlet*: 'Ai vostri giochi'. Verdi: *Nabucco*: 'Ben io t'invenni'.
Conductor: Rescigno.

24 March, Cinema Monumental, Madrid.
Bellini: *Norma*: 'Casta diva'.
Verdi: *Il Trovatore*: 'D'amor sull'ali rosee'.
Boito: *Mefistofele*: 'L'altra notte'.
Thomas: *Hamlet*: 'Ai vostri giochi'.
Conductor: Morelli.

10 June, Covent Garden, London.*
Bellini: *I Puritani*: 'Qui la voce'.
Conductor: Pritchard.

CONCERT TOUR
11 October, Municipal Auditorium, Birmingham.
14 October, Municipal Auditorium, Atlanta.
17 October, Forum, Montreal.
21 October, Maple Leaf Garden, Toronto.
15 November, Public Music House, Cleveland.
18 November, Masonic Auditorium, Detroit.
22 November, Constitution Hall, Washington.
26 November, War Memorial Opera House, San Francisco.
29 November, Kiel Auditorium, St Louis.
Spontini: *La Vestale*: 'Tu che invoco'.
Verdi: *Macbeth*: 'Vieni t'affreta'.
Rossini: *Il Barbiere di Siviglia*: 'Una voce poco fa'.
Boito: *Mefistofele*: 'L'altra notte'.
Puccini: *La Bohème*: 'Quando me'n vo'.
Thomas: *Hamlet*: 'A vos jeux, mes amis'.
Conductor: Rescigno.

19 December, Paris Opera.
Bellini: *Norma*: 'Sedisiose voci', 'Casta diva', 'Fine al rito', 'Ah! bello a me ritorna'.
Verdi: *Il Trovatore*: 'D'amor sull'ali rosee'; 'Miserere'.**
Rossini: *Il Barbiere di Siviglia*: 'Una voce poco fa'.
Puccini: *Tosca*. Act II. With Tito Gobbi, Albert Lance, Louis Rialland, Jean-Paul Hurteau.
Conductor: Sebastian.

1959
11 January, Kiel Auditorium, St Louis.
Concert. Programme/conductor as detailed 11-10 to 29-11-58.

* Callas appeared as part of bill for the Covent Garden Centenary.
** Duet with Albert Lance.

24 January, Academy of Music, Philadelphia.
Boito: *Mefistofele*: 'L'altra notte'.
Rossini: *Il Barbiere di Siviglia*: 'Una voce poco fa'.
Thomas: *Hamlet*: 'A vos jeux, mes amis'.
Conductor: Ormandy.

27 January, Carnegie Hall, New York.
29 January, Constitution Hall, Washington.
Bellini: *Il Pirata* (concert performance).
Imogene: Maria Callas, Ernesto: Constantino Ego, Gualtiero: Pier Miranda Ferraro, Itulbo: Glade Peterson.
Conductor: Nicola Rescigno.

2 May, Téatro de la Zarzuela, Madrid.
Mozart: *Don Giovanni*: 'Non mi dir'.
Verdi: *Macbeth*: 'Vieni t'affretta'.
Rossini: *Semiramide*: 'Bel raggio', Ponchiello: *La Gioconda*: 'Suicidio!'
Bellini: *Il Pirata*: 'Col sorriso'.
Conductor: Rescigno.

5 May, Téatro del Liceo, Barcelona.
Verdi: *Don Carlos*: 'Tuche le vanità'.
Bolto: *Mefistofele*: 'L'altra notte'.
Rossini: *Il Barbiere di Siviglia*: 'Una voce poco fa'.
Puccini: *Tosca*: Vissi d'arte, *La Bohème*: 'Quando m'en vo'.
Bellini: *Il Pirata*: 'Col sorriso'.
Conductor: Rescigno.

CONCERT TOUR
15 May, Musikhalle, Hamburg.
19 May, Liederhalle, Stuttgart.
21 May, Deutsche Museum, Munich.
24 May, Kursaal, Wiesbaden.
Spontini: *La Vestale*: 'Tu che invoco'.
Verdi: *Macbeth*: 'Vieni t'affretta'.
Rossini: *Il Barbiere di Siviglia*: 'Una voce poco fa'.
Verdi: *Don Carlos*: 'Tu che le vanità'.
Bellini: *Il Pirata*: 'Col sorriso'.
Conductor: Rescigno.

11 July, Concertgebouw, Amsterdam.
14 July, Théâtre de la Monnaie, Brussels.
Spontini: *La Vestale*: 'Tu che invoco'.
Verdi: *Ernani*: 'Ernani involami', *Don Carlos*: 'Tu che la vanità'.

Bellini: *Il Pirata*: 'Col sorriso'.
Conductor: Rescigno.

17 September, Coliseo Albia, Bilbao.
Verdi: *Don Carlos*: 'Tu che le vanità'.
Thomas: *Hamlet*: 'A vos jeux, mes amis.'
Verdi: *Ernani*: 'Ernani involami', Bellini: *Il Pirata*: 'Col sorriso'.
Conductor: Rescigno.

23 September, Royal Festival Hall, London.
Verdi: *Don Carlos*: 'Tu che le vanità'.
Bellini: *Il Pirata*: 'Col sorriso'.
Thomas: *Hamlet*: 'A vos jeux, mes amis', Verdi: *Macbeth*: 'Una macchia'.
Conductor: Rescigno.

23 October, Titiana Palast, Berlin.
Mozart: *Don Giovanni*: 'Non mi dir'.
Verdi: *Ernani*: 'Ernani involami', *Don Carlos*: 'Tu che le vanità'.
Thomas: *Hamlet*: 'A vos jeux, mes amis'.
Conductor: Rescigno.

28 October, Loew's Midland Theater, Kansas City.
Mozart: *Don Giovanni*: 'Non mi dir'.
Donizetti: *Lucia di Lammermoor*: 'Regnava nel silenzio'.
Verdi: *Ernani*: 'Ernani involami', Bellini: *Il Parata*: 'Col sorriso'.
Conductor: Rescigno.

1961
30 May, St James's Palace, London.
Bellini: *Norma*: 'Casta diva', Massenet: *Le Cid*: 'Pleurez mes yeux'.
Verdi: *Don Carlos*: 'Tu che le vanità'.
Boito: *Mefistofele*: 'L'altra notte'.
Pianist: Sargent.

1962
27 February, Royal Festival Hall, London.
Weber: *Oberon*: 'Ocean, thou mighty monster'.
Massenet: *Le Cid*: 'Pleurez mes yeux'.
Rossini: *La Cenerentola*: 'Nacqui all'affanno'.
Verdi: *Don Carlos*: 'O don fatale', *Macbeth*: 'La luce langue'.
Donizetti: *Anna Bolena*: 'Al dolce guidami'.
Conductor: Prêtre.

CONCERT TOUR
12 March, Deutsche Museum, Munich.

16 March, Musikhalle, Hamburg.
19 March, Städtischer Saalbau, Essen.
23 March, Beethoven Halle, Bonn.
Verdi: *Don Carlos*: 'O don fatale'.
Massenet: *Le Cid*: 'Pleurez mes yeux'.
Rossini: *La Cenerentola*: 'Nacqui all'affanno'.
Bizet: *Carmen*: 'Habañera', 'Séguedille'.
Verdi: *Ernani*: 'Ernani involami'.
Conductor: Prêtre.

19 May, Madison Square Garden, New York.
Bizet: *Carmen*: 'Habañera', 'Séquedille'.
Pianist: Wilson.

1963
CONCERT TOUR
17 May, Deutsche Opera, Berlin.
20 May, Rheinhalle, Düsseldorf.
23 May, Liederhalle, Stuttgart.
31 May, Royal Festival Hall, London.
5 June, Théâtre des Champs-Elysées, Paris.*
Falkoner Centre, Copenhagen.
Rossini: *Semiramide*: 'Bel raggio', Bellini: *Norma*: 'Casta diva'.
Verdi: *Nabucco*: 'Ben io t'invenni'.
Puccini: *La Bohème*: 'Quando m'en vo', *Madama Butterfly*: 'Tu, tu'.
Piccolo iddio, *Gianni Schicchi*: 'O mio babbino caro'.
Conductor: Prêtre.

1973
CONCERT TOUR. With Giuseppe di Stefano.
25 October, Hamburg. 29 October, Berlin. 2 November, Düsseldorf. 6
November, Munich. 9 November, Frankfurt. 12 November, Mannheim.
20 November, Madrid. 26 November & 2 December, London. 7
December, Paris. 11 December, Amsterdam.
Donizetti: *L'Elisir d'Amore*: 'Una parola Adina'.
Gounod: *Faust*: 'O silence! O bonheur ... O nuit d'amour!'.
Bizet: *Carmen*: 'C'est toi, c'est moi'; 'Habañera'.
Verdi: *I Vespri Siciliani*: 'Quale, o prode'.
Mascagni: *Cavalleria Rusticana*: 'Tu qui, Santuzza?'; 'Voi lo sapete'.

* In Paris, 'Casta diva' was dropped and the following added to the programme:
  Rossini: *La Cenerentola*: 'Nacqui all'affano', Massenet: *Werther*: 'Air des lettres',
  Manon: 'Adieu notre petite table'.

Verdi: *La Forza del Destino*: 'Ah! per sempre'.
Verdi: *Don Carlo*: 'Io vengo a domandar'; 'Tu che la vanità'.
Ponchielli: *La Gioconda*: 'Suicidio'. Verdi: *Tosca*: 'Vissi d'arte'.
Puccini: *Manon Lescaut*: 'Sola, perduta, abbandonata'.
Puccini: *Gianni Schicchi*: 'O mio babbino caro'.
Massenet: *Werther*: 'Air des lettres'; *Manon*: 'Adieu, notre petite table'.
Puccini: *La Bohème*: 'Si, si chiamano Mimi'.
Pianist: Newton/Sutherland.

1974
CONCERT TOUR. With Giuseppe di Stefano.
20 January, Milan (private). 23 January, Stuttgart. 11 February, Philadelphia. 21 February, Toronto. 24 February, Washington. 27 February, Boston. 2 March, Chicago. 5 March, New York. 9 March, Detroit. 12 March, Dallas. 21 March, Miami Beach. 4 April, Columbus. 9 April, Brookville LI. 15 April, New York. 18 April, Cincinatti. 24 April, Seattle. 27 April, Portland. 1 May, Vancouver. 5 May, Los Angeles. 9 May, San Francisco. 13 May, Montreal. 5 & 8 October, Seoul. 12, 19 & 27 October, Tokyo. 24 October, Fukuoka. 2 November, Osaka. 7 November, Hiroshima. 11 November, Sapporo.
Pianist: Sutherland. Programme as 1973.

Appendix II

Maria Callas: Opera Performances

1939
2 April, Olympia Theatre, Athens.
Mascagni: *Cavalleria Rusticana*. (Student production) (Santuzza)
Callas, Semeriotis, Copanou, Atheneos, Euthemiadou.
Conductor unknown.

1940
16 June, Odeon Concert Hall, Athens.
Puccini: *Suor Angelica*. (Suor Angelica).
Also performed 27 November, National Theatre. No other details.

1941
21 January, Palace Theatre, Athens.
Von Suppé: *Boccace*. (Beatrice).
Also performed 3 July, Park Summer Theatre. No other details.

1942
27 August, 8 September, Summer Theatre, Athens.
Puccini: *Tosca*. (Floria Tosca).
Callas, Dellendas*, Calogeras**
Conductor unknown.

1943 19 February, Royal Theatre, Athens. Kalomiras: *Ho Protomastoras* (The Master Builder).
Callas sang in the chorus during the Intermezzo between Acts One and Two.

* Replaced by Couroussopoulos and ** Xirellis in 2nd perf.

17 July, Summer Theatre, Athens.
Puccini: *Tosca*
Callas, Dellendas, Xirellis.
Conductor unknown.

1944
22, 23, 30 April, 4, 7, 10 May, Olympia Theatre, Athens.
d'Albert: *Tiefland*. (Martha).
Callas, Mangliveras, Dellendas.
Conductor unknown.

21 May, Olympia Theatre, Athens.
Mascagni: *Cavalleria Rusticana*. (Santuzza).
Callas, Dellendas, Tsoubris, Courahani.
Conductor: Karalivanos.
29, 30 July, Herodes Atticus Amphitheatre, Athens.
d'Albert: *Ho Protomastoras*. (Smaragda).
Callas, Mangliveras, Tsoubris.
Conductor: Kalomiras.

14, 19 August, Herodes Atticus Amphitheatre, Athens.
Beethoven: *Fidelio*. (Sung in Greek)(Leonora).
Callas, Dellendas, Mangliveras, Vlachopoulou.
Conductor: Hörner.

1945
14 March, Olympia Theatre, Athens.
d'Albert: *Tiefland*. (Martha).
No other details.

5 September, Summer Theatre, Athens.
Millöcker: *Der Bettelstudent*. (Laura).
No other details. Callas abandoned the subsequent performances of this production when she left Greece for the United States.

1947
2, 5, 10, 14, 17 August, Arena, Verona.
Ponchielli: *La Gioconda* (Gioconda).
Callas, Nicolai, Rossi-Lemeni, Tucker, Tagliabue, Canali.
Conductor: Serafin.

30 December, 3, 8, 11 January, La Fenice, Venice.
Wagner: *Tristan und Isolde* (Sung in Italian) (Isolde).

Callas, Barbieri, Christoff, Torres, Tasso.
Conductor: Serafin.

1948
29, 31 January, 3, 8, 10 February, La Fenice, Venice.
Puccini: *Turandot*. (Turandot).
Callas, Rizzieri, Soler, Carmassi.
Conductor: Sanzogno.

11, 14 March, Puccini Theatre, Udine.
Puccini: *Turandot*.
Callas, Ottani, Soler, Maionica.
Conductor: de Fabritiis.

17, 20, 21, 25 April, Politeama Rossetti, Trieste.
Verdi: *La Forza del Destino*. (Leonora)
Callas, Canali, Vertecchi, Franci, Siepi, Parenti.
Conductor: Serpo.

12, 14, 16 May, Grattacielo, Genoa.
Wagner: *Tristan und Isolde*. (Sung in Italian). (Isolde).
Callas, Nicolai, Rossi-Lemeni, Torres, Lorenz.
Conductor: Serafin.

4, 6, 11 July, Terme di Caracalla, Rome.
Puccini: *Turandot*.
Callas, Montanari, Masini, Flamini.
Conductor: de Fabritiis.

27 July, 1, 5, 9 August, Arena, Verona.
Puccini: *Turandot*.
Callas, Rossi-Lemeni, Rizzieri, de Cecco, Salvarezza, Tognoli.
Conductor: Votto.

11, 14 August, Carlo Felice, Genoa.
Puccini: *Turandot*.
Callas, del Monaco, Salvarezza, Maionica.
Conductor: Montanari.

18, 19, 23, 25 September, Lyric Theatre, Turin.
Verdi: *Aida*. (Aida).
Callas, Nicolai, Colasanti, Turrini, de Falchi.
Conductor: Serafin.

19, 21, 24 October, Sociale Theatre, Rovigo.
Verdi: *Aida*.
Callas, Pirazzini, Turrini, Viaro.
Conductor: Berretoni.

Mid-November, Pisa.
Puccini: *Turandot*.
Callas, Campagno. Conductor: de Ruggero. No other details.

30 November, 5 December, Communale Theatre, Florence.
Bellini: *Norma*. (Norma).
Callas, Barbieri, Picchi, Siepi.
Conductor: Serafin.

1949
8, 12, 14, 16 January, La Fenice, Venice.
Wagner: *Die Walküre*. (Sung in Italian). (Brünnhilde).
Callas, Magnoni, Pini, Voyer, Torres, Dominici.
Conductor: Serafin.

19, 22, 23 January, La Fenice, Venice.
Bellini: *I Puritani*. (Elvira).
Callas, Christoff, Pirino, Savarese.
Conductor: Serafin.

28 January, 10 February, Téatro Massimo, Palermo.
Wagner: *Die Walküre*. (Sung in Italian).
Callas, Mangoni, Sani, Voyer, Neri, Carmassi.
Conductor: Molinari-Pradelli.

12, 16, 18, 20 February, Téatro San Carlo, Naples.
Puccini: *Turandot*.
Callas, Montanari, Petri, R. Gigli.
Conductor: Perlea.

26 February, 2, 5, 8 March, Opera House, Rome.
Wagner: *Parsifal*. (Sung in Italian). (Kundry).
Callas, Siepi, Beirer, Cortis.
Conductor: Serafin.

20, 29 May, 11, 22 June, Téatro Colón, Buenos Aires.
Puccini: *Turandot*.
Callas, del Monaco, Arizmendi, Zanin/Rossi-Lemeni.
Conductor: Serafin.

17, 19, 25, 29 June, Téatro Colón, Buenos Aires.
Bellini: *Norma*.
Callas, Barbieri, Rossi-Lemeni, Vela, Damiani.
Conductor: Serafin.

2 July, Téatro Colón, Buenos Aires.
Verdi: *Aida*.
Callas, Barbieri, Rossi-Lemeni, Vela, Damiani.
Conductor: Serafin.

20, 22, 27 December, Téatro San Carlo, Naples.
Verdi: *Narbucco*. (Abigaille).
Callas, Pini, Sinimberghi, Bechi, Neroni.
Conductor: Gui.

1950
13, 15, 19 January, La Fenice, Venice.
Bellini: *Norma*.
Callas, Nicolai, Penno, Pasero.
Conductor: Votto.

2, 7 February, Téatro Grande, Brescia.
Verdi: *Aida*.
Callas, del Monaco, Pini, Protti.
Conductor: Erede.

6, 9, 19, 25, 28 February, Opera House, Rome.
Wagner: *Tristan und Isolde*. (Sung in Italian).
Callas, Nicolai, Seider, Franci, Neri/Nerone.
Conductor: Serafin.

23, 26 February, 2, 4, 7 March, Opera House, Rome.
Bellini: *Norma*.
Callas, Stignani, Massini, Neri, Cassinelli.
Conductor: Serafin.

16, 19, 22, 25 March, Téatro Massimo Bellini, Catania.
Bellini: *Norma*.
Callas, Gardino, Picchi, Stefanoni.
Conductor: Berretoni.

2, 5, 18 April, La Scala, Milan.
Verdi: *Aida*.

Callas (replacing Renata Tebaldi), Barbieri, del Monaco, de Falchi, Protti.
Conductor: Capuana.

27, 30 April, 2, 4 May, Téatro San Carlo, Naples.
Verdi: *Aida*.
Callas, Picchi, Stignani, Savarese.

23, 27 May, Palacio de Bellas Artes, Mexico City.
Bellini: *Norma*.
Callas, Baum, Simionato, Moscona.
Conductor: Picco.

30 May, 3, 15 June, Palacio de Bellas Artes, Mexico City.
Verdi: *Aida*.
Callas, Baum/Filippeschi, Simionato, Weede.
Conductor: Picco.

8, 10 June, Palacio de Bellas Artes, Mexico City.
Puccini: *Tosca*.
Callas, Weede, Filippeschi.
Conductor: Mugnai.

20, 24, 27 June, Palacio de Bellas Artes, Mexico City.
Verdi: *Il Trovatore*. (Leonora).
Callas, Baum, Moscona, Simionato, Warren/Petroff.
Conductor: Picco.

22 September, Téatro Nuovo, Salsomaggiore.
Puccini: *Tosca*.
Callas, Pelizzoni, Inghilleri.
Conductor: Questa.

24 September, Téatro Duse, Bologna.
Puccini: *Tosca*.
Callas, Turrini, Azzolini.
Conductor: Questa.

2 October, Opera House, Rome.
Verdi: *Aida*.
Callas, Picchi, Stignani, Neri, de Falchi.
Conductor: Bellezza.

7, 8 October, Téatro Verdi, Pisa.
Puccini: *Tosca*.

Callas, Masini, Polli.
Conductor: Santarelli.

19, 22, 25, 29 October, Téatro Eliseo, Rome.
Rossini: *Il Turco in Italia*. (Fiorilla).
Callas, Valletti, Stabile, Canali.
Conductor: Gavazzeni.

1951
14, 16, 20 January, Téatro Comunale, Florence.
Verdi: *La Traviata*. (Violetta).
Callas, Mascherini, Albanese.
Conductor: Serafin.

27, 30 January, 1 February, Téatro San Carlo, Naples.
Verdi: *Il Trovatore*.
Callas, Lauri-Volpi/Vertecchi, Elmo, Tajo, Silveri.
Conductor: Serafin.

15, 20 February, Téatro Massimo, Palermo.
Bellini: *Norma*.
Callas, Nicolai, Neri, Gavarini.
Conductor: Ghione.

28 February, Téatro Comunale, Reggio Calabre.
Verdi: *Aida*.
Callas, Pirazzini, Soler, Manca-Serra.
Conductor: del Cupolo.

14, 18 March, Téatro Massimo, Cagliari.
Verdi: *La Traviata*.
Callas, Capora, Polli.
Conductor: Molinari-Pradelli.

26, 30 May, 2, 5 June, Téatro Comunale, Florence.
Verdi: *I Vespri Siciliani*. (Elena).
Callas, Kokolios-Bardi, Mascherini, Christoff, Carmassi.
Conductor: Kleiber.

9, 10 June, Téatro La Pergola, Florence.
Haydn: *Orfeo ed Euridice*. (Euridice).
Callas, Tygeson, Christoff.
Conductor: Kleiber.

3, 7, 10 July, Palacio de Bellas Artes, Mexico City.
Verdi: *Aida*.
Callas, del Monaco, Taddei, Dominguez.
Conductor: de Fabritiis.

17, 19, 21, 22 July, Palacio de Bellas Artes, Mexico City.
Verdi: *La Traviata*.
Callas, Valetti, Taddei/Morelli.
Conductor: de Fabritiis.

7 September, Municipal Theatre, Sao Paulo.
Bellini: *Norma*.
Callas, Barbieri, Picchi, Rossi-Lemeni.
Conductor: Serafin.

9 September, Municipal Theatre, Sao Paulo.
Verdi: *La Traviata*.
Callas, de Stefano, Gobbi.
Conductor: Serafin.

12, 16 September, Municipal Theatre, Rio de Janeiro.
Bellini: *Norma*.
Callas, Nicolai, Picchi, Christoff.
Conductor: Votto.

24 September, Municipal Theatre, Rio de Janeiro.
Puccini: *Tosca*.
Callas, Poggi, Silveri.
Conductor: Votto.

28, 30 September, Municipal Theatre, Rio de Janeiro.
Verdi: *La Traviata*.
Callas, Possi, Salsedo.
Conductor: Gaioni.

20, 23 October, Téatro Donizetti, Bergamo.
Verdi: *La Traviata*.
Callas, Prandelli, Fabbri.
Conductor: Giulini.

3, 6, 17, 20 November, Téatro Massimo Bellini, Catania.
Bellini: *Norma*.
Callas, Simionato, Penno, Christoff/Wolovski.
Conductor: Ghione.

8, 11, 13, 16 November, Téatro Massimo Bellini, Catania.
Bellini: *I Puritani*.
Callas, Tagliabue, Christoff, Wenkow.
Conductor: Wolf-Ferrari.

7, 9, 12, 16, 19, 27 December, 3 January, La Scala, Milan.
Verdi: *I Vespri Siciliani*.
Callas, Mascherini, Christoff/Modesti, Quadri, Conley.
Conductor: de Sabata.

29 December, Téatro Regio, Parma.
Verdi: *La Traviata*.
Callas, Pola, Savarese.
Conductor: de Fabritiis.

1952
9, 11 January, Téatro Comunale, Florence.
Bellini: *I Puritani*.
Callas, Tagliabue, Rossi-Lemeni, Conley.
Conductor: Serafin.

16, 19, 23, 27, 29 January, 2, 7, 10 February, 14 April, La Scala, Milan.
Bellini: *Norma*.
Callas, Stignani, Rossi-Lemeni, Penno.
Conductor: Ghione.

12, 14, 16 March, Téatro Massimo Bellini, Catania.
Verdi: *La Traviata*.
Callas, Mascherini, Campora.
Conductor: Molinari-Pradelli.

2, 5, 7, 9 April, La Scala, Milan.
Mozart: *Die Entführung aus dem Serail*. (Constanze).
Callas, Munteanu, Prandelli, Baccaloni, Menotti/Duval.
Conductor: Perlea.

26, 29 April, 4 May, Téatro Comunale, Florence.
Rossini: *Armida*. (Armida).
Callas, Albanese, Ziliani, Salvarezza, Filippeschi, Raimondi.
Conductor: Serafin.

2, 6, 11 May, Opera House, Rome.
Bellini: *I Puritani*.

Callas, Lauri-Volpi/Pirino, Silveri, Neri.
Conductor: Santini.

29, 31 May, Palacio de Bellas Artes, Mexico City.
Bellini: *I Puritani*.
Callas, di Stefano, Campolonghi, Silva.
Conductor: Picco.

3, 7 June, Palacia de Bellas Artes, Mexico City.
Verdi: *La Traviata*.
Callas, di Stefano, Campolonghi.
Conductor: Mugnai.

10, 14, 26 June, Palacio de Bellas Artes, Mexico City.
Donizetti: *Lucia di Lammermoor*. (Lucia).
Callas, di Stefano, Campolonghi, Silva.
Conductor: Picco.

17, 21 June, Palacio de Bellas Artes, Mexico City.
Verdi: *Rigoletto*. (Gilda).
Callas, di Stefano, Campolonghi, Garcia, Ruffino.
Conductor: Mugnai.

28 June, 1 July, Palacio de Bellas Artes, Mexico City.
Puccini: *Tosca*.
Callas, di Stefano, Campolonghi.
Conductor: Picco.

19, 23 July, Arena, Verona.
Ponchielli: *La Gioconda*.
Callas, Nicolai, Poggi, Tajo, Canali, Inghilleri.
Conductor: Votto.

2, 5, 10, 14 August.
Verdi: *La Traviata*.
Callas, Mascherini, Campora.
Conductor: Molinari-Pradelli.

8, 10, 13, 18, 20 November, Covent Garden, London.
Bellini: *Norma*.
Callaas, Stignani, Picchi, Sutherland, Vaghi.
Conductor: Gui/Pritchard.

7, 9, 11, 14, 17 December, La Scala, Milan.
Verdi: *Macbeth*. (Lady Macbeth).
Callas, Mascherini, Penno, Tajo/Modesti, Dello-Pergola.
Conductor: de Sabata.

26, 28, 30 December, 1, 3 January, 19 February, La Scala, Milan.
Ponchielli: *La Gioconda*.
Callas, Stignani, di Stefano, Tagliabue, Tajo/Modesti, Danielli.
Conductor: Votto.

1953
8, 10 January, La Fenice, Venice.
Verdi: *La Traviata*.
Callas, Albanese, Savarese, Tagliabue.
Conductor: Questa.

15, 18, 21 January, Opera House, Rome.
Verdi: *La Traviata*.
Callas, Albanese, Savarese.
Conductor: Santini.

25, 28 January, 5, 8 February, Téatro Comunale, Florence.
Donizetti: *Lucia di Lammermoor*.
Callas, Lauri-Volpi, di Stefano, Arié, Bastianini.
Conductor: Ghione.

23, 26, 28 February, 24, 29 March, La Scala, Milan.
Verdi: *Il Trovatore*.
Callas, Stignani, Penno, Tagliabue, Modesti.
Conductor: Votto.

14, 17 March, Téatro Carlo Felice, Genoa.
Donizetti: *Lucia di Lammermoor*.
Callas, di Stefano, Mascherini.
Conductor: Ghione.

9, 12, 15, 18 April, Opera House, Rome.
Bellini: *Norma*.
Callas, Barbieri, Corelli, Neri.
Conductor: Santini.

21, 23 April, Téatro Massimo Bellini, Catania.
Donizetti: *Lucia di Lammermoor*.

Callas, Taddei, Arié, Turrini.
Conductor: de Fabritiis.

7, 10, 12 May, Téatro Comunale, Florence.
Cherubini: *Medea*. (Medea).
Callas, Guichandut, Tucci, Petri, Barbieri.
Conductor: Gui.

19, 21, 24 May, Opera House, Rome.
Donizetti: *Lucia di Lammermoor*.
Callas, Poggi, Guelfi, Cassinelli.
Conductor: Gavazzeni.

4, 6, 10 June, Covent Garden, London.
Verdi: *Aida*.
Callas, Baum, Simionato, Walters.
Conductor: Barbirolli.

15, 17, 20, 23 June, Covent Garden, London.
Bellini: *Norma*.
Callas, Simionato, Picchi, Neri, Sutherland.
Conductor: Pritchard.

26, 29 June, 1 July, Covent Garden, London.
Verdi: *Il Trovatore*.
Callas, Simionato, Walters, Langdon, Johnston.
Conductor: Erede.

23, 25, 28, 30 July, 8 August, Arena, Verona.
Verdi: *Aida*.
Callas, del Monaco/Filippeschi/Zambruno, Pirazzini, Protti/Malaspina.
Conductor: Serafin.

15 August, Arena, Verona.
Verdi: *Il Trovatore*.
Callas, Danielli, Zambruno, Protti, Malonica.
Conductor: Molinari-Pradelli.

19, 22, 23, 29 November, Téatro Verdi, Trieste.
Bellini: *Norma*.
Callas, Nicolai, Corelli, Christoff, Ronchini, Botteghelli.
Conductor: Votto.

10, 12, 29 December, 2, 6 January, La Scala, Milan.
Cherubini: *Medea*
Callas, Barbieri, Penno, Modesti, Nach.
Conductor: Bernstein.

16, 19, 23 December, Opera House, Rome.
Verdi: *Il Trovatore*.
Callas, Barbieri/Pirazzini, Lauri-Volpi, Silveri, Neri.
Conductor: Santini.

1954
18, 21, 24, 27, 31 January, 5, 7 February, La Scala, Milan.
Donizetti: *Lucia di Lammermoor*.
Callas, di Stefano/Poggi, Panerai, Modesti.
Conductor: Karajan.

13, 16, 21 February, La Fenice, Venice.
Donizetti: *Lucia di Lammermoor*.
Callas, Bastianini, Infantino, Tozzi.
Conductor: Questa.

2, 4, 7 March, La Fenice, Venice.
Cherubini: *Medea*.
Callas, Tucci, Pirazzini, Gavarini, Tozzi.

10, 15, 17 March, Téatro Carlo Felice, Genoa.
Puccini: *Tosca*.
Callas, Ortica, Guelfi.
Conductor: Ghione.

4, 6, 15, 20 April, La Scala, Milan.
Gluck: *Alceste* (Alceste).
Callas, Gavarini, Silveri, Panerai, Zaccaria.
Conductor: Giulini.

12, 17, 23, 25, 27 April, La Scala, Milan.
Verdi: *Don Carlo* (Elisabetta).
Callas, Mascherini, Rossi-Lemeni, Stignani, Ortica.
Conductor: Votto.

23, 26 May, Téatro Alighieri, Ravenna.
Verdi: *La Forza del Destino*.
Callas, del Monaco, Modesti, Gardino, Protti.
Conductor: Ghione.

15, 20, 25 July, Arena, Verona.
Boito: *Mefistofele*. (Margherita).
Callas, di Stefano, Tagliavini, de Cecco/de Cavalieri, Rossi-Lemeni.
Conductor: Votto.

6, 9 October, Téatro Donizetti, Bergamo.
Donizetti: *Lucia de Lammermoor*.
Callas, Savarese, Tagliavini, Maionica.
Conductor: Molinari-Pradelli.

1, 5 November, Civic Opera House, Chicago.
Bellini: *Norma*.
Callas, Simionato, Picchi, Rossi-Lemeni.
Conductor: Rescigno.

8, 12 November, Civic Opera House, Chicago.
Verdi: *La Traviata*.
Callas, Gobbi, Simoneau.
Conductor: Rescigno.

15, 17 November, Civic Opera House, Chicago.
Donizetti: *Lucia di Lammermoor*.
Conductor: Rescigno.

7, 9, 12, 16, 18 December, La Scala, Milan.
Spontini: *La Vestale* (Giulia).
Callas, Corelli, Rossi-Lemeni, Stignani, Sordello.
Conductor: Votto.

1955
8, 10, 13, 16 January, 3, 6 February, La Scala, Milan.
Giordano: *Andrea Chénier* (Maddalena).
Callas, del Monaco/Ortica, Taddei/Protti.
Conductor: Votto.

22, 25, 27, 30 January, Rome Opera.
Cherubini: *Medea*.
Callas, Barbieri, Christoff, Albanese, Tucci.
Conductor: Santini.

5, 8, 13, 16, 19, 24, 30 March, 12, 24, 27 April, La Scala, Milan.
Bellini: *La Sonnambula* (Amina).
Callas, Ratti, Modesti/Zaccaria, Valetti.
Conductor: Bernstein.

15, 18, 21, 23 April, 4 May, La Scala, Milan.
Rossini: *Il Turco in Italia*.
Callas, Gardino, Valetti, Stabile, Rossi-Lemeni, Calabrese.
Conductor: Gavazzeni.

28, 31 May, 5, 7 June, La Scala, Milan.
Verdi: *La Traviata*.
Callas, di Stefano, Bastianini, Prandelli.
Conductor: Giulini.

29 September, 2 October, Staatsoper, Berlin.
Donizetti: *Lucia di Lammermoor*
Callas, di Stefano/Zampieri, Panerai, Zaccaria.
Conductor: Karajan.

31 October, 2 November, Civic Opera House, Chicago.
Bellini: *I Puritani*.
Callas, di Stefano, Bastianini, Rossi-Lemeni.
Conductor: Rescigno.

5, 8 November, Civic Opera House, Chicago.
Verdi: *Il Trovatore*.
Callas, Björling, Stignani/Truner, Bastianini/Weede, Wildermann.
Conductor: Rescigno.

11, 14, 17 November, Civic Opera House, Chicago.
Puccini: *Madama Butterfly* (Cio-Cio-San).
Callas, di Stefano, Weede, Alberts.
Conductor: Rescigno.

7, 11, 14, 17, 21, 29 December, 1, 5, 8 January, La Scala, Milan.
Bellini: *Norma*.
Callas, Simionato/Nicolai, del Monaco, Zaccaria.

1956
19, 23, 26, 29 January, 2, 5, 18, 26 February, 9 March, 5, 14, 18, 21, 25, 27, 29 April, 6 May, La Scala, Milan.
Verdi: *La Traviata*.
Callas, Raimondi, Bastianini/Tagliabue, Protti/Colzani.
Conductor: Giulini/Tonini.

16, 21 February, 3, 6, 15 March, La Scala, Milan.
Rossini: *Il Barbiere di Siviglia* (Rosina).

Callas, Gobbi, Alva/Monti, Luise/Badioli, Rossi-Lemeni.
Conductor: Giulini.

22, 24, 27 March, Téatro San Carlo, Naples.
Donizetti: *Lucia di Lammermoor*.
Callas, Raimondi, Panerai, Zerbini.

21, 23, 27, 30 May, 1, 3 June, La Scala, Milan.
Giodano: *Fedora* (Fedora).
Callas, Corelli, Zanolli, Colzani.
Conductor: Gavazzeni.

12, 14, 16 June, Staatsoper, Vienna.
Donizetti: *Lucia di Lammermoor*.
Callas, di Stefano, Panerai, Zaccaria.
Conductor: Karajan.

29 October, 3, 7, 10, 22 November, Metropolitan Opera House, New York.
Bellini: *Norma*.
Callas, Barbieri, del Monaco/Baum, Siepi/Moscona.
Conductor: Cleva.

15, 19 November, Metropolitan Opera House, New York.
Puccini: *Tosca*.
Callas, London, Campora.
Conductor: Mitropoulos.

27 November, Academy of Music, Philadelphia.
Bellini: *Norma*.
Callas, Barbieri, Baum, Moscona.
Conductor: Cleva.

3, 8, 14, 19 December, Metropolitan Opera House, New York.
Donizetti: *Lucia di Lammermoor*.
Callas, Campora/Tucker, Sordello/Valentino, Moscona.
Conductor: Cleva.

1957
2, 6 February, Covent Garden, London.
Bellini: *Norma*.
Callas, Stignani, Zaccaria, Vertecchi, Collier.
Conductor: Pritchard.

2, 7, 10, 12, 17, 20 March, La Scala, Milan.
Bellini: *La Sonnambula*.

Callas, Monti/Spini, Ratti, Zaccaria, Cossotto.
Conductor: Votto.

14, 17, 20, 24, 27, 30 April, 5 May, La Scala, Milan.
Donizetti: *Anna Bolena* (Anna).
Callas, Simionato, Rossi-Lemeni, Raimondi, Carturan, Rumbo.
Conductor: Gavazzeni.

1, 3, 5, 10 June, La Scala, Milan.
Gluck: *Iphigénie en Tauride* (Iphigenia).
Callas, Dondi, Albanese, Colzani.
Conductor: Sanzogno.

4, 6 July, Operhaus, Cologne.
Bellini: *La Sonnambula*.
Callas, Monti, Zaccaria, Cossotto.
Conductor: Votto.

19, 21, 26, 29 August, King's Theatre, Edinburgh.
Bellini: *La Sonnambula*.
Callas, Monti, Zaccaria, Cossotto.
Conductor: Votto.

7, 10, 16, 19, 22 December, La Scala, Milan.
Verdi: *Un Ballo in Maschera* (Amelia).
Callas, Simionato, di Stefano, Ratti, Bastianini.
Conductor: Gavazzeni.

1958
2 January, La Scala, Milan.*
Bellini: *Norma*.
Callas, Corelli, Pirazzini, Neri.
Conductor: Santini.

6, 10 February, Metropolitan Opera House, New York.
Verdi: *La Traviata*.
Callas, Campori/Barioni, Zanassi.
Conductor: Cleva.

13, 20, 25 February, Metropolitan Opera House, New York.

* Callas abandoned the performance after Act One and was replaced in the three
  subsequent performances by Anita Cerquetti.

Donizetti: *Lucia di Lammermoor*.
Callas, Bergonzi/Fernandi, Sereni, Moscona/Scott, Tozzi.
Conductor: Cleva.

28 February, 5 March, Metropolitan Opera House, New York.
Puccini: *Tosca*.
Callas, Tucker, London/Cassell.
Conductor: Mitropoulos.

27, 30 March, Téatro Sao Carlos, Lisbon.
Verdi: *La Traviata*.
Callas, Ktaus, Sereni.
Conductor: Ghione.

9, 13, 16, 19, 23 April, La Scala, Milan.
Donizetti: *Anna Bolena*.
Callas, Simionato, Raimondi, Carturan, Siepi.
Conductor: Gavazzeni.

19, 22, 25, 28, 31 May, La Scala, Milan.
Bellini: *Il Pirata* (Imogene).
Callas, Corelli, Bastianini.
Conductor: Votto.

20, 23, 26, 28, 30 June, Covent Garden, London.
Verdi: *La Traviata*.
Callas, Valletti, Zanassi.
Conductor: Rescigno.

31 October, 2 November, Civic Opera House, Dallas.
Verdi: *La Traviata*.
Callas, Taddei, Filacuridi.
Conductor: Rescigno.

6, 8 November, Civic Opera House, Dallas.
Cherubini: *Medea*.
Callas, Berganza, Vickers, Zaccaria.
Conductor: Rescigno.

1959
17, 22, 24, 27, 30 June, Covent Garden, London.
Cherubini: *Medea*.
Callas, Vickers, Cossotto, Zaccaria.
Conductor: Rescigno.

6, 8 November, Civic Opera House, Dallas.
Donizetti: *Lucia di Lammermoor*.
Callas, Raimondi, Bastianini, Zaccaria.
Conductor: Rescigno.

19, 21 November, Civic Opera House, Dallas.
Cherubini: *Medea*.
Callas, Vickers, Zaccaria, Williams, Merriman.
Conductor: Rescigno.

1960
24, 28 August, Epidaurus Amphitheatre.
Bellini: *Norma*.
Callas, Morforniou, Picchi, Mazzoli.
Conductor: Serafin.

7, 10, 14, 18, 21 December, La Scala, Milan.
Donizetti: *Poliuto* (Paolina).
Callas, Corelli, Bastianini, Zaccaria.
Conductor: Votto/Tonini.

1961
6, 13 August, Epidaurus Amphitheatre.
Cherubini: *Medea*.
Callas, Morforniou, Vickers, Modesti.
Conductor: Glantzi.

11, 14, 20 December, La Scala, Milan.
Cherubini: *Medea*.
Callas, Simionato, Vickers, Ghiaurov, Tosini/Rizzoli.
Conductor: Schippers.

1962
23 May, 3 June, La Scala, Milan.
Cherubini: *Medea*.
Callas, Vickers, Simionato, Ghiaurov, Rizzoli.
Conductor: Schippers.

1964
21, 24, 27, 30 January, 1, 5 February, Covent Garden, London.
Puccini: *Tosca*.
Callas, Cioni, Gobbi.
Conductor: Cillario.

22, 25, 31 May, 6, 10, 14, 19, 24 June, Paris Opera.
Bellini: *Norma.*
Callas, Cossotto, Craig/Corelli, Vinco.
Conductor: Prêtre.

1965
19, 22, 26 February, 1, 3, 5, 8, 10, 13 March, Paris Opera.
Puccini: *Tosca.*
Callas, Cioni, Gobbi.
Conductor: Prêtre/Rescigno.

19, 25 March, Metropolitan Opera House, New York.
Puccini: *Tosca.*
Callas, Corelli/Tucker, Gobbi.
Conductor: Cleva.

14, 17, 21, 24, 29 (minus Act IV), Paris Opera.
Bellini: *Norma.*
Callas, Simionato/Cossotto, Cecchele, Vinco.
Conductor: Prêtre.

5 July, Covent Garden, London.
Puccini: *Tosca.*
Callas, Cioni, Gobbi.
Conductor: Prêtre.

Appendix III

Maria Callas: Recordings

1935
4 July: *Madama Butterfly*: 'Un bel di vedremo'.
Tape recording preceded by speaking voice of 'Nina Foresti'.

1939
July: *Gianni Schicchi*: 'O mio babbino caro'. No other details.

1947
30 December: *Tristan Und Isolde*, Venice.
Pirated live recording. See Appendix II for details.

1949
7 March, Turin radio recital.
Pirated live recording. See Appendix IV for details.
Mid-March: *Norma*: 'Casta diva'*
              Norma: 'Ah! bello a me ritorno'.*
              Cetra, Italy, 78 rpm, R 300–41
Mid-March: *I Puritani*: 'Oh rendetemi la speme . . . Qui la voce'.*
              I Puritani: 'Vien diletto e in ciel la luna'
              Cetra, Italy, 78 rpm, R 300–43
Mid-March: *Tristano e Isotta*: 'Liebestod'. (sung in Italian)*
              Tristano e Isotta: 'Morte d'Isotta'.*
              Cetra, Italy, 78 rpm, CB 20481.

* With the Turin Radio Orchestra, conductor Arturo Basile

20 May: *Turandot*. Buenos Aires.
Pirated live recording. Details in Appendix IV.

17 June: *Norma*. Buenos Aires.
Pirated live recording. Details in Appendix II.

31 October: *Recital*. Verona.
Pirated live recording. Details in Appendix I.

20 December: *Nabucco*. Naples.
Pirated live recording. Details in Appendix II. Part of this was reissued on GREEN LINE CDCLC 5015/1/2/3 (box-set) in 1989.

1950
23 May: *Norma*. Mexico City.
Pirated live recording. Details in Appendix II.

30 May & 3 June: *Aida*. Mexico City.
Pirated live recordings. Details in Appendix II.

8 June: *Tosca*. Mexico City.
Pirated live recording. Details in Appendix II.

20 June: *Il Trovatore*. Mexico City.
Pirated live recording. Details in Appendix II.

2 October: *Aida*. Rome.
Pirated live recording. Details in Appendix II.

20 November: *Parsifal*. Rome.
Broadcast studio performance. Details in Appendix IV.
Released 1951 on PENZANCE (LP) FWR 648.

1951
27 January: *Il Trovatore*. Naples.
Pirated live recording. Details in Appendix II.

12 March: *Recital*, Turin.
Pirated studio recording. Details in Appendix IV.

26 May: *I Vespri Siciliani*. Florence.
Pirated live recording. Details in Appendix II.
Released 1951 on Penzance (LP) FWR 645.

Released 1951 on Penzance (LP) FWR 645
3 July: *Aida*, Mexico City.
Pirated live recording. Details in Appendix II.

17 July: *La Traviata*, Mexico City.
Pirated live recording. Details in Appendix II.

24 September: *Tosca*, Rio de Janeiro.
Pirated live recording. Details in Appendix II.

1952
18 February: *Recital*, Rome.
Pirated live recording. Details in Appendix IV.

26 April: *Armida*, Florence.
Pirated live recording. Details in Appendix II.

29 May: *I Puritani*, Mexico City.
Pirated live recording. Details in Appendix II.

3 June: *La Traviata*, Mexico City.
Pirated live recording. Details in Appendix II.

10, 14 June: *Lucia di Lammermoor*, Mexico City.
Pirated live recording. Details in Appendix II.

17 June: *Rigoletto*, Mexico City.
Pirated live recording. Details in Appendix II.

28 June: *Tosca*, Mexico City.
Pirated live recording. Details in Appendix II.

? August: *Don Giovanni*: Non mi dir.
Test-recording for EMI, cut in Florence.
Conductor: Tullio Serafin.

? September: *La Gioconda*. Turin.
Gioconda: Maria Callas, Laura: Fedora Barbieri, Enzo: Gianni Poggi, La
Cieca: Maria Amadini, Barnaba: Paolo Silveri, Alvise: Giulio Neri.
Orchestra and chorus of *RAI Turin* conducted by Antonino Votto.
CETRA (album) LPC 1241. Released 1952.

? September: *La Traviata*. Turin.
Violetta: Maria Callas, Alfredo: Francesco Albanese, Giorgio: Ugo

Savarese.
Orchestra & chorus of *RAI Turin* conducted by Gabriele Santini.
CETRA (album) LPC 1246. Released 1953.

18 November: *Norma*. London.
Pirated live recording. Details in Appendix II.

7 December: *Macbeth*. Milan.
Lady Macbeth: Maria Callas, Macbeth: Enzo Mascherini, Banquo: Italo
Tajo, Macduff: Gino Penno, Malcolm: Luciano Della Pergola.
Orchestra & Chorus of La Scala, Milan, conducted by Victor de Sabata.
Pirated live recording of performance in Appendix II.
Digitally remastered and re-released 1993. EMI (CD) CMS 64944-2.

1953
? February: *Lucia di Lammermoor*. Florence.
Lucia: Maria Callas, Edgardo: Guiseppi di Stefano, Enrico: Tito Gobbi,
Raimondo: Rafaele Arié, Arturo: Valiano Natali, Alisa: Anna Maria
Canali, Normanno: Gino Sarri.
Orchestra & Chorus of the Maggio Musicale Fiorentino conducted by
Tullio Serafin.
EMI (albums) 33CX 1131–2. Released 1953.

28 February: *Il Trovatore*. Milan.
Pirated live recording. Details in Appendix II.

24–30 March: *I Puritani*.
Elvira: Maria Callas, Arturo: Giuseppe di Stefano, Giorgio: Nicola Rossi-
Lemeni, Riccardo: Rolando Panerai.
Orchestra & Chorus of LaScala, Milan, conducted by Tullio Serafin.
EMI (albums) 33CX 1058–60. Released 1953.

7 May: *Medea*. Florence.
Pirated live performance. Details in Appendix II.

4 June: *Aida*. London.
Pirated live recording. Details in Appendix II.

3–4 August: *Cavalleria Rusticana*.
Santuzza: Maria Callas, Turiddu: Giuseppe di Stefano, Alfio: Rolando
Panerai, Mama Lucia: Ebe Ticozzi.
Orchestra & Chorus of La Scala, Milan, conducted by Tullio Serafin.
EMI (albums) 33CX 1182–3. Released 1954.

COLUMBIA (extracts EP) SEL 1563. Released 1953.
10–21 August: *Tosca*. Milan.
Floria Tosca: Maria Callas, Cavaradossi: Giuseppe di Stefano, Scarpia: Tito Gobbi.
Orchestra & Chorus of La Scala, Milan, conducted by Vittorio de Sabata.
EMI 33CX 1094–5. Released 1953.

19 November: *Norma*. Trieste.
Pirated live recording. Details in Appendix II.
Released 1954 on HISTORIC RECORDINGS (LP) HRE 283.

10 December: *Medea*. Milan.
Pirated live recording. Details in Appendix II.

1954
18 January: *Lucia di Lammermoor*. Milan.
Pirated live recording. Details in Appendix II.

4 April: *Alceste*. Milan.
Pirated live recording. Details in Appendix II.

23 April–3 May: *Norma*. Milan.
Norma: Maria Callas, Adalgisa: Ebe Stignani, Pollione: Mario Filippeschi, Oroveso: Nicola Rossi-Lemeni.
Orchestra & Chorus of La Scala, Milan, conducted by Tullio Serafin.
EMI 33CX 1179–81. Released 1954.

27 May–17 June: *I Pagliacci*. Milan.
Nedda: Maria Callas, Canio: Giuseppe di Stefano, Tonio: Tito Gobbi, Silvio: Rolando Panerai, Beppe: Nicola Monti.
Orchestra & Chorus of La Scala, Milan, conducted by Tullio Serafin.
EMI 33CXS 1211–2. Released 1954.

17–27 August: *La Forza Del Destino*. Milan.
Leonora: Maria Callas, Preziosilla: Elena Nicolai, Alvaro: Richard Tucker, Don Carlo: Carlo Tagliabue, Padre Guardiano: Nicola Rossi-Lemeni.
Orchestra & Chorus of La Scala, Milan, conducted by Tullio Serafin.
EMI 33CX 1258–60. Released 1954.

31 August–8 September: *Il Turco In Italia*. Milan.
Fiorilla: Maria Callas, Zaida: Iolanda Gardino, Selim: Nicola Rossi-Lemeni, Geronio: Franco Calabrese, Poet: Mariano Stabile, Narciso: Nicolai Gedda.

Orchestra & Chorus of La Scala, Milan, conducted by Gianandrea Gavazzeni.
EMI 33SX 1289–91. Released 1954.

15–21 September: *Puccini Heroines*. London.*
Manon Lescaut: 'In quelle trine morbide'; 'Sola, perduta abbandonata'.
La Bohème: 'Mi chiamano Mimi'; 'Donde lieta usci'.
Madame Butterfly: 'Un bel di vedremo'; 'Tu, tu, piccolo Iddio'.
Suor Angelica: Senza mamma *Gianni Schicchi*: 'O mio babbino caro'.
Turandot: 'Signore, ascolta'; 'In questa reggia'; 'Tu che di gel sei cinta'.
EMI 33CX 1204. Released 1954.

15–21 September: *MARIA CALLAS SINGS OPERATIC ARIAS*. London.*
Adriana Lecouvreur: 'Ecco: respiro appena' . . . 'Io son l'umile ancella'; 'Poveri fiori'.
La Wally: 'Ebben? N'andro lontana.'
Andrea Chènier: 'La mamma morta'; *Mefistofele*: 'L'altra notte'.
Il Barbiere di Siviglia: 'Una voce poco fa'.
Dinorah: 'Ombra leggiera'; *Lakmé*: 'Dov'è l'Indiana bruna'.
I Vespri Siciliani: 'Mercè, dilette amiche'.
EMI 33CX 1231. Released 1954.

7 December: *La Vestale*. Milan.
Pirated live recording. Details in Appendix II.

27 December: *Recital*. San Remo.
Pirated studio recording. Details in Appendix IV.

1955
8 January: *Andréa Chenier*. Milan.
Pirated live recording. Details in Appendix II.

5 March: *La Sonnambula*. Milan.
Pirated live recording. Details in Appendix II.

28 May: *La Traviata*. Milan.
Pirated live recording. Details in Appendix II.

12 June: *Callas at La Scala*. Milan.
La Sonnambula: 'Come per me'; 'An non credea'.*

* Both albums: Philharmonia Orchestra conducted by Tullio Serafin.

I Puritani: 'Oh rendetemi la speme' . . . 'Qui la voce'; 'Vien deletto e in ciel la luna'.*
Medea: 'Dei tuo figli'.*
La Vestale: 'Tu che invoco'; 'O nume tutelar'; 'Caro oggetto'.
Orchestra & Chorus of La Scala, Milan, conducted by Tullio Serafin/Antonino Votto.
EMI 33CX 1540. Released 1955.

29 June: *Norma*. Rome.
Norma: Maria Callas, Pollione: Mario del Monaco, Oroveso: Giuseppe Modesti, Adalgisa: Ebe Stignani, Clotile: Rina Cavallari.
Orchestra & Chorus of Rome Opera conducted by Tullio Serafin.
Pirated live recording of performance in Appendix IV.
Digitally remastered and re-released 1995.
EUROPA MUSICA (CD) 051-014.

1–6 August: *Madama Butterfly*. Milan.
Cio-Cio-San: Maria Callas, Suzuki: Lucia Danieli, Pinkerton: Nicolai Gedda, Sharpless: Mario Borriello.
Orchestra & Chorus of La Scala, Milan, conducted by Herbert von Karajan.
EMI 33CX 1296-8. Released 1955.

10–24 August: *Aida*. Milan.
Aida: Maria Callas, Amneris: Fedora Barbieri, Radames: Richard Tucker, Amonasro: Tito Gobbi.
Orchestra & Chorus of La Scala, Milan, conducted by Tullio Serafin.
EMI 33CX 1318-20. Released 1955.

3–16 September: *Rigoletto*. Milan.
Gilda: Maria Callas, Duke: Giuseppe di Stefano, Rigoletto: Tito Gobbi, Sparafucile: Nicola Zaccaria.
Orchestra & Chorus of La Scala, Milan, conducted by Tullio Serafin.
EMI 33CX 1324-6. Released 1955.

29 September: *Lucia di Lammermoor*. Berlin.
Pirated recording. Details in Appendix II.
Digitally remastered and re-released 1990. EMI (CD) CMS 7-63631-2

7 December: *Norma*. Milan.
Pirated live recording. Details in Appendix II.

* Taken from the complete recording of the opera.

1956
19 January: *La Traviata*. Milan.
Pirated live recording. Details in Appendix II.

16 February: *Il Barbiere di Siviglia*. Milan.
Pirated live recording. Details in Appendix II.

22 March: *Lucia di Lammermoor*. Naples.
Pirated live recording. Details in Appendix II.

3–9 August: *Il Trovatore*. Milan.
Leonora: Maria Callas, Azucena: Fedora Barbieri. Manrico: Giuseppe di Stefano, Di Luna: Rolando Panerai, Ferrando: Nicola Zaccaria.
Orchestra & Chorus of La Scala, Milan, conducted by Herbert von Karajan.
EMI 33CX 1483-5. Released 1956.

20–25 August, 3–4 September: *La Bohème*. Milan.
Mimi: Maria Callas, Musetta: Anna Moffo, Rodolfo: Giuseppe di Stefano, Marcello: Rolando Panerai.
Orchestra & Chorus of La Scala, Milan, conducted by Tullio Serafin.
EMI 33CX 1464-5. Released 1955.

4–12 September: *Un Ballo In Maschera*. Milan.
Amelia: Maria Callas, Ulrica: Fedora Barbieri, Oscar: Eugenia Ratti, Riccardo: Giuseppe di Stefano, Renato: Tito Gobbi.
Orchestra & Chorus of La Scala, Milan, conducted by Antonino Votto.
EMI 33CX 1472-4. Released 1956.

27 September: *Recital*. Milan.
Pirated live recording. Details in Appendix IV.

25 November: *Tosca* (excerpts from Act II). New York.
Pirated recording of television broadcast. Details in Appendix V.

8 December: *Lucia di Lammermoor*. New York.
Pirated live recording. Details in Appendix II.

1957
7–14 February: *Il Barbiere Di Siviglia*. London.
Rosina: Maria Callas, Figaro: Tito Gobbi, Almaviva: Luigi Alva, Bartolo: Nicola Zaccaria.

Philharmonia Orchestra & Chorus conducted by Alceo Galliera.
EMI 33CX 1507-9. Released 1957.

3–9 March: *La Sonnambula*. Milan.
Amina: Maria Callas, Elvino: Nicola Monti, Teresa: Fiorenza Cossotto,
Lisa: Eugenia Ratti, Rodolfo: Nicola Zaccaria.
Orchestra & Chorus of La Scala, Milan, conducted by Antonino Votto.
EMI 33CX 1469-71. Released 1957.

14 April: *Anna Bolena*. Milan.
Pirated live recording. Details in Appendix II.
Digitally remastered and re-released in 1993. EMI CMS 7-64941-2.

1 June: *Iphigénie en Tauride*. Milan.
Pirated live recording. Details in Appendix II.

26 June: *Lucia di Lammermoor*. Rome.
Pirated live recording. Details in Appendix II.

4 July: *La Sonnambula*. Cologne.
Pirated live recording. Details in Appendix II.

9–15 July: *Turandot*. Milan.
Cio-Cio-San: Maria Callas, Liù: Elisabeth Schwarzkopf, Calaf: Eugenio
Fernandi, Timur: Nicola Zaccaria.
Orchestra & Chorus of La Scala, Milan, conducted by Tullio Serafin.
EMI 33CX 1555-7. Released 1957.

18–27 July: *Manon Lescaut*. Milan.
Manon: Maria Callas, Des Grieux: Giuseppe di Stefano, Lescauat: Giulio
Fioravanti.
EMI 33CX 1583-5. Released 1957.

5 August: *Recital*. Athens.
Pirated live recording. Details in Appendix I.

21 August: *La Sonnambula*. Edinburgh.
Pirated live recording. Details in Appendix II.
12–19 September: *Medea*. Milan.
Medea: Maria Callas, Neris: Miriam Pirzzini, Glauce: Renata Scotto,
Jason: Mirto Picchi, Creonte: Giuseppe Modesti.
Orchestra & Chorus of La Scala, Milan, conducted by Tullio Serafin.
RICORDI, subsequently reissued by EMI, 1957, 33SX 1618-20.

20 November: *Concert Rehearsal*. Dallas.*
Die Entführung aus dem Serail: 'Tutte le torture'.
I Puritani: 'Qui la voce', *Macbeth*: 'Vieni t'affretta'.
La Traviata: 'Ah, fors'è lui', *Anna Bolena*: 'Al dolce guidami'.
Dallas Symphony Orchestra, conducted by Nicola Rescigno.
Pirated recording.

7 December: *Un Ballo In Maschera*. Milan.
Pirated live recording. Details in Appendix II.

1958
2 January: *Norma*. Rome.
Pirated live recording. Details in Appendix II.

27 March: *La Traviata*. Lisbon.
Pirated live recording. Details in Appendix II.
Digitally remastered and re-released 1993?. EMI CDS 7-49187-8.

17 June: *Recital*. London.
Pirated live recording. Details in Appendix V.

20 June: *La Traviata*. London.
Pirated live recording. Details in Appendix II.

23 September: *Recital*. London.
Pirated live recording. Details in Appendix V.

19–24 September: *Callas Portrays Verdi Heroines*. London.**
Macbeth: 'Vieni t'affretta'; 'La luce langue'; 'Una macchia'.
Nabucco: 'Ben io t'invenni'; *Ernani*: 'Ernani involami'.
Don Carlos: 'Tu che le vanitá'.
EMI 33CX 1628. Released 1959.

24–25 September: *Callas Mad Scenes*. London.**
Anna Bolena: 'Piangete voi; 'Al dolce guidami'.

Hamlet: 'A vos jeux, mes amis' . . . 'Partagez-vous mes fleurs'; 'Et main-tenant écoutez ma chanson'.
Il Pirata: 'Oh! s'io potessi' . . . 'Col sorriso'.
EMI 33CX 1645. Released 1959.

* Rehearsal taped at State Fair Music Hall ** Both albums: Philharmonia
  Orchestra & Chorus conducted by Nicola Rescigno.

6 November: *Medea*. Dallas.
Pirated live recording. Details in Appendix II.

19 December: *Recital*. Paris.
Pirated live recording. Details in Appendix I.

1959
27 January: *Il Pirata*. New York.
Pirated live recording. Details in Appendix I.
Digitally remastered and re-released 1993. EMI CMS 7-64938-2.

16–21 March: *Lucia di Lammermoor*. London.
Lucia: Maria Callas, Edgardo: Ferrucio Tagliavini, Raimondo: Bernard Ladysz, Enrico: Piero Cappuccilli.
London Philharmonia Orchestra & Chorus conducted by Tullio Serafin.
EMI 33CX 1723-4. Released 1959.

15 May: *Recital*. Hamburg.
Pirated live recording. Details in Appendix I.

19 May: *Recital*. Stuttgart.
Pirated live recording. Details in Appendix I.

30 June: *Medea*. London.
Pirated live recording. Details in Appendix II.

11 July: *Recital*. Amsterdam.
Pirated live recording. Details in Appendix I.

5–10 September: *La Gioconda*. Milan.
Gioconda: Maria Callas, Enzo; Pier Miranda Ferraro, Laura: Fiorenza Cossotto, Barnaba: Piero Cappuccilli, Alvisa: Ivo Vinco.
Orchestra & Chorus of La Scala, Milan, conducted by Antonini Votto.
EMI 33CX 1706-8. Released 1960.

23 September: *Recital*. London.
Pirated live recording. Details in Appendix I.

3 October: Recital. London.
Pirated live recording. Details in Appendix V.

1960

? July: *Arias*. London.*

Semiramide: 'Bel raggio', *Armida*: 'D'amor al dolce impero'.

I Vespri Siciliani: 'Arrigo! ah parli a un core'.

Philharmonia Orchestra conducted by Antonio Tonini.

5–12 July: *Norma*. Milan.

Norma: Maria Callas, Adalgisa: Christa Ludwig, Pollione: Franco Corelli, Oroveso: Nicola Zaccaria.

Orchestra & Chorus of La Scala Milan, conducted by Tullio Serafin.

EMI 33CX 1766-8. Released 1961.

7 December: *Poliuto*. Milan.

Pirated live recording. Details in Appendix II.

1961

28–31 March, 4–5 April: *Callas À Paris*. Paris.

Orphée: 'J'ai perdu mon Eurydice', *Alceste*: 'Divinités du Styx'.

Carmen: 'Habañera', 'Séguedille'.

Samson and Delilah: 'Printemps qui commence', 'Amour viens aider', 'Mon coeur s'ouvre à ta voix'. *Romeo and Juliet*: 'Je veux vivre'.

Mignon: 'Je suis Titania', *Le Cid*: 'Pleurez mes yeux', *Louise*: 'Depuis le jour'.

Orchestre Radiodiffusion Française conducted by Georges Prêtre.

EMI 33CX 1771. Released 1961.

? November: *Artas*. London.**

Il Pirata: 'Sorgete', *Lucrezia Borgia*: 'Com'è bello'.

La Cenerentola: 'Nacqui all'affanno', *William Tell*: 'Selva opaca'.

Anna Bolena: 'Legger potessi in me', *Semiramide*: 'Bel raggio'.

London Philharmonia Orchestra conducted by Antonio Tonino.

11 December: *Medea*. Milan.

Pirated live recording. Details in Appendix II.

1962

27 February: *Recital*. London.

Pirated live recording. Details in Appendix I.

16 March: *Recital*. Hamburg.

Pirated live recording. Details in Appendix I.

* Unpublished in Callas's lifetime. ** All unpublished in Callas's lifetime save for *Il Pirata*.

? April: *Arias*. London.*
Oberon: 'Ocean, thou mighty monster', *Don Carlos*: 'O don fatale'.
La Cenerentola: 'Nacqui all'affano'.
Conductor: Antonio Tonini.

19 May: *Recital*. New York.
Pirated live recording. Details in Appendix I.

4 November: *Recital*. London.
Pirated live recording. Details in Appendix V.

1963
3–8 May: *Callas À Paris II*. Paris.
Iphigénie en Tauride: 'Malheureuse Iphigénie'.
La Damnation de Faust: 'D'amour l'ardente flamme'.
Les Pêcheurs de Perles: 'Comme autrefois'.
Manon: 'Adieu notre petite table', 'Je marche sur tous les chemins'.
Werther: 'Air des lettres', *Faust*: 'Il était un roi de Thulé', 'Ah! je ris'.
Orchestre Société des Concerts du Conservatoire conducted by Georges
Prêtre.
EMI 33CX 1858. Released 1963.

17 May: *Quando m'en vo*. Berlin.
Pirated live extract. Details in Appendix I.

23 May: *Recital*: Stuttgart.
Pirated live recording. Details in Appendix I.

31 May: *Bel raggio*. London.
Pirated live extract. Details in Appendix I.

5 June: *Recital*. Paris.
Pirated live recording. Details in Appendix I.

6-23 December & 8 January 1964: *Maria Callas Sings Mozart, Beethoven &
Weber Arias*.
'Ah! Perfido!' (Beethoven), *Oberon*: 'Ocean, thou mighty monster'.
Don Giovanni: 'Or sai che l'onore', 'Non mi dir', 'Mi tradi'.
Le Nozze di Figaro: 'Porgi amor'.

* Not published in Callas's lifetime.

Orchestre Société des Concerts du Conservatoire conducted by Nicola Rescigno.
EMI 33CX 1900. Released 1964.

17–27 December & 20–21 January 1964: *Callas Portrays Verdi Heroines II*.
Otello: 'Salce, salce', 'Ave Maria'.
Aroldo: 'Ah! degli scanni'; 'Ciel, ch'io respiri'.
Don Carlo: 'O don fatale: Non pianger, mia compagna'.
Orchestre Société des Concerts du Conservatoire conducted by Nicola Rescigno.
EMI 33CX 1910. Released 1964.

4–23 December & 13–24 April 1964: *Maria Callas Sings Arias by Rossini & Donizetti*.
La Cenerentola: 'Nacqui all'affano'.
William Tell: 'Selva opaca', *Semiramide*. 'Bel raggio'.
La Fille du Régiment: 'Convien partir'.
Lucrezia Borgia: 'Com'è bello'. *L'Elisir d'Amore*: 'Prendi, per me'.
Orchestre Société des Concerts du Conservatoire conducted by Nicola Resigno.
EMI 33CX 1923. Released 1964.

1964
24 January: *Tosca*. London.
Pirated live recording. Details in Appendix II.

21 February & 7–22 April: *Recital*. Paris.
Attila: 'Liberamente or piangi'.*
I Lombardi: 'Se vano è il pregare';* 'Te vergin santa'.***
Aida: 'Ritorna vincitor'.*
Il Trovatore: 'Tacea la notte';** 'D'amor sull'ali rosee'.***
Un Ballo in Maschera: 'Ecco l'orrido campo';** 'Morrò, ma prima in grazia'.**
I Vespri Siciliani: 'Arrigo! ah parle ad un core'.*
Orchestre Société des Concerts du Conservatoire conducted by Nicola Rescigno.

25 June: *Recital*. Paris.
Callas is known to have recorded duets from *Poliuto, Don Carlo, I Puritani, Un Ballo In Maschera* and *Il Pirata* with Franco Corelli, though all that survives of this session is *Aida*: 'Pur ti riveggo'.

* published 1972 ** published 1978 *** published 1992

Orchestre du Théâtre National de l'Opéra de Paris conducted by Georges Prêtre.
Released 1990.

6–20 July: *Carmen*. Paris.
Carmen: Maria Callas, Don José: Nicolai Gedda, Micaëla: Andréa Guiot, Escamillo: Robert Massard.
Orchestre du Théâtre National de l'Opéra de Paris/Choeurs René Duclos conducted by Georges Prêtre.
EMI AN 140. Released 1964.

3–14 December: *Tosca*. Paris.
Floria Tosca: Maria Callas, Cavaradossi: Carlo Bergonzi, Scarpia: Tito Gobbi, Spoletta: Renato Ercolani.
Orchestre Société des Concerts du Conservatoire conducted by Georges Prêtre.
EMI AN 149-50. Released 1965.

1965
1 & 3 March; *Tosca*. Paris.
Pirated live recording. Details in Appendix II.

19 & 25 March; *Tosca*. New York.
Pirated live recording. Details in Appendix II.

14, 17, 21, 29 May: *Norma*. Paris.
Pirated live recording. Details in Appendix II.

1969
February & March: *Verdi Recital*.
Il Corsaro: 'Non so le tetre imaggini'; 'Vola talor'.
Attila: 'Liberamente or piangi'.
I Vespri Siciliani: 'Arrigo! ah parli a un core'.
I Lombardi: 'Te vergin santa'.
Orchestre Société des Concerts du Conservatoire conducted by Nicola Rescigno.
Released 1978.

1972
November & December, plus March 1973: *Duets With Di Stefano*. London.
Don Carlos: 'Io vengo a domandar', *I Vespri Siciliani*: 'Qual prode', *Otello*: 'Già nella notte densa', *Aida*: 'Pur ti riveggo'.
La Forza del Destino: 'Ah! per sempre'.

London Symphony Orchestra conducted by Antonio de Almeida.
PHILIPS. All unreleased.

1973 & 1974
Pirated live recordings are known to exist of all the Callas/di Stefano
'farewell' concerts.

Maria Callas: Radio Appearances

1940
3 April, *Radio Athens*.
Callas sang duets from *La Gioconda, Norma* and *Aida* with Arda Mandikian.

1943
22 April, *Radio Athens*.
Pergolesi: *Stabat Mater*. With Arda Mandikian.
Conductor: G. Lycoudis.

1947
2 August, *Italia Radio*.
Puccini: *La Gioconda*. Verona. See Appendix II.

30 December, *Italian Radio*.
Puccini: *Tristan Und Isolde*. Venice. See Appendix II.

1948
29 January, *Italian Radio*.
Puccini: *Turandot*. Venice. See Appendix II.

1949
7 March, *RAI, Turin*.
Wagner: *Tristan Und Isolde*: 'Liebestod' (sung in Italian).
Bellini: *Norma*: 'Casta diva'. *I Puritani*: 'Qui la voce'.
Verdi: *Aida*: 'O patria mia'.
Conductor: Molinari-Pradelli.

20 May, *Radio Argentina*.
Puccini: *Turandot*. Buenos Aires. See Appendix II.

20 December, *Radio Italia*.
Verdi: *Nabucco*. Naples. See Appendices II & III.

24 November, *RAI Turin*
Puccini: *Tosca*: Act 2, *Manon Lescaut*: Act 4.
With Campagnano. Conductor: Baroni.

1950
13 March, *RAI Turin*.
Weber: *Oberon*: 'Ocean! Thou mighty monster', Verdi: *La Traviata*; 'Ah, fors'è lui', *Il Trovatore*: 'D'amor sull'ali rosee'. Meyerbeer: *Dinorah*: 'Ombra leggera'.
Conductor: Alfredo Simonetto.

23 May, *Mexico Radio*.
Bellini: *Norma*. Mexico City. See Appendices II & III.

30 May, *Mexico Radio*.
Verdi: *Aida*. Mexico City. See Appendices II & III.

8 June, *Mexico Radio*.
Puccini: *Tosca*. Mexico City. See Appendices II & III.

20 June, *Mexico Radio*.
Verdi: *Il Trovatore*. Mexico City. See Appendices II & III.

24 September, *Radio Italia*.
Puccini: *Tosca*. Bologna. See Appendix II.

2 October, *Radio Italia*.
Verdi: *Aida*. Rome. See Appendix II.

20, 21 November, *RAI Rome*.
Wagner: *Parsifal*. (Sung in Italian).
Kundry: Maria Callas, Parsifal: Africo Baldelli, Gurnemanz: Boris Christoff, Titurel: Dimitri Lopatto, Amfortas: Rolando Panerai, Klingsor: Giuseppi Modesti.
Conductor: Vittorio Gui.

1951
27 January, *Radio Italia*.

Verdi: *Il Trovatore*. Naples. See Appendix II.

12 March, *RAI Turin*.
Verdi: *Un Ballo in Maschera*; 'Ecco l'orrido campo'.
Thomas: *Mignon*: 'Io son Titania'.
Weber: *Der Freischütz*: 'Leise, leise'. Proch: *Variations*.
Conductor: Wolf-Ferrari.

26 May, *Italian Radio*.
Verdi: *I Vespri Siciliani*. Florence. See Appendix II.

3 July, *Radio Mexico*.
Verdi: *Aida*. Mexico City. See Appendix II.

15 July, *Radio Mexico*.
Verdi: *La Forza del Destino*: 'Pace, pace'.
Verdi: *Un Ballo in Maschera*: 'Morrò, ma prima in grazia'.
Conductor: Oliviero de Fabritiis.

17 July, *Radio Mexico*.
Verdi: *La Traviata*. Mexico City. See Appendix II.

24 September, *Brazilian Radio*.
Puccini: *Tosca*. Rio de Janeiro. See Appendix II.

1952
18 February, *RAI Rome*.
Verdi: *Macbeth*: 'Vieni t'affretta'; *Nabucco*: 'Ben io t'invenni'.
Donizetti: *Lucia di Lammermoor*: 'Ardon gli incensi'.
Delibes: *Lakmé*: 'Dov'è l'indiana bruna'.
Conductor: Oliviero de Fabritiis.

26 April, *Italian Radio*.
Rossini: *Armida*. Florence. See Appendix II.

29 May, *Mexico Radio*.
Bellini: *I Puritani*. Mexico City. See Appendix II.

10 June, *Mexico Radio*.
Donizetti: *Lucia di Lammermoor*. Mexico City. See Appendix II.

17 June, *Mexico Radio*.
Verdi: *Rigoletto*. Mexico City. See Appendix II.

28 June, *Mexico Radio*.
Puccini: *Tosca*. Mexico City. See Appendix II.

8 November, *BBC Radio*.
Bellini: *Norma*. London. See Appendix II.

7 December, *Italian Radio*.
Verdi: *Macbeth*. Milan. See Appendix II.

1953
23 February, *Italian Radio*.
Verdi: *Il Trovatore*. Milan. See Appendix II.

7 May, *Italian Radio*.
Cherubini: *Medea*. Florence. See Appendix II.

4 June, *BBC Radio*.
Verdi: *Aida*. London. See Appendix II.

19 November, *Italian Radio*.
Bellini: *Norma*. Trieste. See Appendix II.

10 December, *Italian Radio*.
Cherubini: *Medea*. See Appendix II.

1954
18 January, *Italian Radio*.
Donizetti: *Lucia di Lammermoor*. Milan. See Appendix II.

4 April, *Italian Radio*.
Gluck: *Alceste*. Milan. See Appendix II.

7 December, *Italian Radio*.
Spontini: *La Vestale*. Milan. See Appendix II.

27 December, *RAI San Remo*.
Mozart: *Die Entführung aus dem Serail*: 'Tutte le torture'.
Meyerbeer: *Dinorah*: 'Ombra leggiera'.
Charpentier: *Louise*: 'Depuis le jour.'
Rossini: *Armida*: 'D'amore al doce impero'.
Conductor: Alfredo Simonetto.

1955
8 January, *Italian Radio*
Giordano: *Andrea Chénier*. Milan. See Appendix II.
5 March, *Italian Radio*.
Bellini: *La Sonnambula*. Milan. See Appendix II.

28 May, *Italian Radio*.
Verdi: *La Traviata*. Milan. See Appendix II.

29 June: *RAI Rome*.
Bellini: *Norma*.
Norma: Maria Callas, Adalgisa: Ebe Stignani, Pollione: Mario del Monaco, Oroveso: Giuseppe Modesti.
Conductor: Tullio Serafin.

29 September: *Berlin Radio*.
Donizetti: *Lucia di Lammermoor*. Berlin. See Appendix II.

7 December: *Italian Radio*.
Bellini: *Norma*. Milan. See Appendix II.

1956
19 January: *Italian Radio*.
Verdi: *La Traviata*. Milan. See Appendix II.

16 February: *Italian Radio*.
Rossini: *Il Barbiere di Siviglia*. Milan. See Appendix II.

22 March: *Italian Radio*.
Donizetti: *Lucia di Lammermoor*. Naples. See Appendix II.

27 September: *RAI Milan*.
Spontini: *La Vestale*: 'Tu che invoco'.
Rossini: *Semiramide*: 'Bel raggio'.
Thomas: *Hamlet*: 'Ai vostri giochi'.
Bellini: *I Puritani*: 'Vieni al tempo'.
Conductor: Alfredo Simonetto.

3 December: *NBC Radio*.
Donizetti: *Lucia di Lammermoor*. New York. See Appendix II.

1957
2 March: *Italian Radio*.
Bellini: *La Sonnambula*. Milan. See Appendix II.

14 April: *Italian Radio.*
Donizetti: *Anna Bolena.* Milan. See Appendix II.

1 June: *Italian Radio.*
Gluck: *Iphigénie en Tauride.* Milan. See Appendix II.

26 June: *RAI Rome.*
Donizetti: *Lucia di Lammermoor.*
Lucia: Maria Callas, Edgardo: Eugenio Fernandi, Enrico: Rolando Panerai, Raimondo: Giuseppe Modesti.
Conductor: Tullio Serafin.

4 July, *German Radio.*
Bellini: *La Sonnambula.* Cologne. See Appendix II.

5 August: *Athens Radio.*
Recital. See Appendix I.

19 August, *BBC Radio.*
Bellini: *La Sonnambula.* Edinburgh. See Appendix II.

21 November, *American Radio.*
Recital: Dallas. See Appendix I.

7 December: *Italian Radio.*
Verdi: *Un Ballo in Maschera.* Milan. See Appendix II.

1958
2 January: *RAI Rome.*
Bellini: *Norma.* See Appendix II.

27 March: *Portuguese Radio.*
Verdi: *La Traviata.* Lisbon. See Appendix II.

20 June: *BBC Radio.*
Verdi: *La Traviata.* London. See Appendix II.

19 December: *French Radio.*
Recital: Paris. See Appendix I.

1959
15, 19 May: *German Radio.*
Recitals: Hamburg & Stuttgart. See Appendix I.

17 June: *BBC Radio.*
Cherubini: *Medea.* London. See Appendix II.

23 September: *BBC Radio.*
Recital: London. See Appendix I.

3 October: *BBC Radio.*
Recital: London. See Appendix V.

1960
7 December: *Italian Radio.*
Donizetti: *Poliuto.* Milan. See Appendix II.

1961
30 May: *BBC Radio.*
Recital. London. See Appendix I.

11 December: *Italian Radio.*
Cherubini: *Medea.* Milan. See Appendix II.

1962
16 March: *German Radio.*
Recital. Hamburg. See Appendix I.

19 May: *CBS Radio.*
Kennedy Concert. New York. See Appendix I.

1963
17 May: *German Radio.*
Recital. Berlin. See Appendix I.

23 May. *German Radio.*
Recital. Stuttgart. See Appendix I.

31 May: *BBC Radio.*
Recital. London. See Appendix I.

5 June: *French Radio.*
Recital. Paris. See Appendix I.

1964
21 January: *BBC Radio.*
Tosca. London. See Appendix II.

1965
19 February: *French Radio*.
Tosca. Paris. See Appendix II.
19 March: *CBS Radio*.
Tosca. New York. See Appendix II.

14 May: *French Radio*.
Norma. Paris. See Appendix II.

5 July: *BBC Radio*.
Tosca. London. See Appendix II.

1973 & 1974
Most of the Callas/di Stefano 'farewell' concerts were broadcast on the radio, but there are no exact details regarding dates, etc, as some were not broadcast live and others were heavily edited and passed around the US radio network.

Appendix V

Maria Callas: Television & Film Appearances

1952
7 December. Italian Television.
Verdi: *Macbeth*. Milan. See Appendix II.

1956
25 November. CBS Television.
Puccini: *Tosca*. Extracts from Act Two.
The Ed Sullivan Show.
With George London. Conductor: Dimitri Mitropoulos.

1957
31 December. Italian Television.
Bellini: *Norma*: 'Casta diva'.

1958
? January. NBS Television.
Person To Person. In conversation with Ed Murrow. New York.

26 February NBC Television.
The Hy Gardner Show. Chat-show, New York. With George Callas.

17 June. BBC Television.
Tosca: Vissi d'arte, *Il Barbiere di Siviglia*.
Conductor: John Pritchard.

23 September. BBC Television.
Madama Butterfly: 'Un bel di', *Norma*: 'Casta diva'.
Conductor: John Pritchard.

1959
3 October. BBC Television.
Puccini: *La Bohème*: 'Si, mi chiamano Mimi'.
Boito: *Mefistofele*: 'L'altra notte'.
Conductor: Sir Malcolm Sargent.

1962
19 May, NBC Television.
Concert for Kennedy. Details in Appendix I.

4 November. BBC Television.
Lew Grade's *The Golden Hour*.
Verdi: *Don Carlos*: 'Tu che le vanità'.
Bizet: *Carmen*: 'Habañera', 'Séguedille'.
Conductor: Georges Prêtre.

1964
9 February. BBC Television.
Puccini: *Tosca* (Act II).
Callas, Cioni, Gobbi. Broadcast from Covent Garden.
Conductor: Cillario.

1965
12 May. French Television.
Les Grandes Interprètes, presented by Bernard Gavoty.
Massenet: *Manon*: 'Adieu notre petite table'.
Bellini: *La Sonnambula*: 'Ah, non credea'.
Puccini: *Gianni Schicchi*: 'O mio babbino caro'.
Duparc: 'Invitation au voyage' (the latter not broadcast).
Conductor: Georges Prêtre.

1965
September. British Home Entertainments.
Tosca, directed by Franco Zeffirelli.
Callas made a colour screen-test with Tito Gobbi and recorded part of score with Gobbi and Renato Cioni but the project was abandoned.

1968
Late autumn. BBC Television.

The Callas Conversations. Two interview programmes with Lord Harewood.
Photography: Ken Westbury/John Baker.
Editor: Bill Harris. Executive producer: John Culshaw.
Director: Barrie Gavin.

1969

Summer – early autumn. San Marco/Les Film Number One/Janus *Medea*.
Director: Pier Paolo Pasolini.
Producer: Franco Rossellini.
Director of photography: Ennio Guarnieri.
Production director: Fernando Franchi.
Costumes: Piero Tosi.
Medea: Maria Callas; Jason: Giuseppe Gentile. With Massimo Girotti, Laurent Terzieff, Margareth Clementi, Paul Jabara, Gerard Weiss, Sergio Tramonti, Luigi Barbini, Gianpaolo Duregon, Luigi Masironi, Michelangelo Masironi, Gianni Brandizi, Franco Jacobbi, Anna Maria Chio, Piera Degli Esposti, Mirella Panfili, Graziella Chiarcossi.

1974

Summer. Zeffirelli-Visconti Productions.
Love, Love, Sarah! The two producers set up this venture to film three episodes in the life of Sarah Bernhardt with Callas in the title role. No other stars were signed up. Callas made the screen test in Versailles, but the film was abandoned.

Addenda

During the production of this book, and to commemorate the 20th anniversary of Callas's death, EMI Classics re-released her entire catalogue, repackaged and digitally remastered.

Phase 1:

Bellini: *Norma*	CDS 5 56271 2
Bellini: *I Puritani*	CDS 5 56275 2
Bellini: *La Sonnambula*	CDS 5 56278 2
Bizet: *Carmen*	CDS 5 56281 2
Donizetti: *Lucia di Lammermoor*	CDS 5 56284 2
Leoncavallo/Mascagni: *Pagliacci/Cavalleria Rusticana*	CDS 5 56287 2
Ponchielli: *La Gioconda*	CDS 5 56291 2
Puccini: *La Bohème*	CDS 5 56295 2
Puccini: *Madama Butterfly*	CDS 5 56298 2
Puccini: *Manon Lescaut*	CDS 5 56301 2
Puccini: *Tosca*	CDS 5 56304 2
Puccini: *Turandot*	CDS 5 56307 2
Rossini: *Il Barbiere di Siviglia*	CDS 5 56310 2
Rossini: *Il Turco in Italia*	CDS 5 56313 2
Verdi: *Aida*	CDS 5 56316 2
Verdi: *Un Ballo in Maschera*	CDS 5 56320 2
Verdi: *La Forza del Destino*	CDS 5 56323 2
Verdi: *Rigoletto*	CDS 5 56327 2

Verdi: *La Traviata*   CDS 5 56330 2
Verdi: *Il Trovatore*   CDS 5 56333 2

Interview: 'Maria Callas in conversation with Edward Downes'. Originally broadcast in the USA in two parts during the intermissions of the Metropolitan Opera broadcasts on 30 December 1967 and 13 January 1968. CDM 5 65822 2

Phase 2:

Donizetti: *Poliuto**   CMS 5 65448 2
Bellini: *Norma*   CMS 5 66428 2
Bellini: *Il Pirata*   CMS 5 66432 2
Cherubini: *Medea*   CMS 5 66435 2
Donizetti: *Lucia*   CMS 5 66438 2
Donizetti: *Lucia*   CMS 5 66441 2
Donizetti: *Anna Bolena*   CMS 5 66471 2
Puccini: *Tosca*   CMS 5 66444 2
Verdi: *Macbeth*   CMS 5 66447 2
Verdi: *La Traviata*   CMS 5 66450 2

Maria Callas Puccini Arias   CDM 5 66463 2
Callas at La Scala   CDM 5 66457 2
Maria Callas Lyric and Coloratura Arias   CDM 5 66458 2
Maria Callas Mozart, Beethoven, Weber Arias   CDM 5 66465 2
Callas Mad Scenes   CDM 5 66459 2
Callas Rossini and Donizetti Arias   CDM 5 66464 2
Maria Callas Verdi Arias Vol I   CDM 5 66460 2
Maria Callas Verdi Arias Vol II   CDM 5 66461 2
Maria Callas Verdi Arias Vol III   CDM 5 66462 2
Callas à Paris Vol I   CDM 5 66466 2
Maria Callas à Paris Vol II   CDM 5 66467 2
Maria Callas, The EMI Rarities   CMS 5 66468 2
Maria Callas, Live in Concert   CZS 5 72030 2

Phase 3:

This is a re-issue of nine compact discs, catalogue numbers unknown at time of going to press: *Norma*, (x2), *Carmen*, *Tosca*, *La Traviata*, *Lucia di Lammermoor*, (x2), *Madama Butterfly*, *Il Barbiere di Siviglia*.

* Radio broadcast, December 1960, of La Scala première.

Clubs

The Maria Callas International Club,
Administrator: John L. Pettitt,
Home Farm House, Menston,
Ilkley LS29 6BB, West Yorkshire

The Callas Circle,
Founder: Steven Mathers,
64 Empire Court, North End Road,
Wembley Park,
Middlesex HA9 OAQ

Major Interview Sources

Bing, Rudolph, *The Times*, October 1972.
Caballé, Montserrat, with David Bret, June 1997.
Callas, Maria, *Oggi*, January and February 1957, with Anita Pensotti.
Callas, Maria, American TV, January 1958, with Ed Murrow.
Callas, Maria, American TV, February 1958, with Hy Gardner.
Callas, Maria, French radio, February 1965, with Micheline Banzet.
Callas, Maria, French TV, May 1965, with Bernard Gavoty.
Callas, Maria, CBS Radio, December 1967, with Edward Downes.
Callas, Maria, *Life* magazine, November 1964, with Peter Dragadze.
Callas, Maria, *Sunday Times*, March 1961, with Derek Prouse.
Callas, Maria, BBC TV, late 1968, with Lord Harewood.
Callas, Maria, *Observer*, February 1990, with Kenneth Harris.
Callas, Maria, New York TV, February 1974, with Mike Wallace.
Callas, Maria, New York TV, April 1974, with Barbara Walters.
Sutherland, Robert, *Sunday Telegraph*, September and October 1980.
Tebaldi, Renata, *Sunday Telegraph*, August 1991, with Mel Cooper.
Zeffirelli, Franco, *Sunday Times*, September 1986.

Great Britain: *Guardian, Daily Mail, Observer, Sunday Telegraph, Daily Telegraph, London Life, Illustrated London News, Tatler, Gay Times, Gay Gazette*, London *Evening Standard, Daily Express, Daily Mirror, Opera*.

United States: *Philadelphia Enquirer, New York Times, Chicago Tribune, Opera News, Musical America, Music and Musicians, High Fidelity, Opera Annual, Dallas Morning News, New York Herald Tribune, Time, Washington Post, Life, Saturday Review, Chicago American, The New Yorker, Atlanta Constitution.*

Italy: *Corriere della Sera, Corriere Lombardo, Corriere del Teatro, Corriere del Popolo.*

Mexico: *Excelsior.*

Germany: *Der Tagesspieler.*

France: *France-Soir, Le Monde, Le Figaro, Arts, L'Avant Scène.*

Greece: *Vradyni, Deutsche Nachrichten in Griechenland.*

Bibliography: Primary and Secondary Sources

Ardoin, John, *The Callas Legacy*, Duckworth, 1977.

Ardoin, John, *Callas at Juilliard*, Robson Books, 1987.

Ardoin, John and Fitzgerald, Gerald, *Callas*, Thames & Hudson, 1974.

Bozhkoff, Atanas, *Boris Christoff*, Robson Books, 1991.

Callas, Evangelia, *My Daughter Maria Callas*, Fleet, 1960.

Callas, Jackie, *Sisters*, Macmillan, 1989.

Galatopoulis, Stelios, *Callas, La Divina*, Dent, 1966.

Gobbi, Tito, *My Life*, Macdonald & Jane's, 1979.

Jelinek, George, *Callas, Portrait of a Prima Donna*, Dover, 1986.

Lowe, David A., *Callas As They Saw Her*, Robson Books, 1987.

Meneghini, Giovanni Battista, *My Wife Maria Callas*, Farrar, Strauss & Giroux, 1982.

Normand, Roger and Bret, David, *Le Ring*, unpublished.

Scott, Michael, *Maria Meneghini Callas*, Simon & Schuster, 1991.

Segalini, Sergio, *Callas: Les Images d'une Voix*, van der Welde, 1979.

Stancioff, Nadia, *Maria Callas Remembered*, Sidgwick & Jackson, 1988.

Stassinopoulis, Ariana, *Maria, Beyond the Callas Legend*, Weidenfeld & Nicolson, 1980.

Stirling, Monica, *Visconti, a Screen Of Time*, Harcourt, Brace & Jovanovich, 1979.

Wallace, Irving, *Secret Sex Lives*, Chancellor Press, 1981.

Wisneski, Henry, *Callas, the Art Behind the Legend*, Doubleday, 1975.

And also:

Franco Abbiati, Roger Baker, Ian Ball, Alan Blyth, Jacques Bourgeois, Allessandro Cannavo, Neville Cardus, Claudia Cassidy, Teodoro Celli,

Anne de Courcy, Roger Dettmer, Placido Domingo, Richard Dyer, Sydney Edwards, Lady Rachel Ellenborough, Mabel Elliott, Ronald Eyer, Michael Field, Janet Flanner, Olga Franklyn, John Freeman, Michel Glotz, Trudy Goth, Richard Gray, Jeanne Handzic, Friedrich Herzog, Philip Hope-Wallace, Newell Jenkins, Cynthia Jolly, Frank Johnson, Junius, Solomon Khan, Irving Kolodon, Alexandra Lalaouni, J.W. Lambert, Walter Legge, George London, William Mann, Eric Mason, Steven Mathers, Henry Miller, Bayan Northcott, Keith Nurse, Werner Oehlmann, Mariano Paes, Eve Perrick, John Pettit, Andrew Porter, Giuseppe Pugliese, Mario Quaglia, Seymour Raven, Charles Reid, Alan Rich, Harold Rosenthal, Wintrop Sargeant, Signe Scanzoni, Harold Schonberg, Elizabeth Schwarzkopf, Desmond Shawe-Taylor, Cecil Smith, Robin Smith, Joan Sutherland, Howard Talley, Howard Taubman, Peter Thompson, Sir John Tooley, Harry Weaver, Paul Webster.

Index